CREATORS OF MODERN CHINA

100 Lives from Empire to Republic 1796–1912

天津高等女學堂大演操

CREATORS OF MODERN CHINA

100 Lives from Empire to Republic 1796–1912

Edited by Jessica Harrison-Hall and Julia Lovell

Thames
&Hudson

The British
Museum

CONTENTS

Page 2. Unidentified artist, *Training at the Tianjin Girls' High School* (detail), *c.* 1905–20. Woodblock print, ink and colours on paper. Height 58.3 cm, width 94 cm. British Museum, London. Collected by Jean-Paul Dubosc.
Page 4. Qingkuan et al., *Battle Scene from the Muslim Rebellions in Shaanxi, Gansu and Xinjiang Provinces* (detail), *c.* 1875–1908. Ink and colours on silk. Height 143 cm, width 315 cm. Mactaggart Collection in the University of Alberta, Edmonton.

INTRODUCTION

JESSICA HARRISON-HALL AND JULIA LOVELL

History is made, and made memorable, by individuals. Through telling one hundred extraordinary lives, this book aims to characterize and humanize a century of Chinese experience that for decades was dismissed in both Sinophone and non-Sinophone accounts as an epoch of stagnation, decline and failure, sandwiched between the glories of the 18th-century 'High Qing' and the epochal transformations of the 20th and 21st centuries. But the experiences of the 'long 19th century', between the end of the reign of the Qianlong emperor and the abdication of the last emperor, Puyi, form a crucial bridge to Chinese modernity. Across these 116 years, the imperial state fundamentally re-envisioned its role: it transformed from a light-touch, understaffed bureaucracy, to a centralizing, interventionist state. The borders of contemporary China firmed up: Qing frontier rule in, for example, Xinjiang shifted from taking the form of a culturally devolved protectorate, to asserting over this ethnically diverse region sovereign ownership and integration into central government. Political participation expanded, especially on the part of the Han Chinese majority. Government and governed engaged in new debates about the balance of power between monarch and bureaucracy – the fundamentals of constitutionalism. High politics, elite culture and everyday life opened to global influences and exchanges. Artistic and literary traditions were challenged, dismantled, added to and remade – the amalgam of and dislocation between old and new generated a cosmopolitan cultural modernity. Historians have long identified the May Fourth–New Culture era (c. 1915–25) as the crucible of Chinese transformation, when the politics, culture and society of China became mobilized into a modern (republican) nation. But many of the standout changes associated with this period began in the late Qing: the shift towards the vernacular as the language of publishing and education; exposure to and voracious consumption of global news and culture; arguments for feminist emancipation and ethnic autonomy; a new understanding of China not as a world in itself, but as a nation in the world. Through the biographies of one hundred people who experienced China's long 19th century, this volume aspires to convey both the external and internal cataclysms suffered by the country, and the diverse, innovative responses that these crises generated.

This volume juxtaposes lives that are reflective of the political, social, cultural and ethnic diversity of the late empire – rulers, statesmen, soldiers, artists, writers, entertainers and craftspeople, conservatives and dissenters, anti-quarians and modernists. (Indeed, almost all the lives recounted fall into at least two such categories.) This book combines written biographies with images – portraits in many media, emblematic objects – that powerfully and poignantly evoke the visual and material worlds of the individuals featured.

The biographies are grouped here into eight sections. Rather than arranged by strict chronology of birth or professional category alone, they are sometimes curated according to their relationship to one another. For example, in the 'Court' section, emperors and empresses are accompanied by their eunuchs and enter-tainers. Daoists, Buddhists, Muslims and Christians follow the order in which those religions developed in China. Militarists – soldiers, martyrs, mercenaries and pirates – are sequenced according to the major 19th-century conflicts in which they participated. Artists and literary observers are grouped by genre: calligraphers, epigraphers, painters, illustrators, photographers, poets, writers, translators, chroniclers, travellers. The book's business people cover entre-preneurs, media tycoons, financiers and commodity traders, arranged broadly chronologically, but also reflecting the mid-century shift of international trade from Guangzhou in the south, to Shanghai on the east coast. Statespeople – who include here administrators, reformers, diplomats and political think-ers – are presented in the order in which their work affected late Qing China. Our final section – 'Makers' – features industrialists, craftspeople, folklorists, archaeologists and doctors.

The selection of which lives to feature was challenging; as editors we could, naturally, have produced an entirely different book by choosing other, similarly compelling lives. The current volume is of course not the final version of a col-lective biography of China's 19th century; the editors hope that other selections will follow, that will introduce readers to yet more of this period's extraordinary human diversity. We strove in particular to represent the experiences of women and non-Han Chinese (the multi-ethnic nature of Qing China had a deep impact on 19th-century, and indeed subsequent, history); but there remains scope for the inclusion of many more lives. The book as a whole is very much an interna-tional, collective endeavour, involving experts from fourteen countries in Asia, Europe, Australia and North America, and from multiple disciplines: art, cultural, economic, intellectual, material and political historians, as well as librarians and museum curators, all steeped in the textual, visual and material cultures of the late empire. The range of sources consulted for individual biographies reflects the global, multidisciplinary nature of this writing community. We would like to warmly thank our contributors for bringing to life this collage of voices and expe-riences, Wenyuan Xin for her expert translations, and also the scholars who generously advised on the book's design and structure.

1

THE COURT

EMPERORS, EMPRESSES, EUNUCHS, COURTIERS AND ENTERTAINERS

Our narrative of major court figures begins with the abdication, in 1796, of the Qianlong emperor, whose reign is regarded as a high point in Qing history. It concludes in 1912 when the boy Xuantong emperor, known as Puyi or the last emperor, abdicated following the Xinhai Revolution, ending some 2,000 years of dynastic rule. In the early 1800s, the Qing court, with the emperor at the helm, controlled, through a bureaucratic network, vast territories and a population of over 300 million people.

Qing rulers were not Han Chinese but ethnically distinct Manchus, whose homeland is now part of north-east China. In 1644, Manchu armies invaded the Ming empire and established the Qing dynasty. Between 1796 and 1912, six emperors ruled; however, after 1861, due to a succession of child emperors, Empress Dowager Cixi wielded power behind the throne for fifty years until her death in 1908. Manchu, based on a script used to write Mongolian, was the empire's official language alongside Chinese, Mongolian, Tibetan and Uyghur. As a conquering minority, Qing rulers constantly feared uprisings, and ethnic politics were at the heart of state policy.

It is challenging to write personal biographies of individual emperors, who left no diaries or memoirs. Once they came to the throne, their lives and personalities became indistinguishable from actions and decisions of, and events befalling, the state – whether or not an individual emperor was personally responsible for such twists and turns. But imperial portraits (and the objects and culture favoured by rulers) can be revealing of emperors' personalities and preferences. During this period, images of people at court changed, and arguably the imperial family's self-representations became increasingly Sinicized. For example, court artists were commissioned less frequently to paint emperors in grand-scale military portraits, popular in the period c. 1700 to 1850, and favoured images showing the imperial family engaged in traditional Han cultural pursuits such as reading poetry or writing with a brush.

Qing emperors and their households carried out their duties and relaxed within palace complexes in northern China: the Forbidden City in the heart of Beijing, the summer palaces in and around Beijing, and the Rehe Palace north of the Great Wall in Chengde. Each palace had ritual and devotional spaces, living quarters, household spaces for servicing the palace, and gardens for the emperors' families and guests. Due to prolonged fiscal crisis during the 19th century, relatively few new buildings were added to existing palaces, although some new architectural elements were incorporated, such as Jiaqing's maze of interconnecting rooms or Cixi's 'Crystal Palace' in the Forbidden City. After the Summer Palace (Yuanming yuan) was looted and burned in 1860 by British and French troops, a new Summer Palace (Yihe yuan) was constructed by Cixi, though not without inciting controversy about its perceived extravagance.

Partly due to the advent of photography, during the 1800s both the medium and the distribution of the personal images of the emperors and their wives altered strikingly. In the 1700s, the emperor's face would have been familiar only to the very few who had had a personal audience with him or had seen an official imperial portrait in the ancestral shrine. By the end of the dynasty, the Empress Dowager had her portrait painted for public exhibition at an American trade fair and gave photographs of herself posing with foreign diplomats as presents to her guests.

More than for any other era of dynastic history, we also know about the supporting cast that kept the court running, through palace archives and objects of daily life that have survived. As in the past, eunuchs continued to manage the day-to-day care of the imperial family and supplies of luxury goods and clothing, and to support entertainments such as opera within the palace. During the second half of the 19th century, the cultural form known as Peking Opera became particularly popular at court. Male actors, playing male and female roles, were invited to perform on specially constructed stages. Most famous of these were Tan Xinpei and Wang Yaoqing. Both actors were immortalized by a Beijing-based Muslim snuff-bottle painter, who created photographic likenesses of the actors on the inside surface of rock crystal bottles. Courtiers such as Yu Rongling, with experience of travelling abroad, introduced foreign fashions and dances to the court.

The late Qing court is often imagined as a locus of luxury living and palace intrigue, but it played a vital role in shaping China. Emperors and regents struggled with challenges across the empire: overpopulation, overextended territories, insufficient funds from taxation, environmental exhaustion, and the aggressive expansion of Europe, the United States and, later, Japan. Misjudgments about the threat posed by the West meant Qing modernization lagged behind its closest regional competitor, Japan. Yet the regencies of the 1860s to 1880s oversaw military and fiscal modernization that enabled the dynasty to survive far longer than external observers expected. Ultimately, however, the successive political, military, economic and cultural crises of China's 'long 19th century' generated contestation over state modernization and political organization that led to the collapse of imperial, dynastic rule in 1912. **JHH**

1. THE JIAQING EMPEROR

嘉慶帝 (*r.* 1796–1820)

UNDER-ESTIMATED RULER

On a crisp winter's day in February 1796, the 35-year-old Prince Jia of the First Rank ascended the throne during a lavish succession ceremony held in the Forbidden City. Given the name Yongyan (literally 'everlasting gem') at birth, Prince Jia was the fifteenth son of the Qianlong emperor (*r.* 1736–1795), hailing from the House of Aisin Gioro, the Manchu clan who had established the Qing dynasty a century and a half earlier in 1644. Yongyan's transition from Prince Jia to the Jiaqing emperor was unusual due to the physical presence of his predecessor. Earlier that day, Qianlong had abdicated willingly in an orchestrated move that broke with convention, honouring his grandfather, the Kangxi emperor, by stepping down before surpassing the sixty-one years he had ruled. Through the solemn act of conferring to his son the grand heirloom seal of state – a large and heavy piece of the finest spinach-green jade with a delicate carving of a five-clawed dragon – Qianlong assumed the title 'retired emperor' (*taishang huangdi*).

In theory, Qianlong would retreat and allow his son to rule. In reality, Jiaqing remained subordinate, bound by the strictures of filiality and ceremony, as well as by the powerful influence of Qianlong's most-favoured official, the Svengali-like Heshen (1750–1799). The trappings of the title were Jiaqing's, but not yet the honour, nor the power. Two courts were effectively maintained, two sets of court diaries and two calendars kept, so that the final four years of the 18th century were dogged by confusion as to whether these were the first of the Jiaqing era or the last of his predecessor's. Forced to swallow his pride out of respect for his father, Jiaqing dedicated himself to studying the classics of the Confucian literary canon and carrying out whichever imperial duties came his way.

Qianlong died in February of 1799. Yet Jiaqing's inability to shake off his father's yoke continues to permeate history books, popular fiction and TV dramas. In English and Chinese narratives alike, he is associated with 'the beginning of the end', the emperor who presided over China's descent into its 'century of humiliation'. He is characterized as pleasure-loving and incompetent, a slovenly man who is rumoured to have died of an obesity-induced stroke while travelling to his north-east summer retreat in 1820. This depiction contrasts starkly with popular ones of Kangxi as the mighty Manchu warrior-hunter, and Qianlong the cultured philosopher-thinker. Even in his own lifetime, Jiaqing proved highly unpopular, surviving not one, but two assassination attempts carried out in broad daylight at the gates of the Forbidden City.

These plots against Jiaqing's life were emblematic of a broader pattern of unrest, ushering in a series of popular uprisings that reshaped government and society, almost destroying the Qing, decades before the 1911 Revolution forced the abdication of the

Unidentified court artist, *The Jiaqing Emperor in his Study*, c. 1820. Hanging scroll, ink and colours on silk. Height 224 cm, width 174 cm. The Palace Museum, Beijing.

last emperor. The most serious of these was the White Lotus, a fragmented insurrection launched in 1794 by millenarian Buddhists and supported by a disaffected population. Military blunders and brutal government suppression led to tens of thousands of deaths, destabilizing large swathes of central Qing China. The deeply disturbed Qianlong was assured of positive progress by Heshen; this untruth, combined with Qianlong's gullibility, led Jiaqing to the uncharacteristically candid confession of his father's senility in official records. Arguably, it was only due to a change in tactics under Jiaqing that this sprawling rebellion was finally ended in 1806. This action drained the imperial coffers, however, and its legacy inspired countless further insurgencies, including the Eight Trigrams uprising – marked by its attempt at regicide in 1813 – representing one of the most direct threats to imperial rule in Qing history.

Jiaqing unquestionably ruled over a significant inflection point in Chinese imperial history. Armed rebellions were just one problem he faced. An explosion of the Qing population through the 18th century had led to serious food shortages, exacerbated by numerous natural disasters. Price inflation, rampant corruption, economically damaging piracy along the southern coast, and religious unrest, especially in the borderlands added during Qianlong's 'Ten Great Campaigns', made matters worse. Trade in opium expanded dramatically. Repeated prohibitions in 1800 and 1813 were unsuccessful, the legacy of which (a growing narcotics crisis) would be handed on to Jiaqing's successor, the Daoguang emperor.

To paint a picture of an emperor devoid of any agency or aspiration for reform would do a disservice to Jiaqing, however. Beyond his effective response to the White Lotus, Jiaqing initiated what later came to be referred to as the 'Jiaqing Reforms' (1799–1805), an elaborate restructuring of the court, the civil service and the treasury that garnered considerable excitement among literati.

His contemporaries described him as an attentive, clear-headed man, who self-deprecatingly referred to himself as a 'youthful monarch' who 'doesn't know enough'. His assertive, if not ruthless actions upon his father's death proved otherwise. Within days of Qianlong's demise, he charged Heshen with corruption and abuses of power, stripped him of his titles and property, and ordered him to commit suicide. Through a series of powerful ideological attacks, Jiaqing singled out Heshen as the venom that had seeped into the soul of Qing government. Eliminating this 'primary evil' thus became a highly symbolic act that demonstrated the throne's commitment to eradicating bureaucratic corruption and restoring probity and efficacy in government.

To make these reforms more palatable, Jiaqing was at pains to present a narrative of unbroken continuity with the imperial mission and values of his Qing forefathers. He obsessed over imperial ceremony and institutions, insisted on strictly following protocols passed down by his predecessors, and upheld traditions associated with Manchu identity, including imperial hunts, and inspection tours in 1805, 1812 and 1818. Jiaqing's successors, by contrast, would go on to abolish both hunts and tours.

In the cultural sphere too, Jiaqing emphasized continuity to promote stability. Under his supervision, the imperial printing workshops' output of illustrated books and catalogues was second only to that under his father. Qianlong had created inventories of the courtly collections as a way of standardizing a particular imperial aesthetic; Jiaqing compiled these into printed compendia for wider dissemination. Such publications shape our understanding of Qing court art to this day. Jiaqing was an indefatigable scholar of the Chinese classics, his 15,267 poems making him the second most prolific emperor-poet in Chinese history after Qianlong. His compositions reveal a monarch seemingly concerned for the future of his realm and its peoples.

It is debatable just how successful Jiaqing's attempts at reform in the guise of continuity were. His inclusion of local elites in infrastructure building and administration, his relative tolerance for critique beyond the court, and his reform agenda certainly increased Chinese literati engagement, paving the way for future intellectual movements of the 1860s to 1900s. Instead of assigning to Jiaqing a narrative of decline, then, we ought perhaps to look to the actions of his reign to understand how the Qing were able to survive another hundred years.

Ricarda Brosch

2. THE DAOGUANG EMPEROR

道光帝 (r. 1821–1850)

RULER FORCED TO OPEN CHINA TO WESTERN POWERS

On 16 September 1782, the future Daoguang emperor was born in the Hall of Harvesting Fragrance in the Forbidden City. He was the second son of Prince Yongyan, who later ruled as the Jiaqing emperor (r. 1796–1820). His mother, Lady Hitara (1760–1797), was Yongyan's primary consort, known posthumously as Empress Xiaoshurui. His given name was originally Mianning, but after he was enthroned as the Daoguang emperor, he substituted the first character of his name (*mian*, literally meaning 'silk floss') with a less common character (*min*, a rare usage for 'autumn'), in order to make it easier for the populace to observe the taboo against using the characters of the reigning emperor's given name.

Mianning began to attend the palace school after he turned five. His study mainly focused on the Confucian classics, Chinese history and Chinese literature. But the Qianlong and Jiaqing emperors expected the young Mianning to cultivate military as well as civil virtues. At the age of ten, he went hunting with his grandfather and successfully shot a deer. The Qianlong emperor was so pleased that he rewarded Mianning with a *huang magua* (yellow imperial riding jacket) and a *hualing* (type of peacock feather hat decoration), and wrote a poem about his grandson's feat.

In 1799, the Jiaqing emperor secretly designated Mianning heir to the throne. In October 1813, Mianning accompanied his father on a trip to the imperial hunting grounds at Mulan in Manchuria. However, the event was interrupted by heavy rain and he returned ahead of the rest of the party to the Forbidden City in Beijing. On 8 October, millenarian rebels in the Heavenly Principle sect (sometimes also known as the Eight Trigrams) launched an attack on the palace with the support of eunuchs within the imperial court. After receiving news of the attack, Mianning promptly joined and directed the palace's defences. He even killed with his musket two rebels who were climbing over the palace walls. Soon after, imperial guards arrived and put down the insurrection. Delighted with Mianning's extraordinary presence of mind and bravery, the Jiaqing emperor granted him the title of Prince Zhi of the First Rank. After Jiaqing's sudden death at Rehe in September 1820, Mianning was enthroned in the Hall of Supreme Harmony as the Daoguang emperor, and the court declared the following year as the first year of the Daoguang reign.

Unidentified court artist, *Portrait of the Daoguang Emperor on Horseback*, c. 1821–50. Hanging scroll, ink and colours on paper. Height 250 cm, width 156 cm. The Palace Museum, Beijing.

After ascending the throne, the new emperor made significant personnel changes to the Grand Council (the most powerful court institution of government) to ensure his personal authority, improve the functioning of the civil service, and combat corruption. During his thirty-year reign, he promoted frugality at court by setting a personal example. He cancelled the jade tribute previously required from Xinjiang, as well as gifts of lychee trees and year-round tribute orchids from Fujian. He also ended the tradition of imperial hunting at Mulan. A diligent administrator, he involved himself closely with the management of grain tribute, river conservancy and salt administration. He also twice called for an assessment of transport by sea as an alternative to using the Grand Canal for moving grain from the south-east to the north. However, he was short-sighted in making appointments. Despite keeping some capable ministers in his employ such as Yinghe (1771–1839), Tao Shu (1779–1839), Ruan Yuan (1764–1849) and He Changling (1785–1848), he for years relied heavily on two rather mediocre personal advisors, Cao Zhenyong (1755–1835) and Mujangga (1782–1856).

In 1826, Jahangir Khoja (1788–1828), a tribal leader from East Turkestan, led a large-scale rebellion against Qing rule in Xinjiang, destroying Qing garrisons in cities across the west of the region. The Daoguang emperor mobilized imperial forces to suppress this jihad and punished officials in Xinjiang whose brutality and corruption had originally provoked the uprising. In 1827, Jahangir Khoja was captured. The following year a stele was erected in the Imperial Academy (Guozijian) – the empire's highest institution of learning – with an inscription written by Daoguang to celebrate the quelling of the rebellion. The emperor also commissioned a set of portraits of imperial officials and valiant warriors who contributed to the task, and hung them in the Hall of Imperial Brilliance (Ziguang ge), west of the Forbidden City. In 1828, Jahangir Khoja was escorted under guard to the capital, where he was presented to the Qing court in a ceremony held by the emperor at the Meridian Gate of the Forbidden City, and then executed.

Daoguang also had to contend with Britain's expanded influence in East Asia, owing to its emergence, during the middle years of the Qing dynasty, as the world's dominant maritime power. In order to resolve a growing trade deficit with China, at the turn of the 19th century, Britain had begun to facilitate and protect opium smuggling into China (the Qing government had banned the drug in 1729). By the 1830s, British India's opium traffic with China had grown with astonishing speed, leading to Daoguang's decision to suppress the trade in order to halt the drain of silver out of China, and reduce the physical and moral harms of opium addiction. In 1838, he appointed Lin Zexu (1785–1850) – then governor general of Hunan and Hubei – his special imperial commissioner to crack down on smugglers. After travelling to the epicentre of the trade at Guangzhou, in 1839 Lin Zexu confiscated and destroyed a large quantity of opium brought to the south China coast by British traders. When news of the destruction reached the British government that year, it decided to send a fleet to China to recoup the cost of the destroyed opium, and negotiate new trade privileges with the Qing. The First Opium War, as it is now known, lasted two and a half years, and ended when the British fleet sailed up China's east coast to hold the city of Nanjing ransom in summer 1842. After a string of military failures, the Daoguang emperor had no choice but to ratify the Treaty of Nanjing, which extracted from the Qing a war indemnity of 21 million Mexican silver dollars (equivalent to 550 million in today's pounds) and gave British traders the right to live and work in five 'treaty ports' along China's south and east coast. This first treaty with a Western power was soon followed by agreements that gave similar trading privileges to the United States and France. The First Opium War, and the treaties that followed it, thus began the opening of China to Western powers.

In January 1850, the Daoguang emperor's health worsened due to grief and exhaustion after presiding over Empress Dowager Gongci's funeral (she had brought Daoguang up, following the death in 1797 of his birth mother). On 25 February, the ailing emperor summoned a group of senior officials to witness the nomination of his fourth son, Yizhu, as the heir apparent and his sixth son, Yixin, as Prince Gong of the First Rank. Shortly after, the Daoguang emperor died in the Hall of Prudent Virtue in the Yuanming yuan (Old Summer Palace). He is remembered today as a diligent, careful emperor, who struggled with the intense environmental, demographic, financial and social crises prevailing in the empire, and who – distracted by the enormity of these crises – misjudged the threat posed by new, well-armed European forces along the empire's coast.

Zhao Chengling

3. THE XIANFENG EMPEROR

咸豐帝 (r. 1851–1861)

VICTIM AND PERPETRATOR OF QING DECLINE

The Daoguang emperor's successor, whose temple name was Wenzong and personal name Yizhu, ruled under the reign name Xianfeng, meaning 'universal prosperity'; his era was anything but. The devastating Taiping Civil War (1851–64) in south China overlapped with a brutal armed uprising, the Nian Rebellion (1851–68), in the north. Simultaneously, foreign aggression erupted in the Second Opium War (1856–60) and culminated in Anglo-French forces looting and burning the magnificent Yuanming yuan, or Old Summer Palace, in Beijing's north-west suburbs. In 1860, when the Qing ceded a strip of land near the Amur River to Russia, the empire physically shrank. Despite monetary reforms, the Xianfeng emperor's government could not control catastrophic inflation. Xianfeng was unable even to orchestrate a smooth succession: his death was followed by a coup instigated in part by his widow, Empress Dowager Cixi, who went on to dominate court and government until her death in 1908.

Not yet twenty years old when he ascended the throne, and facing so many long-standing crises, it is not surprising that, despite earnest efforts, Xianfeng did not reverse China's misfortunes. His historical reputation has been tarnished by both the humiliating destruction of the Yuanming yuan – still a raw wound for contemporary Chinese nationalists – and his decision to elevate to senior consort the controversial Cixi. Inasmuch as Chinese TV dramas such as the 2005 *Dreams behind the Curtain at Xianfeng's Court* are a barometer of current public opinion, Xianfeng seems to be viewed – with unfair exaggeration – as a crippled, lustful, inept alcoholic. A fairer appraisal might judge him to be a Qing traditionalist, who, although guilty of some grave strategic miscalculations, did not wantonly disregard his imperial duty.

Xianfeng was educated conventionally, studying Manchu, Chinese and Mongolian languages, the Confucian classics, and Manchu military skills including archery and riding. His father, the Daoguang emperor, reputedly named him heir because of his literary acumen. The young Xianfeng was decorously filial and paid appropriate ritual respect to imperial portraits. His mother Empress Xiaoquan died before he was nine years old, so a third-rank consort, Jing Guifei (1812–1855) took over his care.

Unidentified court artist, *Portrait of the Xianfeng Emperor*, c. 1851–61. Hanging scroll, ink and colours on silk. Height 167.1 cm, width 80.5 cm. The Palace Museum, Beijing.

Once enthroned, Xianfeng paid her a daily visit, as he would have done his birth mother had she been alive. Deeply attached to her, in 1855, Xianfeng promoted this foster mother to the highest honour of empress dowager shortly before her death and subsequently mourned her like a parent. Yet, steadfast in following tradition and court hierarchies, he restrained his personal desire to grant her a separate tomb, instead following his father's plan to have her buried with other consorts.

Xianfeng was attentive to political affairs and diligently corresponded with his generals in the field, but his views, especially regarding foreigners, were old-fashioned. He found European requests for diplomatic relations offensive, even though in his last year his senior officials established a prototype for a Foreign Office (the Zongli yamen). Still, this was too late. When foreign forces approached Beijing in 1860 seeking revenge for the Qing's refusal to agree terms in the Second Opium War, he fled to the imperial retreat at Rehe on the pretext of leading the annual hunt. Opponents to his leaving Beijing, including Prince Gong (1833–1898), the emperor's younger brother, stayed to negotiate with the foreign invaders after they looted and burned the Yuanming yuan. Following this catastrophic defeat, Xianfeng was forced to accept the principle of a modern, Western-dominated international system. 'England is an independent sovereign state', he pronounced. 'Let it have equal status with China.'

On a macro level, the destruction of the Yuanming yuan was a symbol of humiliation and foreign subjugation, but it was also an intimate loss for Xianfeng, since it was his birthplace and early home. News of its burning triggered his physical and mental decline. Refusing to return to Beijing, he died at Rehe, weak and inattentive, less than a year later. Although outwardly a foregone conclusion (since Xianfeng had only one surviving son), the succession was not smooth. Rival court factions sparred over regency of the new underage emperor, and a coup led by his widows, empress dowagers Ci'an and Cixi, gave these two women extraordinary power at court, ruling alongside Prince Gong.

A leisure-time court portrait pictures Xianfeng in the prime of his life, staging his image for viewers by signalling his personal propriety and worthiness of respect. Wearing a robe patterned with propitious bats, he sits beneath a Chinese parasol tree, which symbolizes moral rectitude because of its straight trunk. Surrounding roses, bamboo and lotus project messages of longevity, gentlemanly character, purity and peace. Instead of sitting with an open book as was typical for emperors, Xianfeng holds a fashionable snuff bottle and an exquisite feather fan, the latter a likely reference to Zhuge Liang, a renowned military strategist of the Three Kingdoms period (220 to 280 CE) often pictured waving such a fan. The allusion to Zhuge Liang was also designed to communicate the holder's victory, through self-control, over sensual pursuits.

Xianfeng indulged in some pleasures, but his keeping of eighteen consorts was not unusual relative to previous emperors (some of whom had as many as fifty-four). His love life has been distorted in popular imagination due to negative perceptions of

Cixi, who came into his palace as a low-ranking consort and was promoted by him as mother of his only surviving son. Opera was among his greatest passions, and finding the palace opera troupe waning, he agreed for twelve new musicians to join in the year 1855, the first increase in players in almost thirty years; further additions followed. During his exile in Rehe, he watched more than 300 operas, still attending performances just two days before he died.

After Xianfeng's death, his heir, the Tongzhi emperor, followed proper ritual protocol to honour the emperor's memory, but also showed personal affection and reverence for his father. He decreed that some of Xianfeng's personal effects – hair, jewelry, a vermilion brush and a painting – be placed in the eastern Buddha hall of the Hall of Mental Cultivation. These touching remnants and reminders of a life whose premature death was hastened by European aggression towards the Qing seem to emblematize Xianfeng's mixed place in Qing history: though respected as a traditionalist emperor, he was crushingly ineffective in stopping Qing decline.

Jan Stuart

4. THE TONGZHI EMPEROR

同治帝 (*r.* 1862–1874)

PUPPET EMPEROR

After the Xianfeng emperor (*r.* 1851–1861) died in Rehe (present-day Chengde, Hebei province) in 1861, his only surviving son, Zaichun, ascended the throne at the age of six with the reign name of Tongzhi, the eighth emperor of the Qing dynasty to rule China.

Upon the enthronement of the young emperor, the widows of the Xianfeng emperor, the empress Lady Niohuru (1837–1881) and the noble consort Lady Yehe Nara (1835–1908), the birth mother of the Tongzhi emperor, were elevated to the rank of empress dowager with the titles of Ci'an and Cixi respectively. Although both names had strong connotations of kindness, peace and happiness, Empress Dowager Cixi in particular soon evinced an ambition for imperial power. She won the support of Prince Gong (1833–1898), the younger brother of the deceased Xianfeng emperor, and instigated a *coup d'état* in 1861. As a result, Sushun (1816–1861) and another seven ministers appointed by the Xianfeng emperor as regents to his successor were ousted and the two dowager empresses began to co-rule behind the throne. The pre-assigned reign name of Qixiang ('good luck and happiness') was consequently changed to Tongzhi ('ruling together'). The more dominant of the two empresses, Cixi, assumed power as de facto ruler, and the underage emperor became a puppet under her control from the start of his reign in November 1861. This ushered in a new era of female leadership without dynastic precedent.

The boy emperor's primary task was to study. The two dowager empresses appointed a group of prominent and trusted scholar-officials as imperial tutors including Qi Hongzao (1793–1866), Li Hongzao (1820–1897), Weng Tonghe (1830–1904), Woren (1804–1871) and Xu Tong (1819–1900). Although the tutors strove to instil a knowledge of state affairs in the young emperor, he showed little interest in such subjects. At court audiences as a child, the Tongzhi emperor had to sit still for long periods on his large throne and was bewildered by his ministers' numerous reports – a dull, difficult experience which made him reluctant to learn how to govern as a mature, careful emperor. The boy grew up into an ignorant and foppish young man, despite his tutors' years of careful instruction.

According to Qing tradition, at fourteen an emperor was considered mature enough to marry and take up the reins of power. However, upon the Tongzhi emperor's coming of age, Empress Dowager Cixi cited his failure to study diligently as an excuse to continue withholding power until the Tongzhi emperor turned seventeen. In imperial China, marriage marked the transition to adulthood. Empress Dowager Ci'an supported the appointment of Lady Arute (1853–1875), daughter of the brilliant, high-ranking official Chongqi (1829–1900), as empress (primary) consort to the Tongzhi emperor. Cixi's favourite, Lady Fucha (1858–1904), by contrast, received only the lowly position of concubine of the third rank, which irritated the emperor's mother and sowed the seeds of future conflicts between Cixi and Lady Arute. After the imperial wedding on 21 October 1872, Cixi interfered extensively in the lives of the newly wedded couple. The Tongzhi emperor, it is believed, grew disheartened and listless in response, and abandoned himself to sexual overindulgence (though he remained childless).

The Tongzhi reign was a period of critical, dramatic change for the Qing. Conflicts between social classes, ethnic groups, and court and regions that had developed during the previous reign intensified further, and led to successive insurrections, which took years, even decades, to suppress, at great cost to the dynasty. Despite this cataclysmic backdrop, this era is also known as the 'Tongzhi Restoration', in which, under the leadership of individuals such as Cixi and Prince Gong, the Qing court adjusted its diplomatic policies to a more open attitude towards foreign countries, founded modern schools, sent students overseas, opened factories and mines, and built railways. Economically, the government carried out fiscal reforms, which set China on the road to modernization, and won the Qing court temporary respite against internal and external enemies. However, these great changes and reforms had little to do with the Tongzhi emperor himself. Living a life of debauchery and never escaping the overbearing control exercised by Cixi, the Tongzhi emperor became increasingly alienated from his imperial role. As Cixi became more dominant at court, her attitude towards Prince Gong oscillated unsteadily between alliance and antagonism. Cixi used him as a counterweight to balance different powers at court and ensure her own pre-eminence, which led to destabilizing tensions.

On 23 February 1873, a grand ceremony was held on the occasion of the Tongzhi emperor's formal assumption of power. However, in practice the emperor still had to

Unidentified court artist, *Portrait of the Tongzhi Emperor in Buddhist Costume, c.* 1861–75. Hanging scroll, ink and colours on silk. Height 183.5 cm, width 98 cm. The Palace Museum, Beijing.

follow the decisions of the two dowager empresses. He continued to attend his tutors' classes after daily audiences, and was fawned over by an infantilizing group of eunuchs and officials. He therefore had very few chances to handle state affairs. In terms of domestic interventions, the Tongzhi emperor ordered the rebuilding of the imperial garden Yuanming yuan (the Old Summer Palace) as a retreat for Cixi and Ci'an after they relinquished their regencies. This can be read as the emperor's transparent attempt to drive Cixi away so he could rule without her interference.

However, the timing for Tongzhi's plan was inauspicious. Having just emerged from decades of destructive regional rebellions, the empire was still financially over-stretched and struggling to reconstruct. The rebuilding project therefore triggered fierce controversy and was eventually cancelled. The Tongzhi emperor's main contribution to foreign relations came in 1873, when for the first time he received (and accepted diplomatic credentials from) the Japanese ambassador and ministers from Russia, the United States, Britain, France and the Netherlands at an audience in the Pavilion of Purple Light within the Forbidden City.

At the end of 1874, after less than two years in power, the Tongzhi emperor fell ill with smallpox. After a temporary improvement in his health, he caught flu and suddenly died at the age of nineteen. He was, at his death, almost politically powerless at court, and lacking in meaningful political experience. Moreover, the Tongzhi emperor's failure to produce an heir left the court with a serious succession crisis.

Zhu Saihong

5. THE GUANGXU EMPEROR

光緒帝 (r. 1875–1908)

REFORMING EMPEROR

In 1871, in the mansion of Prince Chun (1840–1891) – seventh son of the Daoguang emperor – a boy was born and given the name Zaitian (1871–1908). Four years later, after the Tongzhi emperor (r. 1862–1874) died childless, the succession to the throne became a major issue for the court. Empress Dowager Cixi (1835–1908), the de facto ruler of the Qing empire, was worried that if she selected an older prince, he might evade her control. Therefore, going against traditional succession practices in such situations, she controversially installed the underage Zaitian (of the same generation as the deceased Tongzhi emperor, though fifteen years younger) as the new emperor, so that she could preserve her own power. Zaitian's life was transformed by Cixi's decision.

On the morning following the Tongzhi emperor's death, the four-year-old Zaitian was brought into the Forbidden City while still asleep. After being woken, he was first instructed to perform the morning greeting to the two empress dowagers – Cixi and Ci'an – serving as regents, and then to mourn for the deceased Tongzhi emperor. With the approval of the empress dowagers, the ministers chose 'Guangxu' as the new reign title, a name that translates as 'continuing the ancestors' glories'. The enthronement took place on 25 February 1875. Zaitian sat on the imperial throne in the Hall of Supreme Harmony, while high-ranking nobility and officials performed three kneelings and nine head-knockings and shouted *wansui* ('may you live ten thousand years') to the boy emperor.

Official documents that record the physical appearance of the Guangxu emperor describe him as an intelligent-looking man with a high nose, 'dragon eyes' (a turn of phrase that means large, shining eyes), an oval face and a wide forehead. This description fits with his portraits currently in the Palace Museum, Beijing. A personal diary by a contemporary of the emperor describes Guangxu as a handsome, slender young man over 1.8 metres tall, with a wide mouth and neat white teeth; his face, the diarist also noted, usually had a determined look.

From the age of six, the Guangxu emperor received a formal education in the Chinese classics. His tutor, Weng Tonghe (1830–1904), was a top scholar who obtained the position of *zhuangyuan* (first place in the highest level of the imperial civil service examination) in 1856. In addition to being an excellent academician, Weng was also very open-minded. He taught the boy emperor the texts that constituted the canon of Confucian philosophy and learning, and the essentials of governing state affairs, aiming to bring up an accomplished, well-read future ruler. For his part, the Guangxu emperor was a self-disciplined, thoughtful student. His apparent dedication to strengthening the country and improving the livelihoods of ordinary people drove his famous but ill-fated 1898 reforms.

The Guangxu emperor was declared of age in 1887 when he turned seventeen, at a ceremony in the Hall of Supreme Harmony. However, an unmarried emperor was not considered mature enough to rule in his own right. Therefore, in practice the court still relied on Cixi's decisions on state affairs. When the marriage finally took place, moreover, Cixi selected her niece to be empress, so the dowager regent could still exert influence on the Guangxu emperor. A week after Guangxu's wedding on 25 February 1889, Cixi officially retired from the regency in recognition of the emperor's having formally attained his majority.

In 1894, the previous three decades of modernizing 'Self-Strengthening' underwent a major test, when the First Sino-Japanese War broke out, over a conflict about political domination in Korea. Following China's crushing defeat, the Qing court was forced to sign the Treaty of Shimonoseki with Japan in 1895. Qing China ceded to Japan (among other territories) the province of Taiwan and was forced to pay a war indemnity of 200 million taels of silver (roughly two and a half times the Qing's annual revenue); the treaty also permitted Japan to open factories in China – a major blow to the empire's nascent industrialization. The outcome of the conflict was heartbreaking for a serious young emperor devoted to his country. Shocked and galvanized by this crisis, the 24-year-old emperor decided to carry out unprecedentedly far-reaching reforms to strengthen the Qing empire politically and economically. Radical scholars such as Kang Youwei (1858–1927) and Liang Qichao (1873–1929) were similarly shaken by the defeat and actively campaigned for institutional change in response to the national crisis. Their memorials found favour with the emperor, and on 11 June 1898 the Guangxu emperor, advised by Kang and Liang, issued an imperial Edict Determining the Course of the Country and announced a raft of sweeping reforms. More than 180 further imperial edicts were issued over the ensuing 103 days

Unidentified court artist, *Portrait of the Guangxu Emperor in his Study,* c. 1900–8. Hanging scroll, ink and colours on silk. Height 173.5 cm, width 95.5 cm. The Palace Museum, Beijing.

(the so-called Hundred Days' Reform). These wide-ranging measures included: recruiting talented men into a streamlined national bureaucracy, promoting new schools, abolishing the 'eight-legged' (*bagu*) civil service examination essay, facilitating overseas study, eliminating official sinecures, encouraging greater freedom of political expression, revitalizing industries and modernizing the army. Many historians believe that, if these reforms had been fully implemented, Qing China might have embarked on a successful path to modernization. But the reform plans threatened the interests of powerful officials close to Cixi. These conflicts finally led to a *coup d'état* in autumn 1898, which rescinded all the new policies except for the founding of an Imperial University in Beijing. Many of Guangxu's reform party were arrested, executed or driven into exile. Empress Dowager Cixi now resumed her powers as regent and put the emperor under house arrest in Yingtai, an artificial island on the western shores of the artificial lake of Nanhai in the gardens of the Forbidden City.

In 1900, the Eight-Nation Alliance – including soldiers from Austria–Hungary, the British Empire, France, Germany, Italy, Japan, Russia and the United States – invaded China and occupied the capital, following a protracted siege of foreign communities there by the militarized religious sect known as the Boxers. Cixi with her entourage fled Beijing for the old capital city Xi'an, taking Guangxu with them. The court returned to Beijing in early 1902, after signing a few months earlier the Boxer Protocol, one of the most humiliating agreements forced upon China. During the last nine years of his life, the Guangxu emperor proved unable to emerge from the shadow of the Empress Dowager and died in 1908 at the age of thirty-nine, a day before Cixi herself passed away.

Although the Guangxu emperor was on the throne for thirty-three years, his power was short-lived. For most of his reign, Cixi maintained an iron grip over the court. The Guangxu emperor had many political ideals, but unfortunately none of them was realized. Although many of Guangxu's reform policies were enacted by Cixi after the cataclysm of the Boxer War, this was too late to save the Qing dynasty. Three years after the Guangxu emperor's death, the Qing empire collapsed.

Ren Wanping

6. IMPERIAL CONSORT KESHUN

恪順皇貴妃 (1876–1900)

POLEMICALLY ROMANTICIZED CONCUBINE

Imperial Noble Consort Keshun, better known in China as Consort Zhen, was the most beloved concubine of the Guangxu emperor (1871–1908, r. 1875–1908). Like most imperial consorts, very little is known of her beyond the basic standardized biographical accounts in the *Draft History of the Qing* and *Four Genealogies of the Imperial Family of the Qing Dynasty*. While we do not even know her given birth name, and no credible image of her true likeness exists, this lack of information has done little to dampen the public's appetite for her story. Consort Zhen's passionate relationship with the emperor and tragic early death at the age of twenty-four during the bloody Boxer War (1899–1901) have been romanticized in countless dramatic works in print, on stage and on screen.

According to accounts by two late Qing scholars, Shang Yanying (1871–1960) and Hu Sijing (1869–1922), Consort Zhen was beautiful, clever, open-minded and artistically talented. She loved to dress up in men's clothes and was an influential unofficial advisor to the emperor regarding court affairs. Some scholars believe she championed the use of Western photographic technology in the harem, commissioning many photographic portraits of herself and the emperor. Ironically, just one possible photograph of her exists today. The identification of the sitter in the photograph (first published in 1960) as Consort Zhen is still under debate. (A previous photograph identified as Consort Zhen published in 1930 by the Palace Museum, Beijing, was later identified as an unrelated woman.) Empress Dowager Cixi (1835–1908) is thought to have destroyed all photographs of the Guangxu emperor and his favourite consort soon after the emperor's failed Hundred Days' Reform and her own *coup d'état* in 1898.

Consort Zhen was the daughter of Changxu (n.d.), former Vice Minister of Revenue on the Right, from the Tatara clan under the Manchu Bordered Red Banner. In 1888, at the age of twelve, the young Lady Tatara and her half-sister, who later became known as Consort Jin (1873–1924), were appointed concubines to the Guangxu emperor. The honorific title of Zhen, which means 'precious', was awarded alongside the rank of *pin* (imperial consort of the fifth rank). The twenty-year-old Lady Yehe Nara (1868–1913), who was also the niece of Empress Dowager Cixi, later known as Empress Dowager Longyu, was selected as the Guangxu emperor's empress. However, Zhen *pin* was the emperor's favourite.

The emperor must have been excited about the nomination of his first *xiunü* ('Beautiful Women') for imperial consorts, as marriage formalized his adulthood and would require the transfer of power from Cixi to him. According to palace rules, this selection process could have been held in 1885 (and subsequently every three years). It is thought that Cixi deliberately delayed and prolonged the proceedings, which started in 1886 and lasted until 1888, so that the wedding could not be held until 1889, three years after Guangxu officially came of age.

Palace legend suggests that the five finalists in the *xiunü* selection also included another two sisters who had been educated in Europe, the daughters of another banner official named Dexin (n.d.) of the Fuca clan. The Guangxu emperor, perhaps fascinated by their worldly knowledge, attempted to select one as his empress but was eventually overruled by Cixi, and the Fuca sisters were swiftly sent home. Cixi was thought to admire Consort Zhen at first as she recognized herself in the young, beautiful and clever girl. However, while Consort Zhen quickly became the emperor's favourite, she was unable to maintain the favour of his powerful aunt and stepmother Cixi, who was disappointed by Consort Zhen's inability, or refusal, to temper the emperor's radical ideas.

Nonetheless, at the age of eighteen Consort Zhen was elevated to *fei* (imperial consort of the fourth rank), the highest imperial rank she achieved during her lifetime and the title she has been commonly known by since her death. However, in the

The Palace Museum in Beijing first published this photograph in 1960, identifying it as the 'Portrait of Noble Consort Zhen'. The Palace Museum, Beijing.

same year and likely on Cixi's command, Consort Zhen was stripped, beaten and demoted to *guiren* (consort of the sixth rank). According to Hu Sijing and Shang Yanying, Cixi discovered Consort Zhen had been accepting bribes to fund her extravagant lifestyle in return for recommending unqualified candidates to the emperor for official appointments. Consort Zhen's brother and many of her eunuchs were punished in this incident, and as collateral damage, Consort Zhen's half-sister Consort Jin was also demoted. Happily for Consort Zhen, this punishment was temporary, and both sisters were reinstated as *fei* the following year. But after a bitter power struggle between Cixi and the Guangxu emperor ended with the emperor's failed reforms (and alleged palace coup) in 1898, the Empress Dowager regained control of the court, and Consort Zhen and the emperor were put under house arrest, probably never seeing each other again.

Members of the Qing court were forced to flee the Forbidden City in 1900 during the Boxer War and Eight-Nation Alliance invasion of Beijing; Cixi and Guangxu took refuge in Xi'an in the north-west. Amid the chaos of the retreat, the 24-year-old Consort Zhen 'drowned in a well' inside the imperial grounds (at least according to the official *Draft History of the Qing*, largely compiled between 1914 and 1927). Some believe she committed suicide to avoid suffering and humiliation if she were to be captured by Boxer rebels or by foreigners. Others, including both Shang Yanying and Cixi's palace maid He Rong'er (n.d.), suggest Consort Zhen was forced into the well by the senior eunuch Cui Yugui (1860–1926), at Cixi's command.

After Cixi and the Guangxu emperor returned to Beijing in late 1901, Consort Zhen was posthumously awarded the honorary title of *guifei* (consort of the third rank). However, she was buried among palace maids below her rank and remained there even after Cixi's death in 1908. Finally, in 1913, two years after the end of the Qing dynasty, Consort Zhen was reburied close to the Guangxu emperor's newly completed mausoleum as an imperial consort. This was on the order of her half-sister Consort Jin, by then known as the Imperial Noble Consort Duankang, who had become one of the most senior women at court as a stepmother to the two-year-old last emperor Puyi (1906–1967, r. 1909–1912) following the death of his adoptive mother, Empress Dowager Longyu. Consort Zhen did not receive her final honorary title until a decade after the fall of the Qing and two decades after her death in 1921, when Puyi promoted her to Imperial Noble Consort Keshun, possibly as part of the imperial customs celebrating his wedding the following year.

In popular dramas, including plays, novels, films and television series, Consort Zhen is often depicted as the heroic victim who was punished for supporting the plans of her beloved husband, the Guangxu emperor, to modernize China. The power-hungry Empress Dowager Cixi and her niece, the empress of the Guangxu emperor, are in turn portrayed as villains who were threatened by the emperor's political allies, and jealous of the love between Consort Zhen and the emperor. Consort Zhen's alleged transgression in accepting bribes for official positions, or the Guangxu emperor's alleged willingness to agree to Cixi's murder during the 1898 palace coup, are usually overlooked and the true complexities of these dynamic relationships forgotten.

Yingbai Fu

7. EMPRESS DOWAGER CIXI

慈禧太后 (1835–1908)

CONTROVERSIAL FEMALE RULER

Empress Dowager Cixi ruled the Qing empire during the most turbulent period of modern Chinese history. A contemporary of Queen Victoria, this formidable Manchu woman, and her regency between 1856 and 1908, have generated much historical controversy.

A daughter of the Manchu Yehe Nara clan, the future Cixi was born in 1835. She became a consort of the Xianfeng emperor (r. 1851–1861) in 1852, and bore his sole male heir in 1856, which led to her promotion to second-rank consort. She received the title of Empress Dowager Cixi when her five-year-old son succeeded the throne as the Tongzhi emperor (r. 1862–1874). At this point, Cixi began her political career as co-regent with Xianfeng's empresses Ci'an (1837–1881) and brother Yixin (Prince Gong, 1833–1898) but soon became the dominant power at court. When the newly wedded Tongzhi emperor died of smallpox in 1875 without having produced a son, Cixi secured her regency by electing her three-year-old nephew to succeed as the Guangxu emperor (r. 1875–1908). Although Guangxu began personal rule in 1889, Cixi maintained her political influence, and resumed her regency after crushing his radical Hundred Days' Reform in 1898. She stayed in power until she and her nephew died within two days of each other in 1908.

Cixi was a capable ruler and a supporter of Westernization. She promoted adept Han Chinese officials who quelled the Taiping Civil War (1851–64), a conflict that critically damaged the landscape and economy of southern China. The large-scale Westernizing reforms that took place during her regency modernized Chinese military, industrial and taxation systems, and enabled the empire to start recovering from the domestic upheavals and foreign aggression that the Qing regime had suffered in the 19th century. The so-called 'Tongzhi Restoration' (c. 1861–74) marked the last revival of Qing imperial power; the government even expanded its territory and re-integrated Xinjiang into the empire as a province in 1884. Cixi was also open to modernizing the Qing monarchy. Plans to model the Qing monarchy after the Japanese Meiji government were under way towards the end of her regency. These late Qing debates about governance underpinned the country's transformation into a modern nation state in the subsequent Republican era.

Cixi encouraged women's education and was an avid patron of the arts. For the first time in Chinese history, the Empress Dowager officially appointed professional women court artists. She sent the woman embroiderer Shen Shou (1874–1921) to Japan to study its modernization of training and manufacturing practices. Cixi even endorsed China's first women's college, which opened in 1908. Culturally, Cixi's patronage revitalized Qing court art production and ushered in new fashions, coloured by her expertise in theatrical performance and design. Thanks to her adoption and adaptation of previous Qing emperors' image-making tactics, she left behind a robust collection of portraits across multiple media (ink, oil painting and photography), some of which incorporated her Buddhist practice of the Guanyin (Bodhisattva Avalokiteśvara) cult. She commissioned several images of herself dressed as the deity, exemplified by the *Heart Sūtra* cover. Her forebear, the Qianlong emperor (r. 1735–1795), had similarly mastered the art of inserting his likeness into the image of Bodhisattva Mañjuśrī to visualize his projection of an absolute authority encompassing both the secular and the sacred realms. By uniting herself with the female form of Guanyin, Cixi created a gendered, feminine version of such power projection. Cixi's serious, grandiloquent patronage of art suggests that she regarded herself as the matriarch of the reigning Aisin Gioro family. Fascinatingly, the exhibition of her portrait in oils, painted by American portraitist Katharine Carl

Unidentified court artist, Empress Dowager Cixi, 1860s or 1870s. The imperial, yellow-ground dragon robe, snuff bottle and archer's thumb ring are all authoritative symbols of male Manchu identity. Hanging scroll, ink and colour on paper. With mount: height 199.5 cm, width 102.2 cm. Image: height 130.5 cm, width 67.5 cm. The Palace Museum, Beijing.

(1865–1938), at the Saint Louis World's Fair in 1904, marked the first public, international exposure and dissemination of the image of a ruler of China.

However, Cixi was also a ruthless and ultimately conservative politician, who denied China the chance to engage in full-scale Westernization. She delayed the personal rule of the Tongzhi and Guangxu emperors and quashed the latter's Hundred Days' Reform, an ambitiously modernizing project. Rumour also has it that she embezzled the navy budget to reconstruct the Yihe yuan – her personal pleasure palace – dedicated to her sixtieth birthday celebration; this diversion of funds, it is alleged, directly caused the Qing's humiliating defeat by Japan in 1895. Cixi's decision to support the Boxers – an anti-Christian, anti-Western secret society who besieged foreign communities across north China in 1900 – triggered the invasion of Beijing by the Eight-Nation Alliance, which forced the imperial family to flee to Xi'an in the north-west between 1900 and 1902. In private, anecdotes of her indulgence in luxury goods and pampering of her close eunuchs were widely circulated.

Prevailing negative images of Cixi arguably result from the deep-rooted distrust of women wielding political power at the heart of Chinese patriarchal governance. The modern publishing industry – which first emerged during her regency – fuelled such perceptions, eventually generating a mainstream, demonizing narrative that has since dominated public memory. The legitimacy of Cixi's regency is indeed questionable. Imperial consorts were forbidden to participate in court politics. According to Qing imperial convention, the deceased monarch's empress, in this case, Ci'an, should have been the only empress dowager. Cixi's appointment came a few days after the appointment of Ci'an, apparently (implausibly) requested by the succeeding child emperor. Such an unusual beginning to her engagement with court politics had a lasting impact on perceptions of the legitimacy of her regency, as her policy moves were often interpreted as ruthless power grabs. This hostile discourse travelled far beyond the Qing empire after Cixi's suppression of the Hundred Days' Reform. Reports alleging her intention to assassinate Guangxu and ascend the throne even made Western media headlines in publications such as *The New York Times*.

A more balanced portrayal might argue that Cixi certainly enjoyed power, but also felt its weight and responsibility, and used it to safeguard the Qing imperial patriarchy. This mentality explains why the de facto ruler of *fin-de-siècle* China maintained her title of empress dowager regent throughout her political career and did not declare herself the second female monarch in dynastic China.

Ying-chen Peng

8. PUYI AND WANRONG

溥儀和婉容
(Puyi 1906–1967, *r.* 1909–1912 and Wanrong 1906–1946)

LAST EMPEROR AND EMPRESS

China's millennia of dynastic history came to an end when Empress Dowager Longyu (1868–1913) announced in 1912 the abdication of the six-year-old Xuantong emperor (Aisin Gioro Puyi, 1906–1967). In the next few decades, Puyi (the last emperor) and his wife Wanrong (also known as Empress Xiaoke) struggled to adapt to chaotically changing times and preserve the legacy of the Qing empire, which continued to shape their personal lives and the history of China deep into the 20th century.

In 1908 the de facto ruler Empress Dowager Cixi (1835–1908) made her two-year-old grand-nephew, Puyi, heir to the childless Guangxu emperor (r. 1875–1908). Puyi was part of an intricate web of family ties Cixi had been building since the 1860s to cement her grip on power. Puyi's paternal grandfather and Guangxu's father, Yixuan (1840–1891), had married Cixi's sister; moreover, Puyi's maternal grandfather was Cixi's loyal minister Ronglu (1836–1903).

Puyi's nominal reign lasted for three years. The boy emperor was supported by his father Zaifeng (1883–1951) as his regent, and by Empress Dowager Longyu, wife of the previous emperor, Guangxu. After the Xinhai Revolution, which overthrew the Qing dynasty, Puyi acted as a non-sovereign monarch from 1912 to 1924. The provisional Republican government granted him such privileges as keeping his imperial title and living inside the Forbidden City. Puyi seemed to enjoy a

The last emperor and empress, each holding a camera, photographed inside the Forbidden City, between 1923 and 1924. The Palace Museum, Beijing.

relatively peaceful boyhood and adolescence inside the palace bubble of courtiers and attendants.

In 1922, the sixteen-year-old Puyi married Wanrong, a beautiful, well-educated and spirited young woman he picked from a set of photographs shown him as part of the imperial-bride selection process. The couple embraced cosmopolitanism, which had been a defining feature of the multilingual Qing court culture for centuries. They were the first Qing emperor and empress to adopt English names. Under the tutelage of the British diplomat Reginald Johnston (1874–1938), Puyi developed a fascination with the telephone, cut off his queue (for centuries, a badge of Manchu identity imposed on all men in Qing China) and expelled a large number of eunuchs from the palace. The young empress was tutored (in English and history, among other subjects) by an American, Isabel Ingram (1902–1988), and enjoyed jazz and Western cuisine. Bicycles, a piano and a bathtub graced her palace residence. Like Cixi, the young couple took a strong interest in photography and became the first imperial couple to be photographed and filmed in China. As the Oscar-winning film *The Last Emperor* shows, the perceived glamour of their royal lifestyle continued to capture popular imagination deep into the 20th century and beyond.

Although a modern woman and style icon from an elite Manchu family, Wanrong did not escape the fate of many Qing palace ladies. She was confined first to the Forbidden City, and later to the couple's residential compounds in Tianjin and Changchun under the surveillance of Japanese guards. On their wedding night, Puyi left her alone in their dark red bedroom. Later, Wanrong, estranged from Puyi, reportedly had an affair with their bodyguard, and even bore an illegitimate child. At the age of thirty-nine, Wanrong died in prison, suffering from opium addiction and other health conditions. Her tragic ending resembles that of Lady Nara (1718–1766), the demoted empress of the Qianlong emperor: both were reviled in history as disobedient, mentally ill women, and both passed away in disgrace.

Puyi married four other women, becoming the first and only monarch in Chinese history to be divorced by his wife. In 1931, his unhappy consort Wenxiu (1909–1953) signed a divorce settlement agreement, striking another heavy blow to the sanctity of Qing imperial institutions, where the emperor traditionally controlled his court women. Puyi himself, quite possibly homosexual, impotent or both, died childless, putting a full stop to this final, sad chapter of Qing history.

The republic that succeeded the Qing was marred by political instability, and in 1917 the Qing loyalist general Zhang Xun (1854–1923) launched a failed attempt to restore Puyi to the emperorship. Puyi's own hopes of regaining the throne were shattered in 1924, when the warlord Feng Yuxiang (1882–1948) evicted him from the Forbidden City, an event that enabled the transformation of the palace into the Palace Museum.

As part of their plan to expand their sphere of influence in China, Japanese diplomats and military officers lured the disillusioned Puyi – who hoped that Japan would support his restoration as emperor – to take refuge in the Japanese concession in

Tianjin, where he and Wanrong enjoyed the novelties and amenities of modern life. After the Japanese army invaded and occupied the Qing's old ancestral homeland Manchuria, following the pretext of the 1931 Mukden Incident, Puyi secretly travelled to Changchun in the north-east, where he was installed in 1932 as Chief Executive of Manchukuo, a puppet state of Japan. Two years later, he was made Emperor of the Great Manchu Empire, another entity tightly controlled by Japan.

In the 1930s and 1940s, the Japanese military state in Manchuria carefully manipulated the couple's images and activities to erode their Qing identity and suit the Japanese colonial and propagandist agenda. At his 1934 coronation ceremony, Puyi was not allowed to wear his court ceremonial robe, symbolic of his rulership of the Qing state. Puyi visited Japan in 1935, becoming the first Qing 'emperor' to travel internationally, reversing the centuries-old tradition that the ruler of the Great Qing should only receive emissaries from other countries in his own land. Wanrong, meanwhile, gradually disappeared from the public eye, probably due to her failing health and uncooperative attitude towards the controlling Japanese army.

As Japan launched full-scale war on China after 1937, Puyi still dreamed that he would follow in the steps of his great ancestors, who in 1644 swept down from the north-east to conquer Beijing and establish there the seat of the Qing government. After the defeat of Japan in World War II, however, Puyi had to renounce his throne once more. But Soviet troops intercepted him on his way to exile in Japan and placed him under detention in the Soviet Union. Wanrong, left behind by her husband, was captured by Communist guerrillas and soon died. In 1950, Puyi was sent back to China, where he learned for the first time of the death of Wanrong four years earlier. He found himself a prisoner again, but this time the subject of a Communist experiment to turn this former emperor into a re-educated member of the proletariat. Back in China after 1950, he learned how to tie his own shoelaces and to wash his face. In 1959, Puyi was released thanks to a special amnesty from Mao Zedong (1893–1976). After working in various jobs, including gardening and editing, Puyi died of kidney cancer at the age of sixty-one.

Throughout their lives, Puyi and Wanrong remained prisoners, first of their marriage and of Qing imperial institutions, later of the political agendas of the successive states that laid claim to China after the fall of the Qing.

In his autobiography Puyi lamented,

If her [Wanrong's] fate was not predestined at the time of her birth, it was certainly set when she married me. I have often thought that if she had divorced me in Tianjin as Wenxiu did, she might have escaped it still.

Daisy Yiyou Wang

9. LI LIANYING

李連英 (1848–1911)

CELEBRATED PALACE EUNUCH

Li Lianying's life deserves attention because, as one of the individuals who made Empress Dowager Cixi (1835–1908)'s court dominance possible, he personifies the crucial role played by the institution of eunuchs in 19th-century China. His career also usefully shifts our focus from the powerful, prominent individuals that history has conventionally deemed significant, to the marginalized servants who enable such people. Eunuchs were rarely castrated as adults but usually as children. Enormous suffering was inflicted on their bodies and their own sexuality erased to enable them to enter the space of the court – the heartland of imperial power – in a socially subordinate position. In such a way, the desexualized Li dedicated his life to serve the needs and ambitions of both his family and the Empress Dowager.

Li Lianying was born in 1848 in Lijia village, Dacheng county, in today's Hebei province, a region from which many Qing-dynasty eunuchs came. His given name was Yingtai (literally 'talented and lofty') and the name is still used today by the family's descendants. His grandfather and father worked as 'leather-fleshers' in Beijing, preparing animal hides by removing the flesh from the skin. According to the epitaph on Li's tomb, in 1856, the nine-year-old Yingtai was sent to the court as a eunuch. Multiple explanations for this decision exist. The popular narrative – retold in many anecdotes, unofficial histories, plays and even films – claims that Li's parents sent him to the court as a servant due to their extreme poverty. But a story passed down by the Li family indicates that his grandfather and father's decision was based on a prediction from a fortune teller, who told them that Li was predestined to become a monk or eunuch. If he disregarded this prophecy and instead lived as a layperson, his entire family would have suffered. According to the fortune teller, then, Li needed to sacrifice his identity as a man to safeguard his relatives. After his castration, the family preserved his male genitalia as a treasured relic and mummified them in a wooden case, which they placed inside a wicker container for measuring rice (*sheng*) suspended over a beam inside their house. Since *sheng* in Chinese also means 'rise up', the family pulled the *sheng* container slightly closer towards the beam every year as a ritual to wish for Yingtai's promotion at the palace. During his more than five decades of service, Li not only protected the entire family (if the fortune teller's prediction is to be believed) but also enriched them, through the earnings, profits from various businesses and farms, gifts, and bribery that life at court made possible.

At court, Li Lianying was given a new, official name, Li Jinxi (Jinxi literally means 'presenting happiness'). It was common practice to give eunuchs names containing characters for happiness or with other positive connotations, as such nomenclature was designed to embue their bodies and daily service to the dynasty

Yu Xunling (1874–1943), *The Empress Dowager Cixi in the Guise of Avalokiteśvara*, 1903. Glass plate negative. Height 24.1 cm, width 17.8 cm. Freer Gallery of Art and Arthur M. Sackler Gallery Archives, Smithsonian Institution, Washington, DC.

with auspiciousness. In 1860, when the Xianfeng emperor (r. 1851–1861) and his imperial entourage fled to Rehe before British and French allied forces invaded Beijing during the Second Opium War, the twelve-year-old Li started to serve Cixi. At that time Cixi was Xianfeng's second-rank consort and mother of his only son; Li was responsible for basic housework such as sweeping, serving food and grinding ink-sticks. Intelligent, hard-working and careful, he progressively learned to fathom how Cixi thought, eventually winning her trust and favour. As Li grew to adulthood, it is reasonable to assume that he also mastered various court protocols and learned from mistakes made by fellow senior eunuchs. For example, in September 1869, An Dehai

(1844–1869), Cixi's chief eunuch during the 1860s, was executed, due to alleged violations of palace rules. As early as 1866, Cixi gave Li a new palace name: Lianying, meaning 'continuing to blossom', a reference to Li's flourishing career, as well as, importantly, reflecting Cixi's own seemingly unassailable power. Li Lianying thrived in his role supporting Cixi as de facto ruler in the last three decades of the 19th century. In 1874, at the age of twenty-six, he was appointed the superintendent in the Palace of Gathering Excellence (Chuxiu gong). By 1894, the year of Cixi's sixtieth birthday, on the first day of the lunar new year, the Empress Dowager flouted protocol limiting the honour and position that could be accorded to a eunuch, and awarded Li with the hat finial and peacock feather usually presented to a senior official, indicating the high regard in which she held him.

The strong bond between the Empress Dowager and Li Lianying was demonstrated again in the role Li played in Cixi's self-identification with Guanyin, the Bodhisattva of Compassion. Court artists portrayed Cixi as the deity Guanyin in a wide range of media and formats including painted hanging scrolls, religious texts such as the *Heart Sutra* (transcribed by herself) and photographs shot by Yu Xunling (1874–1943) in front of a carefully staged setting in the new Summer Palace (Yihe yuan). In these images, Li performed as one or another of Guanyin's attendants, such as Guanyin's acolyte Sudhana, the guardian Wei Tuo or an accompanying Arhat (a Buddhist enlightened being). In the montage opposite, Li Lianying (right) wears the theatrical armour and headdress appropriate to a male martial arts character, while performing the role of Wei Tuo. He holds a *vajra* sword in his right hand and makes a gesture of prayer with his left. The subject of his prayer is Empress Dowager Cixi, who appears in the middle of the tableau, posing simultaneously as Guanyin, the most popular of all female Buddhist deities, and the empire's most powerful female sovereign. Li's supporting role enhances the deification of Cixi and projection of her political authority. In this staged scenario, he thus symbolically enacts the role he played in real life.

After Cixi passed away in November 1908, Li Lianying handled the arrangements for the Empress Dowager's final appearance in her coffin. He staged Cixi's posthumous sovereignty by dressing her in extravagant funerary clothes, placing her on elaborate bedding, and surrounding her with precious burial goods. Though the layout might have been planned by Cixi herself when she was living, it was Li Lianying who implemented her will. After Li had mourned Cixi for a hundred days and with permission from Empress Dowager Longyu (1868–1913) – who, as widow of the Guangxu emperor, succeeded Cixi as the senior woman at court – he retired and left the Forbidden City. Just three years later, on 4 March (the fourth day of the second lunar month) in 1911, he died suddenly; some speculated he overdosed on opium or even that he was assassinated. In 1966, during the Cultural Revolution, his tomb in the Enjizhuang eunuchs' cemetery in Beijing was opened and only his head was found. But who beheaded him and why remains a mystery.

Yuhang Li

10. YU RONGLING

裕容齡 (1882–1973)

DIPLOMAT'S DAUGHTER WHO BROUGHT
MODERN DANCE TO CHINA

Yu Rongling, aka Mlle Nellie Yu Keng, and later Princess Shou-shan (married name, Madame Dan Pao-Chao) is claimed by dance historiography as 'China's first modern dancer'. The widely travelled daughter of a Chinese diplomat, in 1904, she entertained the court of Empress Dowager Cixi with the 'Greek' dance she had studied in Paris, in classes taught by Isadora Duncan herself.

Yu Rongling in Paris in 1902, in 'Rose and Butterfly', a dance popularized that year by American performer Loie Fuller (1862–1928). The photograph appeared in the Chinese magazine, *New Observations*, in 1957. SOAS Library, London.

While China's dynastic upheavals at the start of the 20th century were of dramatic global consequence, their domestic impact informed radical hybrid and intercultural modern identities, afforded by expanding circuits of cultural exchange. Nevertheless, there remains something extraordinary, if not surreal, about the notion of a Manchu princess performing Duncanesque 'free dance' before an admiring Cixi and the assembled ladies and eunuchs of her court. Dismissed in the *Washington Times* as the vogueish impulse of the 'fickle' Dowager, even now the story of Yu Rongling's performance challenges inherited perceptions of a rigidly traditional Qing court, invulnerable to the assaults of modernity.

The daughter of Yu Keng (Yugeng), Cixi's Minister for Foreign Affairs, Yu Rongling (Nellie) along with her younger sister Yu Derling (Lizzie) was appointed lady-in-waiting to the empress on the family's return from Yu Keng's posting in Paris. Some fifteen months later, on 16 June 1904, Rongling gave a gala presentation at the Summer Palace in Beijing, accompanied by both court musicians and a Western orchestra brought from Tianjin. She performed a Chinese 'Ruyi' dance in Manchu dress (*ruyi* is a sceptre or staff symbolizing good fortune), then a tarantella in a Spanish gown and tasselled shawl, and finally the 'Greek' dance for which she wore an ancient Egyptian-style costume.

Yu Keng's daughters were uniquely positioned to serve as cultural go-betweens. Their mother, Louisa Pierson, was the bilingual daughter of a Boston-born merchant in Shanghai and his Han Chinese wife. That the Yus' marriage was a love match is indicative of Yu Keng's remarkably progressive beliefs, according to which he would raise his daughters. The sisters, like their two brothers, were schooled in Western arts and literature as well as the Chinese classics. The family took up residence at the Chinese legation at 4, Avenue Hoche in late summer of 1899. Their entrance to Parisian society was curtailed, however, by events back in China. Among rumblings of Boxer atrocities, false reports that the French Minister to China, Stéphen Pichon, had been assassinated in Beijing provoked a hysterical response in the French press, putting Yu Keng in a difficult diplomatic position. His response was to formally cultivate French artistic and literary figures, the legation soon becoming a cultural hub whose influence on Parisian society would counteract hostile feelings towards China. The atmosphere of her father's 'Europeanized' embassy provided an enabling environment for Rongling's aesthetic education. A piano was installed, and a teacher brought in from the Paris Conservatoire. Yu Derling left a record of their classes with Isadora Duncan, noting how her 'taller, more talented sister' was favoured for inclusion in Duncan's performances of 'Greek interpretations'. This was a crucial period of pedagogical experiment for Duncan, which would result in her seminal manifesto, *The Dancer of the Future* (1903). Duncan's public performances were noted in the social calendar of the international press, as was the inclusion of her 'talented pupil from China, Miss Nellie Yu'. Subsequently, Rongling's demonstrations of her dancing skills at diplomatic events organized by Yu Keng were recognized by the Paris correspondent of the British *Observer* as 'a sign of the appeasement which has come over the relations of China with Europe'.

The potential utility of dance in diplomacy was first sensed by Yu Keng during his ambassadorial posting to Tokyo (1895–99). Rongling gave an impromptu performance of a kabuki dance, 'Tsuru Kame' ('Crane and Tortoise'), that she had learned from a servant without her parents' knowledge. It so impressed the assembled Japanese dignitaries that afterwards a professional dancer was hired to give her formal training. The positive, widely disseminated media profile of the Yus' much-photographed eldest daughter would play no small part in re-focusing the 'yellow peril' rhetoric of the Boxer era (1899–1901). The society columns of syndicated papers typically remarked on her 'perfect type of Chinese beauty' accentuated by 'the modish costume of the French woman of fashion'.

Yu Keng recognized that the salons and drawing rooms of Paris were places where political alliances were consolidated. We would now recognize this promotion of arts and entertainment among a cosmopolitan aristocracy that circulated between Paris, London, New York and, increasingly, the Far East as the development of soft power. Indeed, it was Cixi's recognition of the need to restore her reputation with the Western world after her controversial support of the Boxers that lay behind her adoption of dance as a weapon in her diplomatic armoury. Cixi took her lead from those of China's reformists for whom cultural renewal and nation-building were intertwined, but who, not unlike Duncan, saw the source of artistic renewal not abroad but in China's own past. Having explained something of Duncan's philosophy of movement and her revival of Greek dance which, as Rongling described, was 'creating the new, as well reviving the old', Cixi requested she do the same for Chinese dance. Rongling, now honoured with the dynastic title *junzhu* (which translates as 'princess'), embarked upon a counterpart to Duncan's project. She researched Ming court dance, folk dances and classical Japanese dance, and sourced Chinese painting and Peking Opera for movement styles, creating in her repertoire three 'Chinese' dances – 'Dance of the Lotus Blossom Fairy', 'Fan Dance' and 'Ruyi Dance'.

Informed by the international encounters of a Chinese cosmopolitan elite, older Chinese cultural forms were transformed by individuals like Yu Rongling. Driven by a political impulse quite antithetical to Duncan's, Cixi's initiatives to modernize Chinese dance paved the way for dance to play a central role in the development of modern Chinese culture through the 20th century. Yu Rongling's transition from dance classes in belle-époque Paris to her eventual appointment as Mistress of Ceremonies to the Nationalist Government of the Republic of China after 1912 is an illuminating episode in China's re-positioning on the global stage in the early 20th century.

Anne Witchard

11. TAN XINPEI

譚鑫培 (1847–1917)

FIRST MODERN CHINESE OPERA STAR

Tan Xinpei's life and career embodied Chinese modernity in its Janus-faced contradictions, straddling the last hurrah of the opera-crazy Manchu court and the ever accelerating dominance of Peking Opera after the Qing's demise and the onset of the Republic. He is regarded as the greatest Peking Opera performer of his generation and a pivotal figure in the development of individual schools (*pai*) centred on a single master's performing style and repertory. Such was his influence that it was also said: 'All singers model themselves on Tan Xinpei'.

He specialized in the *laosheng* (bearded, mature male) role, the most respectable and prestigious role-type for actors in a profession that was still socially debased in the 19th century and remained so well into the 20th century. He earned the title 'King of the Actors' for his masterful amalgamation of the *wusheng* (military male) role with the *laosheng* role; for his innovative, varied, improvisational singing style, which freely adopted elements from other role-types and operatic genres; and for his dominance in the acting world both on and off the stage over more than thirty years. His lionization, economic clout, patronage network and broad fan base would not be rivalled until Mei Lanfang (1894–1961) and the star power of the female impersonator (male *dan*) role took over in the 1920s.

Born in Hubei, in today's Wuchang, Tan came from an acting family. His father Tan Zhidao (1808–1887) specialized in the *laodan* (mature female) role. Since Tan *père*'s stage moniker was Jiaotian ('Heaven Shouter'), presumably for his clarion voice that reached the skies, Tan *fils* was nicknamed Xiao Jiaotian ('Heaven Shouter Junior'). As a child, he began his formal operatic training at an opera school (*keban*) in the capital, where he studied the *laosheng* role, but, after his voice broke, switched to *wusheng*. Eventually he joined the Sanqing Troupe, where he became a protégé of Cheng Changgeng (1811–1880), the most famous *laosheng* of his generation. It was not unusual for 19th-century actors to learn more than one role-type, and alternate as circumstances dictated, but Tan's superb skills in them all gave him special versatility, and room to innovate within the system to develop new subtypes, as well as a distinct acting and singing style of his own. In 1887, at the height of his prowess, he founded his own company, the Tongchun Troupe, but he always remained more concerned with enhancing his own career than the welfare of his troupe.

The game changer was Tan's official appointment in 1890 by the Imperial Court Theatre Bureau (Shengping shu) to the post of civilian tutor (*minji jiaoxi*) in the court's Outer School (Waixue) for performers. At court, he joined other premier Peking Opera stars of the day, such as fellow *laosheng* Sun Juxian (1841–1931) and Yang Yuelou (1844–1889), with whom he had performed to great acclaim on the stages of the

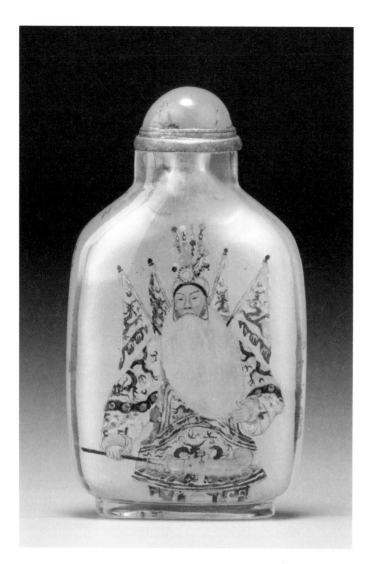

Ma Shaoxuan (1894–1932), inside-painted snuff bottle with a portrait of Tan Xinpei as General Huang Zhong in *Dingjun Mountain*, c. 1900–10. Height 6.2 cm. Water, Pine and Stone Retreat Collection. Photograph by Nick Moss.

capital. The appointment did not preclude gigs outside the palace, and the added cachet of a court post only increased an actor's demand in the public theatres and private salons of the city. A civilian tutor's duties included training eunuch actors in the Inner School (Neixue), overseeing palace productions, and helping update the court repertory of opera scripts from the outmoded Kunqu and Yiyang styles into the now fashionable *pihuang* (Peking Opera) style. His main role, however, was to perform on request for the avid and discerning Peking Opera buff Empress Dowager Cixi, who kept abreast of the latest trends and hottest commercial stars in the capital. Tan Xinpei became her favourite and was even granted an official title of the fourth rank. As Tan recalled, the Empress Dowager enjoyed throwing curve balls, having her actors take on ridiculous roles outside their specialization and deliberately giving them insufficient time to prepare. Performing under her sharp eye and catering to her creative demands helped him hone his skills, swift reflexes and star persona, not to mention greatly increasing his reputation, power and wealth. The cross-fertilization and symbiotic relation between the court theatre and the commercial Beijing stage in the late 19th century, in which Tan Xinpei played such a key role, helped propel Peking Opera's later ascension to the status of China's national theatre (*guoju*), both domestically and internationally.

Tan Xinpei's performing repertory is said to have encompassed over 300 operas, old plays that he adapted rather than new ones written for him. Like so many 19th-century actors, he had no formal schooling and was functionally illiterate, relying on memory and embodied knowledge rather than book learning. In this respect, he resembled the bulk of his compatriots in 19th-century China, who learned history mainly from the opera stage. Among Tan's most celebrated roles, still performed today, were heroic generals or military wizards in historical dramas about the warring Three Kingdoms (220–80 CE) or the Northern Song (960–1127 CE) generals of the Yang family. The heroic male figures in these plays set during past epochs of civil war or foreign invasion would have had resonance for audiences in the late Qing, when the dynasty was under such internal and external assault.

Tan Xinpei may have played the righteous hero on stage, but he was not known as especially morally upstanding or politically engaged off stage. At the time of the Boxer Rebellion against foreigners, and the Eight-Nation Alliance's defeat of the Qing army and occupation of Beijing, a sarcastic ditty criticizing the city's infatuation with operatic heroes is said to have made the rounds: 'Who cares if the nation is up or down? "Heaven Shouter Junior" is playing in town!'

Like many late Qing actors, Tan was addicted to opium and an avid gambler, but this did not prevent him from becoming president of the Actors' Guild in 1912, with all the honour and recognition from the theatre community that this position conferred. The last performance he gave was a private command occasion organized for Lu Rongting (1859–1928), the warlord of Guangxi, on the latter's visit to Beijing in April 1917. This was a sign of the times, since by then China had embarked on the warlord era (1916–28), in which the country was split into regions controlled by different military cliques. For this powerful military commander, Tan played his signature role of the loyal Northern Song general Yang Yanzhao in *Hongyang Cavern*. Soon after, Tan fell ill and died.

Tan Xinpei had eight sons and four daughters. Although he attracted disciples, his theatrical legacy was directly passed down through his sons, grandsons and great-grandsons, particularly his fifth son, Tan Xiaopei (1883–1953), grandson Tan Fuying (1906–1977) and great-grandson Tan Yuantao (1929–2020), all of who became Peking Opera stars.

Today, outside of Peking Opera, Tan Xinpei is sometimes identified as the star of the first Chinese-made film. Supposedly shot in Beijing in 1905, 1907 or 1908, and screened in a public theatre to great acclaim, the footage, ostensibly long lost, is said to have consisted of three solo-fighting sequences from the Peking Opera *Dingjun*

Mountain, featuring Tan as General Huang Zhong of the Three Kingdoms period. An iconic, widely reprinted photograph of Tan costumed as the heroic general, which also provided the model for the inside-painted snuff-bottle portrait of Tan, is sometimes even presented as a still from the film. Recent research, however, indicates that the film is most likely apocryphal. The story of the film's existence did not first appear in print until 1938, and then only as a short anonymous item in the Shanghai weekly magazine *Cinema* based on hearsay credited to an unnamed play-wright. Over the years, the story was successively elaborated and embellished and is now enshrined as fact in many histories of Chinese film. Tan Xinpei's alleged role in the birth of Chinese cinema even inspired a feature film entitled *Shadow Magic*, directed by Ann Hu (Xu Anhua) in 2000.

As well as having studio photographs taken in theatrical costume, Tan recorded arias for Pathé. Some phonograph records survive, but only those dating from 1908 and 1912 are regarded as authentic. The counterfeits (some sung by his son Tan Xiaopei), however, attest again to the magic of Tan Xinpei's name.

Judith T. Zeitlin

12. WANG YAOQING

王瑶卿 (1881–1954)

PEKING OPERA ARTIST AND MASTER TEACHER

Wang Yaoqing's life trajectory captures the radical social and artistic transformation of female impersonators (and actors more generally) in China from playthings to professionals over the first half of the 20th century. He started his career in a 'private residence' (*siyu*), or brothel, for boy actors in the late Qing, but ended it as the head-master of the most prestigious conservatory for Chinese opera training under the newly established People's Republic of China. Despite the personal tragedies that punctuated his life, he was an important agent of this change, paving the way for the next generation of Peking Opera female impersonators to play young female leads well into their sixties, with important implications for how Peking Opera, and its actors, came to be appreciated socially and aesthetically.

Wang was born into a multi-generational family of opera actors in the waning years of the Qing dynasty. Acting at the time was a career of last resort, due to a longstanding stigma associated with entertainers, and especially those who cross-dressed to play the female roles. These youths doubled as high-class 'call boys' for powerful and wealthy patrons. After losing his father at the age of ten, Wang began apprenticing in the *dan*, or young female lead, role-type in the up-and-coming *pihuang* opera, a genre that would soon come to be known as Peking Opera. He enters the historical record in the late Qing as the 'primus' in the 'flower list' of 1894, a sign that his winning looks and emerging performance skills were recognized by the aficionados who wrote guides to opera in Beijing. (Creating 'flower lists' was a literati amusement in which aficionados evaluated the best boy actors, and which archly borrowed the terminology of the imperial civil service examination rankings.) Sometime in 1896, a certain high-ranking official purchased Wang out of his contract with his school-cum-brothel, and set him up with a wife. Thereafter, Wang gathered at least three pupils in his own private training house. He was a pragmatist and the *siyu* system was his habitus; it would not be until another mode of organizing the trade of acting became thinkable that he would come to denounce such practices.

That same streak of pragmatism likely accounts for his artistic innovations. Coming of age essentially orphaned, Wang was pushed by exigency to train with many different *dan* actors, and so he learned to perform both demure *qingyi* ('blue-gown') leading lady and more vivacious *huadan* ('flowery *dan*') roles, shifting towards the *daoma dan* ('sword-and-horse martial female') role-type as his voice began to fail. His crossover style won him fans and critics alike, and set a precedent for the hybrid *huashan* ('multi-coloured smock') role-type that would be mainstreamed by the most successful *dan* actors of the Republican era.

Between 1894 and 1902, Wang moved between the best troupes in the capital. His fame captured the attention of the Qing court; starting in 1902, he was frequently summoned to the palace to perform. In 1905, Wang commenced a longstanding collaboration with the famous *laosheng* (older male lead), Tan Xinpei (1847–1917), gaining the respect of the notoriously cantankerous actor. By the first decade of the 20th century, Wang was at the height of his popularity, widely acclaimed by audiences in Beijing for his signature performances in leading lady roles in the Peking Opera repertoire.

With the fall of the Qing, Wang leveraged his stardom for social advocacy: he rejected use of the *qiao* (stilt-like shoes worn by the *dan* to imitate the look of bound feet) as demeaning to women, and he actively worked to raise the status of actors. In 1912, he joined with fellow *dan* actor Tian Jiyun (1865–1925) to petition the new political authorities in Beijing to outlaw the *siyu* system. Despite the considerable outcry from powerful opera patrons – so fierce that Tian was temporarily jailed – the new Republican government ultimately granted their request.

In the second decade of the 20th century, Wang gravitated to playing martial female roles (involving less singing) to camouflage his increasing vocal deficiencies. By 1924, Wang's voice had become so damaged – Republican-era tabloids gossiped that opium addiction was to blame – that he retired from the stage. He devoted his next thirty years to teaching and collaborating with playwrights and actors to update the existing repertory and create new operas. He gained the accolade 'Master Teacher to All' for coaching over a hundred actors (both men and women) – most famously the four predominant male *dan* of the Republican era: Mei Lanfang (1894–1961), Cheng Yanqiu (1904–1958), Xun Huisheng (1900–1968) and Shang Xiaoyun (1900–1976). In the 20th century, efforts to tame the eroticism of cross-dressing Chinese opera

Ma Shaoxuan (1894–1932), inside-painted rock-crystal snuff bottle, *c*. 1900–10. Wang Yaoqing is depicted wearing a woman's Manchu court headdress and silk jacket. He plays one of his signature roles, the Liao dynasty's Princess Iron Mirror from operas within the Generals of the Yang Family story cycle. Height 6.2 cm. Water, Pine and Stone Retreat Collection. Photograph by Nick Moss.

performers – much associated with the careers of these four stars – began, in fact, with their teacher, Wang Yaoqing. It was not until this next generation of opera actors, however, that most male *dan* continued to perform the role-type into middle age and beyond, consciously drawing upon new discourses and social movements – both domestic and foreign – to transform themselves from 'playthings' of the rich and mighty into modern theatre artists. This social elevation had aesthetic implications, too. Looks gave way to singing, and verisimilitude to aestheticism, as the chief criteria for evaluating the talents of opera actors; this led to an increased emphasis on *listening to* rather than watching Peking Opera (at least in Beijing).

Even as Wang receded to the wings as a performer, his networks forged with erudite fans during his early years served him well in navigating his personal transition into a modern professional. He collaborated with some of the most eminent men of letters of the Republican era, including, among others, the Master of Red Bean House (literary alias for former Manchu noble Putong, who was a highly accomplished amateur opera singer in his own right) to craft new operas, with the Master as lyricist and Wang as 'musical director'. Through his student Cheng Yanqiu, Wang was named an advisor to *Dramaturgy Monthly*, a journal on Chinese opera, and later became both instructor and board member for the Beijing branch of Cheng's modern-style opera training school. With each new venture, Wang's stature as an artist rose, even as the Republican-era mosquito press pitied his widower status, his hard-to-kick habits, and the untimely death of his devoted daughter (also an accomplished actress).

Towards the end of his life, once again, politics intervened to reshape Wang's livelihood and legacy. With the founding of the People's Republic of China (PRC) in 1949, the new regime created the National Academy of Chinese Theatre Arts. Wang was invited to serve as honorary advisor and instructor, and he worked collaboratively with leftist literary luminary Tian Han (1898–1968) to create a new opera based on the White Snake legend. In 1951, Wang was appointed headmaster of the academy, although his tenure was soon cut short by a debilitating stroke. After his death in 1954, he was remembered fondly by his many former students. Indeed, something of a hagiography has grown up around Wang in PRC opera scholarship. The contradictions in his life tend to be glossed over in favour of a simple, triumphalist narrative. And yet, it is precisely the complexity of a life torn between survivalist pragmatism and creative idealism – all played out against the backdrop of the dizzying shifts in political fortunes and social hierarchies from the late Qing to the mid-20th century – that made him so representative of his age.

Andrea S. Goldman

2

RELIGIOUS FIGURES

DAOISTS, BUDDHISTS, MUSLIMS
AND CHRISTIANS

The nature and structures of religious life in late imperial China contrasted sharply with the organized, monotheistic Christianity of Europe and the United States during the same period. Late imperial belief, from the Ming dynasty onwards, has generally been described as syncretic, with three major sets of teachings coexisting and sometimes coalescing: Buddhism, Daoism and Confucianism. Beliefs and practices associated with these teachings varied across different social classes, groups and needs. There were also large Muslim communities, especially in the south-west and north-west. Catholicism was tolerated by early Qing emperors, then proscribed in the 18th century; Christian churches did not establish a substantial presence until the 19th century.

This religious syncretism began with the ruling dynasty, the Qing, which harnessed Manchurian, Mongolian, Tibetan and Chinese religious ideas and practices to shore up its authority over the different ethnicities that the empire encompassed. In public, Qing emperors sponsored cults and practices that had formed the core of Chinese statecraft for centuries: the annual sacrifices at the Temple of Heaven, directly south of the Forbidden City in Beijing, represented a blend of Confucian and Daoist beliefs designed to guarantee the benevolence of Heaven and good harvests. The civil service examination system reinstated by the Qing in the late 17th century aimed to indoctrinate the empire's millions of subjects in the virtues promoted by the Confucian canon (obedience, loyalty, thrift and hard work). While the Confucian state cults conducted worship only of the impersonal sacred forces of Heaven and Earth, the imperial family participated in a range of other faiths. To bolster their authority in the protectorate of Tibet, Qing rulers also advertised themselves as Tibetan Buddhist kings. In private, within family and court settings, the Qing were even more eclectic. The imperial city contained two Manchu *tangse* shrines, including 'spirit poles' through which shamans communicated with Qing ancestors. Individual members of the imperial family held their own beliefs in Daoist goddesses, Buddhist bodhisattvas. Cixi was particularly renowned for her multi-faith patronage.

This wide-ranging approach to faith was replicated at many levels of Qing society throughout the empire (with the exception of the Manchu shamanic cults, from which Han Chinese communities were excluded). Both elite and ordinary believers deployed religion for a variety of purposes: to communicate with the dead and explain the afterlife, to cure disease, to understand the future. Different teachings were seen as more effective or appropriate for different purposes. At the most local level, religious life was organized around temples, devoted to particular deities (historical heroes and ancestors, gods and goddesses linked loosely or tightly to one of the Three Teachings), and at which Buddhist or Daoist priests, or spirit mediums, sometimes conducted rituals. Secular and religious duties often blurred into each other, with temples serving as the organizational hubs for welfare, conflict dispute and flood management, as well as rituals.

As social and economic conflict grew at the end of the 18th century, so did religiously inflected rebellions and wars, beginning with the White Lotus and Eight Trigrams rebellions, which arose from ancient millenarian beliefs. The most dramatic religious dislocations in China's 'long 19th century' sprang from frictions between the Qing state and organized faiths: especially Christianity and Islam. Islam had existed, if not always dominated, in the north-west of the Qing empire for about a millennium before the 19th century. As Qing military and political power waned, social, economic and religious conflicts between the Qing and Muslim communities in the south-west and north-west intensified and periodically erupted into war. In the 1820s, a tribal leader from East Turkestan declared jihad against the Qing. Between 1860 and 1878, rebellions by Muslim peoples in Gansu and Xinjiang against the perceived injustices of infidel Qing rule led to the effective secession of those parts of the Qing empire, and Muslim-dominated political structures replaced the repulsed Qing administration. For ten years, Xinjiang became an independent Muslim state, while Muslim political networks controlled major cities in Gansu. However, the Qing state fought back, and by the end of the century had introduced increasingly Sinicizing, controlling policies over its Muslim populations.

Following the Qing empire's defeat in the First Opium War in 1842, French negotiators succeeded in lifting a prohibition on Christianity, and Christian missionary activity in China boomed over the next half century. The dissemination of Christian teachings fed into the most destructive conflict of China's 19th century, the Taiping Civil War. A delusional schoolteacher called Hong Xiuquan convinced himself he was Jesus Christ's younger brother and led an insurrection that cost, directly and indirectly, between 20 and 70 million lives. The ideology behind the Taiping Civil War (1851–64) was a direct response to missionary preaching – a tract by the evangelist Liang Fa. The later Boxer War (1899–1901) – and the suffering and destruction that ensued – was partly provoked by missionary manoeuvres to seize land and protect 'Christian' felons from local justice. Older, more established faiths such as Buddhism, under the reviving leadership of figures like Yang Wenhui, also took nourishment from the greater opportunity afforded in the late 19th century for dialogue with the West, to build links of cultural and religious understanding between China and the rest of the world. JL

13. MIN YIDE

閔一得 (1749–1836)

HEALER, MYSTIC AND FOUNDER OF AN
ELITE SPIRIT-WRITING NETWORK

Min Yide was born into a prominent gentry family based south of the prefectural city of Huzhou in the heart of the Jiangnan region. His father Min Daxia (1716–1792) was a provincial civil service laureate and served the Qing government as a local official in charge of education. Both are mentioned, briefly, in the Min clan genealogy, which devotes more attention to other members who rose to higher ranks. Min Yide, however, building on the social capital and networks of his family, gradually rose to considerable fame as a spiritual teacher and as the manager of a temple based at Jin'gaishan, a nearby hill where the Mins had long built and maintained graves and hermitages.

This temple was devoted to Patriarch Lü (the immortal Lü Dongbin), the most prominent god among elite spirit-writing cults in this region. Spirit-writing allowed adepts to ask questions and receive all kinds of texts from the gods, who would take them as disciples and train them in various self-cultivation and self-divinization regimens. The temple had been busy providing ritual services and producing revelations since the 1760s, and continued under Min Yide's leadership.

The Min genealogy, local gazetteers and documents on the religious activities at Jin'gaishan, as well as Min Yide's own abundant writings, all provide rich accounts of his life (his birth year is sometimes given as 1758). The young Min Yide was frail and could hardly walk; he mentions a first Daoist healing experience at the age of nine. When he was thirteen he went, with his elder brother, to study at Jin'gaishan under its resident Daoist master. In 1767, Min Daxia, en route to his new posting, left his son at Tiantaishan, a major sacred mountain site in central Zhejiang. There, thanks to physical therapy, Min Yide was cured of his childhood illnesses by the abbot of the main Daoist monastery, Gao Dongli (d. 1768).

Among the members of this community of Quanzhen ('Complete Reality') school Daoists, Min Yide immediately bonded with Shen Yibing (1708–1786). Shen was both a relative – a cousin of Min Daxia – and a charismatic healer, ritual performer and inner alchemist. In 1768, when Gao Dongli died, Min Yide, then aged twenty, became the disciple of Shen, then aged sixty. Over the next eighteen years, Shen was the primary influence on Min's religious development. Min claimed to have also met various immortals, but he refers constantly to Shen's writings and oral instructions throughout his works, and he later initiated his own disciples by giving them the Quanzhen precepts in front of Shen's statue. Late in life, Min received from Shen, through spirit-writing, two long ritual and doctrinal texts that extolled Shen's role as world saviour.

Meanwhile, Min Yide pursued the life of a scion of an elite family. He prepared for the civil service examinations; he married and had two sons, born in 1781 and 1782. He took residence at and managed the Patriarch Lü temple at Jin'gaishan initially between 1780 and 1784, then went travelling again. He was present when Shen Yibing died in 1786, and Shen continued instructing him up to his last moments.

In 1790, Min was given an official appointment, on the recommendation of a high-ranking relative. He served as expectant magistrate in Yunnan province for a year, a post that left him time to pursue religious experiences; he claims to have been initiated by a mysterious monk from India at Jizushan. His father passed away in early 1792, and, upon hearing the news, Min Yide returned home immediately. He settled near Jin'gaishan for the conventional three-year mourning period. He was planning to travel again, when his mother in turn passed away. He then apparently decided not to resume his official career and to stay at Jin'gaishan.

Portrait of Min Yide (1749–1836), from *Books from the Pavilion Storing Old Works*, first published in 1834. This edition was published in Wuxing in 1904. Height 24 cm. Chinese University of Hong Kong Library.

He abandoned his family, leaving his wife and a relative to raise his two sons, and embarked on a programme of temple expansion. This turned somewhat nightmarish. In 1797, floods nearly washed away the buildings. Undaunted, Min Yide started rebuilding with a donation from a friend from Yunnan. He then ran into acute conflict with other groups claiming their rights over the temple and the land, including Buddhists and local clans. He went to Beijing, and, through family and religious connections, obtained the support of one of the most powerful metropolitan officials, Zhu Gui (1731–1807) – a Patriarch Lü devotee. This apparently settled the matter definitively and opened the way for Min's grand plans for building various shrines and a library.

Min Yide's fame and influence progressively increased. He describes himself as mostly first engaging in self-cultivation retreats, before taking disciples, writing and travelling. He was successful at attracting donors, who paid for the temple as well as roads, bridges and other infrastructure on the mountain. In almost all cases, he had first healed them, and they then regularly came to Jin'gaishan to worship Patriarch Lü, and sometimes stayed for retreats. He ordained these disciples, mostly educated men and women, including scholars, merchants and doctors, as 'lay' Quanzhen Daoists, that is, with a status as clerics but no vow of celibacy.

The ritual techniques Min Yide used to heal patients, and to teach those willing to practise, centred on inner alchemy (*neidan*), which trained adepts to mentally rebuild themselves into a transcendent being. Min practised other spiritual exercises too, including incantations and visualizations of the gods, enabling acquisition of divine powers to make rain, exorcize demons, heal illnesses, and save the souls of the dead from the hells. Unlike some of his fellows and disciples, Min did not enjoy performing spectacular rituals in public, favouring solo performances in his meditation room.

Not all who went to Min Yide for healing or advice became advanced practitioners of his spiritual techniques, but some did; a good example is the celebrated poet and official Chen Wenshu (1771–1843). Chen, exhausted from his official duties and in constant pain, went to him in 1818; Min healed him and took him as a disciple together with several of Chen's female relatives, and all became spirit-writing and alchemical practitioners.

During the last two decades of his life, Min was involved in editing several revealed texts by Patriarch Lü and other immortals, which he combined with his own writings (including commentaries and essays) in two closely related collections, *Sequel to the Daoist Canon* and *Books from the Pavilion Storing Old Works*, both first published by his temple in 1834, shortly before his death. A companion book, *The Mind-Lamp of Jin'gai*, a detailed collection of hagiographies of his predecessors, was completed in 1821. This large oeuvre was regularly reprinted by his spiritual heirs and remains in circulation today. During the second half of the 19th century, the temple at Jin'gaishan generated a vast network of further Patriarch Lü spirit-writing temples and charities, with over seventy branches across the Jiangnan region, some of which are still active.

Vincent Goossaert

14. WANYAN LINQING

完顏麟慶 (1791–1846)

BANNERMAN, OFFICIAL AND AUTHOR

Linqing was a prominent Manchu official of the Wanyan clan. He was a descendant in the 24th generation of Jin Shizong (personal name Wanyan Yong), the fifth emperor of the Jurchen Jin dynasty (r. 1161–1189). In the Manchu Qing dynasty (1644–1912), Linqing's family belonged to the privileged Imperial Household Bond-Servant Division of the Manchu Bordered Yellow Banner. He was a direct descendant of the distinguished Manchu translators Asitan (d. 1683) and Hesu (1652–1718). His father, Tinglu (1772–1820), was a Manchu aristocrat and prefect of Tai'an, Shandong, while his mother, Yun Zhu (1771–1833), was a distinguished Han Chinese poet and painter – a descendant of the famous painter Yun Shouping (1633–1690).

Linqing is most famous for his autobiographical memoir *Wild Goose Tracks in the Snow: An Illustrated Record of my Preordained Life*. In this memoir, he described 240 incidents in his life, each sumptuously illustrated by his artist secretaries. The work is divided into three volumes, each beginning with a portrait of the author, followed by eighty illustrations and accompanying texts. The first volume depicts his life up to the age of forty, and the second his life to fifty. These were first printed in the years 1839 to 1841, but originally without the illustrations. The third volume was completed in 1846, the year Linqing died. His sons Chongshi and Chonghou compiled and printed the memoir as a complete illustrated edition between 1847 and 1850. This first complete edition comprised 1,000 copies, which were brought to Beijing; but the wooden blocks were left in Yangzhou, and were eventually burned by Taiping forces in 1860. The work is highly prized by collectors and historians of woodblock illustration.

The autobiography's title is an allusion to a poem by Su Shi (1037–1101) which compares life to the markings left by a goose on the snow:

> *To what should we compare this human life?*
> *To a wild goose treading on the snow.*
> *The snow retains its tracks for a moment;*
> *The goose flies away and is lost to view.*

(based on Simon Leys's translation)

This image inspired Linqing to conceive of 240 memorable events of his life as so many 'tracks in the snow'; ephemeral yet predestined encounters during his sojourn in this mortal world.

Linqing earned his *jinshi* (the highest level of the civil service examinations) in 1809, thus beginning an extensive civil service career in various parts of the empire.

His early roles included palace writer in the Grand Secretariat, inspector in the Imperial Library, secretary in the War Ministry and compiler of the *Veritable Record* – a detailed, day-by-day chronicle of the events of each emperor's reign period – for the Jiaqing emperor (r. 1796–1820). By 1822, Linqing had been appointed to the post of prefect in Ningguo, Anhui. For his work on the *Veritable Record* he was granted imperial gifts of silk and silver plates, and the honorary rank of circuit intendant. Linqing then became involved with river conservancy for the Kaigui–Chenxu Circuit, Henan. He was promoted, again through imperial favour, to become in turn provincial high commissioner of justice in Henan, provincial high commissioner of finance in Guizhou, and governor of Hubei.

Eventually, Linqing was appointed director general of river conservancy stationed at Huai'an, Jiangsu. He was commended several times for his work in this high-ranking post, despite lacking a technical background in river control. In 1841–2, during the First Opium War, he helped to strengthen defences along the northern bank of the Yangtze River. These merits saved him from disgrace when part of the dyke along the Yellow River under his jurisdiction collapsed in 1842, and as punishment for this disaster he was merely deprived of his ranks and titles.

In 1843, Linqing returned to Beijing where two years earlier he had purchased a garden residence called the Half Acre Garden. This was a 17th-century masterpiece of design, created by the multi-talented Li Yu (1611–1680). Here, in an airy gallery above a grotto in the garden, Linqing established a library he named the Wondrous Realm of Langhuan, where he housed his large collection of books. He would remain in Beijing only three months before receiving orders to go to Zhongmou, Henan, to help repair a serious breach in the dyke there.

Wang Yingfu, *A Banquet under the Cassias to Make Mother Happy*. Linqing hosted this family feast in 1824 to celebrate receiving imperially bestowed gifts of silk and silver plates on becoming a circuit intendant. In *Wild Goose Tracks in the Snow*, volume 1, *xia*, chapter 61. Manchester Rylands Library.

In early 1845, Linqing was made amban, or imperial resident, in the Mongolian city of Urga. However, owing to an affliction in his legs and the cold climate there, he was permitted to return home. In his retirement, Linqing visited the Changping district outside Beijing to recuperate in the hot springs within the grounds of the imperial travelling lodge. He also visited the Ming tombs and Mount Pan, before returning to his garden abode, where by March 1846 he seemed to have recovered from the problem with his legs. However, he passed away just six months later. A few months before he died, Linqing fulfilled his longstanding wish to salute his ancestors at the Jin-dynasty imperial tombs at Mount Fang.

Wild Goose Tracks in the Snow is a memoir steeped in the traditional elite culture of the bannermen, and represents the end of an era, after which almost everything in the Qing Chinese universe would change. It gives precious insight into the daily life of a privileged Manchu official during the 19th century: from practical matters of river control and grain transportation to correspondence with the throne, from pleasure-seeking adventures to intimate family gatherings. Linqing's blow-by-blow account of the Chinese defeat during the First Opium War is an important record of early losses in what would come to be called the 'Century of Humiliation'.

Linqing exemplified the syncretic nature of belief in the Qing dynasty. He enjoyed revealing his familiarity with Buddhist and Daoist lore: he often lodged in Buddhist temples while travelling, and made supplications to the Daoist Patriarch Lü for guidance in decisions such as marriage and choosing the right prescription. At the same time, he was a paragon of Confucianism, who demonstrated special admiration for his mother, and also directed Manchu sacrifices in his Hall of Five Blessings to give thanks for fortunate family events.

He delighted in concluding episodes in his autobiography with an idiosyncratic verse or two of his own poetry, which often juxtapose Buddhist and Daoist symbols freely, such as the following from Chapter 55. This commemorates, after Linqing had made supplications to the local Daoist deity on a sacred mountain, the end of floods that had plagued Huizhou, Anhui, where he was serving as prefect:

This mountain screen of many folds
with its dense dark verdure,
Is a Holy Paradise
for the pursuit of Enlightenment.

Where the Curtain of Pearls waterfall
cascades like mist,
And the clouds of Incense-Burner Peak
diffuse their own perfume.

Transcendental melodies of Pacing the Void
echo throughout the crags,
As we all pay obeisance
to the splendour of Buddha's Light.

Arriving in the Prefecture
I first ascended to this Blessed Realm,
Wishing to pray for Abundance
for all Six of my Districts.
          (based on Yang Tsung-han's translation, in *Wild Goose Tracks in the Snow*)

Other poems celebrate family and friendship by drawing on themes of predestination and reincarnation, such as the following, from Chapter 188, about a butterfly visiting his garden:

Fluttering so happily
high in the sky,
You bring to mind the timeless
butterfly dream of Master Zhuang.

I thank you for thus so kindly
bringing me this moment of Bliss,
To celebrate the completion
of my humble abode.

I grieve that my lady wife is no longer with us
to pour you a libation of wine,
But I am gladdened that my grandson
could salute your fairy presence.

As you brush past the willows,
as you thread through the flowers,
Your soaring flight is surely a portent
of some predestined affinity.

Christina Sanderson

15. YANG WENHUI

楊文會 (1837–1911)

FATHER OF MODERN CHINESE BUDDHISM

Yang Wenhui, also known as Yang Renshan, was a Chinese Buddhist layperson who rose from humble beginnings to become a figure of major importance in modern Chinese history. Yang is best known for helping to revive and reform Chinese Buddhism at the end of the Qing dynasty and for establishing an international network of Buddhists that connected China to Europe, Japan and India. He was born in Anhui province, but was raised in Beijing, where he received a conventional education in the Confucian and Daoist classics. In 1863, his father passed away and he was beset with a severe illness. Around that time, he chanced upon a Buddhist text in a bookstore, *The Awakening of Faith*, and had a conversion-like experience. That text helped him through his difficulties, sparked his interest in Buddhism, and profoundly shaped the course of his life.

Needing to support his family, he went to Nanjing to assist with its reconstruction after the city suffered massive devastation during the Taiping Civil War (1851–64). While there, he established a group of friends with a common interest in Buddhism. He witnessed first-hand how the Taiping Civil War had not only destroyed that city, but also irreparably damaged Buddhism. Temples were razed, images smashed and libraries burned, leading to the loss of a large number of Buddhist scriptures. This dire situation inspired Yang to study Buddhism further, and also initiated a frenzied search for surviving Buddhist texts, which he resolved to collect and reprint.

In 1866, Yang founded the Jinling Scriptural Press – one of his greatest accomplishments – with the aim of publishing lost Buddhist scriptures. Its publications were in the traditional woodblock format, and the press quickly attained a reputation as a printer of high-quality editions. The press has printed over a million copies of texts and remains in existence still today, despite undergoing severe hardship during the

Photograph of Yang
Wenhui. c. 1867–87.
Jinling Buddhist Press
(Jinling kejingchu).

mid-20th century. Yang was never ordained as a Buddhist monk, since he had a negative view of the clergy, but he became an influential lay practitioner who believed that disseminating Buddhist writings was the best way to replace lost scriptures, revive Chinese Buddhism and address the ills of Chinese society.

In 1878, Yang relocated to London to work at the Chinese legation, and he later spent time in Paris. While in London, Yang visited the British Museum and was delighted to discover Buddhist texts that were no longer extant in China. He met and befriended the Japanese Buddhist Nanjō Bunyū (1849–1927), who had been sent to England to study Sanskrit and philosophy at Oxford with Max Müller (the editor of the influential *Sacred Books of the East* series). Throughout their lifelong friendship, Nanjō helped Yang secure hundreds of Buddhist texts that had been lost in China, so he could reprint them at his press. Yang provided Nanjō with Chinese scriptures to assist with his project on a compilation of a supplement to the Buddhist canon in

Japan. This international collaboration was part of a late 19th-century effort to find lost Buddhist texts, especially those in Sanskrit, which had an important influence on the development of modern Western, Japanese and Chinese Buddhist studies.

Yang became a key conduit to the West and encouraged further exchanges between Europe and China. While in England, he was brought face to face with advancements in Western technology. He purchased a microscope, telescope, gramophone and camera, which he brought back to China. Unfortunately, however, Yang's extensive photo archive was destroyed during the War of Resistance Against Japan (1937–45).

After returning to China, Yang remained a node connecting China to other parts of the world. In 1893, for instance, he met the Indian Buddhist Anagarika Dharmapala, who was trying to restore – and reform – Buddhism in India. Dharmapala had founded the Mahā Bodhi Society and had just achieved international renown in the wake of a fiery speech he delivered at the World's Parliament of Religions in Chicago (1893). Yang expressed his desire for more exchanges between India and China, and they shared a vision of spreading Buddhism around the world.

Yang later met the Christian missionary Timothy Richard (1845–1919) and together they produced a translation of *The Awakening of Faith* (1894), the text that had been so important to Yang personally and had become an essential primer of Buddhism in China. This was one of the first substantive collaborations between a Western Christian and a Chinese Buddhist. Yang hoped the translation would help spread Buddhism in the West, but later expressed regret at how Richard had overly 'Christianized' the text.

In 1898, China entered a period of reform that included an effort to turn Buddhist temples into schools as part of China's modernization efforts. Seeking to disseminate information about Buddhism through education, Yang set up a school, the Jetavana Hermitage, opened in 1908 to lay and monastics alike. This is one of the first instances, but not the last, of an institution in which a layperson taught Buddhist monastics and became a model for Buddhist education in China. Yang also wrote the school's textbooks. While only open for little over a year, the Jetavana Hermitage helped to educate the next generation of Buddhist leaders in China, like Taixu (1890–1947) and Ouyang Jingwu (1871–1943). Given Yang's enduring interest in science and technology, it is no surprise that his curriculum was primarily focused on Yogācāra Buddhism, which he, and other Buddhists, thought was the most amenable to modern science and epistemology. Some years after the closing of the Jetavana Hermitage, Yang founded the Buddhist Research Society, which focused on the scholastic study of Buddhism, and reprinting lost and rare Buddhist texts.

After Yang Wenhui died, at the age of seventy-five, he was buried in a pagoda on the site of the Jinling Press, to which he had dedicated his life. Looking back, we can appreciate how Yang's life both reflected and contributed to China's transition to modernity. Yang is remembered today as an important lay reformer of Chinese Buddhism – sometimes referred to as the 'Father of Modern Chinese Buddhism'

– and for his work printing Buddhist scriptures. His life is also noteworthy for the ways he endeavoured to build bridges of cultural exchange, understanding and cooperation, between China and Japan, China and India, and China and the West, during the waning days of the Qing dynasty.

James Robson

16. YUSUF MA DEXIN

馬德新 (1794–1874)

ISLAMIC SCHOLAR AND HAJJI

The route Hajji Yusuf Ma Dexin took on leaving his home town Dali in Yunnan province in 1841 was a mix of the old and the new. First, he joined a caravan of Muslim merchants travelling the old spice routes to cross into Burma (Myanmar). Then he floated downstream on the Irrawaddy by boat, before travelling by steamship, via Calcutta (Kolkata), to the Arabian Peninsula. While there, he not only performed the hajj, but also paused to seek out the birthplace of the Prophet and the famed battlefields of Badr, before travelling on to Medina. He made a point of exploring the

Pages from *Record of a Pilgrimage Journey*, by Yusuf Ma Dexin, translated into Chinese by his disciple Ma Anli, Kunming, 1861. The Kaaba and Masjid al-Haram, or Great Mosque of Mecca (Makkah), in Saudi Arabia are depicted. Woodblock-printed, ink on paper. Cambridge University Library.

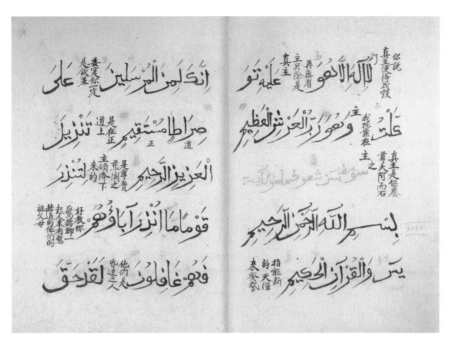

The beginning of Sūrat 36 Yā Sīn from a Qur'an with interlinear Chinese translation, early 19th century. This book was taken by William Gabbett (1810–1866, later major general of the Madras Horse Artillery) from the house of a Muslim admiral in Xiamen during the fall of Xiamen to the British in 1841, at the time of the First Opium War. British Library, London.

regions in which he found himself, visiting Yemen, Jeddah and Damascus, and living for some months in Jerusalem. He went to Cairo twice, staying six months to study at the Al-Azhar University, and wrote admiringly of the society he saw there. He called on the sultan in Istanbul and was granted permission to visit the city's imperial palace. He journeyed to the graves of Muslim holy men and of ancient thinkers such as Galen and Ptolemy. He returned to China in 1849, his hajj having taken him eight years.

When he returned to China, he wrote a book about it: *Record of a Pilgrimage Journey*. As for many of his writings, Ma Dexin composed this work in Arabic and had it translated into Chinese by his disciple Ma Anli (1820–1899) in 1861. Typically, Ma Dexin did not write of the exceptional nature of his travels, but instead wrote a travel guide. *Record of a Pilgrimage Journey* was intended to demystify the hajj, describing the physical route and the details of the journey, in the hope that other Chinese Muslims would be encouraged to set forth. In previous centuries, the hajj had been a distant dream for most Chinese Muslims. The few believers who completed the pilgrimage became legendary teachers, returning with precious texts and initiations into Sufi mysteries. By contrast, Ma Dexin hoped that his pilgrimage (including the steamship) might serve as an example for Chinese Muslims to follow, opening the paths between Muslims in China and their co-religionists elsewhere – a process that has continued to play out over the centuries since.

Born in Dali and a descendant of the first provincial governor of Yunnan, Sayyid 'Ajall Shams al-din Umar al-Bukhari (1211–1279), who had been installed by the

Mongol Yuan dynasty, Ma Dexin came from a family of Islamic clerics. He began his religious education in the usual fashion, studying under an elder at his local mosque. As an adult, already able to read Arabic and Persian, he travelled to Shaanxi to study at a scripture hall under Master Zhou Laoye (*c.* 1770–*c.* 1850), following a tradition that focused on the Chinese-language corpus of Islamic texts, known as the Han kitab. Ma Dexin's hajj brought him fame. On his return, he became head imam of the Huilong madrasa, south of Dali, where he gathered a loyal following of students and disciples. He wrote extensively in Arabic and Chinese, producing textbooks for his students, translating key Persian and Arabic works into Chinese, and authoring works of Islamic philosophy and science. Ma Dexin's approach combined a profound respect for the Sino-Islamic canon with a commitment to methodological Arabic teaching and scholarship. The capstone of his life's work was perhaps his attempt to produce the first systematic translation of the Qur'an into Chinese, a project unfinished at the time of his death.

Ma Dexin's position in Muslim society in Yunnan inevitably drew him into politics. Relations between the Han Chinese and Chinese Muslims (the Hui) in the province had been fraught for decades, and further exacerbated by the tendency of Qing officials to side with the Han in disputes. Escalating violence culminated in the 1856 Massacre of Kunming, in which 8,000 Hui were murdered by Han militias with the sanction of the state. Ma Dexin, as the leading Islamic cleric in Yunnan, helped spread news of the massacre, as Muslims across Yunnan took up arms against the Qing in response. The rebellion spread fast, and the Qing quickly lost control across the province. As religious teacher to several Muslim leaders, Ma Dexin played a key role in mediating between the different rebel factions throughout the course of what became the Panthay Rebellion (1856–73). The precise nature of his involvement remains ambiguous: there are records in which he appears as a rebel leader, but others in which he called for peace. In 1874, a year after the Panthay Rebellion had formally ended, a local official named Cen Yuying (1829–1889) charged Ma Dexin with attempting to foment unrest. Ma Dexin was to be arrested and brought back to Kunming to face charges, but instead the official had him executed on the spot.

Ma Dexin ushered in Chinese Islamic modernity. His hajj speaks to a new, cosmopolitan Islamic world; his career as an educator was dedicated to both Chinese Islamic tradition and preparing his students to meet the Arabic-speaking world. His death, however, indicates the entrenched nature of anti-Muslim prejudice in late Qing China.

Hannah Theaker

17. HONG XIUQUAN

洪秀全 (1814–1864)

INSPIRER OF THE TAIPING

Hong Xiuquan inspired and fought an enormously destructive, fourteen-year civil war, which almost toppled the Qing empire, and drove a decentralization of authority that led directly on to the violent disunity of the 20th century. The traumatic memory of this fragmentation of political power continues to haunt policy calculations in China today.

In 1851, the Heavenly Kingdom of Great Peace (Taiping Tianguo) – often shortened to Taiping in English – launched their war against the Qing dynasty, establishing a capital in the city now called Nanjing in 1853. The Taiping Civil War, which finally ended in 1864, cost between 20 and 70 million direct and indirect lives, within an estimated population of 400 to 450 million people. The original cause of the uprising seems to have been visions experienced by Hong Xiuquan, following his failure to pass the lowest civil service examinations. Born in Guangzhou (Canton), he was of Hakka background – a southern Chinese population group tending to be much poorer than other groups and driven to migration, whose members often worked hard to achieve upward social mobility.

Hong was a typical example of these social ambitions and the frustrations that they engendered. When he failed the examinations for a third time, in 1837, he suffered a mental breakdown that lasted weeks, during which he had numerous visions, before slowly recuperating. When he failed yet again in 1843, he returned to these earlier dreams, and, after rereading a Christian pamphlet he had received in 1836,

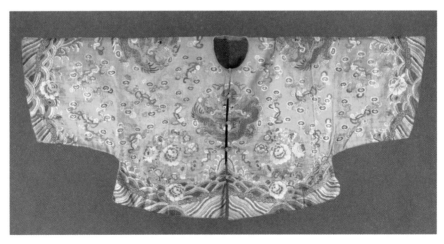

Riding jacket (*magua*) that once belonged to one of the Taiping Heavenly Kings, Nanjing, 1860–64. Embroidered silks on satin. Height 59 cm, width 132 cm. Taiping Heavenly Kingdom History Museum, Nanjing.

Illustration of Hong Xiuquan from *L'insurrection en Chine, depuis son origine jusqu'à la prise de Nankin*, 1853. University of Oxford.

德天

and with the help of a cousin, he developed a coherent narrative in which he had been assigned a heavenly mission by the 'Old Father' (an Old Testament-style Christian God) to destroy evil demons. In his dreams, Hong was given a sword and a seal to serve as his weapons. He also encountered another person, whom he identified as his elder brother Jesus, who would help him in his exorcising mission. In the religious hierarchy of the Taiping movement, Hong would become known as the Younger Brother and derive much of his authority from this claimed kinship. In Hong's visions, the figure of Confucius, so central to traditional Chinese education, was identified as one of the villains in a struggle between good and evil.

Hong Xiuquan was never the real leader – in practical, logistical terms – of the Taiping movement, but certainly provided its essential inspiration. Although, in his original dreams, the overtly Christian dimensions of his envisioned mission remained quite limited, this gradually changed, as Hong and his closest circle expanded their understanding of the religion, though always on their own interpretive terms. Other Taiping believers would add indigenous religious practices to their faith, such as possession by the Old Father (Yahweh or God) and the Elder Brother (Jesus), and ideals about communal life and land reform. After his last examination failure in 1843, Hong Xiuquan baptized himself, and started to engage in iconoclastic behaviour, within the context of southern Chinese society. He threw away the statues of the deities worshipped by his community and, especially important symbolically, he removed the tablet of Confucius from the school where he was teaching. From late summer 1851, the year in which Hong formally proclaimed the founding of the Taiping Heavenly Kingdom, to 1864, when Hong and his followers were besieged by Qing forces trying to destroy them, the Manchu Qing and their representatives were identified as the demons (of Hong's visions) requiring extermination. With this, Hong's message became explicitly one of rebellion against the imperial government.

The work of this rebellion, however, was undertaken by others, above all talented military leaders. In 1853, Taiping armies took control of the old imperial capital of Nanjing, which they occupied until it was reconquered by Qing forces in 1864. Between 1853 and 1864, Hong became increasingly reclusive and unpredictable, for example maintaining a large harem of concubines, while the Taiping rank-and-file were subject to puritanical rules, such as strict segregation of the sexes. In June 1864, a few weeks before Qing forces retook Nanjing, Hong died of unconfirmed causes.

Barend ter Haar

18. LIANG FA

梁發 (1789–1855)

CHINESE EVANGELIST AND FIRST PROTESTANT MINISTER

Liang Fa, or in full Liang Gongfa (Cantonese: Leung Keung-Fah), was born in 1789 in a village in Gaoming (Cantonese: Koming) district in Foshan (Fatshan) municipality, west of Guangzhou. Since he came from a deprived household, his parents could not afford to send him to school until he was eleven. Once there, his teachers did their best to instil a solid sense of classical Confucian morality into the young Liang. Four years later, he followed his family to Guangzhou and eventually became a woodblock cutter. Following the death of his mother in 1810, he devoted himself to woodblock printing, becoming a sought-after expert in the art of carving characters into printing blocks.

It was at this juncture in his life that Liang became acquainted with Robert Morrison (1782–1834), a member of the London Missionary Society (LMS), who had arrived in Guangzhou in 1807 as an employee of the British East India Company. By 1811, Liang had begun to take advantage of the generous pay offered by the LMS to assist Morrison in his major translation project, that of the entire Bible into Chinese, by carving the parables and stories of the Evangelist Luke and of the Apostle Paul into printing blocks. While this long-term work was advancing, Liang also produced a Chinese version of *A True History of the Words and Deeds of the Redeemer* by William Milne (1785–1822), a close colleague of Morrison, and thereby became acquainted with the basic tenets of Christianity. The missionaries must have trusted Liang to no small degree, since the fact that he was assisting in translation work (illegal under the regulations of the Canton System, the set of restrictive rules that had governed

Portrait of Liang Fa from George Hunter McNeur's *China's First Preacher: Liang A-Fa 1789–1855*, published in Shanghai by Kwang Hsueh Publishing House & Oxford University Press (China Agency), 1934.

contact between the Chinese and Europeans in Guangzhou since 1760) and in the propagation of Christianity (prohibited by the Qing since 1724) put the missionaries, and the printers too, at considerable risk. Moreover, Liang was a practising Buddhist, a fact that could have deterred him from collaborating with Christian missionaries from countries with clearly defined, mutually exclusive cultural traditions. However, Liang was open-minded, and worked in a country with deep-rooted tolerance towards different religious traditions. Christianity, after all, had been known in China since at least the 8th century. As Liang approached his twenty-eighth birthday, he went through a period of soul-searching. After he indicated that he was considering conversion, Milne examined his intentions prior to his baptism.

Liang spent the years 1817 to 1818 in Malacca, where, under the pseudonym Xueshanzhe ('Pursuer of Virtue'), he assisted in the publication of the *Chinese Monthly Magazine*, published since 1815 by Milne. Meanwhile, Liang also trained novices in the art of woodblock carving. Upon his return to Guangdong, Liang made himself known to his family and local society as a proselytizing Christian, equipped with a condensed version of the scripture, which he referred to as the *Annotated Summary of the Records of Universal Redemption*. He applied himself so fervently that he was arrested by yamen officials, who forced Liang to pay all the money he had earned in Malacca to them, rather than spend it on his family. Nevertheless, he persevered and made such an impression on his future wife that she too converted. Liang Fa and his wife (a woman with the surname Li) thus became the first Protestant Christian family in China; their son Liang Jinde (1820–1862) was baptized by Robert Morrison in 1823. For the subsequent decade Liang was preoccupied with missionary work and the production of religious pamphlets. When the tensions that would eventually lead to the First Opium War (1839–42) resulted in prohibitive action against both Western missionaries and Chinese preachers, Liang followed the foreign missionaries to Singapore, where he stayed until the outbreak of the war. He would continue his missionary work while based at the missionary Boji Hospital (Pok Tsai Hospital) in Guangzhou until his death in 1855.

Following the demise of William Milne in 1822 and the departure of Robert Morrison in 1826, Liang Fa became the first indigenous missionary in the service of the LMS. In subsequent years, Liang made himself known as an accomplished author of Christian tracts, as well as a preacher. A slow process of conversions among his fellow countrymen ensued, though by the early 1830s the local inhabitants of the Cantonese heartland had become wary of Liang's sermons. Western missionaries, for instance David Abeel and Elijah Bridgman of the American Board of Commissioners for Foreign Missions, were also aware of his talents. Introduced by the newly returned Robert Morrison, Bridgman requested to bring up the young Liang Jinde, who not only studied the Christian faith and Western knowledge, but also learned colloquial English.

Liang's historically most far-reaching contribution was his own synposis of the Christan faith published in 1832, namely, as rendered by a contemporary English missionary, *Good Words Exhorting the Age*. The tract, consisting of excerpts from Morrison's translation of the Bible, as well as Liang's own prose, may have been far from the peak of literary achievement that a literatus trained in classical studies would have been able to accomplish. However, the popularity of the *Exhortations* left an indelible imprint on the history of the late Qing empire. It became part of the socio-religious edifice which Hong Xiuquan (1814–64) built for his Taiping Heavenly Kingdom (1851–64). The egalitarian and eschatological visions that Hong propagated were largely in line with the ideals expressed in the book. The tract also contained strict rules governing the behaviour of women, as well as against the consumption of alcohol and opium, ideas that similarly made their appearance in Taiping government and society. What Liang would have said about the excessive violence of the Taiping militias, or about their racist attitudes against Manchus and Mongols, is not known.

With Liang Fa's missionary work in mind, did he contribute to the modernization of China? In two respects, yes. Despite the thoroughly traditional Confucian social attitudes that permeated his upbringing and writings, the mere fact that he contributed to the indigenization of the (Protestant) Christian enterprise led to the intensification of Sino-Western contacts, that hastened the 'occidentalization' of China during the 19th century. Secondly, Liang's writings influenced the ideological fabric of the Taiping movement, which in turn generated the cataclysmic Taiping Civil War, and led to a radical change in economic and administrative policies, following the eventual victory of the Qing forces in 1864. For better or for worse, Liang Fa's name is thus inextricably entwined with the course taken by China in the 19th century.

Lars Laamann

3

MILITARISTS

SOLDIERS, MARTYRS, MERCENARIES
AND PIRATES

The external and internal wars of China's 'long 19th century' transformed the Qing military. The dynasty began the century with an elite, hereditary force of 'banner armies', descended from those who had enabled the dynasty to conquer China from its north-eastern homeland in the 1640s. Bannermen and their families lived in garrisons kept separate from the majority Han population. The Green Standard Army, of Han Chinese soldiers, was about three times larger than the banner forces but enjoyed much less funding and prestige.

During the first 150 years of Qing rule, its armies more than doubled the dimensions of the empire inherited from the preceding Ming dynasty. But by the beginning of the Jiaqing reign (1796–1820), serious military weaknesses were apparent. Green Standard forces were badly paid and equipped, and – deployed in larger numbers than banner soldiers – failed to suppress a major insurrection, the White Lotus Rebellion, in central China. The stipends paid to bannermen were unable to keep up with empire-wide inflation. Thanks to the 'Pax Manchurica' established in the mid-18th century – the subjugation and absorption of territories north and north-west of the capital in Beijing – the Qing had not felt an imperative to equip its armies with the same cutting-edge technologies that European armies competitively developed during the Napoleonic Wars. (The British war machine was moreover significantly boosted by the state's ability to raise national debt to cover military expenditure.) The Qing also lacked an effective seagoing navy, for it had not required one for more than a hundred years. It therefore struggled to suppress a major piracy crisis (in which Shi Yang played an important part) on its south and east coasts. When a more redoubtable antagonist – the British Navy – attacked its coastlines in 1839, at the start of the First Opium War, the Qing military establishment was battered by the superior guns and warships of the British.

The 1850s to 1860s witnessed conflicts that thoroughly exposed the shakiness of the Qing military – of which Nergingge represented the old guard – and dictated a radical overhaul. The Second Opium War (1856–60) saw the invasion by Anglo-French forces of Beijing, and their sacking of the emperor's Summer Palace. By 1853, most of the prosperous south-east had been occupied by Taiping armies determined to annihilate the Qing. Further rebellions threatened to break off large parts of the south and north-west. The failure of the old banner and Green Standard forces to suppress these insurrections galvanized two radical solutions. First, the Qing accepted help – weapons, training, logistics – from Western powers (Charles Gordon's entry point into Qing warfare). From the 1860s, the Qing opened arsenals and shipyards to modernize its military machine. The crisis of the Taiping and other civil wars also led to the creation of new, regional armies, raised by imperial officials native to those regions. Personal, localist ties made these new armies cohesively loyal to each other and unified them in the war against the Taiping, which these new forces won for the Qing – at appalling human cost, as Huang Shuhua's story attests – in 1864. The men who recruited these regionalist forces – such as Zeng Guofan and Li Hongzhang – were Han Chinese, and their success shifted power and credibility away from the Manchu and Mongol banner forces that had previously dominated the dynasty's war machine.

Despite the time, money and effort expended on modernization of the army – 'Self-Strengthening' – subsequent commentators saw this project as a failure. In 1884–85 and 1894–95, conflicts with the French and Japanese respectively destroyed the Qing's newly minted navy and humiliated its ground forces. Defeat at the hands of Japan in 1895, and the punitive invasion of north China by a joint force drawn from seven Western powers and Japan in 1900, especially, led to a deepening of military reform. In its final decade, the Qing – under the direction of Yuan Shikai – created a thoroughly businesslike, modern New Army: disciplined, ideologically cohesive, well-armed and well-paid. The officer corps was professionalized, through attendance at new military academies, and given new elite status.

But the radical renewal of modernization proved a double-edged sword for the dynasty. On the one hand, the new armies enhanced state power. On the other, the reforms created new breeds of ambitious, modernized men (and also women, such as Qiu Jin) to whom imperial tradition seemed increasingly pointless. Around 1908, pro-republican, revolutionary organizations began infiltrating the new, modernized army: to turn the loyalty of China's military elite to the anti-Manchu cause. Finally, on 9 October 1911, a group of New Army revolutionaries making bombs in Hankou, a city in central China, accidentally detonated one of their explosives. As the Qing set to hunting down the conspirators, the revolutionary ring decided to act quickly before they were arrested and executed. After a day of mutiny in the local barracks, the forces loyal to the Qing were defeated, and the revolt spread chaotically through army headquarters up and down the country. In less than three months of the army abandoning the Qing, a new republic had been founded and the last emperor had abdicated. The New Army that the Qing had built to protect its imperium brought about its demise. JL

19. NERGINGGE

訥爾經額 (1784–1857)

MANCHU OFFICIAL AND MILITARY STRATEGIST

A senior Manchu strategist and official, Nergingge was an emblematically defiant remnant of the old guard in the Qing military, still dedicated to 17th- and 18th-century arts of war, despite the empire's epochal defeat by British gunboats in the First Opium War (1839–1842). His disregard for European military technology notwithstanding, Nergingge's name made it to the Baltic shores of north-east Germany, when officers from the German Navy carried it back from the Boxer War in China in 1900 as an inscription on two cannon. The barrels had been cast half a century earlier in Zhili (the metropolitan province around Beijing) in 1843, the year after the First Opium War, when they were named 'Victory' cannon (though they did not deliver on this promise). It is a supreme irony that Nergingge – albeit in name only – travelled to Europe, as he himself would never have supported the Westernizing Self-Strengthening Movement to reform the army, education and governance, which took off during the 1860s as a reaction to the Qing empire's failed confrontations with British forces during the Opium Wars. By the time of his death in 1857, a few years before Qing diplomats and students started to head West as observers

Archer on horseback, from Nergingge's *Illustrated Explanations of Military Skills*, dated 1843. Height 30 cm. Chinese University of Hong Kong Library.

and students, Nergingge already seemed superannuated. The reforming, post-1860 generations wanted to forget about Nergingge, believing that reactionaries like him had stood in the way of progress for far too long.

The design of the cannon was authored by none other than the Jesuit missionary Father Ferdinand Verbiest (1623–1688) for the court of the Kangxi emperor (r. 1662–1722), but the weapons themselves were cast on Nergingge's orders when he was governor of Zhili (1840–53). This decision shows how deep Nergingge's trust was in Qing military tradition, seemingly wanting to reinforce the old 'Manchu Way', which from 1644 to 1796 had delivered victory upon victory for the court. The cannon were part of Nergingge's broader ambition to resurrect old strategies. Also in 1843, Nergingge received the emperor's approval to publish and disseminate his *Illustrated Explanations of Military Skills*. This picture book of manoeuvres was published to re-discipline the infantry, instructing them to practise their old drills till they knew them like 'the palms of their hands'. Instead of adapting warfare to the new, European enemy (and its formidable gunboats) that had recently appeared on China's coasts, Nergingge looked backwards, to emulate the might of Qi Jiguang (1528–1588), the Ming general who defeated Japanese pirates in the 16th century. Nergingge wanted, the *Illustrated Explanations* declares, to 'turn the weak into the powerful, the cowards into the brave'. However, after the Second Opium War (1856–60) was lost, it was clear that, while the Qing had focused on reinforcing traditional military tactics and weapons within their armies, the British Army had continued to modernize, widening ever further the gap between the two forces. The diplomat Xue Feng (1838–1894) voiced a popular, ridiculing sentiment when he wrote in his *Notes from a Commonplace Hut* (posthumously published in 1897) that Nergingge 'lived like a prince, but knew nothing about warfare'. This was a harsh judgment of a man who devoted his entire life to serving the Qing court and oppressing those who challenged it.

The Manchu Nergingge was born into the Feimo clan within the Plain White Banner. Before turning twenty, he passed the palace examination to become a graduate in translation (*fanyi jinshi*), a degree that had been created to recruit students with strong abilities in Manchu and Mongolian. His career took off, and over half a century, Nergingge served in many posts throughout the empire. He received his first accolade as inspector of Shandong in 1823. While new to the job, he cross-examined an arch-criminal who was refusing to confess to any of his wrongdoings against the empire. But after Nergingge interrogated him 'day and night', the man eventually confessed. An honorary feather – a coveted imperial award – was bestowed upon Nergingge. But decades of turbulence lay ahead, during which the court went from praising to jailing him.

After being promoted, Nergingge became the governor of Shandong. There he contended with the aftermath of floods that had devastated local lives and livelihoods. He pleaded with the court to grant a tax rebate. The court agreed, but in 1836 handed him another formidable challenge: suppressing a violent sectarian anti-Qing uprising in Hunan led by Lan Zhengzun (d. 1850). When officials from the Ministry of Personnel arrived to conduct their regular inspection, it emerged that Nergingge had failed to catch Lan. He received an ultimatum: he was to catch Lan within the year, or face consequences. Nergingge then claimed that his men had chased Lan down and beaten him to death. They presented his clothes as evidence. However, the court was not at all convinced by the old rags. They removed Nergingge from his position immediately and sent him to Tibet, on the furthest edges of the empire.

But Qing governance worked in volatile ways; before long, Nergingge was back in the office of governor. In 1840, when Qishan, the governor of Zhili (the province in which the capital was located), rushed to Canton (Guangzhou) to inspect the damage that the British Army had inflicted on the south coast in the opening engagements of the First Opium War, Nergingge replaced him in the north. As soon as it became clear that Qing policy would not contain the British to the south, Nergingge acted. He started to strengthen camps and garrisons near the capital, building defence posts and barracks, and organizing the artillery and militia. When the British Navy reached Tianjin in 1840, carrying out attacks on the coastline, the court sent Nergingge to resist them. Once in situ, Nergingge observed a worrying shortage of military manpower. He started to recruit tens of thousands of men in the area, ranging from trained infantry to migrant workers. Anticipating the British Army landing on Qing shores, Nergingge ordered trenches to be dug on each side of the river heading inland. Despite his efforts to strengthen the coastal defences of the north, the Qing lost the wider war with the British Army on the south and south-east coasts. Nonetheless, Nergingge's labours were recognized by the court, which appointed him 'tutor to the crown prince' (taizi taibao).

By 1842, the First Opium War was over, but the court knew that new threats were looming domestically as well as from the West. In response, the court entrusted Nergingge to design a manual entitled *Illustrated Explanations of Military Skills*. The resulting book of military drills was a major achievement, at least in the eyes of the Daoguang emperor (r. 1821–1850) and Nergingge. The latter designed training methods that, he believed, would turn the soldiers of the increasingly discredited Green Standard Army (which sat below the elite bannermen in the Qing's military hierarchies), as well as civilian militias, into effective fighting forces. However, both before and after the publication of Nergingge's work, the army was in complete disarray. Contemporaries of Nergingge, such as Zuo Zongtang (1812–1885), recounted that the Green Standard Army was overwhelmed by unskilled civilian volunteers, who had joined hoping to protect themselves and their families from the turmoil intensifying throughout the empire. The drills that Nergingge set out in his book and imposed on this mass of raw recruits would prove utterly ineffective in the Second Opium War (1856–60). Images from the book show soldiers practising pointing their bows while bending their legs (as if on a horse); such exercises taught nothing of the difficult skill of riding while shooting accurately. His instructions for infantry archers were completely inadequate to teach untrained amateurs to fight the modern, post-Napoleonic ships, guns and cannon of European empires, or to defend the Qing in the brutal civil wars of the mid-century. In presenting this manual to his emperor, Nergingge proved that – in Xue Feng's bitterly dismissive words – he 'knew nothing about warfare', or at least nothing that would help the Qing empire reinvent itself in the era of modern, industrial firepower. After being incarcerated in 1853 for failures dealing with the Taiping army's push on north China, Nergingge then faded from public service, and died four years later.

Fresco Sam-Sin

20. SHI YANG

石陽 (c. 1775–1844)

FEMALE PIRATE CHIEF

Control of the South China Sea remains one of the most contentious issues in Asia today. In the long 19th century, it became pivotal to the survival of the Qing, who were not, as is often wrongly assumed, exclusively a land-based power that cared little about the ocean until after the arrival of Western gunboats in the 1840s.

The Qing coastline stretched over 14,000 kilometres from the northern Gulf of Bohai, where the Ming Great Wall meets the East China Sea, to Hainan Island in the south. Security of the coastal frontier was a crucial part of safeguarding the realm. The southern coastline, comprising the modern provinces of Jiangsu, Zhejiang, Fujian, Guangdong and Guangxi, was plagued by pirates, local bandits and smugglers, who operated in large fleets, often with their families on board. Some of these sailors were originally fishermen who were forced into a life of crime through misfortune, and after suffering raids on their own boats or coastal homes.

Pirates smuggled goods, extracted protection money from ships and threatened the security of international traders and diplomatic missions. Fixing this problem, which was not new to the Qing (there had been piracy in the South China Sea throughout imperial history), was the remit of government administrators, posted to coastal cities such as Fuzhou, Xiamen and Guangzhou.

Shi Yang was born in the coastal province of Guangdong at the end of the Qianlong reign, in about 1775. Without family protection, she started her career in her teens as an illiterate and vulnerable sex worker, plying her trade on a floating brothel or pleasure boat, drifting along the Pearl River in Guangzhou. However, she was more fortunate than many of her peers. In 1801, aged twenty-six, she secured her exit from her life as a prostitute by marrying the feared pirate Zheng Yi (1765–1807), and with the support of his family she built a vast pirate army.

Between 1792 and 1802, the Tayson kings of the Vietnamese state employed a Chinese pirate confederation to defend the Sino-Vietnamese border from attack. Following the collapse of the Tayson dynasty and the disbanding of these pirates,

Unknown artists, *Pacifying the South China Sea*, Jiaqing period (1796–1820). A detail shows pirates under siege from Qing soldiers near Lantou Island, Hong Kong. Shi Yang is in the boat with the red flag wearing a red robe. Handscroll, ink and colour on paper. Length 1,820 cm. Hong Kong Maritime Museum.

Zheng Yi and Shi Yang regrouped this confederation to form a formidable southeastern force. The couple controlled the fleet through a strict legal code, with severe penalties, including capital punishment, for rape or desertion. They ruthlessly extorted cash and collected protection money from other ships and made coastal villagers and fishermen slaves if ransoms for them were not paid. Thus, through robbery and blackmail, they paid their vast pirate army, which was grouped into six gangs that were identified by different coloured flags (red, black, white, green, blue and yellow), rather like the Manchu banner system. Zheng Yi and Shi Yang personally headed the Red Flag group.

After her husband died in 1807, Shi Yang became romantically involved with her 21-year-old adopted son, Zhang Bao, and later married him. Nevertheless, she managed to maintain her position of authority within the crucial and largest Red Flag group. In 1809, she captured a British officer, Richard Glasspoole (1788–1846), and his East India Company ship, *The Marquis of Ely*, with seven British sailors on board. The Britons were held for eleven weeks and three days while a ransom was sought, and were forced to fight alongside the pirate army. Glasspoole and the other sailors survived, and he left behind a first-hand account of his time on board the pirate ship. His 'Narrative of his Captivity and Treatment amongst the Ladrones' was first printed in George Wilkinson's *Sketches of Chinese Customs and Manners* (1814).

The pirates posed a significant threat to the Qing. Although their exact numbers are hard to confirm, at the height of her power Shi Yang commanded over 300 ships, manned by at least 17,000 pirates. When their families were also counted, she was in charge of a multi-generational pirate army of some 40,000 souls. To give a comparative idea of the scale of her fleet, the famous English pirate Blackbeard's (d. 1718) largest fleet consisted of just eight ships. Other estimates in the East India Company archives of 1804 state that her total forces were twice those involved in the Spanish Armada – approximately 70,000 pirates, aboard 400 ships. She fought and won battles with the imperial Qing navy, as well as with Portuguese and British sailors.

In 1809, the Jiaqing emperor made a major attempt to tackle piracy and the Qing reluctantly accepted foreign help from the British to bring it under control. Extraordinarily, Shi Yang and her pirate Red Flag Army were pardoned by the Qing government in 1810, and she secured an amnesty for most of her fellow pirates. She was obviously a gifted negotiator and shrewd businesswoman. Having left piracy behind her and secured an official military position for her second husband, she diversified, making money through the salt trade, money-lending and running a string of gambling dens and brothels, with a base in Macao. Despite a life of violence, she died peacefully of old age (for the time) at around sixty-nine.

For nearly two decades, Shi Yang held power over the southern coastal waters. In her prime, she was a ruthless and feared pirate, who led a vast army with her husband, and in later life she became a respectable businesswoman, international negotiator and wife of a military official. Although she may possibly be depicted in the famous scroll of *Pacifying the South China Sea*, no authenticated portraits of her survive. However, there have been many different imaginings of her life in films, television series and books. For example, a character inspired by her and played by Takayo Fischer appears in the 2007 film *Pirates of the Caribbean: At World's End*. In 2003, Ermanno Olmi based the film *Singing behind Screens* on her life. In 2021, the cartoonist Larry Feign published a novel about her, entitled *The Flower Boat Girl: A Novel Based on a True Story*. Most recently, in spring 2022, she was renamed 'Madame Ching' and played by the actor Crystal Yu (b. 1988) in the BBC's *Doctor Who*.

Jessica Harrison-Hall

21. WEI YUAN

魏源 (1794–1857)

VISIONARY OFFICIAL AND WRITER OF A MONUMENTAL STUDY OF QING WARFARE

Born in Shaoyang, Hunan province, Wei Yuan was a solemn, solitary, introverted and precocious boy, with exceptional self-discipline. The story is told that, on the rare occasions that he went out, local dogs would bark wildly at a child they saw so infrequently. In 1802, the eight-year-old Wei Yuan took for the first time the entry-level test of the Chinese civil service examinations (*tongzishi*), which consisted of completing a couplet, for which the examiner (the local magistrate) provided the first line: 'The cup contains the origin of all things' (*Beizhong han taiji*). Wei Yuan promptly responded: 'The abdomen breeds heaven and earth' (*Fuzhong yun qiankun*).

Portrait of Wei Yuan, from Ye Yanlan (1823–1898) and Ye Gongchuo (1881–1968), *Illustrated Biographies of Scholars of the Qing Period*, c. 1840–1900. Album: ink and light colours on paper. Height 26.6 cm, width 17.3 cm. National Museum of China, Beijing.

The magistrate was amazed by the boy's fluent answer, which represented a perfect correspondence for rhythm and content, and impressed by Wei Yuan's prodigious intellectual accomplishment and ambition. The boy advanced quickly through the next level of the civil service examinations, becoming a 'distinguished talent' (*xiucai*) at the young age of thirteen.

Wei Yuan grew up amid the growing political, social and economic turbulence of the Jiaqing and Daoguang eras. In 1813, he began an eight-year sojourn in Beijing, where he became a prominent member of the 'Statecraft' (*jingshi zhixue*) group of scholar-officials, who sought to use their intellects to pursue practical ways of strengthening and enriching the empire. As a young adult, Wei Yuan turned away from the inward-focused Confucianism of Ming-dynasty philosophers such as Wang Yangming (1472–1529) to 'New Text Confucianism' (*jinwen jingxue*), which aimed to deploy the writings of Confucius as a practical guide for governance. Wei Yuan, similarly, believed the primary purpose of academic study was to find useful prescriptions for contemporary problems (*tongjing zhiyong*). In 1822, the second year of the Daoguang reign, he gained second place in the provincial examination competition. In 1825, He Changling (1785–1848), then the provincial administration commissioner of Jiangsu, invited Wei Yuan to compile a 120-volume *Compendium of Statecraft Writing Under the Reigning Dynasty*, an opportunity that Wei Yuan used to put forward proposals about maritime transport and river conservancy. He also advised Tao Zhu (1779–1839), governor general of Jiangsu province, on improving the system for transporting grain from the south-east to the capital, and on flood protection measures. This experience built Wei an academic reputation and a wide network of influential contacts.

Nonetheless, despite his early academic prowess, Wei Yuan did not pass the *jinshi* (the top, metropolitan level of the civil service exam, supposedly guaranteeing the candidate a senior official post) until the age of fifty-one, in 1844. Wei Yuan self-deprecatingly described his belated success, after so many years of failure, as 'an old lady once more becoming the bride'.

After the outbreak of the First Opium War (1839–42), Wei Yuan was offered an official post near the front, as an associate military commissioner to Zhejiang, by Yuqian (1793–1841), a Mongol whom the emperor had appointed his special imperial commissioner to resist the British. Shocked and angered by the Qing's defeat in this conflict, Wei Yuan, by the end of 1842, had quickly compiled the fourteen-volume *Record of Sacred Military Victories*, a massive work of military history that chronicled the almost unbroken string of Qing victories between the time of the dynasty's founder Nurhaci (1559–1626) and the Daoguang emperor (r. 1821–1850), in the hope of galvanizing his elite readership to strengthen the dynasty's failing military system. In 1853, early in the reign of Daoguang's son the Xianfeng emperor, Wei Yuan joined the Buddhist Pure Land sect – an expression of his exhaustion at the turbulence of the empire and public life – and the following year moved his family to Xinghua in Jiangsu province to escape the Taiping Civil War. He died in a monastery in Hangzhou on 26 March 1957, at the age of sixty-three.

In his lifetime, Wei Yuan wrote extensively on a wide range of topics: scripture, ancient poetry, history, literature, Buddhism and geopolitics. But he is best known for his groundbreaking 1844 *Illustrated Treatise on the Maritime Kingdoms*, later acclaimed as China's first modern work of geopolitics. The Qing government's response to the British assault during the First Opium War had been severely hampered by lack of knowledge about Britain and its interests, as a global, colonial power. The *Illustrated*

Treatise enabled mid-century intellectuals to begin to grasp the dimensions and global strategy of the new maritime threat from states such as Britain. Ranging across the politics, economics, military systems, history, geography and culture of multiple Western countries, the work combines older geographical sources with cutting-edge translations of European books, documents and newspapers that Wei Yuan's mentor Lin Zexu (1785–1850) had commissioned while confronting British opium smugglers (and their British government protectors) in Guangzhou at the start of the First Opium War. His purpose, Wei Yuan wrote, 'is to show, to our own advantage, how to use foreigners to fight foreigners, how to make foreigners pacify one another, how to learn the strengths of foreigners in order to control them'. For this achievement, Wei Yuan has been hailed as 'the first to open his eyes to the world in the late Qing'.

The treatise is divided into six sections, each discussing a specific subject. For example, the chapter 'Maps of the World and All Nations' presents nearly one hundred new maps of the world; the chapter 'History and Geography of the World' draws on a range of sources to explain in detail the democratic politics of the United States, including its federal, electoral and parliamentary systems. Using rigorous standards of empirical enquiry, Wei was a trailblazer in uniting Sinophone and Western sources of knowledge about geography, history and politics.

The book also won a readership in Japan, where it had a deep impact. Between 1851 and 1856, it was reprinted twenty-three times in as many as sixteen Japanese translations. Shocked at the Qing's defeat by the British in the First Opium War, Japanese ruling elites learned to be deeply wary of the Western maritime threat. The sense of alarm seeded in Japan by the writings of men like Wei Yuan arguably fed into the greater initiative maintained by Japanese elites, relative to that of the neighbouring Qing, in their relations with the West over coming decades.

Zou Zhenhuan

22. SENGGE RINCHEN

僧格林沁 (1811–1865)

PRINCE AND FORMIDABLE COMMANDER

Sengge Rinchen was a formidable commander who served the Qing dynasty for thirty years. He spent the latter decades of his life eradicating domestic revolts and led Qing troops to defend north China against foreign incursions during the Second Opium War (1856–60). During his lifetime, according to the *Draft History of the Qing*, 'His name inspired awe across the world, and the empire relied on him as if he were its Great Wall.'

He was born into a Khorchin Mongol family within the Borjigid lineage, said to be collaterally descended from Chinggis Khan. The young Daoguang emperor

Unidentified court artist, *Sengge Rinchen and a Hunting Party*, 1850–1900. Handscroll, ink and colours on paper. Height 123 cm, width 261 cm. Capital Museum, Beijing.

(*r.* 1821–1850) clearly thought highly of the fourteen-year-old Sengge Rinchen, appointing him heir to an imperial princedom, where the teenager became a commandery prince (*duoluo junwang*). At twenty-three, he commenced his career in the imperial service as a grand minister in attendance (*yuqian dachen*), and he was subsequently appointed to various high positions in the Eight Banners, the elite, hereditary Qing military force.

His service in the emperor's personal retinue came to an end in 1853, when he was assigned to command imperial troops deployed against the Taiping. The Taiping had consolidated their control of a large, rich area around Nanjing (east China) in the early 1850s. One of the Taiping commanders, Lin Fengxiang (1825–1855), then led his troops on a northern expedition with the intent of capturing the Qing capital at Beijing. Sengge Rinchen halted the Taiping's northern advance and expelled them from the suburbs of Tianjin, the port city that served Beijing. For this, he received the title 'loyal hero' (*tondo baturu*). His relentless southward pursuit of the escaping rebels ended at the fortified town of Lianzhen (some 200 kilometres south of Beijing) in the spring of 1855, where the Taiping entrenched themselves.

There, Sengge Rinchen noticed that the river on which Lianzhen was situated was rising due to heavy rain. He ordered the construction of a dam to block the river and flood the Taiping troops. In their attempt to get away, they were slain without mercy, though Lin Fengxiang was captured alive. For this tactical triumph, Sengge

Rinchen received the title of 'strategically gifted imperial prince' (*bodolgatai cin wang*). Sengge Rinchen's victories may well have saved the Qing dynasty from losing its capital to Taiping forces at one of the most precarious moments of the Taiping Civil War (1851–64).

As a combined Anglo-French force sailed up to Tianjin in 1859 to ratify the treaty that had concluded the initial phase of the Second Opium War, the court called on Sengge Rinchen once more to repel its enemies. The English and French troops found the mouth of the river up to the port blocked. Over the preceding year, Sengge Rinchen had reinforced the twin Dagu Forts on the river. To force entry up to Beijing, the British opened fire on the forts. The Qing troops retaliated with deadly effect. In a memorial to the emperor, Sengge Rinchen recounted how his gunners hit ship after ship, and the sailors on board raised white flags.

Parties of British soldiers landed at low tide, at a substantial distance from the forts. The Qing troops had dug moats in front of the fortified ramparts, filled them with mud, and erected an abatis of iron spikes behind. Sengge Rinchen informed the emperor that he had organized additional groups to engage the British foot soldiers as soon as they reached the moats and British soldiers later described an onslaught of gunfire and arrows. Out of the 600-strong landing party, 200 were killed within moments as they approached the ramparts and sank into the quagmire of mud-filled moats. Altogether, Qing sources reported thirteen ships sunk, and British sources recorded 519 British dead and 456 wounded. *The Times* in London published an article about the confrontation on 16 September 1859, entitled 'The Disaster in China'. It was one of the worst defeats suffered by the British Empire in the 19th century.

The following year, a combined force of Russian, American, French and British ships returned and this time successfully landed and captured Dagu. The emperor had told Sengge Rinchen, 'The foundation of All Under Heaven [meaning the empire] is not located at [that] port (i.e. Dagu), but at the capital. Should you suffer a setback, you must retreat and hold Tianjin.' Sengge Rinchen made a stand at the crucial Bali Bridge east of Beijing. But the combined Western army soundly defeated Sengge Rinchen's troops and even his Mongol cavalry, once considered invincible. Consequentially, the emperor stripped Sengge Rinchen of his titles and princedom. Up to this point in the conflict, Sengge Rinchen and his forces had constituted the primary obstacle to the foreign invasion. The combined armies' victory at Bali Bridge now cleared their path to Beijing. That October, in revenge for Qing forces kidnapping and torturing a negotiating party, Anglo-French forces sacked the Yuanming yuan (Old Summer Palace).

The conclusion of the Second Opium War in 1860 ended only one of the empire's many challenges. As an experienced field commander, Sengge Rinchen was next put in charge of a contingent of Mongol cavalry fielded against the Nian rebels in the north of the empire. As early as November 1860, his achievements against the Nian had earned him the restoration of his titles. His fearsome, highly mobile cavalry forces were almost constantly engaged during the insurrection and often split up to attack multiple pockets of rebels simultaneously. For five years, Sengge Rinchen fought the Nian with great success. In July 1864, the emperor lauded and rewarded Sengge Rinchen and his cavalrymen for 'wholly cleansing the provinces of Zhili and Shandong'. But it was a short-lived accomplishment. Only one year later, the rebels re-entered the north-east province of Shandong. Sengge Rinchen defeated them and, as usual, pursued the routed rebels. However, the Nian led him into an ambush at Caozhou. Sengge Rinchen's continuous forced marches had exhausted his troops and the well-prepared Nian overwhelmed the Mongol cavalry. Wounded eight times, Sengge Rinchen died during the engagement, on 18 May 1865.

His death shocked the court, which decreed three days of mourning. In recognition of Sengge Rinchen's selfless devotion to the dynasty's security, sacrifices to his memory were made in the Imperial Ancestral Temple. His portrait was displayed in the Pavilion of Purple Radiance (Ziguang ge) and a temple was erected in his honour in Beijing, where he was canonized with the encomium 'loyal' (*zhong*). Sengge Rinchen is today remembered most of all for his successes and failures against the Anglo-French forces in the Second Opium War, but to the Qing court, he was an invaluable, practically invincible commander and strategist for three tumultuous decades. After his death, he was commemorated as an exemplary member of the Eight Banners and a loyal servant to the Qing empire in the face of unprecedented external and domestic threats.

Juul Eijk

23. MG CHARLES GORDON

(1833–1885)

BRITISH SOLDIER 'CHINESE' GORDON

The inscription on Charles Gordon's tomb in St Paul's Cathedral insists that during his time in China he 'saved an empire by his warlike genius'. In truth, Gordon had a bit part in suppressing the Taiping, which was mostly the work of Zeng Guofan's (1811–1872) Hunan Army. Gordon was, in his own words, a 'rolling stone who gathers no moss', typical of soldiers of the British Empire moving from place to place fighting the empire's battles.

Gordon's peripatetic existence began at birth. As the son of a major general, he moved with his father's job, growing up in England, Ireland, Scotland and the Ionian Islands. He, and all his brothers, were a fifth generation of army officers. On his return from Corfu, Gordon moved to Woolwich, where he enlisted in the Royal Military Academy around age fifteen.

At twenty-one Gordon was sent to the Crimea where he participated in the siege of Sevastopol and was one of a few junior officers in the Royal Engineers to receive the French Legion of Honour. Following the war, Gordon received surveying commissions delineating the border between the Ottoman Empire and Russia. A highlight of this was tobogganing down Mount Ararat, perhaps beginning his passion for winter sports, which he was to continue when he spent the winter of 1861 ice skating on the frozen Baihe River in Tianjin. On his return from Asia to England, Gordon was appointed second adjutant of the Corps of Royal Engineers at the Chatham Depot. He had been in post for only a year when the failed Anglo-French attack on the Dagu Forts in June 1859 restarted hostilities in China.

Gordon arrived in China in the autumn of 1860, as part of the force despatched to fight the final part of the Second Opium War (1856–60). As he confessed to his mother, he was 'rather late for the amusements', arriving after the fighting had ceased, but in time to be an active participant in the looting of the emperor's Summer Palace (Yuanming yuan). He remained stationed in Tianjin until the summer of 1862, when he was sent south to help defend the Western enclaves in Shanghai from the advancing Taiping forces.

By 1862, British officials regarded the Taiping as a menace that needed eliminating, but after the expense of the Second Opium War the government did not want to fund British involvement in a Chinese civil war. The government's neat solution was to release British troops to train a Chinese force, originally led by American mercenaries, with a view to forming, in the words of John Michel, Commander of British Troops in China, 'the nucleus' of a Chinese army. Gordon was appointed head of the force, which the Qing court dubbed the Ever Victorious Army. So began the mercurial Gordon's tempestuous relationship with Li Hongzhang (1823–1901), governor of Jiangsu and the Qing official responsible for the force.

Gordon's force supported Li in recapturing Suzhou, but Gordon was outraged when he negotiated the surrender of Taiping prisoners, only for Li to have them all executed. He resigned his commission and urged British officials to ask the Qing government for Li's execution as an example to other Chinese officials. Six months later, however, the hatchet had been buried and Gordon was back leading the force and describing Li as 'the best man in the empire'. Gordon left China in 1865, having decommissioned his force. He disliked being called a mercenary almost as much as he disliked his own men. He warned his mother that the British officers of the Ever Victorious Army were 'not gentlemen' and not to answer should they call on her.

Gordon was unlike his peers in that he respected the Qing dynasty's symbolic honours on their own terms. When Gordon distributed Qing medals to his men for their service in China, they returned them, disliking the Qing style and asking for awards that mimicked British medals. Gordon, however, accepted the yellow riding jacket, the uniform of the imperial bodyguard, and proudly told his mother, 'I think the Chinese government trusts me more than any foreigner ever has been trusted'. In fact, Gordon was not the first foreign recipient of the award. The Italian Jesuit Giuseppe Castiglione, who served as a painter to the Qing court, had received it a century earlier.

Valentine 'Val' Prinsep RA (1838–1904), *Portrait of 'Chinese Gordon'*, 1867. Royal Engineers Headquarters Mess, Chatham.

When Gordon returned to China in 1880, as the threat of war with Russia loomed, he allegedly tried to persuade Li to march on Beijing and replace the emperor. Robert Hart (1835–1911), the head of the Imperial Maritime Customs Service, believed that by this point Gordon's grasp on reality was slipping. Gordon did, however, manage to persuade Qing officials their forces were not ready for a war with Russia, probably saving the dynasty from another catastrophic defeat.

The hagiographies written about Gordon and his burial at St Paul's were both a product of his later career. From 1874, Gordon served the Khedive of Egypt, first as governor general of the province of Equatoria, and then as governor general of the Sudan. He returned to England due to ill health in 1880. The British government asked him to return to the Sudan in 1884, to help evacuate Egyptian forces from Khartoum, which was threatened by the Mahdists, followers of Muhammad Al-Mahdī. Gordon ignored his instructions and refused to evacuate, preferring to defend the city. British reinforcements arrived too late, after Gordon had been killed.

The Conservatives gained much political capital in blaming William Gladstone for Gordon's death. Queen Victoria herself was outraged and, perhaps sensing the public mood, outlined her feelings in an uncoded telegram to Gladstone, meaning that anyone, including the press, could read it. When much later, in 1898, Khartoum was recaptured (to stop the French gaining a foothold rather than to avenge Gordon), she commissioned a painting of the memorial held at the site of his death. In popular memory, 'Chinese' Gordon became Gordon of Khartoum.

Jon Chappell

24. HUANG SHUHUA

黃淑華 (1847–1864)

TEENAGE AVENGER AND FEMALE MARTYR

In the autumn of 1864, mere months after imperial forces' reconquest of the rebels' capital at Nanjing and the close of the fourteen-year Taiping Civil War, a traveller in the Hunan town of Xiangxiang stumbled across an appalling spectacle at an inn: three corpses, one man poisoned, another with his throat slit, and a woman hanging from a rafter. On examination, the woman's clothes were all tightly stitched together, a defence against rape. According to other witnesses, the night before, the three had been drinking and laughing together for half the night.

The mystery was resolved by a preface and poems left on the wall of a different inn, where the deceased woman gave an account of how she had reached that place. Huang Shuhua (also known as Huang Wanli) was from the county surrounding Nanjing, daughter of a humble but educated family (both her father and eldest brother were holders of the lowest civil exam degree). She was a child when Nanjing fell to the Taiping armies in 1853. After the conquest, her family supported themselves by farming, refusing to take part in the Taiping-sponsored examinations, but still taught Shuhua to read and write. Her education particularly stressed tales of exemplary martyrs, instructing her that one should not compromise fundamental virtues for the sake of mere survival. Tales of self-sacrifice for the preservation of chastity were a common didactic curriculum for girls, but for her family Shuhua's education was a response to their precarious situation in a city under occupation. Facing this uncertain future, she was not yet betrothed.

In the summer of 1864, when she was sixteen, Huang Shuhua and her family initially rejoiced at the news of the Qing recapture of Nanjing, thinking their long ordeal had ended. But two days later, a soldier broke into their house. Using the justification that those who followed the rebels should not be spared, he killed Shuhua's family, then abducted her and her old friend Jin Meishou, taking them by boat up the Yangtze to his native region of Hunan. Jin drowned herself in the river when threatened with rape. Shuhua contemplated suicide as well but resolved to survive and avenge her family instead. After they shifted to travel by land, her revenge was hindered when her abductor was joined by another man. Resolved to die, but not knowing how or where, she wrote the account on the wall. The crime scene allows readers to infer the end of the story: she had pretended to welcome the men's advances in order to ply them with poisoned wine, then killed herself.

After the traveller who found her copied her poems, over the next three decades, Huang Shuhua's story circulated through different manuscript and print texts: a poster was hung up in Nanjing, scholars documented her in their miscellaneous notes, poets celebrated her, the local histories of both her native place and the place where she died included her, and a playwright dramatized her story. She joined the ranks of the righteous dead chronicled in the great effort of memorial and moral rectification in the post-war years. On the one hand, her slaying of attempted rapists was satisfying, a redress for all the acts of sexual violence never punished. On the other, the timing of her martyrdom and the

Lithographic illustration depicting Huang Shuhua's story, 1895. From Xu E's dramatic adaptation, *Snow on the Pear Blossom*, Scene 10, 'Washing Away Wrong'. In this rendering, she excises her abductor's heart and liver as an offering for her family. Height 18 cm. Harvard University Library, Cambridge, MA.

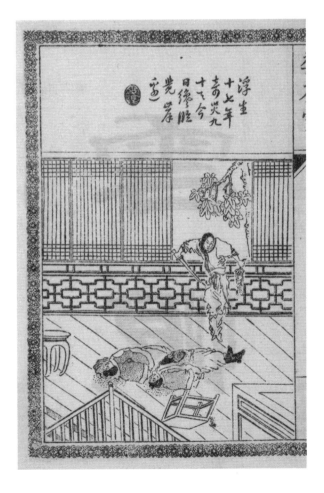

identity of her assailant (as a soldier in Qing government forces) revealed cracks in the project of denigrating the rebels and celebrating the imperial side.

Not only did Huang's family experience no direct violence during the rebels' conquest of Nanjing, by keeping their heads down they even survived in relative peace for a decade. The moment of supposed liberation, by contrast, brought abduction and slaughter. Her assailant was identified as an 'undisciplined soldier' (*luanbing*) not a rebel, and indeed he used the orders for extermination of the Taipings to justify his butchery. Her unassailable position as a chaste martyr allowed those who remembered her to document that the reconquest also took a toll on innocent lives, and 'order' and 'chaos' did not have as clear a historical boundary as official propaganda would insist. Her abductor's provincial origins raise questions about the conduct of Zeng Guofan's (1811–1872) Xiang (Hunan) Army, the 'liberators' of Nanjing.

That Huang Shuhua was able to write her own story, in both poetry and prose, shows the penetration of female literacy into even a relatively humble level of the educated class in her region. Yet her words would not have gone farther than the inn in Hunan without the mediation of a series of men. The virtue of a woman who lived out an expected life course would be lauded by her male kin, or perhaps the other educated men who were hired to write the family's funerary inscriptions. The life story of a martyr, particularly one like Huang Shuhua without an immediate family to preserve her memory, had to move into the (male-dominated) public domain to be recorded.

The Taiping interventions in the Chinese gender and family system – including an examination for talented women, for which Huang Shuhua might have qualified – largely left her untouched. Her concerns were the threat of sexual violence that had faced women during every period of instability in Chinese history. Even in times of peace, the significant labour of conforming to the moral precepts that helped maintain elite family status fell on women: widows, in particular, were exhorted to avoid remarriage, despite financial and familial pressures. In times of war and displacement, the obligation to avoid sexual violation became fatal to women in families who subscribed to such elite cultural conventions, with pre-emptive suicide lauded as the brave and necessary choice. Huang Shuhua is writing less to explain why she died, but why she did not die earlier. Her stitched-together clothes are a claim to integrity as strong as her written words.

It is possible that Shuhua did not even exist, and that her poems are the invention of the male traveller who claimed to be the first witness to discover her death; but hers appears to have been a story that many writers of the post-war decades needed. A generation later, the daughters and grand-daughters of the women who had suffered during the Civil War would be arguing for new standards of female autonomy and education.

Rania Huntington

25. YUAN SHIKAI

袁世凱 (1859–1916)

SOLDIER, REFORMER, PRESIDENT
AND WOULD-BE EMPEROR

Yuan Shikai was born on 16 September 1859 in Xiangcheng county, Henan province, into an elite Han family that had supported the Qing empire for centuries. He shared a generational name with his siblings: *shi*, meaning 'the world'. His given name *kai* denotes 'victory', which was to celebrate the triumph of his great-uncle Yuan Jiasan (1806–1863) over the Nian rebels, who staged one of the 19th century's most significant insurrections against the Qing in north China. When young, Shikai was adopted by his uncle Yuan Baoqing (1825–1873), holder of a *juren* (mid-ranking civil service) degree and a Qing official. Shikai's early years were itinerant, spent in a number of provinces following his foster father's official postings. The sudden death of Yuan Baoqing in 1873 forced the family to return to Xiangcheng. For years, Yuan Shikai studied Confucian classics and even went to Beijing for further instruction. Unfortunately, he failed twice in the civil service examinations, in 1876 and 1879. Yuan's path to leadership in the empire diverged from that of previous generations of scholar-officials: he rose through the ranks as a military man and ended up buying a civil service degree.

Yuan Shikai joined the Anhui Army – one of the special local armies raised to defeat the Taiping Heavenly Kingdom – as a protégé of the celebrated general Wu Changqing (1829–1884) in 1881. The next year, the Imo Mutiny took Wu to Korea at the request of the Korean king. Yuan played a role in suppressing the mutiny, after which he became a commander under Wu. From 1882 to 1894, Yuan lived in Korea, first as an officer and then as the Qing imperial commissioner, safeguarding the traditional tributary relationship between the two countries. Yuan helped train a Korean army and supported the Korean king in his political manoeuvres; in 1884, Yuan assisted in the suppression of the Gapsin Coup and helped the conservatives at the Korean court to regain power. In 1894, on the eve of the First Sino-Japanese War, he left Korea to return to China.

The defeat of China by Japan during the First Sino-Japanese War ignited outrage and panic among educated Chinese, who were electrified by a new sense of empire-wide crisis. Immediately after the war, the Qing court appointed Yuan Shikai to train a modern army in response to this military disaster. Making his headquarters at Xiaozhan near Tianjin, Yuan built this new force along modern Western lines. He hired Western military instructors, and purchased Western weapons and equipment. He recruited qualified, educated men as soldiers, performed regular drills, conducted mock battles, and enforced strict discipline. Visiting Yuan in 1898, British admiral Lord Charles Beresford (1846–1919) was impressed with the results Yuan had achieved.

Yuan surrounded himself with a small group of dedicated military officers, which evolved into the 'Beiyang Clique' – a coterie of powerful militarists who dominated government during the early Republic after 1912. While training a modern army in Xiaozhan, Yuan supported broader movements for political and economic reform under way at the time. Nonetheless, Chinese modernizers and liberals have long demonized him for allegedly betraying radicals such as Kang Youwei (1858–1927), Liang Qichao (1873–1929) and Tan Sitong (1865–1898) during the Hundred Days' Reform and abetting Cixi's putsch against the Guangxu emperor. However, the most up-to-date scholarship has exonerated him from playing a role in Cixi's coup.

Yuan Shikai was governor of Shandong from 1899 to 1901, and governor general of Zhili (the province surrounding Beijing) and imperial minister between 1901 and 1909. While in Shandong, he suppressed Boxer militants, strengthened his own military power base, implemented educational reform including establishing the first provincial university in Shandong, supported Cixi during her flight to Xi'an and her return to Beijing (1900–2), and protected foreign missionaries. In Zhili, he tried to restore social order after the Boxer War, created the first modern police force, oversaw the abolition of the old imperial civil service examination in 1905, built a modern school system, promoted local economic development, supported constitutional reform, and again expanded his military forces. During his short tenure as foreign minister, starting in September 1907, he sought to improve relations with Western countries. But his high political profile provoked the resentment of Manchu nobles who dismissed him on 2 January 1909 – following the death of his supporter, Cixi – after which he lived in Anyang, Henan province, as something of a recluse.

The accidental outbreak of the 1911 Revolution changed the course of Yuan Shikai's life once more, when the Qing court appointed him military commander to suppress the mutinies that began the uprising. But his success in quelling the insurrection was very partial. After a costly assault on the original epicentre of the revolution in Wuhan, he was compelled to conduct peace talks with the revolutionaries, and became their chief intermediary with the Qing dynasty. Although Yuan tried to negotiate a constitutional monarchy, the revolutionaries pushed for republican government. In February 1912, the last Qing emperor, Puyi, abdicated. Recognizing Yuan's political and military pre-eminence – Yuan personally controlled the army garrisons centred in Beijing – the Republic's first provisional president Sun Yat-sen (1866–1925) resigned in February to make way for Yuan. In 1913, one of Sun Yat-sen's close revolutionary comrades – a talented politician called Song Jiaoren (1882–1913) – won the country's first national elections. As he prepared to board a train from Shanghai to Beijing to assemble his cabinet as prime minister, he was assassinated, allegedly on Yuan's orders (although the question of responsibility for the murder remains historically controversial).

During his four-year presidency, Yuan Shikai introduced a series of policies to build a functioning administration and foster economic growth in the new republic, but also became increasingly dictatorial, suppressing the attempts of former

Rio Vius De Sieux, *Photograph of Yuan Shikai (1859–1916), c.* 1915. A military commander as well as a politician, even after he became president of the Republic of China, Yuan Shikai usually dressed in military uniform. University of Bristol.

revolutionaries to limit his powers. In late 1913, he outlawed the Nationalist Party – the successor organization to the key pre-1911 revolutionary organization – and dissolved parliament (the cornerstone of the Republic's representative system) in early 1914. He then promulgated a new constitution that gave him unlimited powers. In early 1915, he faced a diplomatic crisis when Japan presented his government with its Twenty-One Demands, which included extended extraterritoriality and the cession of former German colonies near Qingdao in Shandong. Although Yuan was forced to accept the demands, he revised many to make them less damaging to national interests.

Yuan's attempted dynastic restoration in 1915 was one of his most contentious acts. That year, a supporter of Yuan and ardent monarchist Yang Du (1875–1931) launched a campaign to appoint Yuan emperor. Yuan agreed, convening a puppet 'Representative Assembly', who voted to offer him the title. But Yuan's founding of his new Hongxian dynasty on 1 January 1916 generated fierce national resistance.

The former military governor of Yunnan, Cai E (1882–1916), promptly launched a 'War to Protect the Nation' to oppose Yuan's would-be emperorship. The country's other provinces responded by promptly declaring independence from Yuan's regime; the era of emperors, it seemed, was dead and gone. Yuan abdicated on 23 March, sickened and died on 6 June 1916.

Yuan Shikai is one of the most debated figures of modern China. He has been acclaimed by some as a hero for defending China's national interests, training the first modern army, building a progressive modern school system, establishing a modern police force, supporting constitutional reform, and so forth – at a time when the country was beset by external and internal threats. Others have condemned him as a reactionary, a traitor, a regressive politician, a usurper of the revolution and a ruthless dictator. He was, it is fair to conclude, a talented administrator, who contributed to China's modernization in the late Qing and early Republican eras, and played a crucial role in China's transition from empire to republic, until his fatal error of judgment in attempting to reinstate the emperorship.

Patrick Fuliang Shan

26. QIU JIN

秋瑾 (1875–1907)

POET, FEMINIST AND REVOLUTIONARY

On a hot summer day in July 1904, Qiu Jin boarded a steamship to Japan, joining thousands of Chinese students already there. Like them, she aimed to acquire a modern education overseas at a time when the Qing empire was perceived by many to be hopelessly backward, while Japan had quickly modernized after the Meiji Restoration. This journey would change the trajectory of her life and propel her onto the stage of modern Chinese history.

Qiu Jin was born into a scholar-official family in 1875 at a time when the Qing was beset with internal uprisings and external threats from the Western powers. Like generations of literati daughters, she was taught to read and write by her mother, and grew up exchanging poetry with friends and siblings. A major transition occurred in 1902 when she first came to Beijing with her husband, who was serving as a petty official in the Qing bureaucracy. In the capital, she was exposed to new ideas of freedom and equality, as well as becoming aware of the dire state of China under threat from Western imperialism. In a 1903 poem 'To the Melody "A River Full of Red"', she grappled with her conflicting identities. She was twenty-nine years old at the time, had been married for eight years and was mother of two young children. Chafing under the traditional constraints of womanhood, she wrote of the injustice of having 'been forced to be a lady', when a truer sense of herself, her *xin* (meaning a person's intellectual and emotional capacities, as well as aspirations), was not understood by 'vulgar minds'.

In the call for national salvation, Qiu Jin found the legitimation to breach the traditional gender divide that relegated women to the 'inner chambers'. While in Beijing, she began experimenting at reinventing herself. A photograph taken in early 1904 shows her cross-dressed in a dark Western man's suit with a derby cap on her head. Far from the formal attitude of a proper lady, she is self-consciously theatrical and gazes directly at the camera, as if challenging onlookers with her audacious getup. Although the photograph belongs to the category known as the 'costume shot', in which the sitter puts on a special outfit to enact a dramatic role understood to be distinct from real life, Qiu Jin's costume was neither a studio prop nor limited to a

Photograph of Qiu Jin wearing a Western man's suit, April 1904. National Museum of China, Beijing.

Photograph of Qiu Jin taken in Japan, 1905. Wisconsin Historical Society, Madison.

photographic session: she would continue to cross-dress till the end of her life, whether in a Western suit or the outfit of a Chinese man. As she explained to a Japanese acquaintance, Hattori Shigeko, who recorded it in her memoir of Qiu Jin: 'I want to become strong like men. First, I want to look like them in appearance, and then I will become like them in my psyche.' More than a penchant for dramatic self-presentation and more than revealing a heroic spirit, as later hagiographers would have it, Qiu Jin's cross-dressing was an effort to break away from the lifelong prospect of physical and psychological constraints, which traditional women's attire enforced, by reminding its wearer on a daily basis of the limitations placed on female behaviour.

In response to a call for volunteers to resist the Russian invasion of Manchuria, Qiu Jin adopted the style name Swordswoman of Mirror Lake (Jianhu nüxia) in 1904. Although she did not in fact go to the war front, the national crisis precipitated a process of remaking herself, and, more generally, a re-conceptualization of the role of women in history. In adopting such a name, she was projecting a public persona that indicates her fervent espousal of nationalist and feminist causes. While in Japan, she became an active member in several anti-Manchu revolutionary societies. A photograph taken in Japan in 1905 captures her spirit. Animated by the light that falls slanting across it, her face is alert and unsmiling, her right hand clutching a shiny dagger. Her hair is dressed in a distinctively Nihongami (Japanese looped topknot) style, and her body is enveloped in a voluminous kimono, whose zigzag pattern occupies two-thirds of the photographic space. This photograph was Qiu Jin's favourite, perhaps because it fused so well the Chinese tradition of the swordsman, now reincarnated as Japanese bushido (invoked by the Japanese costume and hairdo), and Russian anarchism bent on overthrowing an oppressive monarchy (indicated by the dagger). At the time it was taken, she had the photograph made into postcards and sent them to family and friends; she also used it as the front cover of the second issue of her periodical, the *Chinese Women's Journal*.

After returning to China in December 1905, Qiu Jin taught briefly at a newly opened women's school, tried her hand at running a feminist journal, and devoted the last year of her life to supporting the republican cause by planning military uprisings against the government. In a letter to a friend, she lamented: 'There have been many men who died for the revolution … but we have not heard of a woman yet, an embarrassment for all of us.' When the uprisings failed and her close comrades were executed, when she knew the Qing soldiers were coming for her, she did not escape to safety, although she had more than enough time to do so. On 15 July 1907, she was executed by beheading.

Qiu Jin's brutal death became a pivotal event that galvanized wide support for the republican revolutionaries. After several more failed uprisings, the Qing empire was finally overthrown in 1911. Qiu Jin was celebrated as one of the most famous martyrs of the revolution, and her last words – 'Autumn wind, autumn rain, fill my heart with sorrow', the opening line of a poem that she would never finish – have been committed to memory by generations of Chinese school children.

Hu Ying

Qin Qinong (n.d.), *Sorrow of Autumn in Hangzhou*, 1907. Painted to commemorate Qiu Jin after her death, this detail shows her tomb by the West Lake, Hangzhou. Inscriptions on the painting record details of her funeral in Chinese and English. Handscroll, ink on paper. Height 31 cm, width 129.8 cm. Zhejiang Provincial Museum, Hangzhou.

4

ARTISTS

CALLIGRAPHERS, EPIGRAPHERS, PAINTERS, ILLUSTRATORS AND PHOTOGRAPHERS

In imperial China, the education system – focused on study of the Confucian textual canon, in preparation for the civil service examinations – produced an elite gentry class that mediated between the state and the people from about 650 CE to 1905. Every civil service examination candidate at local, provincial and national level aimed to gain a position within the state bureaucracy, and thus obtain security, wealth and influence. This system was often described as a meritocracy, because in principle any man could sit the examinations, regardless of birth, age or ethnicity. In reality, success depended on patronage and rigorous exam coaching. By the 19th century, however, this system was beginning to disintegrate, as the state failed to increase official posts to keep pace with growing numbers of examination graduates. As the likelihood of winning an official job dwindled, educated men sought alternative forms of financial and social support, and established new artistic and literary groups. In the closing decades of the dynasty, modern schools opened, teaching a more Westernized curriculum, with subjects such as the natural sciences, European languages and physical education. Universities were founded and some children of the elite went to study overseas.

Until the late 1700s, elite Confucian education was based on the interpretations of medieval thinkers such as Cheng Yi (1033–1107) and Zhu Xi (1130–1200). But the rise of an ardent antiquarianism in the early 19th century led scholars to verify transmitted Confucian texts through researching antique artefacts, such as inscriptions on bronzes. Some intellectuals, including Ruan Yuan, developed extensive collections and built networks of scholars around them. This academic fashion also transformed aesthetic practice. Artists developed new styles of calligraphy based on their study of ancient inscriptions. Although literati had for centuries made rubbings of antiquities, in the 1800s such reproductions circulated more widely and had a greater impact on calligraphic style. Scholar-artists such as Liuzhou invented a new form of three-dimensional rubbing of antique objects, which they incorporated into new painting styles. An original art style called *bapo*, which looks like a collage of scraps but is in fact painted, evolved out of collecting scripts and antiques.

The lives of artists were scarred, and sometimes ended, by the traumatic wars of the 'long 19th century'. Both Tang Yifen and Dai Xi died in the Taiping Civil War (1851–64), fighting for the Qing government in their capacity as soldiers and officials. For survivors, migration necessitated by warfare fragmented personal networks, particularly during the Taiping and Opium Wars of the 1840s to 1860s. Longstanding circles of patronage – often focused on the old cultural heartland of Jiangnan, badly affected by the Civil War – were severed, but the upheaval caused by war could also catalyse innovation. Displaced cultural elites developed new networks and supporters to survive. Younger scholars sought the patronage of older literati to study calligraphic and painterly traditions, as well as the aesthetic legacies of antiquity. Beautiful monochrome ink and colour landscape paintings, fans and albums with themes derived from the natural world, demonstrate that older artistic traditions were not in decline in the 1800s, but sat alongside more 'modern' art. Despite the patriarchal nature of late imperial society, women created their own work and collaborated artistically with their husbands and wider social networks. Women such as Cao Zhenxiu are described as amateur artists and painted to demonstrate their cultural accomplishment, rather than in a 'professional' capacity. Even as the empire found itself under exceptional pressure from external and internal violence, the fin-de-siècle court reinvigorated the genre of battle commemorations with new, epic commissions.

By the mid-19th century, Shanghai had become the epicentre of China's artistic, financial and commercial activities. In just a few years, the port changed from a provincial coastal settlement to a multinational cosmopolitan hub and its population expanded dramatically. This was due substantially to the migration of people displaced by war and the influx of foreigners, as Shanghai became the most important of the new treaty ports opened as a consequence of the First Opium War. Its streets thronged with people of different nationalities and, through education and publishing, a new art style was created, fusing Chinese and Western, scholarly and commercial styles. Artists demonstrated their abilities to reinvent themselves in this hybrid city, created new networks of clients and patrons, and responded to fresh encounters with previously unknown or unfamiliar visual and material culture, and technology. Photography was introduced from the West and had a major impact on portrait painting and the circulation of images. New Western techniques such as lithography were embraced by artists trained also in traditional woodblock printing design, and by new magazines and newspapers in the treaty ports. Far beyond Shanghai, meanwhile, other art forms, such as popular prints and reverse glass paintings, were made in local workshops, reflecting the regional diversity of visual art across the last century of imperial history. JHH

27. DENG SHIRU

鄧石如 (1743–1805)

ANTIQUARIAN MODERNIZER OF CHINESE CALLIGRAPHY

Deng Shiru was a great calligrapher and seal engraver born in Huaining, modern-day Anqing in Anhui province. His original given name was Weiyan; he later took Shiru as a courtesy name. In 1796, when the Jiaqing emperor was enthroned, Deng Shiru had to change his birth name as the second character, *yan*, was taboo because it was used in the emperor's given name, Yongyan. Throughout his life, he used many other pseudonyms including Travelling Daoist (Jiyou daoren), Man Purified by Antiquity (Guhuanzi) and Mountain Man of Wanbai (Wanbai shanren).

His upbringing was quite different from that of many master calligraphers. As he was born into a deprived family, he received no formal education and never took the imperial civil service exams. According to his travel diary (held in Beijing's Palace Museum), after 1772 he began touring the Jiangnan region – traditionally, the cultural centre of the Chinese empire – expanding his social networks and earning a living by selling his artwork. Unlike many of his artistic peers – who combined their aesthetic practice with work in the civil service – Deng was a career calligrapher and seal carver.

Deng Shiru made several original contributions to these two fields. He excelled particularly at seal script (which replicated the angular lines of carved seal inscriptions) and clerical script (characterized by short regular brush strokes). Deng is acclaimed as the founder of *beixue*, or 'stele studies', a new trend in calligraphy that took off in the mid-Qing. A crucial influence on calligraphy of the past three centuries, the stele style imitated ancient stele inscriptions especially from the Qin (221–206 BCE), Han (202 BCE–220 CE) and Northern dynasties (386–581 CE). It fused with and fed off the passion for antiquarianism – visits to ancient sites, art collections and study of antiquities – of the 18th and 19th centuries. Before Deng, calligraphic orthodoxy had been dominated by the 'Model Calligraphy Book' approach, in which calligraphers studied reproductions on silk or paper of Jin dynasty (265–420) writing. By the late 18th century, transmission through repeated copyings had reduced the accuracy of such compendia. Calligraphers of the stele school turned instead to undistorted inscriptions on antiquities (especially bronze vessels and steles) and to the work of previously neglected writers. In making a career as a professional artist, Deng was assisted by Jiangnan's favourable social, cultural and economic environment, which enabled talents from humble backgrounds to make artwork for commercial purposes for constituencies such as a rising mercantile middle class.

Deng's seal and clerical script calligraphy were mostly inspired by calligraphic inscriptions on steles and roof tiles from the Eastern Han (25–220) and Northern Wei (386–534) dynasties, which for centuries had been regarded as antique artefacts rather than models for calligraphy. Breaking with tradition, Deng rediscovered such materials

Huang Jingfeng and Yan Zhubin (both active 1780–1803), *Portrait of Deng Shiru Freeing the Crane*, dated 1803. Hanging scrolls, ink and colour on paper. Probably Anhui. Each height 118 cm, width 60 cm. Anhui Provincial Museum, Hefei.

for his own original art. His greatest contribution to seal-carving lay in his eliminating the technical barrier between seal script calligraphy and seal engraving; his seals innovatively captured – with miniature precision – the shape and style of seal script. But Deng was versatile: he drew inspiration also from 5th- and 6th-century writing, as well as mastering and deploying a more cursive style (which past practitioners had regarded as insufficiently dignified for large-scale works of art). Even the writing equipment that he used, such as goat-hair writing brushes and raw *xuan* (a soft, absorbent paper favoured by painters and calligraphers), was unusual for Chinese calligraphers at the time. His innovations, however, became standard practice among his successors.

Our main source on Deng Shiru's life is *Biography of the Mountain Man of Wanbai* by his friend Bao Shichen (1775–1855). But Bao – a celebrated intellectual and policy advisor – seems to have introduced some fabrications into his narrative, especially regarding Deng's friendship with high-ranking officials. In reality, Deng lived an often impoverished, hand-to-mouth existence, far from circles of political power. His friends and patrons were mainly Jiangnan locals. Between 1791 and 1793, Deng worked for Bi Yuan (1730–1797), a regional governor in central China, but Bi did not particularly value Deng's talent. However, the 19th century's growth in antiquarian studies, sponsored by political luminaries such as Ruan Yuan (1764–1849) and Bao Shichen, brought Deng recognition as a pioneer in incorporating archaic scripts into calligraphic practice. His personal style coincided happily with the transformation of contemporary aesthetic taste. Through the 19th century, Deng thus came to be celebrated as a master of 'stele school' calligraphy and a central figure in Qing art history.

Chen Shuo

28. YI BINGSHOU

伊秉綬 (1754–1815)

CHINESE OFFICIAL, CALLIGRAPHER, EPIGRAPHIST

Yi Bingshou was a dedicated official and brilliant calligrapher active during the reigns of the Qianlong (r. 1735–1795) and Jiaqing (r. 1796–1820) emperors. He lived and worked in several of the most economically and culturally advanced parts of the empire, including Beijing, Guangdong and Jiangsu. He belonged to a generation of scholars who closely modelled their handwriting on ancient engraved stone monuments and promoted the aesthetics of stone carvings as a desirable calligraphic aesthetic. This stylistic revolution, later termed the 'stele school' (*beixue*), advocated the use of calligraphy engraved on ancient steles as the ideal model for Chinese artists to follow. It continues to exercise a profound influence on Chinese calligraphic aesthetics today.

Yi grew up in a prominent gentry family in Ninghua, Fujian province, and was mentored by noted scholar-officials of the 18th century. His father, Yi Chaodong (1729–1807), received several senior appointments from the Qianlong emperor. After serving at the Board of Justice for eighteen years, Yi Chaodong was first promoted to vice minister at the Court of Judicial Review and then to chief minister at the Court of Imperial Entertainments. He also served as an editor for the imperial library project *Complete Library of the Four Treasuries*. As a young scholar, Yi Bingshou visited his father in Beijing, during which time he became acquainted with renowned senior academicians at court. He is said to have studied calligraphy with the Grand Secretary Liu Yong (1720–1805), whose handwriting reinterpreted – with enhanced vigour – the classical styles of Wang Xizhi (303–361) and Su Shi (1037–1101). Between 1785 and 1787, Yi Bingshou worked for Ji Yun (1724–1805), one of the chief editors for the monumental *Complete Library of the Four Treasuries*, and served as tutor to Ji's grandchildren.

Yi joined the imperial civil service at a time of multiplying bureaucratic and social problems. After earning his *jinshi* degree (the highest qualification in the civil service examinations) in 1789, Yi, like his father, began at the Board of Justice and became recognized as 'impartial and empathetic'. In 1798, Yi was awarded the top distinction during a review of capital officials, and he was subsequently promoted to become the prefect of Huizhou – a rank below the level of governor. In this new post, he busied himself with various cultural projects – such as renovating Su Shi's former residence and building up Fenghu Academy, one of the largest educational institutes in Guangdong. But in 1802, when an uprising started in Huizhou and quickly spread across eastern Guangdong, Yi was blamed by his superior for 'losing track of the rebel organization' and was removed from office. After a thorough investigation, however, Yi was pardoned by the Jiaqing emperor and released from jail. In 1805, thanks to the patronage of wealthy maritime merchants in Guangzhou, Yi acquired another appointment as prefect of Yangzhou, where he devoted himself to flood control in the lower Yangtze River region. In addition, he collaborated with the senior scholar-official Ruan Yuan (1764–1849) on a new Yangzhou gazetteer, as well as rebuilding historical sites in the city, such as the mausoleum of Emperor Yang (569–618) of the Sui dynasty (581–618). His honesty and industry in office were widely respected among his colleagues and local scholars.

Yi became an expert in epigraphy through close contact with renowned antiquarians in the circle of Weng Fanggang (1733–1818). A brilliant court academician and bibliophile, Weng was known for his rigorous study of ancient stone inscriptions. He invited Yi up to numerous literary gatherings in Beijing and shared his experiences of examining ancient steles in situ. Yi also maintained a close relationship with Huang Yi (1744–1801), a significant epigraphist, knowledgable about historical monuments in Henan and Shandong. When the distinguished palaeographer Gui Fu (1736–1805) decided to compile a dictionary on the seal script – a style commonly used and standardized during the Qin dynasty (221–206 BCE), Yi was responsible for transcribing

Portrait of Yi Bingshou, from Ye Yanlan (1823–1898) and Ye Gongchuo (1881–1968), *Illustrated Biographies of Scholars of the Qing Period*, c. 1840–1900. Album: ink and light colours on paper. Height 26.6 cm, width 17.3 cm. National Museum of China, Beijing.

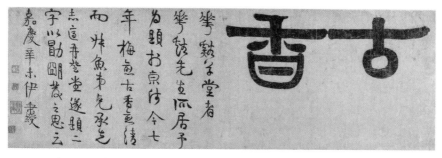

Yi Bingshou (1754–1815), *The Fragrance of Antiquity*, dated to 1811. Horizontal placard scroll, ink on grey paper. Calligraphy: height 39 cm, width 123.8 cm. With mount: height 51 cm, width 149.5 cm, depth 2.2 cm. Princeton University Art Museum.

characters from ancient inscriptions for the publication. This passion for epigraphy was part of the 19th century's broader fashion for 'evidential scholarship' (*kaozheng*), which stressed the importance of careful analysis of ancient texts to the attainment of authentic knowledge of the past. Evidential scholars argued that texts on ancient buildings, steles, bronze vessels and ceramic tiles served as important primary materials that could help correct inaccuracies that historians and editors of antiquity had introduced, and establish the true meanings of Confucian classics.

Yi was recognized as an extraordinary calligrapher within his lifetime. He was most celebrated for his creative interpretation of the quadrate characters of clerical script on Han-dynasty (202 BCE–220 CE) engraved stone monuments. He was especially noted for his study of the *Heng Fang Stele* and *Zhang Qian Stele*, memorial inscriptions to two Han dynasty officials erected in Shandong, in 168 and 186 respectively. Yi particularly admired the former, copying it hundreds of times. The shared features of these two inscriptions, such as the compact structure of their characters and their heavy, bold brushwork, can be observed in many of Yi's extant works. Several court officials were said to have commissioned Yi to write court memorials on their behalf, because the Qianlong emperor was particularly fond of Yi's clerical-script calligraphy. *The Fragrance of Antiquity* is an excellent example of his late style. Dated to 1811, the work was created to commemorate the death of Ye Tingxun (1753–1809), an influential merchant in Guangzhou. Yi's multifaceted knowledge of ancient Chinese writing shines through in the two large characters on the right, which incorporate elements of both seal and clerical scripts. The flowing brush-strokes and dense ink tone bring a strong sense of vigour to the overall composition. Yi's running-script calligraphy – more controlled than standard cursive, freer than regular or clerical script – in the manner of Li Dongyang (1447–1516), a prominent Ming-dynasty official, was also praised by his contemporaries. Kang Youwei (1858–1927), one of the most noted calligraphers of the late Qing, celebrated Yi as a founder of the stele tradition in Chinese calligraphy.

Yan Weitian

29. RUAN YUAN

阮元 (1764–1849)

OUTSTANDING SCHOLAR WITH AN ENCYCLOPAEDIC MIND

An encyclopaedic intellect interested in multiple fields of knowledge, and a senior official who served during the reigns of three emperors (Qianlong, Jiaqing and Daoguang), Ruan Yuan was also a scholar, patron and collector whose vision of antiquity contributed to the emergence of the modern conception of Chinese cultural heritage.

Born into a relatively modest family in Yangzhou, Ruan Yuan counted several officials among his ancestors. The importance given to his education, particularly by his mother, enabled him to pass the highest level of the civil service examinations at the young age of twenty-five, following which he contributed to catalogues of the imperial art collection, in particular those relating to painting and calligraphy. He could thus measure for himself the scope of the immense scholarly and artistic achievements under Qianlong (r. 1736–1795). During his more than forty years of service to the empire, Ruan Yuan also served as governor and governor general in many provinces (including Zhejiang, Henan, Guangdong and Yunnan), ending his career as a member of the Grand Secretariat in the capital, before retiring to his native Yangzhou. Throughout his governorships, he strove to implement policies both ambitious and adapted to the contrasting culture of the regions under his authority.

Bringing together teams of intellectuals and specialists, Ruan Yuan was a central, coordinating figure in multiple collective publishing projects relating to fields of knowledge as diverse as the study of ancient classical texts, history, geography, astronomy, mathematics, literature and epigraphy. The last of these was a discipline about which he was particularly passionate. His editing of such vast, multi-volume publishing projects

Wang Xuehao (1754–1832), *Presenting the Tripod*, 1803 (detail). Ruan Yuan is depicted travelling by boat to present an inscribed Han-dynasty bronze tripod to the monastery on Jiaoshan. Handscroll, ink on paper. Height 33.5 cm, width 89.9 cm. The Metropolitan Museum of Art, New York.

Wang Jun (1816–after 1883), *Album of Ten Sites Associated with Ruan Yuan*, leaf G, dated 1883. According to the painting's inscription, this image shows Ruan Yuan's family temple in Yangzhou, where he composed a text for a stele, with calligraphy (on the stele) done by Gao Kai (1769–1839). Album of ten leaves, ink and colour on paper. Each leaf: height 27.9 cm, width 33.7 cm. The Metropolitan Museum of Art, New York.

illustrated his open-minded conception of what constituted valuable knowledge, as these undertakings encompassed both the Confucian textual canon, which still dominated the education of Chinese scholars of his time, and science and technology. His scientific work innovatively incorporated the contributions of Western scholars.

In these collective projects, as well as in his personal writings, Ruan Yuan projected himself as a representative member of the 'evidential school' of scholarship, which advocated establishing empirical foundations for knowledge through undertaking meticulous analysis of ancient texts, and exerted a profound influence on Chinese intellectual life in the 18th and 19th centuries. Ruan Yuan prized ancient objects and texts as historical sources that enabled scholars to question and verify later, transmitted versions of canonical texts of the 1st millennium BCE.

Ruan Yuan's critical but open approach to the pursuit of knowledge underpinned various academic institutions that he founded in the 1800s and 1820s, such as the Academy of Exegesis of the Classics (Gujingjing she) in Hangzhou or the Sea of Learning Academy (Xuehai tang) in Guangzhou. The continuous influence of the latter on the cultural life of the Guangdong area up until the early 20th century exemplifies the way in which Ruan Yuan made a lasting mark on Chinese intellectual life. At the same time, the creation of libraries within the famous Buddhist Lingyin Temple in Hangzhou and Jiaoshan Temple in Zhenjiang, to which he also entrusted antique objects from his collection, as shown, for example, in Wang Xuehao's (1754–1832) painting *Presenting the Tripod*, helped generate a new, more public and accessible conception of cultural heritage, which foreshadowed the founding of the first public libraries and museums in China.

Ruan Yuan's production and sponsoring of knowledge contributed to development of the arts and archaeology. On the margins of vast projects, which aimed to collect and publish the epigraphic heritage of the territories he administered, he also accumulated an important personal collection. A handscroll by Zhou Zan (n.d.) depicts him surrounded by the ritual vases, ancient weapons and mirrors that constituted this collection. The inscriptions on these objects, reproduced as rubbings, were also included in a catalogue of important contemporary private collections. By collecting objects, and recording and disseminating their images, Ruan Yuan contributed directly to knowledge of the history and culture of ancient China. By taking charge of the transmission of this cultural heritage, he established himself as the first of the great 19th-century collectors (followed by individuals such as Wu Dacheng (1835–1902) and Duanfang (1861–1911)) who promoted antiquarian studies between the peak of the imperial collection at the end of the 18th century and the advent of the first Chinese museums in the 20th century.

Ruan Yuan's promotion of ancient objects and inscriptions directly influenced the artistic creation of his era. In the 19th century, archaic Chinese characters on ancient steles newly discovered by antiquarian aficionados became a crucial inspiration for innovative calligraphers such as Yi Bingshou (1754–1815), He Shaoji (1799–1873) and Zhao Zhiqian (1829–1884). Ruan Yuan's critical guides to such texts asserted, moreover, the authenticity of ancient scripts carved on stone over the calligraphic models transmitted by the literate tradition. This intervention became the theoretical basis on which the calligraphic 'stele school' (*beixue pai*) – championed by intellectuals as diverse as Bao Shichen (1775–1855) and Kang Youwei (1858–1927) – gained prestige. The antiquarian turn in calligraphy extended too into painting, with the emergence of an 'epigraphic school of artists' (*jinshixue huapai*), whose leading representatives – masters like Wu Changshi (1844–1927) and even Qi Baishi (1864–1957) – dominated Chinese painting up to the middle of the 20th century.

Eric Lefebvre

Zhou Zan (n.d.), *Collecting Antiquities*, dated 1803. The painting shows Ruan Yuan (centre), Zhu Weibi and Ruan Changsheng. Handscroll, ink and colours on silk. Height 33.8 cm, width 67.5 cm. National Library of China, Beijing.

30. LIUZHOU

六舟 (1791–1858)

SCHOLAR, MAKER, BELIEVER

When, in the 1910s, the influential scholar and artist Huang Binhong (1865–1955) meditated on the uncertain fate of traditional painting in fast-changing, new China, he proposed to find remedy in the 'study of stone and metal' (*jinshi xue*), an expression generally translated today as antiquarianism. Huang noted that during the Daoguang (1821–1850) and Xianfeng (1851–1861) periods, painters were able to overcome the stale mannerism of the previous generation by turning their attention to the study of ancient inscriptions. If modern scholars have long disagreed with Huang's positive assessment of mid-19th-century painting, most would concur that the period from the 18th century to the mid-19th was indeed a golden age for antiquarian studies. The introduction of new methods of research, the close collaboration between scholars, collectors and specialized craftsmen, which led to the compilation of monumental catalogues still in use today, and the rediscovery of forgotten monuments or texts all marked a turning point in the long history of antiquarian interest in China. Among the most intriguing personalities of the time was Liuzhou, the 'Antiquarian Monk' (*jinshi seng*), traditionally identified as the creator of a startling new process for representing antiquities, the 'full-form rubbing' (*quanxing ta*).

Liuzhou, original name Shi Dashou, was born into a humble household in modern-day Haining, Zhejiang province. At the age of sixteen, he joined the monastic community and spent his early days as a travelling monk, deepening his understanding of the Buddhist Law and his expertise in antique objects stored in monasteries and temples, which, not unlike churches in early modern Europe, served

Liuzhou (1791–1858) and Chen Geng (act. 1821–61), *Cleaning the Lamp*, 1836. Handscroll, ink and colour on paper. Height 31 cm, width 70 cm. Zhejiang Provincial Museum, Hangzhou.

as a training ground for aspiring artists. Liuzhou began to circulate his findings in the form of rubbings, and by the 1820s via striking new creations. In the 1830s he fully mastered this new technique as documented by a remarkable string of highly original works, including the scroll illustrated here, *Cleaning the Lamp*, made in 1836. Liuzhou's innovative skills stirred great interest among collectors across the empire. In 1838, he was invited to the Jigu zhai in Yangzhou, the celebrated residence of Ruan Yuan (1764–1849), then a retired minister and doyen of early 19th-century antiquarians, who became Liuzhou's major patron later in his career. Liuzhou then worked for the equally prominent Chen family in Hangzhou until his death in 1858.

'Full-form rubbing' is an expedient label that denotes what is in fact a laborious process involving several steps and different techniques. Rubbings have a long history in China, and consist of impressions of an object's surface that are obtained by pressing wet paper on a carved stone, letting it dry, then tamping it with an ink-filled cotton ball. Once peeled off, the rubbing appeared as white on the black-inked background and retains everything that exists on the surface worked on: inscriptions and marks, but also the material's natural imperfections and abrasions caused by the passing of time.

Yet, if rubbing was intended as an evocative snapshot of an object's life through time, before Liuzhou, its practice prioritized the legibility of details over the accurate presentation of the object's actual features, volume, and relationship to space. Building on prior experiments, Liuzhou developed instead a multi-part procedure that usually began by casting the vessel's shadow to outline its silhouette on paper. Some parts were then rubbed, and others printed or painted in lustrous black ink. The final effect is astonishing: the three-dimensional object appears as if real within the two-dimensional piece of paper, making viewers feel as if they are standing in front of the actual thing. In the words of Liuzhou's most fervent admirers, his replicas were even better than the original objects.

Exactitude and certainty were not, however, the only goals Liuzhou aspired to achieve with his work. 'Full-form rubbings' entangled audiences in multisensory experiences that amazed viewers of his work, as nothing comparable had ever been accomplished before. Liuzhou often inserted himself in his representations, as in *Cleaning the Lamp*, where two portraits of the monk at work become a measure of and counterpart to two 'portraits' of the ancient vessel, one standing upright and the other upside down. The goose-foot lamp is small; Liuzhou miniaturized himself into a Lilliputian. Another example of such a lamp is found on the desk of Ruan Yuan, in a painting by Zhou Zan (*see* p.107). In other instances, rubbed ancient vessels were reimagined as containers for brilliantly painted cut flowers or branches in compositions destined to attain great popularity in the later 19th century, far beyond the confines of elite antiquarian circles. In other works, Liuzhou stacked up coins, fragments of broken objects, calligraphy samples in semi-abstract and collage-like ensembles. Antiquarian culture of the 19th century did not concern merely the accumulation and reordering of specialized knowledge; it was also about the pleasure of making discoveries, and the personal bonds, rivalry and communion between like-minded individuals. The many inscriptions filling Liuzhou's work evoke long candlelit conversations, travels to far-off places and visits to other enthusiasts' collections; his rubbings capture this peculiar commingling of the scholarly and convivial, and the emotional investments of a generation of Qing scholars.

Liuzhou, unlike his patrons, thought of himself primarily as a maker, as someone possessing specialized skills honed through making that could be quickly mobilized for different tasks. The elevation of artisanal knowledge, a distinct feature of the mid-Qing period, is clearly on display in *Cleaning the Lamp*. Here, Liuzhou's body is fully activated as he stretches to peruse the object or crouches over the inscription, his hands gently running over it, as if to suggest that no understanding of the past is possible without a direct, bodily involvement with things. There was a particular Buddhist dimension to his artwork: he often wrote of the need to rescue ancient Buddhist carvings and statues from oblivion. He understood his attraction for ancient objects in terms of karmic retribution. At a time when ancient Buddhist artefacts were slowly being included in the category of antiquities, having previously been marginalized relative to jades and bronzes, Liuzhou showed that antiquarianism was no longer the exclusive domain of erudite, Neo-Confucian scholars. His painstaking art communicated that the past could be made palpably immediate only through the synergy of eye, hand and the imagination.

Michele Matteini

31. SUN MINGQIU

孫鳴球 (1823–after 1903)

A MASTER OF MASQUERADING

Aesthetic, cultural and intellectual developments of the late Qing instigated the emergence of a new and surprising painting genre called, variously, 'eight brokens' (*bapo*) or 'a pile of brocade ashes' (*jinhuidui*). These paintings depicted, in exacting naturalism, scraps of deteriorating cultural ephemera such as half-burnt calligraphies, worm-eaten book pages and even ripped-open envelopes, all scattered randomly across a paper or silk surface. The artist Sun Mingqiu (style name Zizhen), who most likely hailed from the small town of Gaocheng (located in today's Cangzhou prefecture) in central Hebei province, south of Tianjin, was one of the earliest and finest practitioners of the *bapo* genre. Respect for his work earned him a mention in a catalogue of artists' names dating to the late 19th or early 20th centuries, 'Jottings from the Taoyang Studio', compiled by an as yet unidentified scholar.

Though there are no biographies of Sun, autobiographical inscriptions within his paintings offer clues to his hometown, his life of scholarship – but not officialdom

– and his immersion in Beijing artistic circles. A tiny text on a painting within a painting references his returning home from taking a civil service examination. Though his paintings testify to his deep knowledge of classical texts, there is no evidence that he passed that examination. By the 1880s, Sun was signing his location as Beijing, using the then-popular appellation Dumen ('capital gate'). In the 1890s, he noted his presence at Beijing's book, art supply and antiquities shopping district on Liulichang, at the Songzhuzhai shop (now called Rongbaozhai). The Liulichang shops would have provided him with plenty of material for his intellectual appetite and for his compositions – rubbings, calligraphy, paintings and books.

The earliest known dated *bapo* work by Sun – and, in fact, the earliest yet known *bapo* painting – is a handscroll from 1876. Scattered across its breadth are depictions of worm-eaten papers, fragments of paintings and rubbings, along with a ripped page from a book on ancient coinage. The work is evidence that the *bapo* genre had already reached this mature form by the first years of the Guangxu reign (1875–1908). In later years, Sun Mingqiu further developed his own personal and sophisticated style of *bapo*, represented by the circular album leaf shown here.

Numerous visual art forms, aesthetic interests, intellectual directions and social customs inspired the development of *bapo*. The focus on ancient texts, the collecting of antiquities, calligraphy and rubbings, and even a prevailing belief in the power of images and words, all contributed to its appearance. An earlier genre predating *bapo* presented multiple undamaged works of art in a regular, ordered configuration. Such compositions appeared in both Chinese and Japanese decorative arts as early as the 17th century. *Bapo* took the further step of depicting deteriorating objects, scattered in a random arrangement. The violence, destruction and library conflagrations during the Taiping Civil War (1851–1864) may have provoked such visual storms. This context helps explain the circulation of another designation for this style of composition, 'a pile of brocade ashes', a phrase from a Tang-dynasty poem mourning the destruction of a palace.

In Sun Mingqiu's 1876 work, his textual remnants are damaged and scattered, as if tossed to the winds, but, by the 1890s, as evidenced by numerous works at the Museum of Fine Arts in Boston, at the Museum für Asiatische Kunst in Berlin and at auctions, he had returned to a more orderly composition of generally undamaged antiquities. Some of these works are sets of four or six vertical scrolls, each with one vertical row of objects. Others are circular works, perhaps once mounted as round fans but more likely as album leaves, presenting objects in an ordered arrangement.

In an 1892 work, he presents four objects. At the top is an open folding-fan painting depicting a group of folkloric characters in Chinese popular culture, the Eight Immortals, with a poetic inscription, signed and dated 1892. Below, apparently, are three pages of rubbings: two are texts, and the third is a page from an illustrated catalogue of ancient bronzes. These three pages assertively proclaim a devotion to antiquity, calligraphy and epigraphy, fundamental concerns of the 19th-century scholar and literatus.

Sun Mingqiu (1823–c. 1903), *bapo* painting, 1892. Album leaf, ink and colour on silk. Ø 25 cm. The British Museum, London.

The three 'rubbings', however, are painted, not actual rubbings. By the late 19th century, images of rubbings were being made in a variety of ways. The oldest rubbings, of the purest form, were created by pressing wet paper on a carved stone, letting it dry and then tamping it with an ink-filled cotton ball so that the carved calligraphy or drawings appeared as white on the black-inked background. These rubbings often capture the imperfections of old and damaged stones. To increase the distribution of ancient texts and images, rubbings were also made from wooden boards incised in imitation of stones. In the 1880s, a new technique appeared that came to be known as *yingta*. This process, possibly invented by Sun Mingqiu, was to paint with a brush the likeness of a rubbing. (A work by Sun dating to 1882 already features several *yingta*.) His many examples of this form demonstrate his acute technical abilities, intimate familiarity with classic Chinese masterworks and fascination with calligraphy.

At least two of the *yingta* in this 1892 work are not only not rubbings, but also not even likenesses of actual rubbings. Instead, Sun has re-created the likeness of white-on-black rubbings of damaged stones from printed black-on-white book pages. The central object depicts a rubbing of an ancient three-legged round bronze vessel as recorded in the *Illustrated Catalogue of Examined Antiquity* by Lü Dalin (1046–1092), published in 1092; but the *Illustrated Catalogue*, reprinted many times over the ensuing centuries, was a woodblock-printed book with line illustrations. In presenting the vessel as a rubbing, while seemingly striving for absolute verisimilitude, the artist is, in fact, playing with the viewer's sense of reality.

The text on the right-hand page describes a Qin-dynasty seal, and is from the Ming-dynasty *Seals and Vessels of the Stone Drum Studio* by Yu Zao (act. *c.* 1620–40). Published in 1628, this was a nine-volume, woodblock-printed book. While the book was printed as black text on white paper, Sun reversed the tones, so the text appears to be a rubbing of an ancient stone. To further emphasize the rough quality and age of the stone, he varied the heaviness of his ink to indicate damage on the stone – a stone that never existed.

Sun almost always included his own signature and the date of the painting within one of the elements within the painting. In this case, he wrote date, title, location and his name, along with a poem, across the breadth of the fan painting within the painting. The title is *Wishing Longevity*. Other *bapo* works by Sun done at the same time are entitled *One Hundred Years*, likewise expressing hopes for longevity for the painting's recipient. This phrase is also a word-play, as *sui* ('year') is a homonym of the word for 'broken' or 'fragment', and the paintings themselves are depictions of fragments. With this title, while parading his work as a literati compilation, the artist cleverly reveals yet another level of meaning – mere quotidian birthday wishes.

Nancy Berliner

32. ZHANG YIN

張崟 (1761–1829)

ATMOSPHERIC LANDSCAPE PAINTER

Zhenjiang is an ancient city on the north bank of the Yangtze River, about 200 kilometres from the coast, in the Jiangnan region – a part of China famed for its artistic and literary culture. Its beautiful scenery inspired two famous Song-dynasty artists Mi Fu (1051–1107) and his son Mi Youren (1074–1151) to develop a characteristic, much-imitated style of painting known as 'Mi-Style Cloud-Covered Mountains'. During the mid-Qing, a distinct 'Jingjiang' group of Zhenjiang painters emerged. Zhang Yin was a founding member of this group, who – as the Mis had done for the Song – revitalized the art of landscape painting for the Qing. These Qing artists distanced themselves from artistic conventions of the time, as exemplified by the paintings of the 'Four Wangs' of the early Qing – Wang Shimin (1592–1680), Wang Jian (1609–1677), Wang Hui (1632–1717) and Wang Yuanqi (1642–1715) – who painted landscapes from the confines of their studios, adhering to the techniques and sedate, formulaic compositions of past masters of the 13th century. Instead, the Jingjiang school depicted

Zhang Yin (1761–1829), *Three Mountains in Jingkou*, dated 1827. Handscroll, ink and colour on paper. Height 29.3 cm, width 193 cm. The Palace Museum, Beijing.

actual landscapes from their home region and revived the practice of making direct studies of nature, rather than painting a landscape from imagination.

Zhang Yin was born to a wealthy merchant family. His father, Zhang Zikun (n.d), was an art lover and a passionate collector of paintings and calligraphy. Within his gardens in Zhenjiang, Zhang Zikun built the Room of Clarity and Brilliance, a pavilion where he and his younger brother Zhang Ruoyun (n.d.), also a renowned collector, frequently hosted literati gatherings for wine drinking and other artistic activities. Among the guests were prestigious local literati gentry and artists Wang Wenzhi (1730–1802), Zhou Xupei (n.d.) and Pan Gongshou (1741–1794). Zhang Yin's family background thus gave him opportunities from a young age to study and admire masterpieces of painting and calligraphy, as well as access to tutoring from Wang Wenzhi and Pan Gongshou, whose Buddhist faith had a subtle, long-term influence on Zhang.

Zhang Yin lived at a time when the Qing government enforced policies of ruthless literary inquisition to tighten intellectual and cultural control. This harsh cultural environment, coupled with his father's early death and the family's consequent financial decline, pushed Zhang Yin to retreat to a hermit-like existence in mountain temples. In his youth, he devoted himself to the study of nature and painting, developing talents and skills that eventually had an important, multigenerational influence on the Jingjiang school.

Zhang Yin's artistic thought and practice were heavily influenced by his childhood instructors Wang Wenzhi and Pan Gongshou. Wang was a passionate admirer of Ming-dynasty artists such as Dong Qichang (1555–1636), famous for his theories about art history and classification of painting styles; Shen Zhou (1427–1509), founder of the Wu school of painting that championed the individuality of artistic styles; and Wen Zhengming (1470–1559), poet, calligrapher and artist whose work challenged traditional academic styles of painting. Wang believed that these Ming painters equalled, or even surpassed, the achievements of Song- and Yuan-dynasty masters. His judgments were widely accepted by painters in Zhenjiang. Consequently, Zhang Yin modelled his own landscape painting after that of Shen Zhou and Wen Zhengming. He absorbed the painting traditions of the great masters of landscape painting from the Song and Yuan dynasties (960–1368), and synthesized the 'Northern style', featuring grand panoramic landscapes, with the more refined and delicate 'Southern style' of painting within his own creative vision. But, to a much greater degree than concentrating on artistic models from the past, Zhang Yin went out of his studio to study nature directly, to paint what he saw in real life. He often used strokes with a 'hemp-fibre texture' (*pima cun*) and dot strokes (*dianzi cun*) to execute the shades and textures of southern landscapes. His works are characterized by large-scale, almost majestic landscapes, executed with vigorous brushwork. Pioneered by Zhang Yin, this style was imitated by a long line of eminent artists including Pan Simu (*c.* 1756–1843), Gu Heqing (b. 1766) and Zhou Hao (n.d.).

Canons of Chinese art have arguably underrated Zhang Yin; he has not received the notice that he deserves. But in the long history of Chinese painting, the creative syntheses of the past, emotional immediacy and artistic innovations of his Jingjiang school reversed the decline of mid-Qing landscape painting and underpinned the genre's revival in the 20th century. To scholars of art, and of culture more generally, Zhang's life and career are an important chapter in late imperial history, deserving of further research.

Li Lan

33. QIAN DU

錢杜 (1763–1844)

POET-PAINTER KNOWN FOR HIS FRESH CLASSICISM

For many early 19th-century literati, Qian Du was the premier poet-painter of their generation. But by the time of Qian Du's death, just after the First Opium War (1839–42) and just before the outbreak of the Taiping Civil War (1851–64), the world of privilege into which he was born was disintegrating, along with the set of elite values that supported it. Qian Du's career path and posthumous reception reflect the changing dynamics of the 19th century.

As the seventh son of a high-ranking government official, Qian Du enjoyed many childhood privileges. He was born in the wealthy and cultured Qiantang district of Hangzhou, travelling often to accompany his father to various

Qian Du (1763–1844), *The Pristine and Verdant Garden*, dated 1809. Handscroll, ink and light colour on paper. Height 24.9 cm, width 60.6 cm. The Palace Museum, Beijing.

government postings throughout the empire. As older brothers secured government careers though the civil service examinations, Qian Du devoted his time to poetry and painting, developing a reputation in elite circles for his refined landscapes and blossoming-plum paintings. Qian moved in a cultured network inherited from his father, which included the poet Yuan Mei (1716–1797) and the painter Jin Nong (1687–1763). These social relationships moved across generations. Yuan's son, Yuan Tong (1775–1829), was Qian's lifelong patron, and Qian liked to tell the story of Jin Nong holding him as an infant, as it linked his painting directly to the most renowned artist of the previous generation.

Many of Qian Du's paintings attest to the intergenerational nature of cultural capital. He painted *The Pristine and Verdant Garden* in 1809 for Wang Shitai (n.d.), son-in-law of Yuan Mei and inheritor of a pair of renowned garden estates along the coast of Jiangsu province. In his inscription to the painting, Qian Du recounts stopping at Wang's home on his way back from Yunnan and lingering there for a month writing poems, drinking and relaxing. One day Wang brought out Xi Gang's (1746–1803) *Mountain Retreat of the Jade Tung Trees*, a painting done in 1800 of the garden's most remote pavilion. Finding extra paper mounted with the handscroll, Qian painted a view of the entire garden to complement the earlier painting. Colophons by the most renowned poets, officials, painters and literati of the day – including Ruan Yuan (1764–1849), Guo Lin (1767–1831), Yuan Tong, Chen Wenshu (1771–1843) and several of Qian Du's older brothers – adorn the work. Paintings like this were sites for the documentation and perpetuation of elite social relationships and style (both literary and painterly); they were the means by which literati demonstrated to their peers their cultural depth and refinement. Whereas the moist, heavily textured brushwork of Xi's earlier work enveloped the garden architecture in a monochromatic tradition of landscape painting that could be traced to Yuan-dynasty precedents, Qian Du chose pale colour washes, contrasting patterning and attenuated brushwork to link his work to (and signal an aesthetic lineage

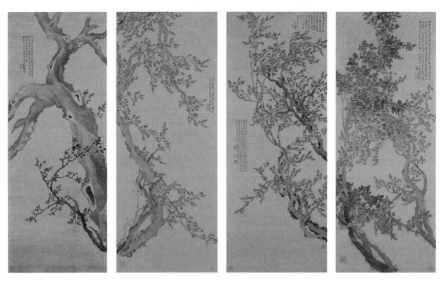

Qian Du (1763–1844), *Plum Blossom*, dated 1841. Set of four hanging scrolls, ink and light colour on paper. Each height 103 cm, width 41 cm. Tianjin Museum.

from) Ming-dynasty painters such as Tang Yin (1470–1524) and Wen Zhengming (1470–1559).

The same people who inscribed Qian Du's handscroll for Wang also helped him to secure work as an aide to various government officials after his father's death. The aide system was a reliable means of income for those who inhabited inherited networks of social privilege but were unable to advance through the civil service examinations. By his late forties, Qian Du had given up this work to make his way through painting and poetry. The publication of two texts, *Songhu's Superfluous Words on Painting* and *Songhu's Reflections on Painting*, mark this transition by presenting Qian's bona fides in the form of theoretical discussions of painting and descriptions of important historical paintings he had seen first-hand. These books further built Qian Du's reputation, and up-and-coming officials like Zhang Jing (1776–1835) sought out the painter to fortify their own statures as men of culture. Some of Qian Du's best work was done for Zhang, who reached the height of his career in the late 1820s and early 1830s as director general of Yellow River and Grand Canal Conservancy.

Towards the end of his life, Qian Du – who had no sons of his own, having abandoned a wife and daughter in his youth – was cared for by his nephew. He still produced high-quality work in his distinctive style of revitalized Ming-dynasty brushwork up to his death at the age of eighty-one, though he was known to employ the help of an assistant (*daibi*) in his later years. A powerful set of four hanging scrolls with blossoming plum branches, painted in 1841, attests to the durability of Qian Du's skills and reputation. Each showcases a different dimension of the ever versatile genre, alternating the use of light colour, subtle ink washes and delicate texturing across four truncated views of suspended branches in bloom. A discussion of the theme in art history accompanies each image, so that, as a set, the four paintings communicate a visual and textual treatise on the legacies of Ming-era plum-blossom painting.

Qian Du's work appealed to his peers for its highly refined brushwork, as well as for the way its forms and textures referenced art history. Qian Du's classicism was not conservativism, however. His aesthetic choices drew from the history of Chinese art in ways that surprised and delighted those around him. His choice of exemplars from the so-called 'Wu school' of the 15th and 16th centuries created a deliberate, artful contrast between his own work and that of the most popular 18th-century painters. Likewise, his advocacy of an 'unstudied' or 'awkward' (*zhuo*) brushwork style aligned his paintings with the contemporaneous trend of epigraphic aesthetics – the appropriation of material and stylistic signs from inscribed stone and metal artefacts dating to the golden age of the Han dynasty (202 BCE–220 CE) and the Six Dynasties (220–589 CE) period. By employing broken brushwork that imitated the worn qualities of classical inscriptions, and by emulating the archaic compositions found on ancient objects, early 19th-century artists claimed to trade in the superfluous affectations of recent painting and calligraphy for a more direct transmission of the roots of Chinese culture.

Qian Du's reputation held for a generation or so after his passing, as writers and painters from the 1850s to the 1880s praised his work and emulated his style, reinforcing his place in the artistic lineages that maintained elite taste. But by the late 19th century, changes set in motion by the havoc of the mid-century Opium Wars and Taiping Civil War unseated these genealogies of style. By the turn of the 20th century, new modern art histories barely mentioned Qian Du. The rarefied, elite world that Qian Du called forth in his images and poems was re-labelled myopic, ossified and self-indulgent, as the artists of his generation – the last to pass before the cataclysms of the mid-19th century – became the scapegoats responsible for a narrative of cultural and political decline that, polemical reformers argued, made the end of the Qing empire inevitable.

Michael J. Hatch

34. CAO ZHENXIU

曹貞秀 (1762–c. 1822)

OUTSTANDING WOMAN CALLIGRAPHER AND PAINTER

A calligrapher, painter and author, Cao Zhenxiu was an active and well-known cultured woman of her time. She was particularly known for her elegant small regular script (*xiao kai*), and was praised by 19th-century writers as the best calligrapher of the dynasty among 'women of the inner chambers' (*guige*), a phrase referring to gentlewomen.

Cao's father, Cao Rui (1732–1793), whose family came from Anhui province, held a military post in the capital, Beijing. Presumably, it was he who, as an art lover, taught

Cao calligraphy and painting. At the age of twenty-three *sui*, she became the second wife of Wang Qisun (1755–1817), a literatus from Suzhou in south-east China who passed the provincial, second level of the civil service examination in 1788. Although he did not achieve great success in officialdom, he was a highly regarded member of the empire's cultural elite. The couple lived in Beijing for a time before eventually returning south. The marriage was apparently a happy one. Husband and wife shared a love for the scholarly arts and they became famed as a cultured, learned couple.

A portrait painting of Cao in the Palace Museum, Beijing, depicts her as a self-possessed married woman of learning and understated refinement. She looks directly at the viewer from behind a circular window in a courtyard, dressed in an unostentatious blue robe. On the table next to her is a dark zither – a reference to her courtesy name Moqin ('ink zither'). Her other hand points to a servant holding a stalk of grain, symbolic of harmony and fecundity – a reference to her marriage. On the left side of the painting runs an inscription written by Wang Qisun. It records that it

Zhou Li (act. late 18th century) and Cao Zhenxiu (1762–*c*. 1822), *Portrait of Cao Zhenxiu*, late 18th century. Hanging scroll, ink and colours on paper. Height 138.8 cm, width 79 cm. The Palace Museum, Beijing.

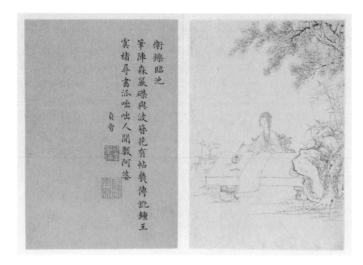

Poem and calligraphy by Cao Zhenxiu (1762– c. 1822), painting by Gai Qi (1773–1828), from *Famous Women*, dated 1799. Album of sixteen leaves, ink on paper. Each image height 24.8 cm, width 16.8 cm. The Metropolitan Museum of Art, New York.

was Cao's idea to ask the painter Zhou Li (act. late 18th century) to paint her portrait, while Wang arranged the occasion by inviting the painter for a drink. Cao then completed the painting by adding bamboo and a crane. This painting shows Cao's confidence in shaping her self-image, and in her own talents to collaborate with a male painter through the intermediary of her husband.

Cao's cultivation and social position put her in contact with notable literary men, including the calligrapher and official Liu Yong (1720–1805), who gave her advice on calligraphy. She received an inscribed plaque from him, as well as from another important calligrapher Gui Fu (1736–1805), a friend of Cao's father, and from Wang Jie (1725–1805), who in time became Grand Secretary. Cao's writings *Drafts from the Pavilion for Writing Rhymes*, published in the early 1800s, record the many inscriptions that she authored for other people's paintings and texts. It reveals her extensive connections with both literary men and women, such as the female poet Chen Duanjing (act. late 18th century) from Jiangsu province and Lady Tongjia (1737–1809), the daughter of a Manchu aristocratic family and wife of a prince.

In her literary work, Cao reveals an awareness of some of the inequalities that women in China faced in life and in the writing of history. In composing the biography of an official's mother, Cao notes, 'A woman who has a special biography [written about her] is a woman of misfortune.' Cao was reflecting on the harsh standards that women were expected to meet in order to be deemed worthy of record by historians, perhaps in response to the extreme forms of female self-sacrifice in the name of filiality and chastity that became prevalent from the Ming dynasty (1368–1644) onwards. Cao's dissatisfaction with restrictive models of female virtue is further suggested in an album in the Metropolitan Museum of Art, New York, dated to 1799. It records sixteen poems composed by Cao on historical and legendary women written in her hand, which she asked the young painter Gai Qi (1773–1828) to illustrate. Among the historical women she wrote about, only two examples are specifically about female virtue. Instead, Cao selected for the most part female scholars and calligraphers, and even a warrior. Her poems on Buddhist, Daoist and popular figures are also interestingly wide-ranging, as she makes references to old age and poverty, in addition to power and beauty.

Moreover, Cao was critical of the lack of recognition in history for female calligraphers. Pondering a Tang-dynasty stele in one of her published writings, she asked: 'Did more than a millennium of gentlewomen truly not produce any accomplished calligraphy? Or is it rather that scholar-officials disparaged and effaced their works?' Cao studied the works of educated women and in particular modelled herself on two early female calligraphers of note – Wu Cailuan (act. 830–845) of the Tang dynasty and Wei Shuo (272–349) of the Eastern Jin.

Cao's passion for the study of calligraphy is evident in her writings, but even an elite woman like her was limited by circumstances. In his preface to Cao's collection of writings, Wang Qisun wrote admiringly and apologetically about his wife's endurance of the couple's humble lifestyle, whereby she had to look after the household and bring up their children herself (including two who died in infancy), all of which affected her ability to practise calligraphy. Cao also once wrote of how physical domestic work had caused her hands to tremble, making it increasingly difficult for her to write in fine script. Nevertheless, Cao had access to a rich cultural world and lived during a relatively prosperous and stable period in Chinese history, prior to the onset of the turbulent 19th century. Her life reflects the growth in female education and flourishing female literary culture that had emerged by the late 16th century in urban centres in China. Through scholarly activities, women like Cao were able to extend their social life beyond the inner chambers, and make the claim that women's talents and work were worthy of record and recognition.

Luk Yu-ping

35. FEI DANXU

費丹旭 (1802–1850)

CELEBRATED ARTIST OF FIGURES FROM LIFE AND LEGEND

Although surviving colophons, catalogues and casual contemporary writings show that Fei Danxu was one of the most celebrated painters of his era, we have relatively little biographical information about him. Born into a family of established professional artists in Huzhou in north Zhejiang province, Fei studied painting as a child. At the age of nineteen, initially in the company of his father Fei Yu (n.d.), he began visiting hubs of artistic activity in the Jiangnan area, south of the Yangtze River. During the last twenty years of his peripatetic life, Fei made repeated return visits to

Fei Danxu (1802–1850), *East Portico Poetry Society* (detail showing self-portrait). The original, completed in late 1832, is now lost. This image is from Sun Yuanchao, *Excellent Portraits by Fei Danxu*, published in Beijing by Renmin meishu chunbanshe, 1959.

Hangzhou and Haining in southern Zhejiang, but Huzhou remained Fei's home base throughout his life, and it was there that he died peacefully.

During extended stays in south Zhejiang, he painted well-known landscapes and sites such as the historic Buddhist temple on Wulin mountain in Hangzhou, as in *Tour of Taoguang Temple*. This group portrait (depicting a visit of 1834) shows five male figures standing with attendants, among groves of bamboo. One of the five figures is the host of the event, Fu'ne Yang'a (1789–1845), the Manchu inspector general of Zhejiang, who requested the visual record from Fei. Fei ends the one-line inscription with the characters *gong bi* ('written with respect'), signalling a sense of distance and acknowledgment of social hierarchy. The portrait is followed by forty-nine colophons (an unusually large number) written by luminaries including Lin Zexu (1785–1850), Xu Baoshan (1790–1838) and Weng Tonghe (1830–1904), indicating the esteem in which Fei's host Wang Yuansun (1794–1836) and his family were held by the contemporary intellectual elite. An unusual feature of this handscroll is the inclusion of a rubbing (inscription dated 1883) of a segment of the painting, carved on stone. Another painting on the same subject by Fei is in the Nanjing Museum.

Fei's surviving oeuvre includes portraits of living male subjects; depictions of female characters in myths and legends, historical narratives and literary works; and eighty-seven illustrations in a Daoist morality book, *Tract on the Hidden Administration [of the deity Wenchang] with Illustrations and Veridical Commentary*, printed on woodblocks in late 1844. The six collaborators on this printed book, including Fei, are represented in, or connected to, two famous handscrolls, *East Portico Poetry Society* (1832) and *Fruit Orchard, Remembrance of the Old* (1849).

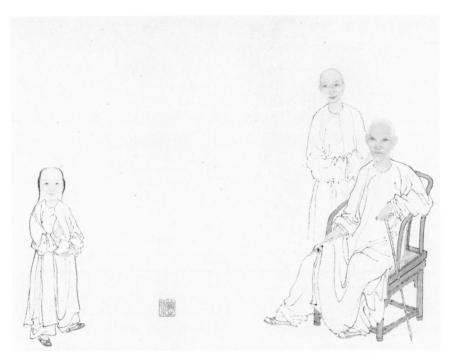

Fei Danxu (1802–1850), *Fruit Orchard, Remembrance of the Old* (detail), 1849. Handscroll, ink and light colour on paper. Height 29 cm, width 105 cm. Zhejiang Provincial Museum, Hangzhou.

The two handscrolls are important because they record professional networks and friendships of the 1830s to 1840s, before the devastation of the Taiping Civil War tore such communities apart. These were not Fei's networks but rather those of his patrons, and centre on the renowned publishing families of Wang Yuansun (1794–1836) in Hangzhou, and Jiang Guangxu (1813–1860) in Haining. They included professional artists; compilers and editors; officials and scholars; bibliophiles and publishers; connoisseurs; and collectors of paintings, calligraphy, rubbings and inscribed antiquities.

In the first of the handscrolls, Fei painted his self-portrait, along with the portraits of twenty-six male members of the East Portico Poetry Society (plus younger male and female attendants) – a copy survives in the collection of the Zhejiang Provincial Museum. Hosted by Wang Yuansun, the East Portico Poetry Society met regularly in the gardens of the Wang family villa to compose poetry. Fei painted the long handscroll in late 1832, towards the end of his three-year stay as a 'paid guest' with the Wang household. During this time, his artistic reputation had prospered, thanks to the support of his mentors. Fei had also studied poetry and calligraphy with the Wang family's friends and associates. Tang Yifen (1778–1853), the official who is rumoured to have introduced Fei to Wang Yuansun, the monk-artist, Liuzhou (1791–1858) and his friend Zhang Tingji (1768–1848), a noted antiquarian and calligrapher who had been a pupil of the famous antiquarian Ruan Yuan (1764–1849), were among the men featured in *East Portico Poetry Society*. Another celebrated scholar and friend of Wang Yuansun included in the gathering was Hu Jing (1769–1845). There is no record of any relationship between Hu and Fei. As one of two early mentors in calligraphy to Fei, Zhang Tingji was a collaborator on the 1844 morality book, as well as one of three male figures represented in the second handscroll, *Fruit Orchard, Remembrance of the Old*. Fei painted this second handscroll in 1849 in the residence of Jiang Guangxu in Haining, with whom Fei had become acquainted probably by 1838.

Fruit Orchard begins with a depiction of landscape seen at a distance, which includes seven small male and female figures of ages ranging from around ten to eighty. One segment shows three male subjects against a plain background: the twelve-year-old son of Jiang Guangxu, Zhang Tingji and Zhang's nephew Zhang Xinyuan (1808–1848). All three were already deceased when Fei created the painting. In an inscription to the left of the scroll, Fei explains that he is memorializing an occasion three years earlier in the same orchard at Jiang's villa, at which the three deceased figures were present. Oddly, their stances and expressions suggest a lack of communication or even awareness of each other; each appears both self-absorbed and to be looking directly at the viewer.

Both during and after his lifetime, Fei Danxu was also famous for his beautiful and unusual paintings of women such as *Confessions in Silk Damask*. In his own time, he was regarded as a poet and artist superior to contemporaries who subsequently became more renowned, such as Ren Xiong (1823–1857). Meanwhile, Ren Bonian (1840–1896) tried to pass himself off as Fei's pupil by means of a play on an adopted name (his artifice was only stopped when Fei's son objected to it). Fei's work may not have the graphic impact of some of his contemporaries – such as Ren Xiong – but it evokes the world and atmosphere of pre-Taiping intellectual life in the empire's cultural heartland.

Marion S. Lee

36. TANG YIFEN

湯貽汾 (1778–1853)

POET, CALLIGRAPHER, PAINTER, COMPOSER, DRAMATIST

Tang Yifen was a native of Wujin, in present-day Changzhou, Jiangsu province. He was a literatus, calligrapher and painter of the late Qing period, much celebrated during his lifetime. Although a career soldier, Tang Yifen was also a masterful poet and painter whose works project a strong sense of moral purpose and integrity.

Like his father and grandfather, Tang Yifen met his end in battle, attending to his official duties. As martyrs on behalf of the Qing empire, these three generations of the Tang family were celebrated by contemporaries for their loyalty. Tang Yifen's grandfather, Tang Dakui (1728–1787), became a *jinshi* – graduate of the highest rung of the civil service examinations – in 1763. In 1787, when serving as the magistrate in

Fengshan county (present-day Gaoxiong), Taiwan, he died along with Tang Yifen's father, Tang Xunye, while fighting an anti-Qing sectarian rebellion. As a reward for his loyalty, Tang Dakui was posthumously promoted to commandant of military fortitude and was granted the hereditary noble rank commander of the fast-as-clouds cavalry, to which the eighteen-year-old Tang Yifen succeeded in the autumn of 1795. The emperor instructed the younger Tang to begin his military career serving under the Viceroy of Liangjiang, one of the Qing's most important regional posts with oversight of much of south-east China. This posting gave Tang Yifen the opportunity to travel around some of the region's most beautiful landscapes: the mountains and rivers of Anhui, and the area surrounding Nanjing. On these journeys he accumulated a wealth of materials and aesthetic experiences that inspired many of his future artistic creations.

In 1803, Tang Yifen was appointed to a senior military command in Jiangsu. Four years later, however, he was dismissed from office after being falsely indicted by his superiors when he refused to participate in their own corruption. Although rehabilitated, Tang Yifen was not reinstated for another two years, when he was offered a post in the garrison armies in Guangzhou. In 1832, the 54-year-old Tang Yifen was promoted to deputy military commander in Zhejiang province, but resigned shortly after due to ill health and retired to Jiangning (present-day Nanjing). There, he toured sites of historical, antiquarian importance and extraordinary natural beauty. But empire-wide events – above all the enormously violent and destructive invasion of the south-east by the forces of the Taiping Heavenly Kingdom – pulled Tang back into active service. That same year, Tang Yifen organized local militia to resist the Taiping army's attack on Nanjing, but his defence failed. He committed suicide by drowning at the age of seventy-four, on the day the city fell to the Taiping; they would make the city their breakaway capital until Qing forces retook it, again with appalling bloodshed, in 1864.

During his lifetime, outside the demands of his military career Tang Yifen was a prolific writer of poetry, lyrics and music, a calligrapher and a painter. In the 20th century, critics acclaimed him as the best poet, calligrapher and painter of his time, and a man of enormous personal rectitude: 'He lived in seclusion lest his name became known to his contemporaries', went one much-repeated judgment. He excelled at landscape painting, with a particular talent for depicting flowers, plum, bamboo, pine and cypress. Tang's 1,417 poems were compiled into a thirty-six-volume series entitled *Collection of Poems from the Secluded Zither Garden* – the name was drawn from the garden he built in his official residence in Shanxi. His lyrics made up a further four volumes. A number of Tang Yifen's paintings have survived and his artistic achievements were seen as so remarkable that the *Draft History of the Qing Dynasty* – completed in the 1920s – described him thus: 'Most of the best-known Qing painters came from the 17th and 18th centuries; only Tang Yifen and Dai Xi stand out in the later period.' His *Chit-Chat on an Autumn Plain*, completed at the age of seventy, depicts a group of recluses chatting and chanting poems amid beautifully tranquil autumnal scenery. Its skilled vertically oriented depiction of the scene, exe-cuted in strong, clean brushstrokes, exemplified the mature Tang's ability to capture atmospherically something of his subjects' inner nature. Tang Yifen was also remark-able for his formal versatility. In addition to writing poetry, he wrote drama, such as *The Legend of the Swordmen*, all the while serving as a senior military officer in Guangdong and Shanxi province.

Tang Yifen also made contributions to discussions of aesthetic theory and artistic technique. His *Analytical Examination of Painting Methods* is a compendium of the great achievements of Ming and Qing painting and also a cogent summary and re-examination of the inaccessibly long and loosely structured manual *Painting Methods* by the celebrated artist Da Chongguang (1623–1692). Combining his own creative experience with older theories about painting, Tang Yifen emphasized the impor-tance of individual study of, and independent creativity in, rendering subjects, especially in landscape painting; this represented a breakthrough in Chinese painting theory, which for several centuries had prioritized the copying of formalized, ideal-ized versions of landscape, over direct observation. In his *Analytical Examination of Painting Methods*, Tang's contemporary Xie Lansheng (1760–1831) likened Da Chong-guang's *Painting Methods* to a *weishang*, an ancient ceremonial garment made of a single

Tang Yifen (1778–1853), *Chit-Chat on an Autumn Plain*, dated 1848/49. Hanging scroll, ink and colours on paper. Height 97 cm, width 47 cm. The Palace Museum, Beijing.

piece of fabric, whose subtle and intricate arguments were difficult to comprehend, whereas Tang Yifen's analysis cut the cloth into individual, graspable pieces then sewed them back together into a smooth, beautiful whole. Tang Yifen, in other words, in both his artistic theory and practice, reinterpreted some of imperial China's most significant ideas about painting for the age in which he lived.

Pan Qing

37. DAI XI

戴熙 (1801–1860)

OFFICIAL AND PAINTER OF LANDSCAPES REAL AND IMAGINED

Dai Xi was among the first generation of scholar-officials born after the death in 1799 of the Qianlong emperor (r. 1736–1795), the dominating figure of China's 18th century. In this sense, Dai was truly a man of the next era – a creature of the 19th century – whose life was defined and delimited by the concerns and cataclysms of that period.

Born to a scholarly Hangzhou family in 1801, Dai showed early promise, achieving the *juren* (mid-level) civil service degree at the age of eighteen and the *jinshi* (highest) civil service qualification at thirty-one. In 1838, he was selected by the Daoguang emperor (r. 1821–1850) to serve in the Southern Studio (*Nan shufang*), an intimate space within the inner quarters of the Forbidden City where the emperor engaged in cultural pursuits with specially selected officials of the Hanlin Academy (the government's elite academic institution). Members of the Southern Studio were chosen for artistic as well as scholarly gifts, and it is likely that Dai's calligraphic and painterly accomplishments were key reasons for his selection.

Later in 1838, Dai was sent to Guangdong to serve as provincial educational commissioner, a post that brought him in direct contact with the worsening opium crisis, which he sought to mitigate by enforcing prohibition of drug use by students. Dai served into 1840 – through the beginning of the First Opium War – before returning to Beijing. In the ensuing years, Dai assumed various duties, including a return stint as educational commissioner in Guangdong from 1845 to 1847. In 1849, pleading illness, he retired to his native Hangzhou.

With his official career seemingly at an end, Dai settled into a peaceful and artistic retirement in Jiangnan. The reverie did not last long, however. In 1853, when Taiping forces took Nanjing, Dai joined with local elders to organize resistance in his native Hangzhou. When Hangzhou was briefly taken by the Taiping army in 1860, Dai gave ultimate expression to his loyalty to the Qing cause by committing suicide through drowning. For this act of sacrifice, Dai was celebrated as a martyr and given the posthumous title 'cultured and loyal' (*wenjie*).

Dai Xi (1801–1860), *Rain-Coming Pavilion by the Stone Bridge at Mt Tiantai*, dated 1848. Handscroll, ink on paper. Image height 34.5, width 142.6 cm. Cleveland Museum of Art.

From an early age, Dai Xi thought deeply about the theory and practice of painting. His father, a passionate practitioner of epigraphic or antiquarian studies (*jinshixue*), collected antiquities, painting and calligraphy, and these objects provided a foundation for the young artist. During his youth, the Hangzhou painting scene was dominated by the legacy of Xi Gang (1746–1803), whose interests served as an early guide for Dai's direction as a painter. Xi was a dedicated adherent of what has been called the Orthodox school (Zhengtong pai), a movement that valorized a select group of 'old master' painters through intensive study and creative adaptation of their styles into new creations. The Orthodox school's defining figures, especially Dong Qichang (1555–1636) and the 'Four Wangs' – Wang Shimin (1592–1680), Wang Jian (1609–1677/88), Wang Hui (1632–1717) and Wang Yuanqi (1642–1715) – were the polestars of Xi Gang's Hangzhou. Though he was too young to learn from Xi directly, Dai did study with several of the elder artist's students, who transmitted their teacher's sensibility to Dai during his formative years. This was how Dai internalized the understanding of art history codified by the Orthodox school, which held that the pathway to developing one's own style was through careful study of a specific canon. An album by the 26-year-old Dai Xi now in the Tianjin Municipal Museum preserves a snapshot of these early studious explorations of various Orthodox school painting techniques; Dai created the album, which he called *A Compendium of Trees and Rocks of the Southern School*, as part of a larger teaching manual designed to instruct students in the proper approach to painting.

As he matured, Dai's general interest in the Orthodox school painters of the early Qing developed into a particular admiration for Yun Shouping (1633–1690). Where earlier generations had compared Yun unfavourably to his friend Wang Hui, especially in matters of landscape, Dai saw a lyrical grace in Yun that offered the perfect counterpoint to Wang's solidity. Just as earlier Orthodox school painters had sought to combine the best of Song- and Yuan-dynasty painting into a 'Great Synthesis', Dai advocated a fusion of Wang and Yun. His intense study of Yun manifests in a lightness of touch and an emphasis on wet brushwork that minimizes contour lines

Portrait of Dai Xi, from Ye
Yanlan (1823–1898) and
Ye Gongchuo (1881–1968),
*Illustrated Biographies of
Scholars of the Qing Period*,
c. 1840–1900. Album, ink
and light colours on paper.
Height 26.6 cm, width
17.3 cm. National Museum
of China, Beijing.

in favour of broad washes, especially in small-scale works made after 1840, such as
the exquisite album painted in 1848 for Zhang Xianghe (1765–1862), now in the
Metropolitan Museum of Art.

Dai Xi also wrote prolifically on painting theory. His most striking contribution,
especially given his early training in Orthodox school circles, was to de-emphasize the
study of old paintings in favour of direct encounters with real landscapes. Particularly
after his service in Guangdong afforded him the opportunity to see the empire first-
hand, Dai argued that painters should look beyond the studio to nature itself as the
key source of artistic inspiration. Fearing that the Orthodox school would lose its
vitality and sink into solipsism without a rebalancing of priorities, Dai urged painters
to 'take creation as one's teacher' (*shifa zaohua*) and to 'take the past as one's teacher
without becoming mired in it' (*shigu er bu nigu*). In this, he offered a gentle presage
of the later, 20th-century critique of the Orthodox school levied by prominent
cultural modernizers such as Chen Duxiu (1879–1942), who criticized antiquarian

self-referentiality as regressive and therefore unsuited to the modern era. While much of Dai's oeuvre may appear conservative at first glance, his reformer's zeal may be seen in his subtly quirky approach to composition, which manifests in unusually large voids and unbroken horizontal masses. Elements such as these, which have little precedent in the Chinese landscape-painting tradition, would seem to be born out of his turn from the studio to the mountains, where he sought a path forward for Chinese painting that would link the power of landscapes real and represented into something original.

Joseph Scheier-Dolberg

38. SU RENSHAN

蘇仁山 (1814–c. 1849)

ICONOCLAST AND WARTIME ARTIST

When Confucius was a criminal judge, he mixed up right and wrong. I say that when Fuxi used yin–yang principles to create civilization, he separated Heaven from Hell. When Confucius, in his Spring and Autumn Annals, *condemned a good person, he turned Heaven into Hell.*

So wrote Su Renshan, an artist from Shunde in Guangzhou, in the 1840s. The forceful words had a visual, as well as textual, power, for they formed part of an inscription on his painting, *Portrait of Fuxi, Confucius, Nuwa and Yinghuo* (currently in the Guangzhou Art Museum). The accusation against Confucius was intended to be read as part of the aesthetic experience of an artwork and radically departs from the usual artist's colophon to a Chinese painting. Unsurprisingly, the main pictorial element was equally unorthodox. Instead of following conventions where gods are auspicious figures and Confucius a moral leader, Su painted a scene about a confrontation. In the painting, the three gods (Fuxi, Nuwa and Yinghuo) are clustered as a family unit facing China's most famous philosopher, whose back is turned towards the audience. Fuxi's hand is raised, perhaps a warning gesture to keep Confucius away, while Yinghuo, pictured here as a young child, hides behind the female god Nuwa.

As an artist based in south China during the First Opium War (1839–42) and the beginnings of the Taiping Civil War (1851–64), Su Renshan was a witness to prevailing violence and socio-political tensions that might indeed have felt like Hell. He used his paintings as vehicles for his frustration at longstanding moralistic hierarchies that had sanctified scholar-officials as guardians of the country's welfare. What emerges are defiant artworks that attack these moral values by overturning established genres, symbols and brushwork methods associated with the ideal of the Confucian 'gentleman'.

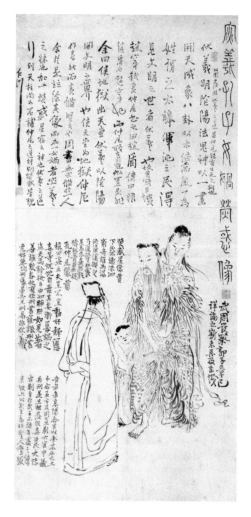

Su Renshan himself was an insider-outsider. He came from a reasonably affluent family in an area with strong clan traditions. As the eldest child of ten, he was expected to continue the family's lineage. Su's wife, married late in life, remained with her family, as was the custom in Shunde where a bride stayed at her maternal home for the first three years of a marriage or until pregnancy. As genealogical records show that Su never produced a son (thereby failing his duty as an eldest son to the lineage), it is unclear if Su's wife ever 'crossed the threshold' into her husband's home. In 1841, aged twenty-seven, Su skipped his third attempt at sitting for the civil service examinations in the city of Guangzhou, and instead set off wandering around Guilin, a part of south China famous for its extraordinary limestone formations. He was always a dreamer, and thus it was not unusual for him to escape domestic and academic obligations by heading into the mountains. However, these were abnormal times. The summer of 1841 saw one of the tensest phases of the First Opium War, with British ships and soldiers besieging Guangzhou. The city was in uproar; conflict between locals and soldiers from other provinces was particularly intense. Had Su sat the examination, he would have witnessed the students hurling their inkstones at the presiding examiner, Yu Baochun (n.d.), who had recently negotiated a deal with the British to back down from a confrontation with the local militia (which included payment of an indemnity of 6 million silver taels). Su's father was so enraged by his son's absenteeism that Su left home (though it is unclear whether this was by compulsion or choice).

It was during this exile period that Su's art matured into an experimental, idiosyncratic style so arrestingly different from the mainstream aesthetics of Chinese painting. He arranged landscapes into zigzag compositions, and turned hanging rocks into upside-down mountains. He sometimes overwhelmed the surface of his pictures with graffiti-like inscriptions. He had a penchant for thin, undulating brushwork with a graphic or pencil-like quality, a technique that was profoundly irreverent towards traditional Chinese brushwork, long regarded as the signature discipline of an artist. *Landscape with Willow* (currently in the Art Museum of the Chinese University of Hong Kong), according to his inscription, referenced the work of the earlier painter Tang Yin (1470–1524), but rather than copying the Ming master's distinctive brushwork (which would have been the usual practice), Su imitated the printed quality of a 'Tang Yin' prototype taken from a painting manual. This is a radical commentary on the importance of the humble manual, which was a tool for less privileged artists without the means of seeing real artworks, in transmitting artistic knowledge. Su pushed the subversive conceit of a painting mimicking a print even further, by exaggerating the size of his own work, which fills a surface over 2.5 metres in height and over a metre in width.

Su was ingenious at reframing the familiar to unsettling effect. One of the strangest paintings of birds in China art, *A Celebration of Myriad Birds*, is based on the well-known painterly theme of 'a hundred birds' that conveys a symbolic message of harmony. Su's version, however, depicted a chaotic cluster of feathered creatures with sharp wings and pointed tails flying against one another. The bottom edge shows a crane whose bent beak renders him mute and a timid-looking eagle staring at the ground. Although Su left no indication of how to decode the painting, one plausible interpretation would be to follow iconographic conventions of reading the eagle as the ruler and the crane as a Confucian gentleman. If this is the case, Su subverted a painterly genre wishing for auspiciousness, into a political critique of leaders ignoring the rowdy disorder of a country in trouble.

Su's satirical works may be unusual in the world of paintings, but find many companions in literature. At the heart of early 19th-century satirical novels such as *The Scholars* by Wu Jingzi (1701–1754), and *Flowers in the Mirror* by Li Ruzhen (1763–1830) was a broader discussion about the nature and role of Confucian scholarship (*ru*) and whether benevolence, righteousness, and textual and ritual competence were still relevant – a question that became ever more urgent as the 19th century progressed.

In 1848, Su returned home, but within a year, his father placed him in a local *yamen* jail for filial impiety. It is unclear why his father took such drastic action and later historians have speculated that Su's political outbursts became more dangerous; or perhaps his father sanctioned Su because he refused to bring his wife back to the family home. It is also unclear how long he stayed in jail, although it was said that the *yamen* officers would bring Su ink and paper so he could continue painting. His last dated artwork was completed while Su was still imprisoned in the winter of 1849–50. Again, in the inscription, Su calls Confucius a bringer of chaos who opened the gates to Hell. These turned out to be prophetic words. Barely a year later, at the end of 1850, a decade of infernal chaos descended on Qing China, when Hong Xiuquan (1814–1864) declared the founding of the Taiping Heavenly Kingdom, initiating a vast civil war that cost between 20 and 70 million lives.

Yeewan Koon

39. JU CHAO

居巢 (1811–1865)

POET AND PAINTER OF LINGNAN

Ju Chao and his cousin Ju Lian (1828–1904), commonly known as the 'two Jus', have been given a notable place in the history of Guangdong painting as masters of the 'flower-and-bird' genre. They developed a refined, decorative style of depicting flora and fauna, with an interest in local cultivars and species, and unconventional subjects. Ju Chao, who enjoyed generous private patronage, was more representative of the scholarly amateur painter. Ju Lian, who learned painting from his older cousin and lived into the 20th century, adapted to the art market and became thoroughly professionalized. He maintained a large studio that some of the most important artists of the Republican era came up through.

The 'Lingnan school', famous for its Japanese-derived 'eclectic' (*zhezhong*) style, was started by Ju Lian's direct or indirect students, Gao Jianfu (1879–1951), Chen Shuren (1884–1948) and Gao Qifeng (1889–1933). They tried to reform Chinese painting with a more scientific approach to form, perspective and lighting, based on their experiences of modern Japanese painting (*nihonga*) rather than Western art. Their common geographical origin gives the school its somewhat ill-fitting name. Lingnan ('south of the mountains') is often used in place of Guangdong, but in its broad sense refers to the far south of China, including Guangdong and Guangxi. There have been attempts to trace the lineage of this modern school back to the two Jus, and see them as the forebears of a regional art school that was at the forefront of China's modernization. In fact, neither Ju Chao nor Ju Lian had the progressive insight of their successors, but they stood at a critical transitional moment in history: one of growing regional awareness and increasing blurring between scholarly and popular tastes. Ju Chao, the scholar-artist, mainly painted vignettes of nature for a circle of literati, but he expanded his subjects beyond the scholar's favourites to include products of Lingnan such as lychee and banana shrub. His detailed, colourful paintings possessed a potential for popular appeal that was later fully explored by Ju Lian.

Ju Chao spent most of his life in the two provinces of Guangdong and Guangxi. Born into a family of minor officials in Panyu, Guangdong, he learned the refined arts of poetry, calligraphy and painting from a young age. His contemporaries praised his poetic as much as – if not more than – his painting talent. Many of his poems are preserved in the collection *Poem Collection from the Hut of Tonight* and the manuscript *Lyrics of Mist and Rain*. A surviving catalogue of Han-dynasty seals, *Genuine Holding of Ancient Seals*, further records his antiquarian interest (very widespread among his peers) and early family exposure to the art of seal carving. Despite their scholarly interests (which usually required moneyed leisure to pursue), Ju Chao's family was,

Ju Chao, *Bird's Nest among Wutong Leaves*, 1859. Folding fan mounted as album leaf, ink and colour on paper. Height 18.4 cm, width 54.5 cm. Art Museum, the Chinese University of Hong Kong.

at best, of modest means. His father served in a minor post in Guangxi, and after his death, the family could hardly support itself.

Not much is known about Ju Chao's early career, but in his thirties, his fate became tied to that of the official Zhang Jingxiu (1823–1864), who fought against the Taiping. Zhang was appointed to office in Guangxi in 1845, retired to his native Guangdong in 1856, and passed away in 1864. From around Zhang's Guangxi appointment until his death, Ju Chao remained his personal advisor, painter in residence and respected guest. This long-time sponsorship offered Ju Chao a comfortable life and the luxury of artistic pursuits. He lived a year longer than his patron, dying in 1865.

In Guangxi, Ju Chao accompanied Zhang Jingxiu as the latter battled Taiping forces. Ju's poems occasionally reflected on the sorrow and brutality of the war, but more often documented the elegant life of a literatus. His paintings of this period are mostly exquisite snapshots of nature, undisturbed by the external world. Whatever sentiments he had about contemporary events were rarely expressed through painting. And even when he had something to say, he hid the message in the symbolism of flowers and fruits, using poetic inscriptions for accentuation. In 1851 Ju Chao made a painting of lotus roots (now in the Chinese University of Hong Kong's Art Museum) to celebrate the triumph of Zhang Jingxiu's army against Taiping forces. Ju was making a pun, since in Chinese 'joints of lotus roots' is pronounced *lianjie*, a homophone for 'successive victories'.

Whether or not Ju Chao was deeply affected by experiences on the frontline of the Taiping Civil War in Guangxi, he withdrew to a life of near complete leisurely retirement after he returned to Guangdong. At one point, this retreat was interrupted by Zhang Jingxiu being called back to office in Jiangxi; Ju Chao, who went with him, lamented in a poem: 'Wandering around without a way of settling, I grow old and have little thought of leaving home'. Some travels notwithstanding, Ju Chao was at his most productive and refined during this late period, achieving a delicate balance between naturalism and lyricism, between descriptive detail and confident handling of the brush. His love for flowers is evident in the number of extant paintings, but sometimes his work shows a deep fascination with the broader vibrant workings of nature.

Bird's Nest among Wutong Leaves, dated 1859, captures the lively moment when a bird is feeding its nestlings, as the other parent watches attentively from a nearby branch. Love and affection overflow from the image. Ju Chao further animates the painting with unusual but charming details. The feeding bird is portrayed from a surprising angle, revealing its round belly and clenched talons. The nest is not built on a branch but wrapped in a large *wutong* leaf. Here on the leaves and branches, Ju Chao applies his special wet-on-wet technique, producing a diaphanous effect that feels embellished, but not excessively so. This technique has come to be known as 'water infusion' (*zhuangshui*), that is, adding water to a wet painted surface to create interesting effects of gradation or volume. Often an outline forms naturally when the water dries. Ju also favoured 'powder infusion' (*zhuangfen*), in which mineral pigments rather than water are added to the surface of wet paint. The two techniques became the trademark of the two Jus and their followers.

Ju Chao's naturalistic portrayal of flowers in the 'boneless' (no-outline) manner is often traced to the tradition of Yun Shouping (1633–1690) – a major landscape and nature painter of the early Qing. Here, however, the particular environment that fostered Ju's art is arguably more significant than any particular stylistic inheritance. The warm and humid climate of Lingnan gave Ju Chao unlimited access to scenes of natural beauty and his work displays an almost indiscriminate love of both cultivated and wild species, including commonplace fruits and vegetables. While taking nature as his model, Ju Chao retained a degree of elegance and restraint that no doubt facilitated the acceptance of his work by literati patrons. He flourished at a time when the orthodoxy of landscape painting and pure ink was giving way to a diversity of expressions influenced by increasing commercialism and regionalism, and his skilful, easy-going versatility reflects this growing fluidity of artistic values.

Xiong Xin

40. YAO XIE

姚燮 (1805–1864)

MAN OF LETTERS AND TRAILBLAZING PATRON

The life and work of Yao Xie are emblematic of the pressures that mid-19th-century events imposed on established modes of artistic production and patronage. Yao came of age in Zhenhai, a suburb of Ningbo, in the 1820s. He was born into a scholarly family of modest means and was known from a young age as a precocious talent in poetry, publishing his first multi-volume collection, *Poetry from the Scattered Shadows Pavilion*, in 1833. This won him significant attention among his peers, and after passing the Zhejiang provincial civil service examinations the next year, he travelled to Beijing to take the final metropolitan exams that would secure him a national-level position in government. Failing his first attempt, he stumbled four more times over the next decade before finally giving up. This inability to ascend the bureaucratic ladder destined Yao to a future of steadily diminishing stability.

During the previous generation, population growth had not been met by a corresponding expansion in government positions, resulting in a bottleneck that curtailed advancement for many of Yao's contemporaries, as well as problematic undergovernment for the empire. Frustration and animosity led some into outright revolt, as, for example, Hong Xiuquan (1814–1864), the leader of the Taiping that would consume China's heartland in the 1850s and early 1860s. Others, like Yao, supported themselves with a combination of tutoring, painting and writing, relying on friends for assistance when opportunities were particularly lean. Over the course of his

Fei Danxu (1802–1850), portrait of Yao Xie surrounded by twelve iconic beauties, titled *Confessions in Silk Damask*, dated 1839. Handscroll, ink and light colour on paper. Height 31cm, width 128.9 cm. The Palace Museum, Beijing.

life, Yao published personal essays, poetry, and a ground-breaking compendium of drama, *A Critical Examination of Drama to the Present*. Yao's reputation among literary scholars today is built largely on this work and his *Supplement and Appendices to the Story of the Stone*, a posthumously published (in 1875) set of commentaries on the famous 18th-century novel *Dream of the Red Chamber*.

An 1839 portrait of Yao Xie by Fei Danxu (1802–1850) catches the poet in the midst of this career transition. In it, twelve young female attendants gravitate towards Yao, bearing various objects representative of elite habits: paper, tea, a wrapped *qin* (zither) and a sword. Fei was the pre-eminent painter of women of his era and, for all the world, the image seems to show Yao as a decadent literatus indulging in the company of courtesans, which he was known to do. Yet the title, *Confessions in Silk Damask*, and the long parallel prose essay Yao penned to accompany the portrait, reveal an extended discourse in Buddhist terms on the interrelated nature of pleasure, perception and knowledge: 'Our bodies are but naked worms, perceiving (the world) in fantasy like a spot of froth on the open seas. Only confession gives rise to the laying aside of delusion and the drawing near of realization. Fei Danxu has painted this image for me where I am but an illusion of reflection and froth, depicting this froth as froth within froth, this reflection as reflection within reflection. The froth churns and churns until the churning stills, the reflections irritate and itch until the irritation is extinguished.' Given Yao's preoccupation with *Dream of the Red Chamber*, a book that also deals with fantasy and impermanence, the women in the image likely represent the iconic Twelve Beauties of Jinling from that book. Fei was renowned for his images of these women, and his painting thus produces another fantasy for Yao, in which Yao becomes the book's central character, Jia Baoyu.

Yao Xie's second collection of poetry, *The Poetry of Fuzhuang*, written between 1833 and 1846, demonstrates the extent of the network of senior statesmen and elite artists he attracted with his writing. It includes work dedicated to established senior poets and painters, such as Chen Wenshu (1771–1843) and Wang Xuehao (1754–1832), to up-and-comers like the calligrapher and official He Shaoji (1799–1873), and to the sons of major statesmen, including Ruan Heng (1783–1859), whose father, Ruan Yuan (1764–1849), was among the most decorated public servants during his lifetime. Yao's book also charts his transition from typical literati themes to more pointed social commentary. In 1841, Yao's wife died, just as he was displaced from his home due to British invasion during the First Opium War (1839–42). The poem 'Entering my Residence in the Prefectural Seat to Find it Occupied and Already without Provisions for Three Days' captures the changing tone of his writing in the face of these troubles: 'Broken books, no rice gruel, and not a neighbour left here to lend us grain. As I continuously sigh over your body, who is here to support us in consolation after your death? Prying mice have eaten cauldrons empty, and wherever I tread, the dirt has blackened. So I go to a corner of the garden for some kindling and pull apart the gate for firewood.' Other poems from this time present scathing critiques of corrupt Chinese troops and inept bureaucrats, as well as images of starvation, flood, drought, martyrdom and displaced refugees.

Despite this upheaval and his inconsistent income, Yao retained the elite social network he built earlier as a promising young poet in the capital and while travelling around Ningbo, Shanghai and Suzhou. Known among his friends as a spendthrift, Yao would often exhaust money from publishing, painting or teaching soon after he

Painting from an unusual and beautiful 120-leaf album by Ren Xiong (1823–1857), with each painting matched to one of Yao Xie's (1805–1864) poems, 1850s. Album, ink and colours on paper. Height 27.3 cm, width 32.5 cm. The Palace Museum, Beijing.

earned it. He frequently reinvested his funds into the social world that supported him by hosting friends and supporting up-and-coming artists like Ren Xiong (1823–1857), a poor but talented painter from rural Zhejiang province.

Yao needed Ren's talent as much as the young artist needed support. Through Yao, Ren met a network of patrons who were so astonished by his versatility that they made new commissions and spread the word of his talent. Through Ren, Yao was able to present his poetry to his friends in innovative ways, allowing him to sell his publications and remain financially solvent. In 1850, Yao invited Ren to live with him for a year, in his grandiloquently named Great Blossoming Plum Mountain Hall. There, among other works, they collaborated on a 120-leaf album of Ren's paintings matched to Yao's poetry. The size of the commission was unheard of at this time, when typical painting albums comprised eight to twelve leaves. For Ren to produce this volume of work, purportedly in a few months, stretched the limits of technique, imagination and stamina. Aside from the dazzling range of subjects and innovative styles, historians find in this collaborative album a precursor to the increasingly commercialized and self-aware artistic conventions of what would later be called the Shanghai school. This loose grouping of artists supporting artists – exemplified by the relationship between Yao and Ren – in the global urban melting pot of late 19th-century Shanghai bears similarities to the fledgling gallery system of mid-19th-century Paris, where old patterns of patronage were likewise giving way to new modes of promoting artists and distributing artworks. Yao died in Shanghai in 1864, just as the new art world he helped to catalyse began to flourish.

Michael J. Hatch

41. REN XIONG

任熊 (1823–1857)

PRODIGIOUSLY INNOVATIVE ARTIST

In his tragically brief but brilliantly productive career, Ren Xiong became a renowned painter and designer of woodblock-printed book illustrations. His inventive and colourful compositions led to his recognition as a leading figure of the mid-19th-century Shanghai school of painting, but he actually resided and worked in several locales in modern Zhejiang province of south-eastern China, as well as the long-established commercial and culture centre of Suzhou.

Ren Xiong trained as a portraitist in his birthplace of Xiaoshan, near Shaoxing in Zhejiang, and painted several notable images of contemporaries, but his life-sized *Self-Portrait* is unprecedented, and one of the most powerful and arresting of all surviving Chinese self-portrayals. His imposing figure is both muscular and gaunt, isolated within an empty space and directly confronting the viewer with an intense gaze and stern expression, and a striking exposure of his upper chest and bare right shoulder. His face and torso are strongly modelled with highlights on his forehead, cheekbones and shoulder, and contrasting flesh-coloured shaded tones, effects similar to hybrid styles of Sino-Western painting practised in Canton (Guangzhou) and at the imperial court in Beijing. The jagged, angular folds of his blue-tinted robe are rendered with a bold linear energy that recalls instead his portraits of ancient swordsmen, local heroes and Daoist immortals for woodblock book illustrations.

The visual and expressive impact of the *Self-Portrait* are augmented by Ren Xiong's long poetic inscription that frames his frontal figure with bold calligraphic text. The poem, as this excerpt reveals, is a plaintive outpouring of disappointment and confusion, provoked by the artist's mirrored self-examination:

> *In the vast world – what lies before my eyes? I smile and bow and go about*
> *flattering people [in hope of] extending connections, but what do I know of the world?*
> *In the great confusion, what is there to hold on to and rely on….More pitiful still:*
> *although the mirror [shows] my black eyebrows exchanged [for white],*
> *and worldly dust covering my white head, I am still like a racing steed*
> *without plans. Historians have not recorded even a single, trivial word about me….*
> *All my glancing eyes see is the boundless void.*

The *Self-Portrait* is undated but was probably painted around 1856, near the end of Ren's life. The 'great confusion' mentioned in his inscription might refer to the Taiping Civil War of the 1850s, which brought displacement, suffering and death to broad regions of south-east China. Ren's self-reported connection-seeking may reflect his general pursuit of success, or more specific patronage relationships. Ren Xiong found a long-term supporter in the poet and official Zhou Xian (1820–1875), who in 1848 invited him to be a guest at his home in Jiaxing, about halfway between Hangzhou and Shanghai, where Ren remained for three years, studying Zhou's art collection and producing paintings for him. Zhou was Ren's frequent companion for the remainder of his life. They travelled together to notable scenic spots, and Zhou wrote an admiring biography of Ren after his early death from tuberculosis. Ren Xiong's famous *Ten Myriads* landscape album of paintings on gold paper lacks a specific dedication but bears an inscription by Zhou Xian. It is represented here by a leaf titled *Ten Thousand Branches of Fragrant Snow*, a poetic conceit for blossoming apricot branches. This leaf combines decorative blue and green mineral colours with repeated patterns of clustered apricot blossoms; like the other leaves in the album, the theme conveys a surfeit of beauty and an elaboration of inventive design. The vista may represent the surroundings of Fragrant Snow Lake near Suzhou, and other leaves suggest references to other scenic locations around Suzhou and Hangzhou where Ren travelled with his associates. Ren Xiong's long relationship with Zhou Xian culminated in his inventive depiction in 1855 of Zhou's *Thatched Hall at Fan Lake*, which was based on Zhou's descriptive essay of his planned garden

莽乾坤眼前何
物翩翩笑側身長繁
覺甚事紛紛攘攘傳此則
談何容易武說這家筆金張
許史到如今能幾遠而悄鏡檢青援座摧自頭一樣奔馳無計
算少年原孤立是趣騎寫古來陳例誰是名豪汪洋何賢哲我也
夏謨笑可嗤青里一宮何以輕記公子憑肩先生肯掉搖蓬起已且放語起舞
全世意巴任恍欺一瞬蕊擦葉涯集右調十二時得長任能偽幹

Ren Xiong (1823–1857), *Self-Portrait*, early 1850s. Hanging scroll, ink and colour on paper. Height 177.5 cm, width 78.8 cm. The Palace Museum, Beijing.

Ren Xiong (1823–1857), *Ten Thousand Branches of Fragrant Snow*, album leaf from *Ten Myriads*. Ink and colour on gold paper. Height 26.3 cm, width 20.5 cm. The Palace Museum, Beijing.

precincts. Ren Xiong had visited Zhou's home both as a long-term guest and episodically, but Zhou never realized his ambitions for an elaborate garden estate, except through Ren's imagined illustration. Like the *Ten Myriads* album, the exceptionally long *Fan Lake* handscroll is couched in the archaistic and decorative blue-and-green manner, crowded with lush details of natural views and pavilions.

Ren Xiong's other major patron was the poet and painter Yao Xie (1805–1864). The two met and travelled together around 1850, and in the following year Ren spent several months in Yao's company as a guest at his villa near the coastal city of Ningbo, working on an ambitious project of illustrations of selected lines from Yao's poems. The result was an unusually large and diverse set of 120 album leaves, divided thematically into genres and subjects, such as supernatural gods, ghosts and demons, mythological figures, activities of gentlewomen, and antique objects, along with landscapes, birds and flowers, insects and animals. Many figures and creatures reference the 17th-century style of Chen Hongshou (1598–1652), another native of Ren Xiong's home region, who was also a source for many of the figure types in Ren's woodblock illustrations. Ren Xiong's inscription on the album for Yao Xie is strongly personalized, revealing his admiration for Yao and his sense of their sympathetic temperaments and talents, an appreciation reciprocated in Yao's equation of Ren's artistry with famous masters of earlier times. Ren's inscription indicates his proud awareness of the distinctiveness of his accomplishment, echoed in the appreciations of later viewers and collectors of its unmatched variety of themes, original conceptions and striking designs. The album sold for a very high price to a noted collector after Yao Xie's death, and was copied several times thereafter, serving as an ongoing source of inspiration for later 19th-century painters.

Richard Vinograd

42. REN YI

Ren Yi 任頤 or Ren Bonian 任伯年 (1840–1896)

SHANGHAI ARTIST AND PORTRAIT PAINTER

Ren Yi, more often known as Ren Bonian, settled in Shanghai in 1868 for the last half of his life, after a somewhat peripatetic early career. He received early training as a painter from his father, Ren Songyun (d. 1861), an aspiring scholar who made his living as a portrait painter. Ren Bonian's youthful regimen included realistic sketches of birds, flowers and animals, as well as portraits of visitors to the family home near Shaoxing, in modern Zhejiang province, south-eastern China. Ren was reported to have been recruited or captured in his youth by forces of the Taiping rebels, for whom he served as a flag bearer. In his mid-twenties, he moved for a time to the coastal port city of Ningbo, and then to Suzhou, a centre of art and commerce where his uncle Ren Xun (c. 1835–1893), also a noted painter, was based.

Ren Bonian thus had experience of several urban and artistic cultures before his relocation to Shanghai, whose rapid growth was fuelled in part by refugees from Taiping turmoil, as well as by the commerce fostered by British, French and American administrations in extraterritorial concession zones, ceded by the Qing empire after the First Opium War (1839–42). The city had become a multi-regional melting pot as well as a cosmopolitan international contact zone, although the foreign populations and changing architectural skyline of the city are not directly represented in Ren Bonian's paintings. Images of frontier characters from literary and historical narratives may be stand-ins for contemporary foreigners, however, and Ren is said to have studied for a time at the arts and crafts academy established by the Jesuits at their Tushanwan Orphanage in the Xujiahui district of Shanghai, and to have used Western pencils in his sketching practices.

Shanghai's status as a centre of trade had the greatest impact on Ren Bonian, who established himself in art-world commerce as a busy professional, selling his paintings through fan shops, creating designs for woodblock-printed books and painting manuals, and spreading his reputation through networks of associates and supporters.

Below. Ren Yi (1840–1896), *Picture of Three Friends*, 1884. Hanging scroll, ink and colour on paper. Height 64.5 cm, width 36.2 cm. The Palace Museum, Beijing.

Right. Ren Yi (1840–1896), *Egrets and Lotus*, 1890. Hanging scroll, golden paint on blue-foiled paper. Height 153 cm, width 41 cm. National Art Museum of China, Beijing.

His best-known self-portrait, titled *Three Friends*, dated to 1884 when Ren was in his mid-forties, portrays him seated in a companionable circle with a man named Zeng Fengji (n.d.) in the centre and Zhu Jintang (act. 1880–1890), the patron and recipient of the group portrait, at the viewer's left. Zhu was the owner of a fan shop and letter-paper store in the French Concession where painters like Ren Bonian could display and sell their works, acting in effect as an art dealer. The title of the group portrait indicates a primarily social relationship, but Ren Bonian's distinctly lower position than the others, at the viewer's right, and his inscribed expression of good fortune at being permitted to sit with the others suggest a certain obsequious deference. The stacks of covered albums and wrapped handscrolls on the table and larger hanging-scroll paintings batched within an adjacent large pot also imply a display of artistic goods for sale, likely including some of Ren's own works. The portrait faces are sharply observed, with something of the fidelity of the emerging contemporary medium of photographic portraiture, but the fluent folds of the sitters' monk-style robes are representative of Ren's signature mode of energetic brushwork.

Ren Bonian painted many portraits of art-world associates, including images of notable fellow painters and calligraphers such as Hu Gongshou (1823–1886), Gao Yong (1850–1921) and Wu Changshi (1844–1927), the latter Ren's student in painting who went on to be a leading figure of the Shanghai school of painting well into the early 20th century. Many are unconventional and inventive portrayals in multiple versions, including characterizations of the artist-subjects costumed as beggars or vagrants, in ways perhaps intended as satires, or as reflections of the precarity of urban careers subject to changing circumstances of patronage and taste. The inscriptions and poems frequently written on such portraits by the artist, his subjects or their associates, serve, like the portrait images, both to commemorate and to establish artistic and social relationships.

Ren Bonian was prolific, with very large numbers of his brightly coloured and dynamic 'bird-and-flower' (images of flora and fauna) or figural narrative compositions still extant. *Egrets and Lotus* is part of a six-scroll set of birds and plants painted in 1890, which are unusual in their gold pigment medium, but representative of Ren Bonian's professional practice in their subject matter and decorative appeal. The subject could be understood as a kind of pictorial rebus equivalent to the auspicious sentiment 'May your path be ever harmonious' (*hehua lusi*), based on the homophonous Chinese pronunciations of that phrase and the egret and lotus motifs. Such functional and popular images were staples of Ren Bonian's production. The implied opulence and showiness of the gold paint medium was designed to appeal to commercially minded city audiences. The dense composition, which requires the viewer's active attention to disentangle the blotchy forms of the egrets from intervening lotus stalks, and the piercing gazes of the birds are formal analogues of the complex visual environments and spectatorial culture of urban Shanghai.

Richard Vinograd

43. ZHAO ZHIQIAN

趙之謙 (1829–1884)

SEAL ARTIST, CALLIGRAPHER AND PAINTER

Born into a humble business family in Shaoxing, modern Zhejiang province, Zhao Zhiqian was one of the most innovative artists of China's 19th century. He studied with the passionate antiquarian scholar and collector Shen Fucan (1779–1850), who inspired Zhao to apply his aesthetic appreciation of ancient bronze and stone inscriptions to his calligraphy and seal carving.

While progressing through the civil service examinations as a young man, for ten years Zhao served as administrator to a frontline commander, Miu Zi (1807–1860), defending against Taiping forces in eastern China. (Miu himself died in battle in 1860.) In 1862, when Zhao's wife and their second and third daughters passed away in his hometown, Taiping attacks on the area made it impossible for Zhao to cross the

Detail of Wang Yuan (act. *c.* 1862–1908), *Portrait of Zhao Zhiqian*, dated 1871. Hanging scroll, ink and colour on paper. Height 106 cm, width 33.7 cm. The Metropolitan Museum of Art, New York.

the frontline for their funerals. Plunged into deep sorrow, Zhao changed his name to Bei'an (literally 'Hut of Sadness'), vowed that he would not remarry and carved a seal with the inscription 'home broken, family gone' (*jiapo renwang*). The pain was so great, he later related, that he lost the desire to live, even while he knew he needed to stay alive to look after the remainder of his family. To pray for his deceased family, in 1864 Zhao carved another seal 'nurturing life through reciting sutras' (*canjing yangnian*), with an image of a bodhisattva in relief on the side, in the style of Buddhist steles of the Northern Wei (386–534 CE). This was the first time that an image complementing the text had been added to the side of a seal stone. This aesthetic innovation was adopted later in the century by artists such as Wu Changshi (1844–1927), Xu Sangeng (1826–1890), Chen Shizeng (1876–1923) and Qi Baishi (1864–1957).

Zhao Zhiqian moved to Beijing in 1863. After failing the highest, metropolitan stage of the civil service examination four times, in 1872, he finally secured an official job as chief editor of the *Gazetteer of Jiangxi* in Nanchang by 'donating' to the government (purchasing such posts became common in the final century of the Qing). He later served as a local magistrate, supporting the Qing army in its war with the French in Fuzhou in 1881 and 1884. Throughout his life (he died in Hangzhou in 1884), the insufficiency of his official's salary left Zhao in constant financial distress; he therefore took commissions for calligraphy, painting and composition of epitaphs in order to live. A piece of calligraphy for a Cantonese client, for example, could earn him twenty silver *liang*, a sum equivalent to a third of his monthly salary.

Zhao Zhiqian's aesthetic discernment and antiquarian style exemplify the continuity and innovation in 19th-century scholars' practices of the 'four accomplishments' (*siyi*) of classical Chinese culture: calligraphy, painting, poetry and seal carving. In his own writings, Zhao acknowledged the impact on his art of pre-Tang-dynasty seals and of the Qing antiquarian scholars – men like Gao Zhixi (1655–1719) and Tong Yu (1721–1782) – who had collected and studied such artefacts.

In his own virtuosic seal carving, Zhao combined the 'cutting blade' techniques of the Zhejiang school with the 'abrasive blade' approach of the Anhui school. Zhejiang seal-makers held the knife vertically upright, pointed it at one end of a stroke and cut forward. This technique required a recurring, rhythmic action, transmitting the strength of the wrist to the seal, with each cut connecting naturally to the previous one. Anhui makers, by contrast, held the knife sideways, pushing the angled knife quickly and continuously, using the power of both wrist and fingertips. Zhao was also indebted to the aesthetic theory and practice of Deng Shiru (1743–1805), who emphasized the importance for seal carvers of calligraphic training and knowledge of ancient scripts. This advocacy sprang from the ardent antiquarianism of the 19th-century Qing empire, and Zhao sought inspiration for his seals from a range of antiquities: Qin-dynasty (221–206 BCE) stone drums, *zhaoban* (plaques announcing official edicts) and bronze weights; Han-dynasty (202 BCE–220 CE) bronze mirrors, lamps and bricks; and coins from the Six Dynasties (220–589 CE) to the Song dynasty (960–1279). His adaptation of diverse ancient styles earned Zhao a unique reputation

Zhao Zhiqian (1829–1884), *Old Pine Tree*, dated 1872. Hanging scroll, ink on paper. Height 176.5 cm, width 96.5 cm. The Palace Museum, Beijing.

in Chinese art history. Zhao's friend and fellow calligrapher Shen Shuyong (1832–1873) praised Zhao for being the first 'in six hundred years to create a new path for the art of seal-carving'.

Just as Zhao's seal carving matured in the mid-1860s, his calligraphy and painting began to develop significantly, inspired by the fluid running script of the Song calligrapher Huang Tingjian (1045–1105) and the discovery of a Northern Wei stone gate inscription. Zhao's calligraphy seems to have been directly nourished by his innovative seal-carving technique: every turn and corner echoes the sharp-edged knife-cut effect he perfected with his seal work. Each brushstroke is evenly positioned, combining the self-confident control of the Northern Wei writing style with the fluid, transient quality (in the left- and right-slanting strokes) of the Song calligraphers Zhao admired.

In his painting *Old Pine Tree*, Zhao reversed the direction of his brushwork (left to right instead of right to left) to paint at speed the tree branches from base to tip, imbuing the image with great dynamism (Bao Shichen – see page 256 – used a similar, 'upturned brush' (*nibi*) effect in his calligraphy). Zhao acknowledged that the application of calligraphic brushwork to painting was not new, but his skill in combining flattened, forceful brushwork with strokes perfected by study of antique scripts enabled Zhao to innovate. Zhao admitted that contemporary audiences struggled to appreciate his painting because he often mixed the styles of Chen Hongshou (1598–1652), Li Fangying (1695–1755) and 'Monk Artist' Jichen (d. 1800) in his work. Chen's painting is characterized by highly controlled yet embellished, even mannered brushwork influenced by antique styles; Li favoured a blunter technique, resulting in somewhat disordered and scruffy brushwork; Jichen, meanwhile, was famed for his fast, outsized calligraphy. Zhao fused these three highly distinct modes of brushwork – controlled, disordered and vigorous – into his pictures and preferred strong, contrasting colours, inspired by the heavy pigments of Tang-dynasty paintings, to complement his archaic calligraphic brushwork.

Zhao Zhiqian infused the multiple creative arts that he practised (seal carving, painting and calligraphy) with antiquarian scholarship, the empirical investigation of antiquities and epigraphic research. This practice of 'antique innovation' left a deep imprint on his contemporaries and successors in the world of Chinese fine arts.

Chia-ling Yang

44. WU CHANGSHI

吳昌碩 (1844-1927)

FOUNDER OF CHINA'S ARTISTIC MODERNISM

By the end of his long life in 1927, Wu Changshi was widely regarded as one of the fledgling Republic's greatest living artists, paired in the aphorism 'Wu of the south, Qi of the north' with the peasant-born master Qi Baishi (1864–1957), who made his name in Beijing. Wu Changshi came from the last generation of men to have been classically educated, a prerequisite to his sitting the civil service examinations and entering the bureaucracy as a scholar-official under the dynastic system. Wu subsequently served sporadically as a minor provincial official under the Qing. A renowned calligrapher and seal carver in the epigraphic, antiquarian 'metal and stone studies' (*jinshixue*) vein, he came to painting only in his thirties. A lifelong connection with the Shanghai school of painting began through his acquaintance with the most brilliant of the late Qing Shanghai masters, Ren Yi (1840–1896), whom he befriended in 1883 and who encouraged him to regard his painting practice as a technical extension of his epigraphic practice of calligraphy. Wu's preferred painting subject was that favourite of the scholarly artist, plum blossom, long celebrated as an anthropomorphic symbol by China's intellectual class for its early annual flowering, often in the adversity of late winter snow.

Wu Changshi (the *shi* is sometimes pronounced *shuo*) was born Wu Jun (style name Junqing) in 1844 to a scholarly family of Anji county in the mountains of Zhejiang

Detail of Wu Changshi (1844–1927) attrib., *Brewing Tea*, dated 1918. Horizontal painting, ink on paper. Height 39.5 cm, width 137.2 cm. The Metropolitan Museum of Art, New York.

province. He passed the entry level of the civil service examinations (*xiucai*) in 1861, aged twenty-two, and married another artistically minded intellectual, Shi Jiu (1848–1917) in 1872. Following his marriage and up to the late 1880s, he gravitated towards the Suzhou and Hangzhou region, which for centuries had been the centre of literary and artistic activity in the empire. His early artistic development was as a seal carver and a calligrapher in all modes including the archaic seal script, studying under two of the most prominent antiquarian Confucian scholars, Yu Yue (1821–1906) and Yang Xian (1819–1896); Wu moved his family to Suzhou to study with Yang in 1882. Wu Dacheng (1835–1902) was another major influence.

The move to Suzhou brought Wu Changshi into the orbit of Ren Yi, who later depicted Wu's precarious life situation as a petty and poorly paid official in a painting of 1888 entitled *A Miserable and Shabby Official*, in which Wu stands facing the viewer in his tatty cold-weather official dress and hat, his hands crossed over his chest. In the same year, Ren did another portrait of Wu, entitled *Enjoying the Shade of the Banana Palms*. In this intimate portrait, Ren pictured Wu in a state of undress in the dog days of summer, exposing a large round belly and looking sweaty and flustered, seeking respite from the heat under the ragged leaves of a banana tree, all in a shabby genteel private garden setting. Appointed county magistrate in Jiangsu Province in 1899, while in his mid-fifties, Wu Changshi resigned after just a month and devoted himself entirely to making a career as an artist, after carving a self-mocking seal with the legend 'one-month magistrate of Andong'.

In 1913, Wu moved to Shanghai, where he became a leading cultural figure, supported by Wang Zhen (1867–1938), a painter, financier and political actor behind the revolution that led to the overthrow of the Qing in 1911. Although within China Wu Changshi is typically associated with the Shanghai school of painters, including Pu Hua (1830–1911), as well as Ren Yi, he only settled in Shanghai in these early and unstable years of the new Republic, experiencing there the chaotic aftermath of the assassination of China's first democratically elected president, Song Jiaoren (1882–1913). In cosmopolitan Shanghai, Wu's international reputation grew. He would be compared with the great Japanese scholar-painter Tomioka Tessai (1837–1924).

Wu's pre-eminence as a Shanghai school painter in the 1920s heyday of global artistic modernism means that his earlier, foundational artistic accomplishments as a poet, seal carver and calligrapher in the archaistic, epigraphic mode are often somewhat overshadowed in assessments of his achievements. Reminders of this dual practice surface variously in his oeuvre, however. We see it, for example, in works combining ink-rubbing 'pictures' of ancient three-dimensional vessels, made by specialist artisans using the *quanxing ta* ('full-form rubbing') technique pioneered by Liuzhou (1791–1858), with painted elements added by Wu, for example flowers or branches placed as if part of an arrangement in the vessel. Wu Changshi's distinctive epigraphic style of calligraphy, comprised of spiky dark brittle brushstrokes, is well known both from standalone works of calligraphy but also from his inscriptions on paintings as well as the twiggy branches that feature in his own paintings.

Ren Yi (1840–1896), *Enjoying the Shade of the Banana Palms*, dated 1888. Portrait of Wu Changshi. Hanging scroll, ink and colours on paper. Height 129.5 cm, width 58.9 cm. Zhejiang Provincial Museum., Hangzhou.

As the modernizing New Culture Movement gained momentum in the late 1910s, influencing the fine arts as well as literature, Shanghai artists including Wu Changshi contributed to a major re-animation of the lineage of individual expressionism in Chinese scholar-painting, the so-called *xieyi* (sketch conceptualism) mode. A short horizontal scroll (*hengzhou*) entitled *Brewing Tea* is signed and dated 1918, the year after Wu became a widower. Although the brushstrokes are not as finely executed as in Wu's other work, it may be attributed to him, pending further research. The horizontal format for display echoes but also progressively breaks out from the scholarly tradition of the handscroll (which would be rolled out horizontally). The inscription colours our reading of the figure of a lone scholar, seemingly transported from an unsullied past into the nostalgic modern image: 'The pines in ageing have come to resemble immortals, / The zither is strung and beckons the Ancients to come'.

Wu Changshi was active up to his death aged eight-three *sui* (eighty-two in the Western system) late in 1927, and much sought after in art circles as a supporter and endorser. The art historian and painter Zheng Chang (Zheng Wuchang, 1894–1952), for instance, solicited Wu's support for his pioneering historiographic study, *A Complete History of Chinese Painting Studies*. When this tome was published in Shanghai in 1929, it featured Wu Changshi's posthumous preface written in his elegant calligraphy. Wu's personal involvement in this canon-setting work helped confirm, in critical circles, Wu's pivotal role in the arts during China's transition from a late dynastic polity to the would-be democratic Republic.

Shane McCausland

45. QINGKUAN

慶寬 (1848–1927)

COURT PAINTER AND QING LOYALIST

In the last ten years of his life, Qingkuan often reminisced about several sets of paintings that he completed in his late thirties to mid-forties while he worked as a court painter in the Imperial Household Department of the former Qing court in Beijing. Those paintings resulted from imperial commissions and documented contemporary events. The first commission came on 30 March 1886 from none other than Empress Dowager Cixi (1835–1908), the de facto ruler of late Qing China. In the edict, he was appointed as the lead artist to produce a large cycle of battle scenes to commemorate civil wars with Taiping, Nian and Hui (Muslim) forces, which had devastated the country for twenty-seven years from 1850 to 1877. Within weeks, he set up a special workshop at the Guangji Temple, and directed twelve painters and a calligrapher selected from the Metropolitan Field Force and other departments to embark on the project. Over the next five years, he and his team diligently studied the official accounts

Qingkuan et al., *Battle Scene from the Muslim Rebellions in Shaanxi, Gansu and Xinjiang Provinces*, c. 1875–1908. Ink and colour on silk. Height 143 cm, width 315 cm. Mactaggart Art Collection, University of Alberta, Edmonton.

of the battles selected for representation – the commendation lists of army personnel; the statutes about military clothing, insignia and weapons; and the geographical records of battlefields – and translated them into a visual chronicle of the wars. When completed, this visual chronicle consisted of epic-scale battle paintings – twenty for the Taiping Civil War, eighteen for that with the Nian, and thirty-five for that with the Hui – each measuring over three metres wide. The paintings represented the conflicts in a heroic style characteristic of 18th-century military paintings. The images were then fittingly displayed and stored in the Ziguang Pavilion, a building designated by the Qianlong emperor (r. 1736–1795) as the site adjacent to the Forbidden City where the dynasty's martial prowess would be commemorated. In line with the 18th-century practice of war memorialization, these paintings were also reproduced in prints, but by now employing a new technology of the 19th century – photography.

In May 1886, a little more than a month after the battle-painting commission began, Qingkuan was again assigned as one of the draughtsmen on a royal inspection tour – accompanying the Manchu Prince Chun – of the coastal defences and the Beiyang Fleet at the Dagu forts, Weihaiwei and Lüshun, in the north-east of the empire. He and another draughtsman subsequently produced twenty sequential images of a mirage at sea they witnessed. In November 1888, deep in the battle-painting project, he was once more entrusted to lead a major commission to document the grand ceremony of the Guangxu emperor's (r. 1875–1908) wedding, which would take place the following year. This commission again required research on relevant court statutes and archives. It took him and his fellow painters from the painting workshop in the Imperial Household Department more than two years to complete the project.

Qingkuan's leading role in these commissions made him effectively the official visual chronicler of the Qing court. Furthermore, his managerial skills and knowledge of the court archives and statutes demonstrated in these projects won him an important administrative post. In 1888, he was appointed vice director of the Silver Vault, the treasury in the Imperial Household Department. Ironically, it was his service in this office that eventually brought about his downfall.

In 1894, he was impeached for corruption and fraudulent bannerman status. The accusation for the former was largely based on his flamboyant lifestyle and his unconventional use of commercial banks in budget-handling at the Silver Vault. The investigation did not yield any substantial evidence to support the corruption charge. Nevertheless, the investigators discovered along the way that he had been born into a civilian Han Chinese family surnamed Zhao. At some point in his youth, he was falsely registered as a bondservant in the Upper Three Banners (part of the elite hereditary Qing military) and acquired a Manchu name Qingkuan, which paved the way to his entering the Imperial Household Department. Qing laws reserved harsh punishment for asserting false bannerman status. Qingkuan was expelled from his office and the banners, his home was searched, and his properties confiscated. A contemporary court official who witnessed the seizure saw it as a real-life enactment of the one inflicted on the protagonist's family described in the classic mid-18th-century novel *Dream of the Red Chamber* by Cao Xueqin (*c.* 1717– *c.* 1763).

Despite such personal and familial suffering, Qingkuan's loyalty to the dynasty did not waver. In the years immediately preceding the fall of the Qing dynasty, he dedicated his life to activities that attempted to stop reform and revolutionary movements both inside and outside the empire. In 1899, a year after the young Guangxu emperor's abortive attempt at institutional reform and modernization, also known as the Hundred Days' Reform, he travelled to Japan on a mission on behalf of the Qing court, together with a colourful, wealthy lottery businessman called Liu Xuexun (1855–1935). Allegedly the trip aimed to study the achievements of the Meiji Restoration. In secret, the two men planned to extradite or assassinate Kang Youwei (1858–1927), one of the chief advocates of the Hundred Days' Reform programme, who had fled to Japan when Empress Dowager Cixi and her supporters launched their coup against Guangxu and his radical associates, and who had lived there in exile since. However, after they were warned by the Japanese embassy in Beijing that the plan had been discovered, they had to give it up. Qingkuan's pursuit of reformers and revolutionaries did not stop there, however. In 1903, he was involved in plotting the seizure of a young reformist named Shen Jin (1872–1903) in Beijing. On the day of the arrest, he personally led the metropolitan police on its mission to capture Shen. Shen's subsequent trial and execution outraged revolutionaries and the international community. *The Times* condemned the execution as 'the most horrible episode in the history of China since the massacres of 1900' during the Boxer War. Chinese revolutionary newspapers exposed the key role that Qingkuan had played in the event.

After the Qing dynasty was finally overthrown by revolutionaries in 1911, and the Republic of China was founded in the following year, Qingkuan withdrew from the public eye and lived a reclusive life. In his home in Beijing, he surrounded himself with objects from various imperial palaces that he had managed to rescue from looting during the Boxer War and Western troops' subsequent occupation of the city in summer 1900. In the last ten years of his life, he returned to painting, which he had abandoned two decades earlier. He painted literati-style landscapes, birds and flowers and gave his work away as gifts to other Qing loyalists in his small circle of friends.

Qingkuan was forgotten by subsequent generations after his death because of his allegiance to the Qing dynasty. The main body of his works represented China's historical events in the second half of the 19th century from the perspective of the Qing court. This vantage point differed dramatically from the narrative constructed by the revolutionary ideologies dominant through much of China's 20th century, which idealized these challengers as revolutionary heroes, rather than seeing them as criminal rebels. Han Chinese revolutionary politics viewed a supporter of the Manchu Qing dynasty such as Qingkuan as a reactionary. Following the muting of politicization in historical research in the 1980s, scholars began to reconsider the lives and careers of an increasing number of Qing loyalists. The case of the controversial court painter Qingkuan is ripe for such re-examination.

Hongxing Zhang

46. WU YOURU

吳友如 (c. 1840–1894)

NEWS ILLUSTRATOR AND PAINTER

The year 1860 was a life-threatening one for many residents in the city of Suzhou. That May, as Taiping forces advanced towards the city, the imperial forces set fire to the suburbs to fend off the attack. The flames consumed the bustling markets outside the city wall for three days. Between then and 2 June, when the city fell to the Taping, many people from Suzhou fled to Shanghai, the sanctuary of the Jiangnan region in the upheaval of the Taiping Civil War. For many refugees, their destination was the foreign concessions outside the Chinese city, an enclave created after the First Opium War (1839–42) when Shanghai opened as a treaty port. Among those refugees was Wu Youru (born Wu Jiayou), just entering adulthood that year.

Hardly any record of Wu Youru's early career survives; all that is known is that he began his art training after his arrival in Shanghai. Despite being a relative late starter with an obscure artistic lineage, when he made his first appearance on the city's art scene in the early to mid-1880s, he displayed tremendous ambition and versatility by embracing the wide range of opportunities that the unique city could offer. In 1880,

Wu Youru (*c.* 1840–1894) et al., *Capture of the Junior Traitor Hong Fuzhen,* 1886–87. Album, ink and colour on paper. Height 50.5 cm, width 87.5 cm. National Palace Museum, Taipei.

commissioned by the Chinese magistrate of the city's Mixed Court, he made a scroll painting of the grand Western-style dinner at the Yu Garden in the Chinese city to celebrate the visit to Shanghai that year of the Prussian prince Albert Wilhelm Heinrich (1862–1929). Soon after, he supplied large numbers of illustrations to a new edition of the vernacular historical novels *Romance of the Three Kingdoms* and *The Account of the States of the Eastern Zhou,* published in 1883. In the meantime, he was also working with the studio Dianshizhai, the city's first commercial photo-lithographic printing house, founded by the British businessman Ernest Major (1841–1908), to produce the picture album *Scenic Views of Shanghai,* advertising the distinctively Sino-Western hybrid city.

His real interest, however, resided in reportage art, an art form that did not yet exist in China. Seeing the European news illustrations of contemporary events around the world from *The Illustrated London News* and *The Graphic* for sale in Shanghai bookstores, and experiencing the sensation of immediacy they produced, he dreamed that he could establish an illustrated newspaper himself one day. Unsurprisingly, then, he became the first illustrator to join the pioneering news magazine *Dianshizhai Pictorial* set up by Major through his studio in spring 1884. The magazine was issued once every ten days, and each issue contained eight double pages of artwork with explanatory text. The first issue appeared on 8 May 1884, with its illustrations entirely provided by Wu. The subjects of the illustrations included scenes from the ongoing Sino-French War in Vietnam; an American submarine; a hot-air balloon; a military drill featuring the explosion of an underwater mine; a bridge collapse, caused by a large crowd of spectators who had gathered to watch a house on fire in Shanghai; a judge having a corpse dug up for the investigation of a suicide case in Suzhou; and a filial son cutting out a piece of his liver to cure his sick father. With accuracy, sensation and entertainment as criteria for selection of topics, the magazine became an instant success. Through the course of his career, Wu provided for the magazine a total of over 440 illustrations.

In 1886, when he was a well-known reportage artist in Shanghai, he received an invitation from Zeng Guoquan (1824–1890), the governor general of Liangjiang, to set up a special workshop in Nanjing to produce a set of battle scenes documenting the Hunan Army's campaign against the Taiping rebels in the middle and lower reaches of the Yangtze River in the 1850s and 1860s. This commission was in turn part of a larger imperial programme initiated by Empress Dowager Cixi (1835–1908) in Beijing to celebrate victory over the Taiping, Nian and Hui (Muslim) forces in the preceding decades. The imperial court had asked Zeng to supply studies of about twelve battles that the Hunan Army had fought under his elder brother Zeng Guofan's (1811–1872) command, which would then be the basis for court painters led by Qingkuan (1848–1927) to produce a final work. In May, Wu Youru took several of his assistants to Nanjing and began to work on the commission. In the next six months, they visited battlefields, read official accounts of battles and made numerous sketches. The result was a set of twelve battle paintings in both scroll and album formats. After Zeng Guoquan's approval, the work was sent to Beijing for presentation to Empress Dowager Cixi.

But the imperial court did not approve and ordered the court artists to make a completely new set of compositions. Rather than conforming to the imperial tradition for war painting established in the 18th century, Wu Youru's submission employed a pictorial language that de-glorified the victory by paying much attention to carnage, destruction, confusion and horror on the battlefield. Furthermore, the set of paintings contained some strange and, to the Qing court, grating images and depictions. In the last painting, *Capture of the Junior Traitor Hong Fuzhen* showing the triumphant procession of the Hunan Army entering the city gate of Shicheng, with Hong Xiuquan's (1814–1864) son captured, Wu Youru did not portray the local Baofu pagoda as it was, but somehow turned it into an obelisk-like stone monument that looked architecturally non-Chinese, out of place and perplexing. Most embarrassing to the Qing government, the submission seemed to give full credit for the victory to Zeng Guofan and his non-regular Hunan Army. This undermined the imperial court's efforts through the commission of the artwork to reshape the memory of the war as a straightforwardly Qing triumph. Contrary to the truth of what had happened, the court wished to promote the idea that imperial virtue, rather than the Hunan Army, had led to victory.

While the original paintings were quietly rejected and disappeared into the palace archives, in 1888, when Wu returned to Shanghai, he circulated his drawings widely through *Dianshizhai Pictorial*. In 1890, now one of the most sought-after artists in the city, he founded his own illustrated news magazine, called *Feiyingge Pictorial*, exclusively publishing illustrations made by himself. Eventually, he came to rescind his close association with reportage art and turned his full attention to classical genres such as historical and religious figures, landscapes, plants and animals, as illustrated news was 'after all a fad that can't pass down through generations'. In 1893, he gave up ownership of the magazine and transferred it to one of his assistants.

Wu Youru has remained hugely popular in China. Shortly after his death from illness, his former colleagues acquired from his family more than a thousand of his drawings, and in 1909 published them as a massive set of albums, entitled *A Treasury of Wu Youru's Drawings*. Since then, the *Treasury* has gone through many editions; its latest – the tenth – was published in 2017. Despite – or perhaps because of – the court's censorship of his battle drawings, he is remembered today as a news artist for all time.

Hongxing Zhang

47. LI SHUTONG

李叔同 (1880–1942)

BRINGER OF WESTERN OIL PAINTING TO CHINA VIA JAPAN

Known primarily as a Western-style art educator in modern China and a Buddhist monk, Li Shutong was a giant of late imperial and early Republican-era culture, who immersed himself seamlessly in both Chinese and European arts. Through his enormously wide-ranging interests and abilities, he built and fostered networks of talented painters, musicians and writers in both China and Japan at the turn of the 20th century.

Li was born in 1880, the third child of a wealthy salt merchant family in Tianjin. His father, Li Shizhen (1813–1884), acquired the *jinshi*, the highest level of the imperial civil service examinations, which entitled him to a senior position. After serving only briefly as an official, however, he resigned to take over the family business and later went into banking. He died when Shutong was five years old, and the young Li was raised by his mother, née Wang (1860–1905). Li was expected to do well academically and studied for the imperial examinations from childhood.

From his late teens, Li took an interest in traditional Chinese arts, and studied poetry and seal engraving. Politically, he was open about his affinity with Kang Youwei's (1858–1927) reformist views on reorganizing Qing government. When the Hundred Days' Reform failed in 1898, Li apparently feared for his own safety and moved from Tianjin to Shanghai, with his mother and wife, née Yu. There, Li joined the Chengnan Literary Society, co-founded the Shanghai Calligraphy and Painting Association and produced the twice-weekly *Calligraphy and Painting Association Journal*, introducing the general public to works created by established traditional Chinese artists.

In 1901, Li entered the Special Division (*teban*) of Nanyang Public College. Established in 1896, the college aimed to introduce European-style modern education on the model of Japanese normal schools, which had been established in Japan for training mainly primary-school teachers to meet the demand for modern, universal public education. The Special Division required students with traditional

Li Shutong (1880–1942), *Self-Portrait*, 1911. Oil painting. Height 60.5 cm, width 45 cm. The University Art Museum, Tokyo University of the Arts.

academic knowledge as well as aspiring to acquire Western learning. Having already started learning English, Li began to study Japanese under the instruction of Cai Yuanpei (1868–1940), who was to become one of the most famous educators of early 20th-century China. Japanese reading ability was encouraged in order to acquire Western knowledge through the plentiful Japanese translations of European books. Li's enrolment was short, however, since many of the students were expelled or walked out following a student protest in 1902 known as the 'ink bottle incident', in which tensions between progressive students and conservative teachers erupted after a student tampered with a teacher's ink bottle.

Li's mother died in 1905. He reportedly organized an unconventional funeral in Tianjin, in which he played the piano and sang a lament for her. That same year, he went as a privately funded student to Japan to study Western painting at the Tokyo Fine Arts School, where he was one of the earliest Chinese students (there were already thousands of Chinese students in other disciplines in Japan). Li's teacher was Kuroda Seiki (1866–1924), French-trained and one of the most influential

Western-style painters in Japan. Li later exhibited his oil paintings in Tokyo at exhibitions organized by Kuroda's art group Hakuba-kai ('White Horse Society', also known by its French name, Cheval Blanc). Four of Li's works were presented: *Rest after Playing the Piano* in the twelfth exhibition (1909), and *Morning*, *Still Life* and *Daylight* in the thirteenth and final exhibition (1910). The Japanese art critics of the time did not review them particularly favourably, but Li's status as a Chinese artist of Western-style painting attracted attention.

While in Tokyo, Li was also active in the arts more generally. In a Japanese newspaper interview, he revealed that he played the violin and many other musical instruments. He admitted that his oral Japanese was not good enough to understand lectures (though his English was); nonetheless, he was friends with Japanese poets of Chinese verse – this indicates how the shared medium of Chinese characters facilitated cultural interaction between Chinese and Japanese literati of the time. In 1906 with his fellow Chinese student Zeng Yannian (b. 1873), he founded a theatre troupe, Shunryūsha, which the following year presented acclaimed productions of *La Dame aux Camélias* and *Uncle Tom's Cabin*. Also in 1906, he published the first Chinese-language music journal *Music Magazine*, which he printed in Tokyo and sent to Shanghai for distribution. A hard-working student, Li received the Tokyo Fine Arts School's 'diligence award'. His graduation work *Self-Portrait* is one of his few surviving paintings. In 2011, his long-lost oil painting *Semi-Nude Woman* (also dating back to his period in Japan) was rediscovered in the collection of the Central Academy of Fine Arts in Beijing.

Upon his return to China, after briefly teaching at a Shanghai girls' school, in 1912 he got a job at Zhejiang First Provincial Normal School as a teacher of art and music. There he introduced the latest methods of teaching Western painting techniques, which he had learned in Tokyo. Notably, he was the first in China to teach life drawing using a male nude model in class. His teaching nurtured the next generation of leaders in art education in China, such as Feng Zikai (1898–1975) and Liu Zhiping (1894–1978). Li was admired by his pupils, not only for his talent and skill, but also for his serious, calm and sincere character. Around this time, he joined the South Society – a large literary society, with revolutionary, nationalist leanings – in Shanghai, and worked on the editorial team of the newspaper *The Pacific News*, as the chief editor of the literary section *Art and Literature*. In Hangzhou, he organized an epigraphy study group with his students.

Li's life as a passionate art educator and multi-art practitioner came to a halt, however, in 1918, when he decided to enter the Buddhist priesthood at Hupao Temple in Hangzhou, taking the new name Hongyi. As a Buddhist priest, he dedicated himself to the rediscovery of old Buddhist scriptures held in temples and elsewhere, collating versions, and then publishing and disseminating them not only within China but also in Japanese universities and libraries. His sutra calligraphy is still highly regarded. He died in 1942, at the age of sixty-one, in Fujian.

Akiko Yano

48. LAI FONG

黎芳 (*c.* 1839–1890)

QING CHINA'S MOST SUCCESSFUL PHOTOGRAPHER

The most successful Chinese photographer of the 19th century, Lai Fong was more commonly known by his studio name, Afong. According to his obituary, Lai moved to Hong Kong from his native Gaoming in Guangdong province to escape the Taiping Civil War (1851–64). While he is sometimes said to have opened a photographic studio in the British colony in 1859, this is difficult to corroborate. He was certainly employed at the Portuguese-run Silveira & Co., which operated between 1865 and 1867, and the first advertisement for Lai's studio at 54 Queen's Road was published in the *Hongkong Daily Press* in April 1870. Lai was naturalized a British subject in 1883, and died in April 1890, having established his studio (the location of which changed many times) as the pre-eminent commercial photographic brand in Hong Kong. The Afong studio survived well into the 20th century under the direction of Lai's eldest son, Lai Yuet-chen (1871–1937).

Portrait of Lai Fong,
titled Afong (Huafang).
c. 1860–80. Albumen print.
Scottish National Portrait
Gallery, Edinburgh.

The famed Scottish photographer John Thomson (1837–1921) claimed that 'a score' of Chinese photographers had established businesses in Queen's Road by 1872. In this intensely competitive environment, the commercial success of the Afong studio can be explained in part by Lai's ability to cater to both Chinese and Western tastes. Photographs attributed to Lai include private studio portraiture for both Chinese and Western subjects; sets of stereotypical 'native types' such as barbers, cobblers and fortune tellers; stereoscopic views; famous sites of Hong Kong; documentary photographs of key events in local history; views and panoramic landscapes, including those of Guangzhou (Canton), Fuzhou and Shantou, and various other private commissions. The Afong studio under Lai also employed a number of Western associates, such as the Danish photographer Emil Riisfeldt (1846–1893), which may have helped to counter initial wariness from Western customers. Thomson mentions in his 1875 book *The Straits of Malacca, Indo-China and China* that a Portuguese assistant was employed by Lai 'to wait upon' European clients. In 1876, Lai advertised that his customers could 'rely upon being treated with the utmost courtesy', now that he had employed the American William Lentz (b. *c.* 1845).

Lai enjoyed considerable renown among Westerners soon after his Queen's Road studio was established. John Thomson believed that Lai's 'exquisite taste… would enable him to make a living even in London'. His *cartes de visite* from the 1870s proudly lay claim to being 'photographer by appointment' to Sir Arthur Kennedy, governor of Hong Kong from 1872 to 1877, and to Grand Duke Alexis of Russia, who had passed through Hong Kong in 1872. By 1886, photographs by Lai and his one-time business partner, the British photographer D. K. Griffith (b. *c.* 1841), were being exhibited at the Colonial and Indian Exhibition in London. More prosaically, the abundance of albums and loose prints from the Afong studio that have found their way into collections throughout the world attest to a commercial success exceeding that of any of Lai's competitors during this turbulent period.

Lai's willingness to embrace opportunity is reflected in his capture of important events of local history, such as the devastating typhoon of September 1874, of which, typically, he boasted the largest and most complete collection of views. Ventures such as this seem to have been particularly profitable. A handwritten price list brought home by a late 19th-century traveller, now in the Royal Asiatic Society collection in London, reveals that the Afong studio prints that document the aftermath of the typhoon commanded prices 20 per cent higher than those of more traditional tourist prints of temples and racecourses. Lai was later commissioned by the Hong Kong Government to photograph the damage caused by the May 1889 typhoon.

Many of Lai's photographs seem to exhibit the hybrid characteristics we might expect of works emanating from the cross-cultural environment in which he practised his art, or, more interestingly, to challenge assumptions behind the photographic conventions of the period to which he himself also contributed. It is hard not to read a studio portrait of a Western man in Chinese dress facing the camera square on as a deliberate play on the 'Chinese' method of portraiture that had been ridiculed for its aesthetic naivety by John Thomson in 1872. The studio portrait of three young labourers placed in an idealized classical European back-drop may be an attempt to disrupt Orientalist narratives that images of Asian 'coolies' popular among Western consumers sought to perpetuate, although, as the scholar Sarah E. Fraser observes, such an attempt seems futile when set against the vast weight of existing imagery.

As in the case of many of the photographers working in Hong Kong during this period, it is often difficult to identify with absolute certainty whether a photograph was produced by Lai himself, one of his studio associates, or another photographer altogether, since it was common for entire collections of prints and negatives to be purchased and subsumed into different studios' collections when businesses closed. Despite the painstaking efforts of scholars, some photographs remain unidentified, and many more with spurious attributions are held in collections worldwide. The much-vaunted size of the Afong collection alone suggests a need for caution before we accept at face value claims of individual responsibility for particular works. Notices published in the late 1880s boast, 'Afong, Photographer, has for sale a Larger, and more Complete Collection of Views than any other Establishment in the Empire of China, and has quite recently added to it some New Selections of Views and Photos of Native Types.' The likelihood that some works were acquired from other sources demands an expansion of the definition of authorship to include the selection and curation of works incorporated within the Afong collection; given that these images helped to shape Chinese and Western views of China for many decades, such a definition only enhances Lai's claim to be a creator of modern China.

.   Stephen McDowall

5

OBSERVERS

WRITERS, POETS, TRANSLATORS AND TRAVELLERS

China's 'long 19th century' saw major changes in literary production. At the start of the era, literature was dominated by the forms of poetry and essay, and by literati writers – a class of men unified by the communal aspiration to pass the civil service examinations (based on meticulous study of canonical books supposedly written or edited by Confucius, and his later intellectual acolytes) and serve as government officials. By the close of the dynasty, in the early 20th century, this class had been replaced by (or had joined) authors and readers reliant on new media and reading communities that developed in the treaty ports. Such authors (including men like Wu Jianren) and readers favoured genres once disreputable, or indeed unheard of: fiction and short, journalistic articles.

Through the first half of the 19th century, even as the political elite worried over the declining capacity of the state to cope with fiscal decline, socio-economic rebellion and European aggressors on the empire's coasts, and contemplated the reforms necessary for political survival, they dedicated themselves to older literary forms: the archaic prose of the Confucian Tongcheng school, or the parallel prose associated with the Six Dynasties (220–589 CE). Some of the most influential translations from Western languages into Chinese were completed by adherents of 'ancient prose', such as the prolific translators Yan Fu and Lin Shu (1852–1924), responsible for popularizing Chinese Social Darwinism and Rider Haggard (1856–1925), respectively. Fashions in poetry also nodded back to much earlier dynasties, such as the Han, Tang and Song (c. 202 BCE–1279 CE). This is a literary parallel to the fervour for antiquarian aesthetics in painting and calligraphy throughout the last century of imperial rule. Literary production in the Qing was multilingual too: the Qing's conquest and absorption of territories stretching from Manchuria, across Mongolia and to Xinjiang, incorporated writers who moved fluently between the languages of those regions and Chinese.

In the second half of the century, treaties forced on the Qing by European empires, the United States and Japan, plus the dislocations driven by massive internal insurrections, created new kinds of writers and readers in post-Opium War treaty ports. By this point, the strains of late imperial life were rendering ever more uncertain the old literati career path into government service. As state payrolls and appointment quotas to the government bureaucracy failed to keep up proportionally with massive population growth, educated men struggled to find official employment. The entrepreneurially minded sought new literary opportunities in Shanghai, the post-Opium War treaty port relatively shielded from the massive violence of the Taiping Civil War (1851–64). The city became the centre of a modern printing industry, and urban readers devoured newspapers, periodicals and tabloids churned out by its presses, written in new styles of Chinese that combined the classical and vernacular language, and freely incorporated foreign words. *Shenbao* – literally, the Shanghai News – was one of the first, founded in 1872 by a British businessman called Ernest Major. Commercial publishers of pictorials embraced the precision and detail offered by lithography, and informed audiences about national and international affairs. New fiction often reflected, with comic sarcasm, the perplexing, frightening, sometimes supernatural strangeness of the late 19th century: the deficiencies of the patriarchy, the quest for female equality, the amoral flamboyance of late 19th-century Shanghai.

As the Qing built up its diplomatic presence abroad after 1866, so ever more literate individuals – men like Wang Tao and Li Gui – travelled beyond China, penning hundreds of first-hand travelogues of worlds far beyond the Qing. Some were written by Han Chinese women, a group whose horizons, in earlier periods of the Qing, had been severely constrained by patriarchal conservatism. The late Qing travel writer Shan Shili, who regularly sojourned abroad with her diplomat husband, not only embraced Japan as 'home', but travelled with great gusto along the Trans-Siberian Railway to Russia. Her writings showcased a confident, intricate knowledge of Roman, Jewish, Byzantine and Catholic art. By experimenting with the novel form of the Western travelogue – for which gendered norms did not exist as strongly as with other literary genres – Shan was able to explore topics usually off-bounds for women: above all, history and politics.

Indeed, one of the major breakthroughs in the scholarship of Chinese literature of the past thirty years has been the exploration of a library of writing by women in late imperial China. These writings have greatly complicated and enriched understandings of Chinese society and culture, and enable us to access women's experiences and insights about both everyday and tumultuous events in the 19th century. In the final years of the dynasty, women poets, writers and translators plunged into public life, intervening on matters of education and even political reform. They devoured knowledge of the world beyond the Qing, and argued powerfully for the right of women to involve themselves in state affairs, and for the need to give girls a well-rounded Chinese and Western education. When a mutiny in Wuhan transformed into a full-scale insurrection – the revolution long desired by nationalists like Zhang Taiyan – educated, highly literate women fought on the frontlines for a new representative republic. **JL**

49. YUN ZHU

恽珠 (1771–1833)

WOMAN POET AND FEMINIST SCHOLAR *AVANT LA LETTRE*

Yun Zhu epitomized the ideal of an elite gentry woman in late imperial China. She not only embodied Confucian norms by playing the roles of talented daughter, solicitous wife and model mother, but also became an accomplished poet, scholar, painter, editor and anthologizer. Her erudition and exemplary conduct earned her the accolade 'a Confucian among women' by her contemporary, the eminent scholar-official Ruan Yuan (1764–1849). In her lifelong endeavour to collect, preserve and publish women's poetry from the beginning of the Qing dynasty (1644–1912) up to her own time, Yun Zhu may be accorded the epithet 'a feminist scholar *avant la lettre*'.

Yun Zhu was born in 1771 to the Yun clan of Yanghu county, Jiangsu province – a lineage that had produced the famous painter Yun Shouping (1633–1690). Her life straddled the late 18th and early 19th centuries, the zenith of late imperial culture before the onset of devastating wars and rebellions that overtook the Qing empire in the mid-19th century. Like many daughters in scholar-official families in this period, Yun Zhu received a many-sided education at home. She was trained in the usual feminine skills, including composing poetry and embroidery. More unusually, her father also commanded her to study the Confucian classics, such as the *Four Books*, the *Classic of Filial Piety* and the ancient lexicon *Er Ya* in the family school, alongside her two elder brothers. Clearly proud of his talented and intelligent youngest child, Yun Yuxiu (d. 1800) himself began to teach Yun Zhu poetry writing from the age of ten. Yun Zhu thus received the foundational education meant for boys in elite families.

Perhaps the most unusual aspect of Yun Zhu's life was her interethnic marriage as a Han Chinese woman to an elite Manchu. While Manchu men were allowed to take Han women as concubines, it was rare for them to marry a Han woman as principal wife. The story goes that, during one of Yun Yuxiu's official posts, the wife of his Manchu colleague was much taken by the teenage Yun Zhu's poetic talent and proposed a betrothal with her son Wanyan Tinglu (1772–1820). Yun Zhu's support of her husband, her filial care of her parents-in-law, and her maternal instruction and influence on her eldest son Wanyan Linqing (1791–1846) – who became a successful official and writer – were duly recorded and celebrated in family records. They show Yun Zhu's broad knowledge and scholarship in various fields of Confucian learning. She read widely also in Daoist and Buddhist texts, wrote on medicine and effective governance, and edited and reprinted a Confucian scholar's philosophical works. Sadly, most of these writings are no longer extant.

On her son Linqing's initiative, Yun Zhu's poetry collection, *Drafts of Poems from Red Fragrance Studio*, was published in 1814 when she was forty-three. After Yun Zhu's stringent selection, the result was a rather slim volume of eighty-four poems, but the contents reveal that Yun Zhu's poetic skills indeed served multiple functions throughout her life. Writing poetry served her self-expressive needs, facilitated social interactions, and deepened and maintained friendships. Her poetry sheds light on intimate aspects of her life experiences, whether matching the rhymes of her father's poems on a particular topic in her juvenilia, capturing quiet moments of contemplation of nature and the seasons in the boudoir and garden, recording travels as a member of the family entourage of her father, husband and, later, her son, or mourning the death of a young daughter and daughter-in-law.

However, she prioritized collecting and anthologizing other women's voices above her own poetic production. As she said to Linqing, 'In future, you don't have to publish my poetry. You should seek out good compositions by women. I will select them for publication in order that they can be transmitted and known broadly.' Yun Zhu herself had apparently kept poems written by women that she came across since her youth and had cultivated a large network of women poets through her travels accompanying first her father, then her husband, and finally, after her husband's death, her son. For the remainder of her life, with the help of Linqing, Yun Zhu was able to gather women's poems from all corners of the empire to realize her vision. Her 1831 anthology *Correct Beginnings: Poetry by Women of Our Dynasty* contained poems by close to a thousand women from across the empire and a range of social groups – from the noble elite to the lower classes, all were included to demonstrate how women's poetry stood as emblems of the Qing empire's civilizing influence. Yun Zhu herself wrote brief biographical notices for each of the women selected. She engaged her daughter-in-law and granddaughters in the editorial process of this anthology and, when her health was failing, charged her granddaughter Wanyan Miaolianbao (1821–1861) with editing the sequel.

Yun Zhu (1771–1833), *Butterfly and Flowers*. Folding fan mounted as album leaf, ink and light colour on paper. Height 16 cm, width 49.2 cm. The Palace Museum, Beijing.

A set of juvenilia verses inscribed on three of her own paintings of flowers and butterflies indicate another skill in Yun Zhu's artistic repertory. Painting was an art long cultivated in the Yun lineage. Since her famous forbear Yun Shouping, the clan had produced several accomplished artists, one of whom was Yun Zhu's aunt Yun Bing (n.d.), a well-known painter of flowers and birds under whom Yun Zhu studied. The poems of female friends attest to drawings of orchids and other flowers that Yun Zhu had painted for them, often on fans, as a token of friendship.

Yun Zhu also compiled, edited and in 1831 published a collection of more than 500 brief biographies of women entitled *Precious Records from Orchid Chambers*, described by Susan Mann as 'one of the first histories of women by a woman'. *Precious Records* was conceived as a 'civilizing project' that demonstrated how the moral and cultural influence of the Qing state extended to the farthest margins of the empire. The temporal scope of the work covered the two millennia from the Han dynasty (202 BCE–220 CE) to Yun Zhu's own time.

A final, intriguing aspect of Yun Zhu's literary life concerns the complex cultural phenomenon of women as readers and even authors of vernacular fiction in the Qing. As a genre, vernacular fiction had been traditionally held in low regard; even as its popularity grew among the scholar-literati class throughout the Ming (1368–1644) and Qing, its readership had been limited to men. However, after China's most famous novel, *Dream of the Red Chamber* by Cao Xueqin (*c.* 1717–*c.* 1763) was first published in 1791, it attracted an unprecedented female readership, including Yun Zhu. Evidence of female readership is most clearly seen in the poems written by women in response to the novel. In 1796, Yun Zhu accompanied her mother-in-law in returning to Beijing from Nanyang, Henan province, where her father-in-law was posted. It was likely in this period in Beijing that Yun Zhu acquired the novel and became an early avid reader, as she wrote two sets of poems, one on the chrysanthemum and the other on the orchid, matching those written by the main protagonists in the novel. More intriguing still, Gao E (*c.* 1738–*c.* 1815), who completed the novel after Cao Xueqin's death, became a close friend of Yun Zhu's son Linqing. Linqing even invited Gao to write a preface for the printing of Yun Zhu's poetry collection in 1814. One scholar has suggested Yun Zhu may have composed her own sequel to the novel. (*Dream* inspired numerous sequels, many by anonymous or pseudonymous authors, which sought to change the narrative and the ending of the original novel.) Further research on this question may reveal other dimensions to Yun Zhu's remarkable literary talents, and to the contributions to vernacular fiction by women writers of the late Qing.

Grace S. Fong

50. GU TAIQING

顧太清 (1799–1877)

GREATEST FEMALE MANCHU POET OF THE QING DYNASTY

Gu Taiqing was a writer, painter and amateur player of the Chinese zither (*qin*). She is generally regarded as the greatest female Manchu poet of the Qing dynasty. At birth she was named Xilin Chun, with her given name Chun meaning 'spring', and surname Xilin, or Sirin Gioro in Manchu, indicating that she belonged to a prominent clan of the Manchu nobility. Her ancestors were warriors who had helped found the Qing empire in the 17th century. Later, they became great states-men and men of letters. But their literary endeavours got them into trouble. In 1755, Gu's grandfather Ocang (1691–1755) was ordered to commit suicide by the Qianlong emperor for having exchanged poems with Hu Zhongzao (1712–1755), a Chinese official accused of inciting ethnic hatred for the Manchus in his poetry.

Because of the disgrace attached to her antecedents, Gu made little mention in her writing of her childhood or of her parents. She probably grew up in a Manchu military camp stationed in the Fragrant Hills, west of the capital Beijing. Despite their straitened circumstances, her family took education seriously: Gu learned to write poetry at a young age, as did her brother and sister. She did not marry until the relatively late age of twenty-six, when she became a concubine to Prince Yihui (1799–1838), who was exactly her age. It is believed that the pair had met and fallen in love before the marriage, a rare occurrence at the time. They were related by a previous marriage: Yihui's grandfather (Qianlong's fifth son, Yongqi) had married a great aunt of Gu's. But Gu's tarnished family name made it difficult for her to be accepted in Yihui's household. All matters related to members of the imperial family had to be approved by the Imperial Clan Court (*zongren fu*). To avoid detection, she took the surname of a Chinese bondservant in Yihui's household and went on the official record as being the bondservant's daughter Gu Chun.

Gu's marriage was a happy one, founded on love and shared interests. She gave birth to three sons and two daughters; after Yihui's first wife died in 1831, he lived with Gu exclusively. Prince Yihui was known for his calligraphy and painting as well as his poetic skills, especially for writing *ci*, a popular form of lyric verse written to fit pre-existing tunes. Although unfamiliar with composing verse of this kind, once guided by her husband, Gu quickly learned and perfected the skill. It is for her *ci* lyrics that Gu became most famous.

Gu also shared her husband's interest in Daoist philosophy. Together, they read Daoist texts, dressed in Daoist attire, and frequented the Daoist White Cloud Temple on the western outskirts of Beijing. She took on the Daoist name Taiqing ('Great Clarity') to complement, in meaning and in sound, her husband's Daoist name Taisu ('Great Simplicity'). She called her poetry collection *Collected Writings from the Pavilion*

Unknown artist, *Madame Taiqing Listening to the Snow*, (c. 1840–1877). Portrait of Gu Taiqing. Private collection.

of Heavenly Wandering, after the name of her residence in the princely mansion, which was inspired by the Daoist classic, the *Zhuangzi*.

It was through her marriage that Gu assumed a new name and identity, under which she wrote eagerly and tirelessly. Most of her poems, amounting to some 835 *shi* (regulated-verse poems) and 335 *ci* (lyric-verse poems), are vignettes of the everyday life of the Manchu nobility: a spring excursion, a beautiful pot of crab-apple blossom, a piece of music skilfully played on the *qin*. Mostly *vers d'occasion*, they are either written to accompany poems by her husband, or addressed to female friends, some of whom were Manchu noblewomen like herself, while others were the daughters and wives of well-known Chinese scholars. Her grandfather's tragic death did little to stop her from socializing and exchanging poems with her Chinese friends. She even started a poetry club with her best friend Shen Shanbao (1808–1862), a well-known female Chinese poet. Their Autumn Red Poetry Club was attended by some of the most talented Manchu and Chinese female poets in the capital. Some of the poems Gu composed during meetings of the poetry club made their way into her novel, a twenty-four-chapter sequel to the 18th-century masterpiece *Dream of the Red Chamber* (also known as *The Story of the Stone* in David Hawkes and John Minford's famous English translation).

Altogether, Gu's writing paints a picture of the leisurely, aristocratic and cultured world of late imperial China, a world which the ensuing century of revolution sought to depose and destroy. But she was not merely a blithe chronicler of the pleasures of a passing age. There is an unmitigated sadness in her writing, brought on by her perilous existence as a Manchu noblewoman: she was entirely dependent on a husband whose fortunes were tied to those of the crumbling empire. This hazardous predicament precipitated a fascination with dreams, the subject of Gu's most famous poems. Vivid, evocative and intangible, it is with these dream poems that Gu reaches the height of her literary brilliance, as, for example, in 'Remembering a Dream':

Mist frames the cold stream,
Moonlight frames the sand.
Aboard my magic raft
I visit an Immortal Realm –
Down the clear brook,
Twin oars cutting through an inkwash of mist.
Past a small bridge, a new scene comes into view:
By the light of the moon,
I behold plum blossom,
Myriads of blossoming plum trees,
Their shadows interwoven,
By the hills,
By the stream,
In the rippling lake,
Their beauty beyond compare.
Roaming through this sea of fragrant snow,
I wake with a start from my dream –
To the hateful cawing of the crows!

Misfortune was to strike when Gu turned forty. After fourteen years of marriage, her husband died in 1838. Three months later, Gu and her children were forced out of the princely mansion by her mother-in-law, who feared Gu and her sons might take the hereditary title from Yihui's eldest son by his first wife. This banishment inflicted serious economic hardship on Gu, not to mention emotional distress. Nonetheless, she continued to write while raising her children and saw them grow up to obtain official ranks or marry into noble families. In 1857, Yihui's eldest son died without children of his own. The family then adopted one of Gu's grandsons as the heir and she returned to the princely mansion where she lived out her remaining years.

At the age of seventy-six, Gu became blind in both eyes. Despite this, she continued to compose poetry by dictating it to an amanuensis. In the last poem in her anthology, 'One Afternoon in the Second Year of Guangxu [1876], I Visited Sunset Temple in a Dream', Gu expresses her reluctance to wake from a pleasant dream:

I found it,
The little Sunset Temple,
Saw the first plum blossoms by the cliff,
The serpentine waters of the stream,
The tiny path winding to a wooden bridge.

I lingered in the wonder of this dream,
Afraid to wake.
The time seemed all too short!
What joy it is to climb mountains,
To sit at the water's edge!
Alas that such dreams are always short-lived!

Gu Taiqing died a year later, aged seventy-eight. The child emperor Guangxu had just turned six that year. Contrary to his reign title meaning 'glorious succession', he was the penultimate member of the Manchu Aisin Gioro clan to reign over China proper.

Annie Luman Ren

51. WU SONGLIANG

吳嵩梁 (1766–1834)

FORGOTTEN 'LYRICAL BUDDHA'

The poet, calligrapher, painter, historian, literary critic and travel writer Wu Songliang was born at Xintian, Jiangxi province, in 1766. His father, Wu Ju'ao (1728–1785), was a government official and also a poet. As a teenager, Wu Songliang came to the notice of Yang Hu (1744–1828), a celebrated literary figure, who befriended him and encouraged his writing; his precocious gifts were also fostered under the guidance of Jiang Shiquan (1725–1785), the leading Jiangxi poet of the day. Throughout his formative years, Wu was therefore steeped in the elite literary culture of the late Qing. He had already composed hundreds of poems when, aged just eighteen, he was a successful candidate in the lowest level civil service examination held at Jinling (present-day Nanjing), on the occasion of the Qianlong emperor's sixth and final 'southern tour' at the beginning of 1784.

In order to prepare for the next stage of the examinations, he moved with his elder brother Wu Kunrong (also a poet) to Beijing, where he enjoyed the patronage of the scholar-official Wang Chang (1725–1806), scholar Weng Fanggang (1733–1818), writer and official Qin Ying (1743–1821), Mongolian poet Faššan (Fashishan, 1753–1813) and man of letters Wu Xiqi (1746–1818). Wu's name was coupled with that of the poet Huang Jingren (1749–1783) as one of the 'Two Outstanding Talents of the Day' (*yishi zhi erjie*).

After the death by drowning of his brother in 1793, Wu supported his mother by working as a tutor at several private academies. Despite repeated attempts, he did not pass the second-level triennial examination until 1800, and never succeeded at the crucial third-level examination, which would have enabled him to obtain a high-ranking official post. In 1802 he was made an 'erudite' (*boshi*) in the Directorate of Education (Guozijian, sometimes also known in English as the Imperial Academy),

Portrait of Wu Songliang, from Ye Yanlan (1823–1898) and Ye Gongchuo (1881–1968), *Illustrated Biographies of Scholars of the Qing Period*, *c.* 1840–1900. Album, ink and light colours on paper, with brocade cover. Height 26.6 cm, width 17.3 cm. National Museum of China, Beijing.

and he later transferred to the Grand Secretariat (the highest internal executive office of the Qing government) as a secretary (*neige zhongshu*). Here he joined four other scholar-officials Gong Zizhen (1792–1841), Wei Yuan (1794–1857), Zong Jichen (1792–1867) and Duanmu Guohu (1773–1817) to become one of the 'Five Celebrities of the Secretariat'. (At the time of the First Opium War, between 1839 and 1842, the first two would become celebrated advocates of a new foreign policy designed to engage with and confront the threat from maritime Britain.)

In 1830, at the advanced age of sixty-four, he was appointed to the magistracy of Qianxi, in Guizhou province, but after falling out with his superiors he was demoted to be sub-prefect of Changzhaiting (Changshun county, also in Guizhou). After acting twice as a civil service examiner, he died in 1834, aged sixty-eight.

Wu's duties in Beijing included the supervision of students from the Chinese dependency of Ryukyu, through whom his name became known overseas. Japanese merchants eagerly bought up fans with his calligraphic inscriptions. In Korea, a shrine containing his likeness was set up in a grove planted with prunus trees – the prunus was one of his favourite plants, and featured extensively in his poems and paintings. (His other favourite plant was the orchid, hence his cognomen Lanxue, 'Orchid in Snow', from a line in a poem by the celebrated 8th-century Tang poet Li Bai.)

Among his contemporaries Wu's reputation as a poet was high. As a young man he had come to the attention of the painter and poet Yuan Mei (1716–1797), with whom he shared the sobriquet 'Lyrical Buddha' (Shi Fo). Yuan particularly praised the clarity, refinement and sonority of Wu's diction. Wu described himself as 'addicted to hills and streams' and he was heavily influenced by earlier nature poets such as Wang Wei (701–761), Li Bai (701–762), Su Shi (1037–1101) and Lu You (1125–1210).

Like his mentor Yuan Mei, Wu encouraged the artistic endeavours of the women in his household. His sister Wu Suyun, first wife Liu Jinqiu, second wife Jiang Wei, and daughters Wu Xuan and Wu Yunhua were all poets or painters. His concubine Yue Yun, a poet and a singer, was admired for her ability to write and paint ambidextrously. When she died in 1811, Wu was distraught and wrote dozens of poems in her memory.

In a preface to one such poem, Wu relates that forty-nine days after Yue Yun's death, she appeared to him in a dream, chanting a well-known phrase from the *Heart Sutra* about the identity of 'form' (*se*) and 'emptiness' (*kong*). In his dream, he responded with a parallel construction on the identity of poetry (*shi*) and painting (*hua*). On waking, he then inscribed the poem on a scroll bearing a portrait of Bodhisattva Avalokiteśvara (Guanyin), painted in 'fine line' (*baimiao*) style by the Ming artist Ding Yunpeng (1547–1628):

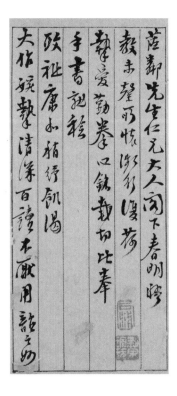

Wu Songliang (1766–1834), letter. Album leaf, ink on paper. Height 19.6 cm, width 9.1 cm. Princeton University Art Museum.

We met in a dream without a doubt;
The wind god was idling far away and all seemed calm.
The heavenly blooms had scattered but their scent was still all-pervasive;
As moon and water commingled I awoke none too late.
Form is emptiness and emptiness is form;
Every poem contains a picture, and every picture a poem.
Now returning to my prayer mat on the ground,
I give thanks to her beauty for being my teacher.

Wu's calligraphic style was influenced by Su Shi and Mi Fu (1051–1107), celebrated for their spontaneity; as an artist he drew inspiration from Wang Meiding (1755–1815), the renowned painter of orchids.

In 1843, some of Wu's admirers published his collected works in thirteen fascicles (more than half of them poetry). In addition to miscellaneous prose, he also wrote influential literary and art criticism, and collaborated in the compilation of the gazetteer (local history) of his native county. He travelled widely and wrote accounts of his journeys in Guangdong and the mountainous regions of Lu shan in Jiangxi and Wuyi shan in Fujian.

Despite his prominence during his lifetime, Wu gradually fell into obscurity after his death. The reprinting of his poems in 2002 has sparked a revival of interest, resulting in several articles in academic journals; paintings and calligraphy by him too occasionally come up for auction. Alongside Zeng Yu (1760–1831) and Yue Jun (1766–1814), Wu Songliang is considered to be one of the three outstanding Jiangxi poets of the early 1800s. Ongoing research into his literary and artistic legacy argues for him to be recognized as one of the leading creative talents in China's long 19th century.

Charles Aylmer

52. WU JIANREN

吴趼人 (1866–1910)

NOVELIST AND NEWSPAPER MAN

Despite a career shortened by his untimely death at the age of forty-four, in a period of little more than half a dozen years, Wu Jianren wrote a number of the most important and influential novels and stories of the 'New Fiction' (*Xin xiaoshuo*) movement inspired by the journal of that name founded by Liang Qichao (1873–1929) in 1902. The New Fiction writers assigned themselves the task of reporting on China's current conditions and problems, as well as hoping to mobilize a mass readership to overcome these difficulties. Prior to his few years devoted to fiction writing, Wu had worked at the Jiangnan Arsenal, that large-scale 'Self-Strengthening' enterprise established by

Zeng Guofan (1811–1872) and Li Hongzhang (1823–1901) in the 1860s. Founded initially to produce weaponry, it expanded its scope over the years to include heavy machinery and ship-building, in addition to sponsoring the publication of translated works on science and technology from English to Chinese. Soon after Wu's arrival in Shanghai in the early 1880s, he began work at the Arsenal as a copyist, eventually working his way up to draughtsman; it was during his years there that he acquired the technical knowledge that features in a number of his works of fiction.

Wu was born in Beijing to a family that had served in government for several generations, although his grandfather was the last of the line to occupy such a position. Probably as a result of their declining fortunes, the family moved to its ancestral home of Foshan in Guangdong province in 1867, where Wu Jianren received his formal education. Following his father's death in Ningbo in 1882, Wu moved to the burgeoning port of Shanghai, where he spent most of the remainder of his life. Obliged by illness to leave his post at the Arsenal, most likely in 1897, he spent the next couple of years nursing his infirmity, emerging after that as editor of a succession of entertainment newspapers, an occupation he later came to regret as having been a waste of time. While he may have regarded it as a detour from his eventual occupation as a creative writer, it is almost certain that his experience as editor brought him into contact with the sort of stories of social events that are the basis for much of his fiction.

It was also during this time that Wu began to be involved in political agitation, speaking at a 1901 rally opposing Russian aggression against China. It may be conjectured that, as someone born in Beijing and raised in Guangdong, who had also lived in Shanghai for two decades, his value as a speaker on that and on subsequent occasions was related to his presumably being fluent in the three most important Chinese languages of his adopted city. In these years he also published essays on current affairs, as well as a pungent set of satirical observations. His political stance was moderate: while critical of the corruption of the Chinese government, he was equally aware of the need to guard national sovereignty against Western incursions, even as he saw an enlightened Confucianism as the key to China's moral revival. Notably, Wu took part as an orator at the 1904–5 demonstrations against the United States making permanent the 1882 Chinese Exclusion Act in 1902; his protest extended to resigning his editorship of an American-owned newspaper in Hankou. The themes of his political essays found their way into his subsequent fiction, although the hopeful perspective with which he tried to imbue his discursive work rarely worked out so well in his fictional depictions of Chinese society.

He shared with such eminent contemporary scholars as Wang Guowei (1877–1927) the conviction that new forms of education incorporating Western knowledge were falling spectacularly short of the hopes that had been invested in them. In a characteristically cynical observation, Wu wrote in one of his satirical pieces: 'I often thought to myself that the reason China is not progressive and open and able to reform is because of a shortage of educated people. Suddenly, however, a different thought came to me: It is precisely because it contains too many educated people that China

Photograph of Wu Jianren raising his hat, with the caption 'Posthumous image [*yixiang*] of Qing novelist Wu Jianren', published in *Baixiang Pengyou*, September 1914.

has been unable to be progressive and open, and to reform.' Wu, however, did not hold himself exempt from such blanket condemnations: 'Wu Jianren of course has not made any progress, but I can clearly see that neither has anyone else.' Each of these observations is closed with the plaintive comment, 'Wu Jianren laments.'

As a key figure in the vibrant fiction-writing and critical community in post-1900 Shanghai, now increasingly able to sustain itself financially via an emerging print culture, Wu incorporated in his novels and stories new literary techniques inspired by Western examples. For instance, his longest and most famous novel, *Strange Events Eyewitnessed over the Last Twenty Years*, which began magazine serialization in late 1903, is marked by the first sustained use of the first-person narrative mode in Chinese literary history, a technique that allows Wu to represent a vivid first-hand reaction to assorted instances of civil and governmental abuse in various parts of China, by no coincidence all places where Wu had personal experience. His 1906 *Strange Injustice to Nine Lives*, an extended jeremiad against what Wu regards as the damaging superstitious belief in geomancy (*fengshui*), incorporates the innovation for Chinese fiction of beginning *in medias res* (that is, in the middle of the story the novel recounts). His *New Story of the Stone*, a fascinating narrative bringing the protagonist of the 18th-century classic *The Story of the Stone* or *Dream of the Red Chamber* back to life in a new age, is clearly indebted to Edward Bellamy's 1888 *Looking Backward, 2000–1887*, which enjoyed much success in a Chinese translation published in 1894, as well as to Jules Verne's *Twenty Thousand Leagues under the Sea*. While these touches of Western influence are unmistakable, Wu is able to weave them into convincing and organic narratives that inventively bring to life the time and place in which they are set.

Wu's own personal favourite was his 1906 ten-chapter novella *Sea of Regret*, unique among his works in not being serialized before publication as a single volume. The story of two young would-be couples whose lives are torn apart by the turmoil surrounding the Boxer Rebellion in Beijing in 1900, it in effect demonstrates the practical futility of the Confucian values Wu holds dear in the face of the chaos endemic to late Qing China. Its careful depiction of the personal feelings of the female protagonist, Dihua, is regarded as having paved the way for the novels of sentiment that came to play such a large role on the Chinese literary stage after Wu's death.

Theodore Huters

53. JAKDAN (ZHAKEDAN)

扎克丹 (*c.* 1780s–after 1848)

TRANSLATOR AND MANCHU POET

Manchu translator and poet of the Plain Red Banner, Jakdan, could not have imagined that he would end up in a volume like this. Had he known, he might have read from one of his poems, 'Song Mumbled Drunkenly', and asked:

Who, me? What is rare about me?
My talent, my capabilities, they are but shadows
What wisdom? I'm unsophisticated.
Powder and fripperies on a tree stump.

He would have protested, explaining that he was hardly important in his own time, gesturing at his clothing – 'a simple wrapping robe' – and his paltry furnishings – his 'chopping board, just shreds and dishes', his 'basin, made of clay, not copper', his 'cold bed' – as evidence of his poverty. He would have said that his work was lowly and his translations inadequate: 'My ability is weak, my capabilities lacking / My Manchu and Chinese writings are basic, I lack skills in archery and shooting from horseback.'

Jakdan could not have guessed that a century and a half after his death he would be regarded as an exceptional Manchu translator and one of the few composers of original Manchu language poetry (or at least one of the few whose work survives). He came to study the Manchu language for practical purposes, noting in the preface to his translation of *Strange Tales from a Chinese Studio* by Pu Songling (1640–1715) that, because his family was poor and he was too stupid (Manchu *mentuhun*) and dull-witted (Manchu *mufuyen*) to study the Confucian classics, he studied Manchu instead, hoping to get an official position. His strategy was a sound one, for the Qing empire always needed translators. The bureaucracy was filled with them: those making sure that all routine memorials (Chinese *tiben*) were in both Manchu and Chinese; and those handling military communications and communications with border regions and with Europeans states such as Russia, where Manchu was often the language used (not least for security reasons, to correspond directly with distant officers in the field, outside Sinophone lines of communication). Jakdan proved his skill through the translation examination in 1826, securing himself a degree as metropolitan graduate in translation and a position as second class secretary of the Board of Works in Mukden (modern Shenyang).

Only two of Jakdan's translations survive. The first is his translation of *Strange Tales*, consisting of 129 stories of haunted houses, immortals, fox women, flower women and the bizarre. Each story is translated in a lucid and lively manner, and the

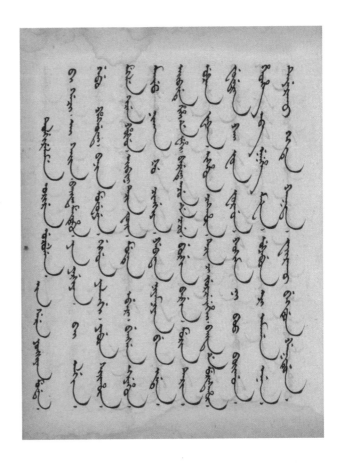

Jakdan (*c.* 1780s–after 1848), first page of the poem 'A Song Mumbled in my Sleep'. The title is the first line (read left to right). The poem is from the poetry collection *Tasty Reads for your Spare Time, juan* 8. Harvard-Yenching Library Rare Books collection, Harvard University, Cambridge, MA.

collection was printed at least twice during the Qing as a bilingual Manchu–Chinese book. His other surviving work is his poetry collection, *Tasty Reads for your Spare Time*, in eight fascicles. The first seven fascicles comprise 345 Manchu translations of Chinese poems by such eminent poets as Du Fu (712–770), Li Bai (701–762) and Su Shi (1037–1101) among many others. The eighth contains twenty-three poems in Manchu, and two poems mixing Manchu and Chinese, all by Jakdan himself. His playful verse showcases the Manchu language at its most lyrical.

Jakdan was not alone in composing Manchu poetry or crafting translations. He sought out 'several teachers and friends' to help him with his *Strange Tales* translation. These included the Manchu teacher and translator Mucihiyan, who collated the collection and contributed a preface, as well as fellow collators Salin of the Manchu Bordered White Banner, and Dasabu of the Bordered Blue Mongol Banner. Kingsi of the Manchu Bordered Red Banner wrote an additional preface and proofread every fascicle, while Deyentai and Canghing (both Manchus of the Plain Red Banner) also contributed a joint preface. His poetry collection received help as well: it was collated by Hai Yu, provincial graduate in translation of the Plain Red Manchu Banner; Jakdan's nephews Sunglin and Sungheo contributed 100 *taels* of silver each to get it printed; and an anonymous person wrote a preface, explaining the difficulties of, and Jakden's expertise in, translating poetry.

Jakdan's work, and his circle of friends and helpers, attests to the popularity of Manchu, even as late as the mid-19th century. While bannermen often used Chinese to compose poetry and novels, and in singing opera, drumsongs and 'bannermen tales' (Chinese *zidishu*), some were also composing poetry in Manchu. At the same time that Manchu was being studied and used by scholars outside the Qing empire – including in Japan, Korea and Europe – bannermen within China were also celebrating the beauty of the Manchu language: how it 'matched yin and yang', how its 'sounds harmonized the major and minor tones', and how, when Chinese literature was translated into Manchu, 'marvellous intents and hidden truths' could be revealed.

No portrait of Jakdan exists today. It is unlikely that he would have been able to afford one, if his poetic grumblings about his poverty – complete with mention of inferior tea and ordinary wine – are to be believed. However, we do know that his surviving translations and poetry were all completed when he was in his seventies, and he seems to have had mixed feelings about aging. His advanced years meant that he had retired from government service, but this freed up his time to translate, as memorialized in his poem 'Writing Offered to the Beard God':

This whitened beard!
It has given me the appearance of an old man, full in years.
Apart from the rest, stranger than others.
My face and eyes are hateful.
My shape and appearance are horrid!
My friends mocked me.

Ministers laughed at me.

After this, my name was no longer kept [on government lists].

Beautiful is my beard!

[…]

The old way of being at peace and at ease.

The original state of being complete and free.

A gourd dipper, one, a basket, one.

My joys are many.

All is because of the kindness of my beard turning white.

Sarah Jessi Bramao-Ramos

54. MANCHU TEACHER OF THE 'ONE HUNDRED LESSONS'

CREATOR OF A MANCHU LINGUISTIC IDENTITY

The author of the *Tanggū Meyen* (Chinese *Qinghua baitiao*, 'One Hundred Lessons') is known to us only by name, Zhi Xin (b. *c.* 1710), but the person who shines through in the ninety-eight lessons as a professional of exceptional character is that of the indefatigable 'Teacher'. The *Tanggū Meyen* is a bilingual Manchu–Chinese language textbook most likely conceived in its earliest form in 1750, then edited into a parallel version as the *Essentials of Manchu* (Chinese *Qingwen zhiyao*) by Fu Jun (1748–1834) and published in the late Qianlong era (*c.* 1789), with printings also documented for 1829 and 1843. Primers such as the *Tanggū Meyen* were continuously edited and reprinted for the benefit of an increasingly 'Sinified' Manchu garrison youth, the contemporary heirs to the elite military force that had originally conquered China for the Qing dynasty. The Teacher's task was to enable the Manchu banner youth to retain a modicum of their ancestral language, which Qing emperors since Qianlong (r. 1736–1795) had fretted was being lost, along with other markers of Manchu identity. The Manchu Teacher knew the world of official duties all too well (and is thus identified as male), but was also thoroughly at home in literary Manchu, using the delicate Manchu language to weave vivid images of thought, nature and urban life. From comments in the lessons, it also emerges that he was directly related to some of his students, indicating a tight network of family connections in 19th-century Manchu garrisons and in the capital Beijing. The Manchus had been the dominant group in the Qing armies that invaded the Ming empire in 1644. The Qing empire's ruling dynasty (Aisin Gioro) was Manchu, and in many ways privileged the Manchu conquest elite. However, the mere fact that the vast majority of the Manchus had been dispersed into 'banner garrisons' throughout China – in theory to maintain the

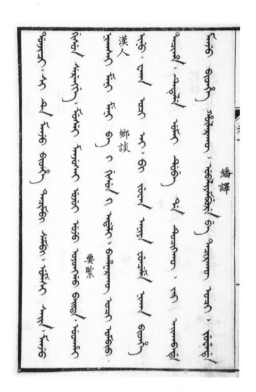

Tanggū Meyen ('One Hundred Lessons'). Printing ink on paper. Height 18.5 cm, width 12 cm. The Palace Museum, Beijing.

security of Qing rule over the Han majority – meant that individual communities were becoming too small to sustain themselves culturally. Throughout the 18th and 19th centuries, Manchu gradually ceased to be the mother tongue of the empire's garrison communities, although the Manchu language was seen as a hallmark of ethnic identity and thus taught up until the end of the Qing era in 1912.

From the very beginning of the Qing empire, active bilingualism became an obligation for all Manchus who aspired to an official career. (The Qing in fact had five official languages: Manchu, Chinese, Mongolian, Tibetan and Uyghur.) Manchu language primers thus dwelled on Confucian virtues and statecraft discourse, which featured prominently in primers such as the *Manju gisun i oyonggo jorin i bithe* (Chinese *Qingwen zhiyao*, 'Important Instructions for the Qing [Manchu] Language'), *Justan bithe* ('Small Notes'), *Manjurame fonjire jabure gisun dehi meyen* ('Questions and Answers on the Manchu Language in Forty Lessons'). However, knowledge of the language for colloquial use depended on domestic story-telling and tuition by local teachers well-versed in the grammar and textual customs of written Manchu. The author of the *Tanggū Meyen*, represented by the Teacher, bears witness to these intellectual currents of the Qing elite, manifesting them with simplicity and elegance. The *Tanggū Meyen* should therefore be regarded as an example of popular Manchu literature in its own right, so popular in fact that in 1924 it was translated into English by Forbes Fraser. The Teacher thus contributed to the Manchu nation-building exercise, both for the sake of the multi-ethnic Qing state as well as for the Manchu banner community after that state collapsed in 1912 (and with it the financial support it had offered for centuries to its banner families).

Since Jules Ferry's (1832–1893) reforms of French schools in 1881, the introduction of a universal school education has been one of the markers of modernity. By this token, the Manchus of the banner (Chinese *qi*, Manchu *gūsa*) communities were 'modern' from the early 18th century. Universal schooling in Manchu language and culture was introduced at this point by both imperial and communal coercion rather than by binding legislation, but proved an effective means of keeping the Manchus' collective identity alive. The 19th century was politically and militarily traumatic for the Manchus in the Qing empire, with a marked rise in anti-Manchu feeling throughout Han Chinese society. While the formidable rebel armies of the Taiping Civil War (1851–64) compared Manchus to diabolical monsters, turn-of-the-century nationalists such as Zou Rong (1885–1905) demanded that all Manchus be expelled from China. Towards the end of the dynasty, the government opened up the Manchurian homeland in the north-east to migration from the Chinese provinces, further weakening the ethnic confidence of the Manchus. Schooling in their ancestral language – still being used for official purposes on a daily basis – provided a sense of cultural continuity, which must have given the beleaguered Manchu banner communities a degree of confidence. The banner schools in Beijing were, at the end of the Qing period, concentrated by the eastern city gate, nicknamed 'College Mile' (Xueyuan lu). Their students were on average between twelve and fifteen years of age; entry was competitive, with clear preference given to candidates of Manchu origin, but also open to Mongolians and Han Chinese. Though elsewhere tuition fees were normal, many of the schools in Beijing were completely free of charge. The *Tanggū Meyen* contributed to the gathering of a Manchu language community, for which the learning of the ancestral tongue meant the creation of a discrete identity.

In terms of pedagogical methodology, Manchu teaching can be compared to today's adult courses, blending topics such as home and working life, remarkable events and news items in order to maintain student engagement. The *Tanggū Meyen* can therefore be characterized as a 'modern' textbook, as opposed to older-style rote learning of grammatical patterns and scriptural phrases. And just like any modern educator, the Teacher does not hide his frustration when the class forgets to do their homework. Lesson 50 – precisely halfway through the volume – is reserved for a warm rebuke to his students: 'This morning,' he grumbles, 'when I made them recite their lessons, every single one was badly prepared. Umming and erring, their mouths wide open, they were speechless or spoke haltingly.' He says to his students: 'Fully grown adults you are soon to be, and I therefore always tell you...harsh words not to harass you, nor to provoke discord. You are my own flesh and bones. All my thoughts are focused on making you educated people. What to do? If I spare no mental effort in teaching you, teaching pursuant to just principles, then I shall have accomplished my aim. To listen to me or not to listen, that is your choice. How can it be mine?'

Lars Laamann

55. INJANNASI

ᠢᠨᠵᠠᠨᠨᠠᠰᠢ (1837–1892)

GROUNDBREAKING MONGOLIAN NOVELIST

Injannasi, son of Wangcinbala, was the creator of a unique and innovative body of fiction in Mongolian, and perhaps the first true 'novelist' in that language. The word 'Mongolia' may conjure up images of steppes, tents and camels, but the branch of the Mongols to which the aristocratic Injannasi belonged had been predominantly agricultural since the 18th century. His father, Wangcinbala (1795–1847), was second-in-command of the Western Tümed Banner, part of the Josotu League, and the family home – a small mansion much like that of a Han Chinese landowner of the period – was situated in today's Beipiao county, Liaoning province, north-east of Beijing. Injannasi was one of eight brothers, and like all members of the Mongolian aristocracy could trace descent back to Temüjin (c. 1162 –1227), the great world conqueror of the 13th century, better known by his title of Chinggis Khan; there were twenty-eight carefully memorialized generations between himself and his mighty ancestor. The princes of the Tümed Mongols had been early adherents of the Manchus, and even in the 19th century still saw themselves as collaborators in the 'Great Enterprise' of Qing rule, rather than as conquered subjects. Their status was bolstered by marriage into the imperial clan, and parts of a surviving porcelain service made most probably for the wedding of an imperial daughter to a Tümed prince attest to this cherished connection. Injannasi was perhaps at that wedding (he certainly knew well the great imperial summer palace at Chengde). The family's loyalty to the dynasty was displayed by Wangcinbala's service in arms in the First Opium War (1839–42), defending the port of Yingkou in 1840 from 'an invasion of the English bandits', as his son remembered it.

Mongolian was one of the five 'official' languages of the Qing empire (along with Manchu, Chinese, Tibetan and Uyghur), enshrined in imperially sponsored dictionaries and compendia, and by the 19th century it had been used to compile a body of chronicle literature, alongside the Mongolian translations of the Buddhist canon of religious texts. Extensive oral literature, usually in the form of song and poetry, also circulated through the vast Mongolian-speaking regions. The first translations from Chinese into Mongolian date from the Yuan period (1271–1368), but these were mostly works of Confucian ethics and statecraft, and it was only in the Qing that Chinese imaginative literature came to be accessible to readers of Mongolian. Translations or free adaptations of major Chinese novels such as *Romance of the Three Kingdoms* and *Water Margin* were produced, alongside versions of crime fiction and short stories, while in 1819 Qasbuu (n.d.) produced the first translation into any language of the great Chinese romantic novel *The Dream of the Red Chamber*, also known in English as *The Story of the Stone*. Most of these works circulated in

Porcelain bowl, probably made to commemorate the marriage in 1842 of a daughter of the Daoguang emperor (r. 1821–1850) to a Mongolian prince of the Tümed banner. Painted with Buddhist emblems and figures in polychrome enamels, with a mark in iron-red on the base in Mongolian reading, *Baragun Tümed*, 'Western Tümed'. Height 6.8 cm, Ø 16.8 cm. The British Museum, London.

manuscript, and most were anonymous, although Injannasi's brother Gülaransa (1820–1851) worked on a Mongolian version of *Water Margin*, and another brother, Süngwaidanjung (1834–1898) was responsible for at least a partial translation of the Chinese historical work *Outline of a Mirror to History* (1172).

Injannasi's first novel, *Tears of the Red Mortals* (i.e. Beauties), written when he was in his early twenties, does not survive in a complete version. The same is true of his largest-scale work, the monumental *Blue Chronicle*, which he first worked on in 1870–71. This account of the glory days of Mongol empire may have been begun by his father; the extant part covers the years 1162 to 1236, from the rise of Temüjin to the eighth year of the Great Khan Ögedei (c. 1186–1241), but it clearly was originally intended to cover the whole of the Yuan dynasty. Drawing on elements from Mongolian chronicle and epic as well as from versions of the 16th-century novel *Romance of the Three Kingdoms* and other Chinese texts, it straddles modern categories like 'fiction' and 'history', in a distinctively Qing Mongolian understanding of the past. It voices the author's pride in being Mongolian, his hostility to the Buddhist religious establishment and to the slurs on Mongols found in Chinese historical writing, as well as his resentment at the theoretically protected status enjoyed by Mongols, which in fact left their culture and their lands constantly at risk of encroachment by Han Chinese commercial interests and settlers. He complains, for example, of the way in which Muslim subjects of the Qing were permitted to sit the crucial civil service examinations, from which the Mongols were excluded.

In the early 1870s, Injannasi also completed his romantic novel *One Storey of the Tower* and its continuation *The Pavilion of Weeping for the Beauties*. These form part of the wider reaction across Qing literature to the phenomenon of the hugely popular *Dream of the Red Chamber*, which spawned numerous continuations, in a genre of high-class 'fan fiction'. Injannasi's two novels incorporate passages of translation from these, as well as from the 1827 historical fantasy *Flowers in the Mirror*, the short stories of Li Yu (1611–1680) and even Tang poetry. Though written in Mongolian, the unique language of his novels would have been incomprehensible to anyone not also familiar with Chinese, and their most likely audience was the multilingual and bicultural social class to which the author himself belonged. Neither was published in Injannasi's lifetime, but instead circulated privately in manuscript.

The social and cultural conflicts of the 19th century directly affected Injannasi, whose lifetime was marked by several revolts of Mongol and Han tenant farmers. His family fortunes were badly hit by failed investment in coal mining, and he died in 1892 in the port of Jinzhou, sheltering there from an uprising of the anti-Qing 'Golden Elixir' religious sect. At his death, he was still revising the *Blue Chronicle*, the publication of which in the 20th century played a significant role in raising consciousness of a Mongolian political and cultural identity, and made Injannasi posthumously one of the key precursors of modern Mongolian literature.

Craig Clunas

56. LU XINYUAN

陸心源 (1834–1894)

INFLUENTIAL COLLECTOR OF ANTIQUARIAN TEXTS

It may seem of minor import that Lu Xinyuan dedicated his life to collecting antiquarian texts and objects, but this was one of many ways that Qing scholar-officials waged a multi-pronged campaign against the chaos engulfing the declining empire in the 19th century. Born in Gui'an (part of modern Wuxing, Zhejiang province), Lu was an intelligent child with an impressive memory. At the age of twenty-five, in 1859, he passed the *juren* (mid-level) civil service examination. The next year, after he failed his *jinshi* (top-level) examination, he was attacked by Nian rebels – whose insurrection had engulfed much of north China – on his trip home from Beijing. From this moment, the incredible violence of the late 1850s and 1860s took priority over his studies. Back in Gui'an, he organized a militia to fend off rebel forces, in the Taiping Civil War. When he actually became an official in 1862, he led troops to 'subdue' an uprising in Xinfeng county, Guangdong. He later, in 1865, suppressed soldiers mutinying against their Qing commanders in Hunan.

His involvement in political affairs, as well as a youth spent admiring the writings of Gu Yanwu (1613–1682), the founder of the 'evidential research group' (*kaozheng xuepai*), meant that Lu, like many of the outstanding minds of his generation, was committed to empirical study. A dominant school of late Qing scholarship, 'evidential research' advocated establishing empirical foundations for knowledge through

Lu Xinyuan's seal portrait, which shows him at the age of forty-five.

undertaking meticulous analysis of ancient texts, rather than relying on edited versions passed down through history (which could contain errors and omissions). Lu belonged to a vast network of practically orientated, high-ranking scholar-officials. His correspondents and friends included Li Hongzhang (1823–1901), Wei Yuan (1794–1857) and Zeng Guoquan (1824–1890). They were united by a common purpose – looking both inwards, towards tradition and history, and outwards, to foreign information and methods, as part of their efforts to revive the empire.

Lu described something of their shared philosophical orientation in a preface to Wei Yuan's writings. He noted that too many scholars were merely obsessed with producing ornate writings, which was a critical weakness of the learning encouraged by the examination system. In contrast, Wei Yuan read 'official manuals from our dynasty, cases, as well as European writings' in order to effect practical change. Capacious reading and meticulous research rather than quiet contemplation would allow scholar-officials to accurately diagnose what had gone wrong in the 19th century.

Lu's empiricist orientation was fed by bibliomania and a drive to collect antiquities. Wherever Lu went, he sought books, rubbings and other artefacts from the past. By the 1870s, he had collected tens of thousands of books – including roughly two hundred titles from the Song (960–1279) and Yuan (1271–1368) dynasties. His library collection, which was divided into three discrete parts, encompassed books of all types and was supplemented by collections of tiles, bronzes and other materials.

Lu's commitment to practical studies – and his personal collections – contributed in no small ways to the development of late Qing scholarship. While it may be tempting to see this as a form of antiquarianism, the questions scholars tried to answer through these materials were linked to contemporary concerns. In his position as collector, Lu reprinted rare editions, produced scholarly studies, and shared his findings widely. In reading his letters to friends, one gets the impression that Lu imagined his home as a sort of semi-public research centre.

Lu Xinyuan (1834–1894), illustration of ancient tiles collected in the Qianbi Pavillion, 1891. Height 25 cm. Waseda University Library, Tokyo.

Lu shared his work with as wide an audience as possible, publicizing his own collection to give scholars a sense of the benefits of material-oriented scholarship. One of his greatest contributions is undoubtedly his annotated bibliography of the rare Song and Yuan editions in his library collection. Sifting through the entries of the 1892 *Catalogue of the Library of Song Editions* is dizzying. In 120 chapters, Lu Xinyuan describes his holdings dating to the 'golden age' of Chinese printing, the Song and Yuan dynasties. One important aspect of this catalogue is that it was written according to some of the new standards developed for bibliographical description. Many of the titles are described with both bio-bibliographical information about authors and compilers as well as physical descriptions of the page layout. Lu's catalogue was one of the foundational texts for establishing modern descriptive standards for Chinese rare books, many aspects of which can be seen in library catalogues today.

After Lu's death, the economic decline of his family in the early 20th century inspired his son to raise revenue by trying to find a better home for the collection. Local officials and the central state were offered the collection. When no domestic buyers emerged, the Japanese magnate Iwasaki Yanosuke (1851–1908), who happened to be in China at the time, offered to purchase the collection. So in 1907 the books were moved to Japan, where they would form one of the most important collections of the Seikadō Library. The loss of the collection, along with contemporaneous reports of the pillaging of Dunhuang in west China by non-Chinese explorers and scholars, were partially responsible for increased government activism in library and museum collection building.

Although Lu Xinyuan has been generally overlooked in recent Western scholarship, his biography exemplifies the techniques used by late Qing intellectuals and officials in their attempts to revitalize the empire. Collections of artefacts and books built in the wake of the Taiping Civil War played a crucial role in helping to redefine late imperial scholarship, laying a foundation for later ideas about museums and libraries, as well as archaeology, in modern China. Stele by stele, tile by tile, and book by book, Lu's collection, and the collections of his friends, provided the material foundation for the scholarly renaissance of the Republican period.

Devin Fitzgerald

57. MŪSĀ SAYRĀMĪ

مؤسا سايرامى (1836–1917)

CHRONICLER OF WAR AND RECONSTRUCTION

On the night of 6 June 1864, the Muslims of the town of Kucha rose up against Qing rule. This rebellion was one of many that year in the north-western, Muslim-majority region of Xinjiang, or East Turkestan. Within months, the Qing lost control of the region. For the next thirteen years, various Muslim powers came and went, each contesting for control over the region's territory and resources, and each making some claim to legitimate rule over its people. That story, and the Qing's reconquest of the region in 1877, are a central episode in the history of the modern Uyghur people, and their homeland of East Turkestan.

Our understanding of this episode today is thanks in large part to the efforts of Mullah Mūsā, son of Mullah 'Īsā b. Mullah 'Azīzkhan Khwāja Sayrāmī. Mūsā Sayrāmī was a young scholar when the uprisings broke out, served as an official in two of the Muslim states, and was an eyewitness to many of the key events of this period. Many years after the reconquest, he penned his most famous work, the *Tārīkh-i Amniyya* ('Chronicle of peace'), and later revised it as the renamed *Tārīkh-i Ḥamīdī* ('Hamidian chronicle'). The book is a masterful history of the Muslim uprisings in the Uyghur homeland in the mid-19th century from the perspective of an autochthonous scholar.

The name 'Sayrāmī' is a *nisba* – a word indicating his place of origin. Mūsā Sayrāmī's ancestors came from Old Sayram, a town in today's Kazakhstan. In the 17th century, the Zunghar Mongols conquered that town and removed many of its people to East Turkestan, which was then part of Zunghar territory. Later, in the 1750s, the Qing conquered the region, and the displaced people of Old Sayram asked to return to their homeland. The Qing refused, and so eventually those people settled a place in a mountain valley in central Xinjiang, near Kucha, that they dubbed New Sayram. The Sayramis were Turkic-speaking and Muslim, and so were linguistically and culturally similar to the people around them. Nevertheless, Mūsā Sayrāmī's sense of a history separate from that of the people of East Turkestan may have informed the critical distance that characterizes his chronicle.

Traumatic experiences of war are probably another reason. From 1847 to 1854, Sayrāmī was educated at the Saqsaq Madrasa (Islamic college) in Kucha, where he studied a broad range of humanistic and mathematical sciences, ranging from Hadith scholarship to astronomy, and he evidently learned not only Arabic and Persian but Urdu. He also befriended his classmate, Maḥmūdīn Khoja (n.d.), a member of a prominent Sufi family that in 1864 came to lead the Kucha rebellion. Sayrāmī, now a madrasa teacher himself, joined the movement as a trusted advisor. However, an early battle left him first imprisoned, then wandering in the wilderness, where he concluded that the world had changed too much for him to return home.

Mūsā Sayrāmī rejoined the Kucha faction and soon began managing Maḥmūdīn's affairs during the latter's rule of the oasis of Uchturfan, gaining fame (to some, notoriety) as a scrupulous and exacting administrator. However, he gradually became disillusioned with the leadership of pious mystics, especially as he was drawn into their infighting and witnessed the corrupting effects of power. Mūsā Sayrāmī recalls in his chronicle how he risked his life to preserve the Kucha faction's rule, only to see these supposedly holy men scheme and feast at the common people's expense. This experience probably informed the critique of power that suffuses Sayrāmī's account.

Page from Mūsā Sayrāmī (1836–1917), *Tārīkh-i Amniyya*, copy made in Kashgar, 1912–13. Height 22.5 cm, width 14 cm. Lund University Library.

Tomb at the shrine of 'Arshuddīn in Kucha, where Sayrāmī took refuge during the Kucha uprisings in 1864. Photograph by Lisa Ross.

Early in the uprisings, one of the Muslim factions vying for control of East Turkestan invited the neighbouring Emirate of Khoqand to send a leader and bring peace to the land. Instead, they received a conquering force led by the military officer Yaʿqūb Beg (1820–1877), who defeated the Kucha faction in 1867 and consolidated his rule.

Mūsā Sayrāmī was captured and enslaved, until it was revealed that he was an experienced administrator. He then spent the remainder of the uprising, until 1877, as a tax collector for an area around the oasis of Aqsu. This vantage point permitted Sayrāmī an exceptionally intimate view of Yaʿqūb Beg's state, its dysfunction, and its effects on local people, and his chronicle evaluates many mid-level officials and details their affairs.

The autobiographical sections of Sayrāmī's chronicle paint a picture of a disillusioned man. He struggles with the violence that the Kucha faction enacted upon other Muslims. He depicts Yaʿqūb Beg as a false saviour corrupted by his increasingly unrestrained rage. Even the ascetic, fanatically pious tax collector under whom Sayrāmī worked comes across as a pathetic and delusional figure. Sayrāmī writes how the people of East Turkestan grew tired of the Khoqandis' exactions and 'cried out for the emperor of China', but also depicts the return of Qing rule as horror and tragedy. He reserves kind words for a select few officials who acted with justice and genuine concern for ordinary people.

Mūsā Sayrāmī reveals little about his own life after 1877, and we may speculate that he was among the petty officials who, as he describes it, compromised and joined the Qing administration. Other sources, now inaccessible to scholars, indicate that he lived in Aqsu from 1879, and some Uyghur accounts assert that he travelled around the region writing poetry and collecting stories.

At some point, Sayrāmī gained a patron named Muḥammad Amīn Bay (n.d.), who was possibly a Russian trade and diplomatic agent, and for whom Sayrāmī penned the original *Tārīkh-i Amniyya* in 1903 as a way to memorialize the events of the Muslim uprisings. The Russian orientalist and imperial administrator Nikolai Pantusov (1849–1909) then had the chronicle printed in Kazan, Tatarstan, in 1905. Meanwhile, Sayrāmī revised his chronicle, evidently prompted in part by foreign visitors. As he did so, new copies were made for other foreign travellers, as well as for readers across the region. Sayrāmī also produced a collection of original poetry that has received scant scholarly attention.

Several factors contributed to Sayrāmī's revision of the *Tārīkh-i Amniyya* as the *Tārīkh-i Ḥamīdī*. One was growing disillusionment with the late Qing era, which no longer seemed like one of 'peace'. Another was his encounter with other Muslim intellectuals, including Qurbān ʿAlī Khālidī (1846–1913) of Tarbaghatai, with whom he discussed Chinese sources among other topics, and the Syrian traveller known as 'Shāmī Damulla' (1870–c. 1932), who strengthened Sayrāmī's scepticism. The latest known version of the *Tārīkh-i Ḥamīdī*'s text dates to 1908, although copies of different versions were made as late as the early 1930s. The text as we know it is a patchwork of sources and arguments revised over the course of many years, held together by Sayrāmī's evolving critical vision. That vision was anchored in the effort to recover lost memory and to explain the rise and tragic fall of Islamic power and the state of the rapidly changing world. Sayrāmī was a critical historian who attempted to make sense of Chinese power through Islamic modes of history writing.

In 1909, Sayrāmī fell ill and was invited to live with his brother in his home village of Toqsun. He subsequently returned to Aksu, although a final bout of illness in 1917 brought him home again. He soon passed away, and a dome was erected over his grave. It was destroyed during the Cultural Revolution (1966–76) but subsequently rebuilt.

A later author, Ghulām Muḥammad Khan (n.d.), wrote a continuation of Mūsā Sayrāmī's chronicle that recounted the events of the world through to 1927. His efforts brought Sayrāmī's ideas of historical change to bear on an even more unfamiliar world, as Eurasian empires fell and new states rose to replace them. By the early 1930s, Sayrāmī's chronicle had become enshrined as a classic in the emerging Uyghur nationalist canon.

Eric Schluessel

58. WANG TAO

王韜 (1828–1897)

JOURNALIST, NEWSPAPER PUBLISHER,
REFORMER, WORLD TRAVELLER

Born into a poor family near Suzhou, in Jiangsu province, Wang Tao was a studious boy and early on showed great literary talent. By the age of nine, he was able to recite by heart the thirteen classic texts that were the foundation of the imperial civil service examination curriculum, for which he was acclaimed as a child prodigy. In 1849, at the age of twenty-one, Wang Tao moved to Shanghai, where he found employment at the London Missionary Society Press, founded by Walter Henry Medhurst (1796–1857). Wang Tao worked there for four years and assisted Medhurst in the collective project of translating the Bible into Chinese; Wang worked on doctrinal sections of the New Testament and all the Old Testament. Much impressed with Wang Tao's talent and his devotion to work, Medhurst praised him as a genius. One of the first to realize the importance of translation in promoting communication between China and the West, and reforming China, Wang devoted much time and energy to introducing Western knowledge into China through writing and translation. During his lifetime, he wrote and translated more than sixty works: on scripture, politics, history and science. As well as non-fiction, he wrote novels, diaries, poetry and letters.

In August 1862, Wang Tao was accused by the Qing government of collusion with the Taiping rebels (it seems that Wang wrote to the Taiping offering his services against the Qing). With the help of British missionaries, Wang Tao escaped to Hong Kong then headed to Western Europe. During his twenty-three years away from China, Wang Tao deepened and broadened his understanding of modernizing Western countries. While in Hong Kong, Wang Tao was invited by James Legge (1815–1897) to help him translate the 'Four Books and the Five Classics' – nine of the core texts of Confucian thought, many attributed to Confucius himself. This enormous translation project – published over the course of the second half of the 19th century – made accessible, for the first time, the Chinese classical canon to Anglophone readers. Wang Tao thus played an important role in a highly significant episode of cultural exchange between China and the West.

In 1867, James Legge returned to Scotland and invited Wang Tao to join him. Wang Tao lived in Europe for more than two years and recorded his experiences in a travel account *Jottings of my Roamings*. As he spent most time in Britain, Wang Tao was able to investigate in depth its political and legal systems, army, popular customs, entertainment, science, technology and education, all of which he described and discussed in his travelogue. Once more, Wang Tao was a transcultural pioneer, this time as an interpreter of Britain to Chinese audiences. He visited Britain seven years before Guo Songtao (1818–1891) arrived as the first Qing ambassador. Wang Tao was also the

蘇京畝宮

The Old Palace in the
Capital of Scotland
(Edinburgh), from Wang
Tao's *Jottings and Drawings
from Carefree Travels*,
facsimile of 1890 edition,
2004. Leiden University
Libraries.

first Chinese person to lecture at the University of Oxford, where he spoke in Chinese about the history of Sino-British contacts, expressed his hopes for improved relations, and encouraged students to devote themselves to public service. During his stay in Britain, Wang Tao gave frequent recitations of classical Chinese poetry, to promote Chinese culture. During his travels across Europe, he attracted much attention as a Chinese person. He recalled that in a bar in Marseilles, for example, the staff bombarded him with questions about his country and were fascinated by his Chinese clothing. He gave a generous assessment of British mores: 'The British are an honest, modest and sincere people, who produce many commodities.... They seldom quarrel with one another, nor do they cheat foreigners. Because they live in harmony with the natives, immigrants seldom feel anxious. The same could not be said for China. Indeed, I have seen very few foreign countries where such customs prevail.'

Wang Tao made several visits to Crystal Palace, the venue of the 1851 Great Exhibition, and attended the International Exposition of 1867 in Paris. Impressed by what he saw, Wang Tao felt that China lagged far behind the West, in terms of technology and governance. He therefore proposed a number of practical reforms, designed to modernize China. Wang Tao's first-hand experience of Europe also made him a celebrity in East Asia. His detailed account of the 1870–71 Franco-Prussian War not only won him a pardon from the Qing government, after it impressed senior officials such as Li Hongzhang (1823–1901); it also gained a wide readership among Japanese intellectuals. During an invited stay in Japan, Wang Tao came to know several famous contemporary scholars, including the renowned historian Oka Senjin (1833–1914), who personally admired Wang Tao's knowledge of the West and accompanied him around Japan. This visit generated another travelogue, *Journey to Japan*, an influential comparative analysis of the politics, economy and culture of 19th-century China and Japan.

In 1874, Wang Tao founded *Universal Circulating Herald* in Hong Kong, the first Chinese-language daily newspaper run by Chinese people and the first to focus on current affairs both inside and outside China. It had an active reform agenda, calling for the overhaul of China's political, social and educational systems. In 1884, Wang Tao, at the age of fifty-six, returned to Shanghai where, for the last thirteen years of his life, he served as editor for China's first modern newspaper, *Shenbao*, and founded and directed respectively a publishing house and a college with a Westernized curriculum. Wang Tao was an emblematic, groundbreaking cosmopolitan of the late Qing, operating for much of his life along the 'Hong Kong–Shanghai corridor', two places where Chinese and Western cultures met, and – the Western snobbery and racism of both cities notwithstanding – innovative cultural and political agendas became possible.

Pan Qing

59. SHAN SHILI

單士厘 (1858–1945)

POET, TRAVEL WRITER, PROTO-FEMINIST

Born into an upper-class family near Shanghai, Shan Shili did not go to school in the modern sense, but she had a very lively mind. After the death of her mother, when she was ten or eleven, her father and an uncle on her mother's side took over her education, in both classical and modern subjects. This education left her well equipped to carry out research on women of the Ming (1368–1644) and Qing (1644–1912) and to write poetry in classical forms and language. These practices sustained her throughout her lifetime. She was the author of *A Continuation of Correct Beginnings: Poetry by Women of our Dynasty*, published 1911–18, a supplement to the work of Yun Zhu (1771–1833), and a collection of personal poetry, *Draft Poems of Shouci Studio*, published posthumously in 1986, among other works along these lines. The poetry shows many signs of modern thinking, as when it expresses the hope that China's 20th century will be a century of women, but the writing style should be described as traditional, since it follows old-style line lengths and linguistic patterns.

The work for which Shan is best known, however, lies in a completely different area. Her *Record of a Journey in 1903* is a diary about travel with her husband, Qian Xun (1853–1927). A diplomat under the Qing, Qian had the job of escorting a group of Chinese students to Japan that year. Later he joined the Qing's diplomatic staff in Moscow, but he escorted students on this trip too, all in service of Zhang Zhidong's (1837–1909) effort to promote modernization (of which foreign education was an important part). Qian encouraged his wife to come on both trips and to keep a diary, which would be aimed at other Chinese women, and which might enlighten them about the modern world. Influenced by the radical journalist Liang Qichao (1873–1929) and others, Qian and Shan hoped to draw China's women away from traditional thinking, which confined their attention to the home and left them ignorant of world affairs. Properly inspired, as Qian and Shan saw it, they might become forward-looking mothers and educate their children in ways that would strengthen China.

Shan's youthful habit of reading about travel left her well prepared for this assignment. Furthermore, between 1899 and 1903, the couple resided in Japan with their two sons, one of Qian's daughters by another woman, and a daughter-in-law, then enrolled in Shimoda Utako's (1854–1936) famed school for elite Chinese women in Tokyo. While in Japan, Shan read Japanese travelogues to improve her facility in Japanese. Some of these were about travels across Russia. (Qian and Shan's son, Qian Daosun (1887–1966), would later become a leading translator of Japanese literature into Chinese.)

Record of a Journey in 1903 actually covers two trips. The first is a boat journey home from Japan to China and back, on the eve of a trip to Russia. The second is about travel by train, a new phenomenon in East Asia and even newer in Eastern Siberia. It begins with a boat trip from Tokyo to Vladivostok, then continues by train to Korea, to Manchuria and Mongolia, through Russia, past Irkutsk, all the way to Moscow and St Petersburg. Each segment means a new gauge of track and a shift to a new train, hence many opportunities for confusion over seats and status.

The first trip, to the Shanghai area, brings out Shan's concerns about China's poor performance internationally, in comparison with Japan's greater skill in foreign affairs. Shan also comments about Japanese women, whom she feels make a better model for China than Western women because of their greater modesty and deference to men. The Russia trip manifests a pronouncedly anti-Russian bias, partly because of Russian imperialist attitudes towards China, but partly because the Russians did not respect Shan's class privileges as the Japanese had done. When it came to reserving seats and handling luggage, the Japanese were far superior, in Shan's view. Again she comments on women's issues, especially foot-binding, which she states emphatically Chinese women should oppose. At the same time, she displays considerable interest in and knowledge of the sites she passes, even when she transits at night and is unable to see relevant features. Under these circumstances, she draws on prior reading, or even quotes at length from (translated) Japanese travelogues,

Photograph of Shan Shili at the age of eighty-one, thirty-six years after she wrote her *Travels in the Year 1903*, a diary about travelling with her husband, Qian Xun. The image was included in *Draft Poems of Shouci Studio*, published posthumously in 1986.

to fill in the blanks. All the while, she is extremely deferential to her husband, seldom voicing an opinion without couching it in his terms. Nonetheless, *Record of a Journey in 1903* is path-breaking in several respects. The landscape Shan traverses would have been new to Chinese woman readers, as was her cautious support for women's issues, and her vivid descriptions of travel by train.

Shan Shili is clearly a transitional figure. One sees this in her attitudes, but also in her travelogue's language, which is classical Chinese. She makes no effort to reach average people in a vernacular Chinese, an aim which the May Fourth–New Culture Movement of the 1910s and 1920s would later pursue. Although the mission of *Record of a Journey in 1903* is reformist, in many respects Shan remained a gentle-woman of the old school. Subsequently, from 1909 to 1910, Shan wrote a second work on travel, *Writings in Retirement*, which describes her trip to Rome and its environs with her husband and son. Although it introduces readers to the art, architecture and history of the locale, it is not as gripping as *Record of a Journey in 1903*, perhaps because it lacks the immediacy of a diary, or perhaps because Shan is not travelling by train. It is also rather eclectic in form and content, with some writing by her son Daosun and an essay on Marco Polo, but nonetheless part of Shan's legacy as a travel writer. Shan and Qian also travelled to the Netherlands, but this is not recorded in the travelogue, though it does feature in one of her poems. Shan continued to write to the end of her life. Her last dated poem is from 1942, and her final published prose work came out in 1944.

Ellen B. Widmer

60. LI GUI

李圭 (1842–1903)

SURVIVOR AND CIRCUMNAVIGATOR

On 10 May 1876, Li Gui, a Chinese clerk in the Qing Imperial Maritime Customs Service, boarded a steamship owned by the Mitsubishi Company of Japan in Shanghai. After a brief visit to Japan, he travelled to San Francisco by steamship, and continued onward via the Transcontinental Railroad to Philadelphia, the site of the Centennial Exhibition, the first World's Fair to be held in the United States. At this spectacular event, thirty-seven countries displayed artisanal, industrial and natural products to enhance trade, celebrate the 100th anniversary of the founding of the United States, and promote international understanding. Li Gui stayed in Philadelphia for several months, observing the Centennial Exhibition, visiting local institutions, and travelling by train to nearby cities on the East Coast. While there, he had his photograph taken for a calling card. (Later, in 1879, back in Ningbo, in eastern China, he signed one of the cards and gave it to an American commissioner at the Maritime Customs Service. The image came full circle: the card is now housed in an album of photographic calling cards held at Harvard University.)

On 26 October 1876, Li boarded the American Line's steamship, the *Lord Clive*, at Philadelphia and travelled to London, Paris and Marseilles. At Marseilles, he transferred to a French passenger and mail ship, and after making stops at Suez, Aden, Ceylon, Singapore, Saigon and Hong Kong, he returned to Shanghai. The Maritime Customs Service, whose mostly foreign staff organized the Chinese exhibition at the Centennial Exposition, sent Li on this journey to observe and report on what he saw for readers back home. He did so through columns in Shanghai's most important Chinese language newspaper, *Shenbao*, using the byline 'The Circumnavigator', and later in a book, *The New Record of a Trip around the World*, published in 1878 with financial support from the Maritime Customs Service. The book featured a preface by the empire's most powerful official, Li Hongzhang (1823–1901), which presents the book as an introduction to commerce, diplomacy, transportation and military machines. Advertisements, excerpts, diary entries and reprints suggest that the book enjoyed commercial success and cultural influence beyond official circles. This was still true a century later, in 1981, when it was included in the post-Cultural Revolution *Walking towards the World Collectanea* as a harbinger of China's Reform and Opening-Up, initiated by Deng Xiaoping.

Li Gui's adventure made him something of a celebrity in China in his own time. Moreover, he was participating in a new global fad for circumnavigation made possible by the opening of the American Transcontinental Railroad and the Suez Canal. He inhabited a moment defined by new possibilities, as well as debilitating challenges. He travelled in a world of rapid change, widespread uncertainty and considerable optimism; a world, however, in which war globally defined recent memory. The infrastructure and inventions that made the 'modern global system' possible arguably appeared as new, marvellous and disruptive to many Europeans and Americans, as they did to Li Gui.

The idea of travelling 'around the world' in comfort and luxury seemed novel and exciting to almost anyone alive in 1876. Thomas Cook had only recently begun to promote circumnavigation as tourism. Luxury hotels with electric lights and running water at the new steamship hubs dazzled visitors, and not merely those from China. Jules Verne's novel *Around the World in Eighty Days* was published just five years before Li Gui's *New Record*, as was William Simpson's *Meeting the Sun: A Journey All Round the World*. The sensational race around the world by female journalists Nellie Bly (1864–1922) and Elizabeth Bisland (1861–1929) lay more than a decade in the future. The set itinerary for such trips came into being during the 1870s, with the completion of the Suez Canal and the Transcontinental Railroad across the United States in 1869, and the linking of the railways across India in 1870. Moreover, as Li Gui seems to have well understood, this smaller and faster globe was born in the aftermath of the devastating violence that characterized the mid-19th century globally.

Li Gui was born in 1842 in a village not far from the city of Nanjing. He experienced first-hand the suffering associated with China's devastating Taiping Civil War (1851–64). As a very young man, he lost his mother, wife and baby daughter to the conflict; he survived by serving as a secretary in the Taiping administrative establishment. He documented these experiences in his later memoir, *A Record of Pondering Pain*, published in 1880. Produced after his return from overseas and enthusiastically announced in the Shanghai newspaper *Shenbao*, the memoir is typical of other writings about the war: it describes a world of pain for an audience of literate survivors and former refugees, many of whom sought reintegration and opportunity in the post-war restoration.

The book's emotionally powerful contents are mixed up with post-war political imperatives and the author's ambitions. A notice in *Shenbao* observed that its author should not be excluded from official service. Li's desire for exoneration seems built into the very structure of *Pondering Pain*: he served the Taiping only under duress, he sought opportunities to flee, he suffered greatly, and regretted having grown out his hair like his captors. Wartime experience also expanded Li Gui's professional

Li Gui's *carte de visite*, photograph taken at the studio of Gerlach & Fromhagen, Philadelphia, Pennsylvania, United States, in 1876. The card is signed by Li Gui and was given to his colleague Edward Bangs Drew in Ningbo on 23 August 1879. Edward Bangs Drew Collection, Harvard-Yenching Library, Harvard University, Cambridge, MA.

horizons by entangling him in the hybrid extra-bureaucratic institutional networks of the war's victors. *Pondering Pain* reminds readers that any account of 'cosmopolitan encounters', 'treaty ports' and 'Self-Strengthening' in the late 19th century must also reflect the extent to which civil war shaped actors and events of the times.

Li Gui's insights into past pain and futuristic wonders manifest awareness of a shared global experience of war and recovery, an understanding of the unevenness of 'Western' development, and confidence in the accessibility of mechanical marvels. He also demonstrates a striking confidence in himself as a Chinese man of the world. Li publicized his activities in new media. He became a celebrity for circumnavigating the globe, wrote a memoir that established his loyalty to the Qing (having also served a hostile, breakaway regime), and built a reputation as a foreign affairs expert through his patronage networks and in the newspapers. By his own report, he was accepted in elite society in a world where class evidently could modulate racial exclusion, and at a time when those enamoured of impossible utopian visions of an interconnected globe thought somehow that technology, including weapons, might overcome the wars of recent memory.

Tobie Meyer Fong

61. HUANG ZUNXIAN

黃遵憲 (1848–1905)

POET AND DIPLOMAT

Huang Xunxian was born into a wealthy Hakka family from Jiayingzhou, present-day Meizhou, in north-east Guangdong. Huang's father, Huang Hongzao (1828–1891), was a bureaucrat who enjoyed a distinguished career in the service of the Qing state. Huang Zunxian followed in his father's footsteps. After passing the mid-level civil service *juren* examination in 1877, Huang was posted to the Qing state's embassy in Tokyo, learned Japanese and had frequent discussions with Japanese intellectuals. For much of the 1880s, Huang's published first-hand observations of the country constituted an important source of information for late Qing intellectuals on newly centralized, modernizing Japan – a state that would become a crucial model for the Qing empire's own path to reform.

In 1882, he was appointed consul general in San Francisco, arriving shortly after the United States Congress had passed the Chinese Exclusion Act, which remained in place until 1943. In the middle of the 19th century Chinese people emigrated to California in response to the American demand for labour. But a political and media campaign to exclude them from America and from US citizenship had started in around 1850. This campaign had partially realized its goals by 1870 with the Naturalization Act, which denied Chinese people the right to naturalization. The Exclusion Act of 1882 represented its full realization. Huang was outraged by such laws and their consequences for his compatriots. As consul, he threw himself into defending the interests of those who were subject to incessant racism and police harassment. He consecrated several poems to the issue, and his long poem *Expelling the Visitor* on the exclusion of those the Americans perceived to be 'Chinese', deals not merely with anti-Asian racism in California, but with US rapaciousness in regard to native American lands, as well as China's incapacity to protect its people. The poem is a tour de force. Similarly, in a poem on the presidential election of 1884, two years after the promulgation of the Exclusion Act, Huang reminds his readers of the United States' betrayal of its Founding Fathers' principles:

Alas! George Washington!
It is nearly a hundred years now
Since the flag of independence was raised
And oppressive rule was overthrown.
Red and yellow and black and white
Were all to be treated as one.

Portrait of Huang Zunxian,
from Ye Yanlan (1823–
1898) and Ye Gongchuo
(1881–1968), *Illustrated
Biographies of Scholars
of the Qing Period*,
c. 1840–1900. Album, ink
and light colours on paper.
Height 26.6 cm, width
17.3 cm. National Museum
of China, Beijing.

Huang was stationed in California until 1889, and, in 1890, was appointed counsellor at the legation in London. The following year, he became consul general in Singapore. Given a domestic posting in 1897, he became embroiled in the abortive Hundred Days' Reform of 1898. A vociferous supporter of constitutional government as a solution to the Qing state's problems, in particular the territorial encroachment of foreign powers, he had been a favourite of the now powerless Guangxu emperor (r. 1875–1908). With the intervention of high-ranking Japanese and Western officials, he escaped the fate of his fellow poet and reformist Tan Sitong (1865–1898), who was beheaded. However, Huang's career was at an end, and he retired to Jiayingzhou, where he lived out the rest of his days.

Acknowledged by many as the predecessor of the modern Chinese poetry movement, Huang coined the slogan: 'My hand writes what my mouth says; how can antiquity restrain me?' This now often quoted phrase, which was seen to herald the initial, revolutionary rupture with China's long poetic tradition, says more about what was considered radical at the time than it does of Huang's success in crafting a malleable, poetic style responsive both to modern society and modern speech. In the original literary Chinese, the phrase illustrates the difficulty scholar-poets had in breaking free from the traditional idiom, for it is written in the old literary language rather than the vernacular.

The journalist and radical intellectual Liang Qichao (1873–1929) thought Huang the major figure of the 'poetic revolution' (*shijie geming*) of the turn of the century (which itself foreshadowed the May Fourth era's more radical modernization of poetry in the 1910s and 1920s). Liang himself was far from convinced that poetry should be written in a purely vernacular language, and in his own poetry 'new imported things' (objects, ideas and words from the modern West and Japan) confront classical expression and conventional allusions. Huang's continued use of the traditional literary language and its allusions notwithstanding, literary scholars have credited Huang as making a significant contribution to opening Sinophone poetry to a foreign-inflected modernity, and as starting to create a new and viable poetic medium suitable for an emerging modern nation. Nonetheless, even while Huang expressed a commitment to the idea of a revolution in poetry and incorporated modern, Western elements into his writing, he remained intimately attached to old forms and language.

His poem 'Writing a True Record of London' contains numerous allusions to the classical literary heritage: stock phrases from the poetry of the Tang lyricist Du Fu (712–770 CE), the *Shiji* (China's earliest canonical history published 1st century BCE), and the *Han shu* (the *c.* 3rd-century CE chronicle of the Han dynasty). Similarly, in the poem 'Walking in the London Fog', the poet employs a gamut of traditional words and phrases from the classical canon. This latter poem seems to allude to a dictum cited in one of Liang Qichao's writings: 'The sun never sets on the British Empire.' While this might be read as a concession to contemporary reality, it can also be seen as Huang embedding literary references into his poetry (a long-established classical convention). It is a measure of the entrenched and conservative nature of contemporary poetic taste that, to the average elite reader, the incorporation of foreign themes and place names would have been seen as an adventurous and modern departure, even without the abandonment of Chinese metrics and the recourse to allusive composition.

While literary scholars may emphasize Huang's contribution in introducing into contemporary poetry descriptions of foreign lands, cultures and technology, towards the end of his life he acknowledged his failure: 'In my youth I loved to write poetry and wildly proposed the idea of creating a new realm of poetry. However, my talent was limited, and I was not able to bring my words to fruition.' Today, Huang Zunxian is perhaps best remembered for his accomplishments as both a diplomat and a poet who expressed empathy with the plight of migrants, who criticized the hypocrisy of foreign powers, and who bewailed the weakness of his own government.

Gregory B. Lee

62. YAN FU

嚴復 (1854–1921)

POLYMATH WHO AWAKENED A GENERATION

The renowned Chinese military officer, educator, newspaper editor, translator and writer Yan Fu was born in Fuzhou, Fujian province. From his earliest years, Yan not only received instruction in medicine, the profession of both his father and his grandfather, but also became embedded in the cosmopolitan world of Fuzhou harbour. He thus combined global consciousness with a commitment to practical knowledge. In 1866, Yan matriculated into the Fuzhou Navy Yard School, where he studied navigation. He graduated with high honours in 1871. From 1877 to 1879, as part of an early cohort of overseas students, he attended the Royal Naval College, Greenwich, in London, where he studied naval command. His curriculum included mechanics, chemistry, physics, mathematics, navigation and current international military affairs. At Greenwich, Yan also had the opportunity to observe British society at first hand. He commented on the contrasts between Chinese and British ways and grew interested in the workings of Western civilization. In the summer of 1879, Yan Fu returned to China to start teaching at Fuzhou. He moved to the Northern Naval College at Tianjin the following year, and served there for about twenty years, becoming superintendent in 1893. He then served as president of Fudan University (1906–7) and Peking University (1912) – that decade, the latter became the intellectual heartland of a Westernizing cultural reform movement. Yan also directed the Qing government's Translation Bureau (1909–11).

China's humiliating defeat by Japan in 1895 prompted Yan Fu to advocate social and political reforms. The primary vehicles for his enlightenment project were translations of Western works and a newspaper, *National News Daily (Guowen bao)*, modelled after *The Times* of London. With these works, he sought to demonstrate that Western wealth and power did not lie in Western technological advances, but in the ideas and institutions that lay behind these techniques. He translated into classical Chinese Western works, notably Thomas Huxley's *Evolution and Ethics*, Adam Smith's *The Wealth of Nations*, John Stuart Mill's *On Liberty*, Herbert Spencer's *Study of Sociology*, Edward Jenks's *A History of Politics*, Montesquieu's *The Spirit of the Laws*, the first part of Mill's *System of Logic* and William Stanley Jevons's *Science Primers: Logic*, which together came to be known in Chinese as 'Eight Famous Books Translated by Yan Fu'. (He did not translate Karl Marx's works, as they were not politically in keeping with his overall project.) Yan's translations offered their own subtle modifications of the ideas of Spencer and Mill, adapting them to Chinese philosophical concepts through careful choice of equivalent language. For example, he translated Huxley's *Evolution and Ethics* as *The Theory of Heavenly Evolution (Tianyan lun)*: the Chinese name omits the 'ethics' of the original title, since in traditional Chinese philosophy *tian* 'heaven' implies both the cosmos and the source of all morality. He rendered Mill's *On Liberty* as *On the Boundary between Self and Group* (*Qunji quanjie lun*), emphasizing the importance of a balanced relationship between individual and collective.

Yan also emphasized the need to preserve Confucian ethical values – which he understood as important resources for cultivating inner, spiritual ideals – in China's social and political evolution. For Yan, human beings were unique among animals for their combination of group solidarity, personal conscience and enlightened self-interest. He encouraged Chinese people to understand natural evolution as a model through which to strengthen their virtue, wisdom and physical fitness, and to preserve them from their present crisis. Yan also criticized Mill's championing of individualism. He instead advocated for the liberal ideal of a democratic society based on the 'positive freedom' of individuals pursuing their personal interests, while guided by an enlightened elite who had virtue and wisdom instilled into them, becoming altruistic and patriotic through education. For Yan, the struggle for survival depended on the cohesion of the group, and the Chinese needed to bond themselves into the same kind of social and political unit that had enabled Western nations and Japan to

Portrait of Yan Fu, 1905. The photograph was taken in England, and bears his English signature 'Yen Fuk'.

modernize and strengthen themselves. This implied a modern nation, with laws, institutions, rites and rituals that would integrate the Chinese people into a common political endeavour. Like many of his intellectual peers, Yan was determined to synthesize two ideals: the freedom, prosperity and power exemplified by the West, and a vision of morality rooted in Confucian values. His translations exerted tremendous influence on Chinese intellectuals both in his own time and subsequently. It is said that in the late Qing and early Republican period, more than 500 memoirs were published by various educated men, and very few of them were not influenced in some way by Yan Fu's translations such as *Theory of Heavenly Evolution*.

Yan's understanding of social Darwinism convinced him that change must come through a gradual shift, not from revolution (hence his aversion to Marx). In the chaotic years after the Chinese revolution of 1911, he opposed republicanism in China and supported Yuan Shikai in the latter's attempt to restore the monarchy. In his later years, Yan rejected his earlier, positive positions regarding Western thought and turned increasingly to Confucianism and ancient Chinese culture. During this period, he also devoted himself to 'psychical research' (spiritualism, the wisdom of the soul, deities, ghosts, spirit photography, life after death and other mysterious phenomena), accepting Herbert Spencer's 'agnosticism'. Yan Fu came to believe that religion and science were not in conflict, and that psychical research could open up a new field of science. He criticized the iconoclasm of the modernizing, Westernizing May Fourth–New Culture Movement of the 1910s and 1920s, and mocked 'New Literary Revolutionaries' such as Hu Shi (1891–1962) and Chen Duxiu (1879–1942). Yan also achieved renown for his theory of translation. He emphasized three important elements in translation – 'faithfulness, expressiveness and elegance' – which became guiding principles for the practice in modern China. He was furthermore recognized in his lifetime as a poet, and posthumously as a calligrapher. Before he passed away, he designed a tomb for himself with four characters on it: *Weishi zhian* ('adjusting to the trends of the world is the only path to serenity'). This epitaph may stand as his advice to future generations of Chinese people.

Yan Fu transformed the intellectual horizons of the turbulent eras of the late Qing and early Republic, through his translations into exquisite classical Chinese of major European works of political and social science, and his mediation between such geographically and culturally remote traditions of thought.

Max K. W. Huang

63. SARAH PIKE CONGER

(1843–1932)

SURVIVOR OF THE 1900 SIEGE, FRIEND OF CIXI

Sarah Jane Pike was born in Ohio on 24 July 1843 and attended Lombard College in Illinois, an institution that her parents helped to found. While there, she made the unorthodox choice for a woman of the time to study astronomy (which meant that when she moved to Beijing in her fifties, its centuries-old imperial observatory was among her favourite places to visit). In 1866 she married Edwin H. Conger and after marriage was known as Sarah Pike Conger. She settled with her husband in Iowa, where Edwin worked as an attorney, served for a time as state treasurer, and then was elected to congress. In the 1890s, he became a diplomat, posted to first Brazil and then China. Sarah went with him to Rio de Janeiro and then, in 1898, moved on with him to Beijing, where Edwin began a stint as the chief American envoy to the Qing court. In 1900, Sarah had the most dramatic experience of her life, when she became one of more than a thousand foreigners from around the world who were trapped in the capital's Legation Quarter for fifty-five days, pinned there by a joint force of Boxer insurgents and Qing troops from 20 June until the international Eight-Nation Alliance took control of the city in the middle of August.

Before Sarah Pike Conger moved abroad, she played a significant role in temperance activities and gave birth to a son (who died young) and a daughter. She also became an early Christian Scientist and corresponded with the sect's founder Mary Baker Eddy

Photographer unknown, *Ladies and Children of the Diplomatic Corps before Going to the Audience of the Emperor and Empress Dowager*, January 1902. Silver collodion print. Freer Gallery of Art and Arthur M. Sackler Gallery Archives, Smithsonian Institution, Washington, DC.

(1821–1910). Her sojourn in the Qing empire provided her with subject matter for two books. *Letters from China* (1907), the better known one, is a collection of missives mostly written just before, during or soon after the Boxer War. It has attracted the attention of many scholars because of the details it provides about the siege, and Sarah's later leading role in, and thoughts about, an unusual diplomatic endeavour: meetings between wives of foreign envoys and Empress Dowager Cixi (1835–1908). Her second book, *Old China and Young America* (1913), was written with young readers in mind.

The Congers' Beijing household included two young women in their twenties: the couple's daughter (Laura) and a niece of Edwin's. After the siege began, the household, like many other foreigners, moved to the British Legation, the biggest Western compound and easiest to defend. It was while there that Sarah wrote the letters that have been mined most diligently by scholars for insights on this major event in Chinese international relations. Most of these letters – as well as others she wrote before the siege about Chinese customs and views of Christianity, among other topics, and the ones she wrote after the siege – were addressed to relatives at home. Some were reprinted in periodicals before they appeared in her first book.

Conger often looks severe in photographs, but this is deceptive. She was a warm, open-minded person. Proof of this came in two ways after the siege. First, in a September 1900 letter she expressed a fear that foreigners might take an 'eye for an eye' approach to China, when a spirit of Christian forgiveness was needed. She felt that, as despicable as the Boxer actions had been, it was important to remember that the movement was partly motivated by an understandable desire of Chinese people to control their own fate and their own land. The brutal campaigns of reprisal to come proved that her worry was justified. Second, she not only helped arrange the

Portrait of Mrs Conger from a report on the Boxer War published in the *Kansas City Star*, 13 July, 1900. Hoover Institution Library, Stanford University.

Xunling (1874–1943), *The Empress Dowager Cixi with Foreign Envoys' Wives* (detail), 1903–5. The detail shows Sarah Pike Conger with Cixi in the Leshou tang in the Yihe yuan (New Summer Palace). Freer Gallery of Art and Arthur M. Sackler Gallery Archives, Smithsonian Institution, Washington, DC.

meetings between wives of diplomats and Cixi that took place soon after the empress returned to Beijing from her temporary exile in Xi'an at the close of the siege, but also grew to feel affection for that powerful woman who had backed the Boxers and hence had played a key role in imperilling the lives of the Congers.

It is worth noting that Sarah Conger, if largely forgotten now, was for a while extremely famous. For a time during the summer of 1900, she might have been the most talked about – and worried about – woman in America. She was also one of the most widely recognized, since images of her face appeared in newspapers regularly. What brought her this fame was not anything Sarah did, but rather the belief among many people, for about two weeks that summer, that she had been murdered, along with the other members of her household and indeed all of Beijing's foreigners. Photographs and drawings of her appeared on the front pages of many newspapers accompanying stories about an alleged late June or early July Boxer massacre that made the capital's streets run red with foreign blood. Large portraits of supposed victims ran in the press and obituary-like accounts of the lives of these foreigners accompanied the images, sometimes noting that it was not certain they were dead. On the American side of the Atlantic, the Congers got more attention than any other victims, and memorial services were planned for them. In the Midwest, more than a thousand Christian Scientists gathered in a prayer meeting to beseech God specifically to spare Sarah. Meanwhile, in London, where newspapers had focused more on British imagined victims such as Edwin Conger's counterpart Sir Claude MacDonald and his family, a date was set for a mass funeral at St Paul's. After weeks when the Legation Quarter was cut off from communication with the outside world, Edwin managed to get word out that there had been no massacre. The memorial services were cancelled – or, rather, in the St Paul's case, postponed, as fear remained that, even though there had been no early July massacre, an actual massacre could still take place before the Eight-Nation Alliance reached Beijing. (It did not.)

Sarah's letters from the siege express the belief that God will protect her from harm, but not surprisingly they have an anxious tone. Once the siege is lifted, she naturally sounds happier. The arrival of the Alliance put an end to the threat to the lives of all members of the Conger household, and also led to Laura Conger and her cousin meeting soldiers who would soon become their husbands.

After the siege, Sarah hoped that foreigners would come to empathize more with China's people, and the Qing court would realize it should not have backed the Boxers. The first goal led her to write her second book, long after leaving China; the second is evident in her efforts, before she departed, to engage with the Empress Dowager and other women of the Qing. She became convinced the empress realized the errors of her ways in 1900, and when, years later, news reached Sarah that the empress had died, she expressed deep sadness at the loss of someone she thought a dear friend.

Jeffrey Wasserstrom

64. ZHANG TAIYAN

章太炎 (1869–1936)

PHILOLOGIST, REVOLUTIONARY, FOUNDER OF NATIONAL LEARNING

Zhang Taiyan (also Zhang Binglin) is most famous for his denunciations of the Manchu minority who ruled the Qing dynasty. However, he was also a scholar of 'national learning' (study of a Chinese national heritage), a revolutionary and a Buddhist.

Zhang was born on 20 January 1869, in Yuhang prefecture, Zhejiang (south-east China). He later recollected that some of his earliest influences came from his maternal grandfather, Zhu Youqian, who taught him to read the Chinese classics. Zhang grew up and came of age in an era in which the Qing dynasty's Han Chinese minority were renewing their sense of the ethnic 'otherness' from their Qing Manchu rulers, in the context of intensifying socio-economic tensions. In his *Autobiography*, Zhang explains that, at a young age, he learned about the distinction between the Manchus

Photograph of Zhang Taiyan
(1869–1936) in Tokyo,
c. 1906–1911.

and the Han, and describes how moved he was when reading about the Ming (1368–1644), the last ethnically Han dynasty to rule China. He was especially impressed by 'Ming loyalists': scholars born during the Ming, whose lives and careers also stretched into the period of Manchu rule (1644–1912), and yet who constantly dreamed of a return to the Ming. Zhang was influenced in particular by Gu Yanwu (1613–1682) and Huang Zongxi (1610–1695), both well-known for advocating local autonomy in the context of imperial government.

Although early in his life Zhang immersed himself in classical learning and proved a precocious student, he never succeeded in passing the official examinations, which would have secured for him a job in the government. In 1883, when Zhang was fourteen years old, his father told him to take the local district examinations, but Zhang was unable to do so due to a fit of epilepsy a few minutes prior to the test. Zhang would never again take imperial examinations, and some suggest that Zhang's later, radical criticism of the examination system and imperial government was related to this early experience. In the years that followed, Zhang continued to study the classics, without aiming to take the examinations (preparation for which generally channelled candidates towards intellectual conformism); this allowed him the intellectual freedom to mobilize classical ideas against existing structures of power.

To understand the power structures that Zhang criticized, we must briefly mention some of the setbacks that the Qing dynasty faced in the mid-19th century. Beginning with the First Opium War (1839–42), Qing China was defeated in successive conflicts with Western powers. Although this fostered a sense of technological inferiority to the West, government officials still did not want to respond by fundamentally altering their culture. The senior statesman Zhang Zhidong (1837–1909) pithily expressed this 'conservative modernization' approach in his formulation 'Chinese learning as substance, Western learning as application' (*Zhongti xiyong*). This idea held that Western technologies could be imported, but that the Chinese Confucian system of culture and government should remain at its core. The approach was realized in the Self-Strengthening Movement of the 1860s to 1890s, during which staunchly Confucian officials such as Zeng Guofan (1811–1872) oversaw the introduction of Western military and industrial technologies into China.

The validity of this policy was fundamentally challenged after 1895, when China lost the Sino-Japanese War. This defeat discredited much of the Self-Strengthening project, and generated a powerful sense of national crisis, for Chinese intellectuals for centuries had viewed Japan as a cultural tributary, or junior partner. After the Sino-Japanese War, Chinese thinkers sought more radical ways of catching up with the politically and militarily strong nations of Western Europe and Japan. This new brand of radical late Qing politics split between reformers and revolutionaries. Reformers like Kang Youwei (1858–1927) attempted to modernize politics from within the Qing imperial system and transform China into a constitutional monarchy. Zhang Taiyan and his fractious, revolutionary peers, on the other hand, aimed to overthrow the Manchu-led Qing dynasty and create a republic based on their image of Western political systems. Their ideal of a republic entailed overcoming the dynastic system and developing Western-style institutions including parliaments. In this context, Zhang published a famous critique of Confucius.

In 1903, Zhang wrote an approving preface to an inflammatory, anti-Manchu pamphlet called *The Revolutionary Army*, by a young revolutionary called Zou Rong (1885–1905). A Shanghai extraterritorial court tried and sentenced Zhang to three years' imprisonment and Zou to two (if they had been tried by a Qing court, they would surely have been executed). Zou died in prison in 1905, but Zhang was able to survive the experience through, he claimed, avidly reading Yogācāra Buddhist texts. During his years in jail, Zhang began to question narratives of evolution and develop instead a theory of violent anti-Manchu revolution that stressed the cultural particularity of the path taken by the (Chinese) nation, rather than subscribing to a single model of universal progress. In other words, he argued that the Chinese needed to return to a specific identity, namely a pre-Qing Han identity, rather than affirm a universal, evolutionary vision of history. For Zhang, revolution was about return rather than progress. Parallel to this belief, he championed the idea of 'national learning', namely repackaging Chinese history and culture into a cohesive body of knowledge to provoke patriotism.

After Zhang was released from prison, in 1906, he fled to Japan and began drawing on Yogācāra Buddhism to formulate a critique of modernity and linear time. This was part of his effort to rethink the significance of Chinese traditional thought, by examining non-Confucian resources, such as Buddhism and Daoism. In these writings, Zhang used concepts such as karma to argue that history does not inevitably progress to greater levels of development, but rather that the good and bad progress equally. In one of his most famous texts, *A Discussion of the Equalization of Things*, first published in 1910, Zhang synthesized Buddhism and the Daoist philosophy of Zhuangzi to formulate an alternative theory of equality and difference in both politics and philosophy. Zhang professed not only an equality between all human beings, but of all things, inanimate and animate (which seems prescient given concerns about the environment today). At the human level, he argued that freedom must be both individual and collective: individuals must be allowed to flourish for the well-being of the collective. Such a world requires institutions different from the modern capitalist nation state and for this reason, Zhang penned attacks on state power – in this he differed from reformers such as Yan Fu (1854–1921) and Liang Qichao (1873–1929), who believed passionately in the need for a strong, unified state. However, he also saw the necessity of a collective anti-colonial nationalism to resist imperialism wherever it existed.

After the 1911 Revolution, Zhang continued to write and was respected as a scholar of national learning until 1936, when he died of nasopharyngeal cancer. During most of his life he made a living by teaching about national learning, editing journals such as the *People's Journal* (published in Tokyo) and briefly advising officials during the Republic. However, like many famous late Qing intellectuals after the founding of the Republic, he was sometimes seen as an older, conservative voice, out of step with modern politics. Nonetheless, his ideas about national learning, his readings of classics and his critique of modernity continued to influence subsequent generations. Most famously, Lu Xun (1881–1936) – the 'father of modern Chinese literature' – continued Zhang's legacy by being both critical of mainstream readings of the Chinese tradition and developing a critical stance towards (Western) modernity. Both men excavated neglected traditions in China to formulate a new global culture. This scepticism towards both established Chinese values and Western ones accounts for their originality, but also makes them hard to categorize within Chinese intellectual history.

Viren Murthy

65. NAITŌ KONAN

内藤湖南 (1866–1934)

FAMOUS AND CONTROVERSIAL JAPANESE
HISTORIAN OF CHINA

Naitō Konan was born Naitō Torajirō into a scholarly family in northern Honshū, Japan. His father had chosen his son's given name to match that of his personal hero, the famed rebel Yoshida Shōin, or Torajirō (1830–1859), also born in the year of the tiger, but three cycles earlier. (Yoshida's rebellion was part of his domain's opposition to the shogunate's 'appeasement' of the West following the arrival in 1853 of American Commander Matthew Perry's (1794–1858) 'black ships' to demand trade concessions from Japan.) As a young man, Naitō received much the same sort of education that someone of a comparable scholarly family in China would have received, mastering the Chinese classics and commentaries at a relatively young age. Meanwhile, he was also exposed to the parallel Japanese tradition. But the route into government service in the Meiji government was closed off to him because the new regime was dominated by a small number of domains which had engineered the Restoration, and his domain was not among them. After teaching for a short period, in the 1890s, he turned to the vibrant press, which was at that time prominently anti-government.

Naitō wrote extensively for the *Ōsaka asahi shinbun* and other newspapers and magazines, including the pro-Buddhist *Meikyō shinshi* and later *Nihonjin*, on a wide range of political and cultural topics. In the mid-1890s he completed his first book, *Historical Discussion of Modern Scholarship*, published in 1897, the same year that he published his first volume on a Chinese subject, *Zhuge Liang*, about the eponymous early medieval statesman and military strategist. That year he also set out to take on a year-long job in Japan's new (after the defeat of China in the Sino-Japanese War of 1894–95) colony of Taiwan as editor of the daily *Taiwan nippō*.

As his speciality in journalism as well as book-length publishing was China-oriented, his work caught the eye of the Faculty of Letters at Japan's Second National University in Kyoto. In 1906 he was invited to join the new Department of East Asian Studies there and assume its first chair. Since he had never attended university himself, there was an issue in that he had no advanced degrees. When this was brought to the attention of the Ministry of Education in Tokyo, the response was 'even Confucius would need to have graduated from the Imperial University' (there was only one at the time, in Tokyo) to hold the position for which he had been nominated. So, he promptly penned a thesis, and the following year began teaching.

Most humanities scholars at the time in Japan concentrated their attention on the past and looked askance at journalism and contemporary commentary. Coming

Photograph of Naitō Konan in his home garden, 9 April 1934. Published in *Toyo Bijutsu*, vol. 21, 1935.

from that world, however, Naitō continued, on occasion, to write for the press, and until the end of his life remained attentive to contemporary political and cultural events. He thus delivered a series of lectures on the fall of the Qing dynasty in 1911, but, as he was accustomed, related contemporary events to history, often going back many centuries to attempt to make sense of the present day. It was in this lecture series that Naitō first outlined his thesis that the modern era in Chinese history dated (roughly) to the start of the Song dynasty in the late tenth century. That China had entered modernity almost a millennium before the 1911 Revolution was a theory not at all current at the time. He would spend the rest of his life shoring it up from numerous historical perspectives – and his students would carry on these tasks for another generation.

What did he mean, then, by 'modern'? He argued that the collapse of the Qing in 1911–12 was not merely the end of a dynasty, as had happened many times before, but also the end of the dynastic form of government in China. The advent of the Song had marked the end of aristocracy, as none of the great aristocratic houses preceding it survived thereafter. He pictured this earlier transition as the end of aristocracy and its replacement with monarchical autocracy – that is, beginning with the Song, the emperor had no impediments from fellow aristocrats to hamper his authoritarian style. But, interestingly, this also meant, in Naitō's reasoning, that the common people began to emerge and partake in government and culture. Without aristocrats to staff a bureaucracy and run the empire, the emperor now needed a new source of talent, and the examination system (until then almost entirely for aristocrats) was now open (and in theory meritocratic) for virtually all males. Naitō demonstrated how in numerous areas of culture, there was an increasingly wide array of commoners writing, painting, composing, and in many other ways contributing to intellectual life.

The 1911 Revolution, he opined, brought monarchical autocracy to an end, and he foresaw the development of a republic in China, as so many Chinese desired. He also associated the contemporary era with an increasing lack of interest in politics; this would create trouble, especially posthumously in the wake of World War II, as he had occasionally suggested that China should relinquish governmental control to an international body and concentrate on 'culture'. His unilinear view of history held that when a society entered modernity (as, he believed, China's had done a millennium earlier), politics and culture went in different directions: China, since the Song, had developed separate geographical centres for politics and culture (in the late Qing, for example, the political capital was in Beijing, while the heartland of cultural production was in Jiangnan, on the east coast). According to Naitō, by the early 20th century, China was thus far ahead of the rest of the world, and its primary concern should be cultural development. Concern with politics was for countries that lagged behind China's stage of development. He often claimed that the Western world was historically far behind China, based on this theoretical historical trajectory along which, he believed, all national–cultural entities travel. He also placed Japan behind China.

Many Chinese people in the 1910s and 1920s were deeply angered by Japan's actions on the Asian mainland, and anti-Japanese boycotts and demonstrations became a regular part of life. This not only dismayed Naitō, as he always imagined China and Japan marching forward together and being mutually reliant; it also incensed him and he condemned those he saw as the student rabble-rousers behind the demonstrations who, he believed, did not know their own nation's history and culture.

At the very end of his life, after retiring from Kyoto University, he approvingly wrote several pieces about the newly established Japanese-sponsored state of Manchukuo, in the old Manchurian homeland of the Qing, from which Japan would launch full-scale war on Asia between the 1930s and 1940s. He even entertained the Chinese prime minister of that puppet state at his retirement home. This would not win him accolades, although he did at the time make clear that this new state should sever all ties to the Japanese military. In fact, Manchukuo was largely propped up by the Guandong Army – the section of the Japanese military that oversaw the Japanese occupation of north-east China – making his admonition all but impossible.

Naitō Konan is now best remembered for his thesis on the long-range periodization of Chinese history and modernity, a view that has influenced several generations of scholars in Japan, China and the West.

Joshua A. Fogel

6

BUSINESS PEOPLE

COMMODITY TRADERS, FINANCIERS, ENTREPRENEURS AND MEDIA TYCOONS

At the end of the 18th century, Qing China was one of the largest, most prosperous and commercialized empires in the world. A lazy stereotype arguably still exists in the West that 'Confucian' Chinese culture was inimical to, and suppressed, business enterprise. The economic history of the 19th century robustly rebuts that view.

It must be acknowledged, however, that the Qing empire faced redoubtable economic challenges at the start of the 19th century. The empire was approaching its limits, as demographic explosion led to fierce competition for work and resources, ecological degradation, price rises, bureaucratic chaos and corruption. State finances had been run down by the extravagance of the Qianlong emperor (r. 1736–1795), and his expensive taste for military campaigns. A burgeoning culture of official corruption helped drive the eruption of the Jiaqing reign's first major crisis, the White Lotus Rebellion. Its suppression cost the Qing treasury some 120 million ounces of silver – two and a half times annual income during the Qianlong reign. The state's finances never fully recovered, battered even further by yet larger scale domestic insurrections later in the 19th century, and by the acquisitive aggression of European and Japanese powers. The opium trade facilitated and driven by British interests in India, especially, fuelled drug consumption in China that helped drain the country of silver. The first two conflicts (the Opium Wars) between the Qing and foreign powers set the principle by which the Qing treasury would have to pay out vast indemnities simply because they had lost a war. Particularly from the 1880s, when such indemnities became increasingly punitive, the growing indebtedness of the Qing state jeopardized necessary but expensive reform and modernization. The terms of treaties from 1842 onwards also prevented the Qing government from setting its own tariffs and enabled Western nation states to dump surplus manufactures on China, to the detriment of domestic industrialization.

The majority of the population – around 94 per cent – lived in the countryside, and many lived a precarious, hand-to-mouth existence. Rural populations suffered appallingly from the devastation caused by conflicts such as the Taiping Civil War (1851–64) and by natural disasters such as floods, droughts and the spread of epidemic disease.

But great private wealth existed in other parts of the late Qing economy: above all, in trade and banking. In the 1830s, China was home to the wealthiest man in the world, the leading Canton (Guangzhou) trader with European merchants, Wu Bingjian. The careers of Wu and many other prosperous merchants during the rest of the century illuminated the profits to be made through international collaborations. Even before the First Opium War (1839–42), the port of Canton hosted thriving cosmopolitan communities of traders (Indians, Europeans, Americans). With the opening of Shanghai and other treaty ports after 1842, these communities grew in number and wealth. Baghdadi Jewish businessmen like Silas Hardoon made their fortunes in Shanghai, and apprenticed Chinese merchants who would become successful in their own right.

In the second half of the 19th century, modern technology and transport (electricity, lithography, trains, steamships) transformed eastern coastal cities and longstanding manufacturing industries such as publishing, tea, porcelain and silk. Banking and financial services boomed. Urbanization increased, swollen by refugees fleeing civil violence. Thanks partly to state sponsorship, industrialization also intensified in the closing decades of the 19th century. Chinese and non-Chinese entrepreneurs built new businesses, both in traditional industries and in new enterprises – such as Ernest Major and Di Baoxian in the commercial press – employing new technologies and materials. The harsh terms of the 1895 Treaty of Shimonoseki have often been seen as exemplifying Japanese military, political and economic aggression towards China. But more beneficial economic and cultural relations between the two countries were also possible, embodied by men like Kishida Ginkō.

As had been the case for centuries, control of the salt trade and its monopolies remained big business. This industry was an important source of tax revenue for the government and a major opportunity for entrepreneurial landowners to make substantial profits. Hu Xueyan began his career as a salt merchant but rose to become one of the century's most celebrated banking innovators, integrating China into global financial markets (and negotiating foreign loans for the Qing, thereby funding wars that safeguarded the empire from disintegration). Remarkable women – such as Zhou Ying (Widow Anwu) – challenged conventions preventing female participation in public life, to manage (with great skill and success) sprawling, multiregional business empires.

Despite grotesque disparities between the richest and poorest, the wealthy of 19th-century Qing society were also capable of impressively dynamic organization and mobilization. The early 1800s saw the emergence of the 'benevolent hall', a new kind of philanthropic organization, outside government control, sponsored by businessmen. They offered emergency aid, in times of natural disasters or war, in an effort to alleviate the most egregious sufferings of the urban poor. In a context of demographic explosion and chronic under-government, such individuals provided community support and infrastructure – banks, factories, schools, hospitals, disaster relief – beyond that offered by the state. **JHH**

66. WU BINGJIAN

伍秉鑑 (1769–1843)

WEALTHIEST MAN IN THE WORLD IN THE 1830s

Wu Bingjian, better known in the west as 'Houqua', or sometimes 'Howqua', was the most successful Chinese merchant of his day. As leader of the Cohong (Gonghang), the guild of Chinese traders that had been authorized in the late 18th century by the Qing court to oversee trade with Western merchants at Canton (Guangzhou), he was once the richest man in the world. In 1834, Wu's personal wealth was estimated at 26 million Mexican silver dollars (£6.24 million then, around £680 million today). To put this wealth in perspective, the contemporary European financier Nathan Rothschild held capital equivalent to US $5.3 million (around £1.06 million) in 1828. Wu's extraordinary ability to maintain a complex balance between his business interests, the Qing court and his Western partners, made him the most important player in Western countries' trade with China for over half a century.

Wu Bingjian was born in Canton in 1769, a sixth-generation member of the Wu family. His ancestors were originally from Fujian but moved to Canton at the beginning of the Qing period to become merchants. In 1757, a series of official Qing court policies made Canton the sole port city for European traders, restricting the latter to dealings with a monopolistic guild of Chinese merchants known as the 'Hong'; this greatly increased commercial opportunities for Hong merchant families like the Wus. The family already featured prominently in the records of European trading companies, especially those of the British East India Company (EIC), and in 1788 the nineteen-year-old Bingjian started trading with the EIC himself. On taking charge of the family business in 1801 after his brother's death, he further consolidated his relationship with the EIC. As both supplier of goods and provider of finance, he became the Company's most important partner in China. By the 1820s, Wu Bingjian was already the primary supplier of capital to the EIC, as well as the most regular lender of capital to other Hong merchants, who were often in debt to their Western trading partners.

When Americans joined the China trade in 1784, Wu further diversified his business, becoming the pivotal figure within the globalized China trade. Through his remarkable acumen in identifying profitable opportunities, he redirected his goods and capital to US markets. He not only became the dominant seller of goods to American traders, but also managed to invest in US financial markets. Over time, his wealth was invested in American railways through both John Murray Forbes and Robert Forbes, who were partners in the opium trading house Russell & Co. By the early 1830s, Wu had also set up independent trade networks in India with Parsi merchants, selling Chinese silk and cassia (Chinese cinnamon) – the latter was used in medicine, for flavouring tea, and in cookery.

Wu made huge efforts to sustain close ties with his American contemporaries, inviting them to his beautiful gardens on the south bank of Canton's Pearl River, as well as presenting portraits of himself as gifts to his most important long-distance trade partners. Both his gardens and his portraits became iconic of the China trade, the latter treated as treasured souvenirs by Western visitors to China in the first decades of the 19th century.

An oil painting in the Metropolitan Museum of Art, *Houqua*, represents an example of Wu Bingjian's widely circulated image. The portrait was originally attributed to George Chinnery (1774–1852), an English portrait and landscape painter who spent most of his life in Asia, especially in Macao, not far from the trading centre at Canton. This was because the composition and style are very similar to Chinnery's portrait of Wu that was exhibited in the Royal Academy in 1831 and is now housed in the HSBC collection in Hong Kong. Chinnery's depiction (to 19th-century British eyes, an exotic subject) in a European style captivated audiences beyond the Royal Academy exhibition, and similar depictions of Wu began to proliferate soon after.

Possibly by Esther Speakman (1823–1875), in the style of George Chinnery (1774–1852), *Houqua. c.* 1843. Oil on canvas. Height 63.5 cm, width 47.3 cm. The Metropolitan Museum of Art, New York.

The portrait in the Metropolitan Museum of Art is one of many such variants. In a style characteristic of Chinnery compositions, Wu is depicted seated in a nicely furnished area, wearing formal Hong merchant attire. His gaze is directed towards the viewer, with his right leg crossed over the left. The elaborate details of the background, such as the sophisticated carved wooden frame, the fine incense burner on his right, the decorative lantern and his red Mandarin cap, project his enormous wealth and status. Wu became the most famous Chinese merchant of his day not just for his business acumen, but also because many similar portraits of him were distributed across the United States. Those portraits might have been copied overseas without Wu's knowledge, but made him a visually familiar and therefore an accessible figure in Western commerce and media. A writer for *The Australian* wrote, 'His name was a symbol of the integrity of the Chinese, a mark of genuineness and excellence that few traders could do without.' (Wu was particularly popular among Western traders for offering assistance to foreign merchants who 'found themselves financially embarrassed'.)

At the outbreak of the First Opium War in 1839, Wu actively solicited donations and funded the construction of fortresses and warships to defend Canton. In 1841, he donated an American ship and 260,000 taels of silver (about $7 million in contemporary terms) to support the Qing military effort. A year later, British troops defeated the Qing government and the Canton system collapsed. Defeat in the First Opium War ended the Hong merchants' trade monopoly and forced China to open new ports along the south and east coasts. By the provisions of the Treaty of Nanjing that concluded the First Opium War, Qing China was required to pay Britain a large indemnity, to which Wu once more made substantial contributions. He died soon after the end of the First Opium War, at the age of seventy-four, his name still revered by his Western business partners. After his death in 1843, a 582-ton clipper ship was named after him, and his wax effigy was displayed at Madame Tussaud's in London, where for decades he remained the only Asian individual featured.

Tang Hui

67. SIR JAMSETJEE JEJEEBHOY

(1783–1859)

PARSI-INDIAN BUSINESSMAN AND PHILANTHROPIST

The portrait shown below presents the wealthy 19th-century Indian Parsi businessman, Sir Jamsetjee Jejeebhoy, with his Chinese secretary at his side. That a merchant in Bombay (Mumbai) should have had in his employ a Chinese secretary testifies to the voluminous trading links between India and China in that era. These trading links contributed in no small measure to the globalization of the Chinese economy.

They also played a major role in the growth and development of Bombay as India's premier commercial and later industrial centre.

It is perhaps not well known that scores of Indian merchants and firms thronged the Canton–Macau region from the late 18th to the mid-19th centuries, engaged in a lucrative trade based mainly on the export of raw cotton and opium from India. Jamsetjee Jejeebhoy was one of the most successful among them, establishing the fabulously wealthy firm of Jamsetjee Jejeebhoy & Sons. Born in the western Indian town of Navsari in 1783, Jamsetjee Jejeebhoy arrived in Bombay in his teens to join his uncle's bottle-selling business. His move to British-controlled Bombay coincided with the upturn in the trade with China from that port. Many aspiring young men, particularly from the enterprising Parsi community, embarked on risky journeys to the China coast in the hope of making quick profits. Acting as an agent for his uncle, Jamsetjee sailed on his first voyage to China in 1799. By 1806, he had completed five trips to China, in quick succession. It was his fourth voyage, however, that proved to be most significant for his career as a China trader. As a result of the Napoleonic Wars, the ship was seized by the French and diverted in the opposite direction, towards Africa. In the course of the extended journey, Jamsetjee became friends with the young assistant ship's surgeon, William Jardine (1784–1843), who later became one of the most formidable British opium merchants on the China coast.

After 1806, Jamsetjee Jejeebhoy did not venture to China himself but directed his thriving and expanding commercial empire from Bombay. His friendship with Jardine evolved into a long-lasting and successful partnership between his firm in Bombay and what later became Jardine, Matheson & Co. By the second decade of the 19th century, the raw cotton trade between India and China entered a period of stagnation and was overtaken by the trade in opium. Unlike the Patna variety of opium from eastern India, which was grown under the monopoly control of the British East India Company, the production and distribution of Malwa opium from western India was largely in the hands of private Indian cultivators and traders. A large number of merchants and speculators from Bombay, big and small, engaged in the export of Malwa opium to China through Jamsetjee Jejeebhoy's firm. Because of Jamsetjee's dominant position in the trade, about a third of the total opium shipped from Bombay was consigned to his partners at Canton, Jardine, Matheson & Co. In its heyday, his business owned a fleet of ships, which were a familiar sight in the coastal waters off the Canton–Macau region.

Apart from his close connection with William Jardine, Jamsetjee also enjoyed a personal connection with the famous Houqua, or Wu Bingjian (1769–1843), the richest and most powerful of the Chinese 'Hong merchants' who dominated the trade out of the port of Canton (Guangzhou) in the early decades of the 19th century. Jamsetjee carried on a regular correspondence with Houqua, and at one time even engaged in the sale of cassia and pearls on his behalf in Bombay. On Houqua's death, Jamsetjee wrote to his son thanking him for gifting him two portraits of his father.

George Chinnery (1774–1852), *Portrait of Sir Jamsetjee Jejeebhoy with his Chinese Secretary*, n.d.

Parsi merchants like Jamsetjee Jejeebhoy were also responsible for developing a taste for Chinese art and fine products among the elite of Bombay and other parts of India. Their ships often carried Chinese silks, porcelain, furniture and other such items on their return journeys to Bombay. Chinese textiles and embroidery were particularly favoured by Indian customers and gave rise to the characteristic heavily embroidered *gara* sarees worn by Parsi women. Jamsetjee is further believed to have taken the initiative to send weavers from the textile city of Surat in western India to China to learn the art of silk weaving from the masters there. This was the genesis of the *tanchoi* silk weave made famous later by the weavers of Varanasi.

Although Jamsetjee made his fortune from the China trade, and particularly from the illicit trade in opium, in India today he is better remembered for his philanthropy there, and as the founder of some of Bombay's most iconic institutions such as the Sir J. J. Hospital and the Sir J. J. School of Art. His enormous contributions to the development of the city's infrastructure in the 19th century have earned him recognition as one of the most important builders of modern Bombay.

Madhavi Thampi

68. HU XUEYAN

胡雪巖 (1823–1885)

FINANCIER AND MERCHANT

A banking giant collapses, triggering a monumental crisis that paralyses trade, destroys livelihoods and brings the financial system to its knees. It is not New York 2008, but Shanghai 1883. The great Qing banker, the 'Rothschild of China', Hu Xueyan, has failed to the tune of 28 million silver taels, equivalent to £796 million today. To put this figure in context, the reserves of the Qing's Board of Revenue Silver Treasury were only 15.6 million taels at the time.

Financial mavericks are not associated with dynastic China, much less the beleaguered Qing teetering on the brink of collapse in the second half of the 19th century. But the rise and fall of Hu Xueyan (also called Hu Guangyong) is the stuff of legends in China. Without Hu's financial help, the Western Expedition (1867–81) to pacify the north-west and reconquer Xinjiang would probably not have been possible. This was the last imperial campaign of the Qing, and its success saved the empire from dissolution. The resultant honours heaped on Hu earned him the soubriquet the 'Red Hat Merchant', a reference to his dual status as official (distinguished as such by a ruby hat finial) and merchant. In contemporary China, where to get rich is still glorious and entrepreneurs must tread the line between commercial success and official scrutiny, Hu Xueyan has found a new following, thanks to a steady stream of novels and magazine articles, a play, an opera and three major television dramatizations of his life. Ordinary people and the new elite alike identify with Hu Xueyan, because his is a tale of the modern Chinese dream.

The origins of the Red Hat Merchant are obscure; even his birthplace is disputed by the rival south-eastern provinces of Anhui and Zhejiang, which both claim him as their own. The Qing chronicler Chen Daiqing (n.d.) describes how, as a street runner for a bank in Hangzhou, the provincial capital of Zhejiang, Hu gave 500 taels he had just collected for the bank to a poor scholar who did not have the money to purchase an official post. The man turned out to be Wang Youling (1810–1861), who would become the governor of Zhejiang and reward his friend by depositing the official funds of the province in Hu's bank. In a magazine article of 1923, on the other hand, Hu's great-grandson, the painter Hu Yaguang (1901–1986), states that his forebear was apprenticed to a bank whose owner had no sons; upon seeing that Hu was hard-working and resourceful, the owner left him the bank when he died. Whichever account may be correct, and there are others, by the time of Wang Youling's death by his own hand as the Taiping army entered Hangzhou in December 1861, Hu Xueyan was already a well-known 'member of the gentry' of the city and held the official title of *daotai* of Jiangxi province.

Wang's successor was the great general Zuo Zongtang (1812–1885), whose close association with Hu Xueyan would be an important factor in both men's ascent over the next twenty years. This relationship has typically been reduced to one of patronage, where the merchant relied on the official for favour and protection from state exaction. Yet, memorials to the throne and letters to Hu from Zuo reveal the extent to which the Qing government came to rely on bankers and merchants to navigate the modern world dominated by international trade and finance. Between 1867 and

Posthumous portrait of Hu Xueyan painted by Hu Yaguang which appeared in volume 10 of *Banyue* ('The Half Moon') in 1923, the bimonthly literary magazine edited by Zhou Shoujuan (1895–1968).

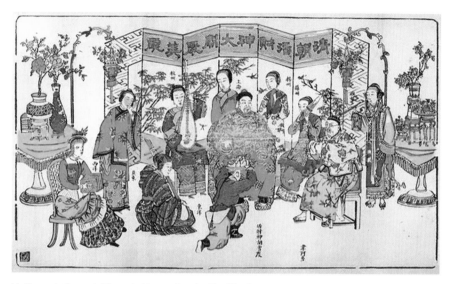

Hu Xueyan is the central figure in this popular print *The Qing Dynasty's Living God of Wealth Opens the Company of Beauties Hall*, Shanghai, c.1900. H. 28 cm, W 48.8 cm. SOAS Library, London.

1881, Hu was given unprecedented powers to negotiate and contract on behalf of the Qing government a series of foreign loans totalling 15.95 million taels from Western lenders including the Hongkong and Shanghai Banking Corporation and Jardine, Matheson. Time and again, the Qing court's own documents describe the loans as a last resort, without which it would not have been able to finance the Western Expedition. The loans were a watershed in Chinese history. Longstanding fiscal principles had prohibited public borrowing, such that sovereign debt, the mainstay of Western public finance, simply did not exist in Qing China. Bonds on Hu's loans were quickly snapped up in markets in London, Hong Kong and Shanghai. For the first time, the Qing could raise money on the international market. In recognition of Hu's contribution, which was deemed to be 'no different to that of a front-line general', the throne granted him the exceptional honour of a yellow riding jacket (*huang magua*). Traditionally bestowed upon the highest officials in the land for outstanding military achievement, this distinction now cemented Hu's position as its leading financier.

Lending to the imperial government was a lucrative business with interest rates hitting 15 per cent per annum, and foreign firms had the monopoly. In response, Hu set up the first joint-stock bank in China, ostensibly to mobilize domestic capital to rival foreign money, in a fit of national fervour. But in reality, the new bank was an investment vehicle for Hu's colossal wealth, which came from the diverse range of concerns that made up his business empire. In the 1878 government loan for 3.5 million taels, Hu's bank provided half the funds, while the Hongkong and Shanghai Banking Corporation supplied the rest. His banking interests, which were the linchpin of his operations, extended far beyond the niche activities of public borrowing, to include commercial lending, collection of customs revenue, remittance of official funds, exchange operations, and looking after the personal fortunes of the great and the good, including Prince Gong and Grand Secretary Wen Yu (d. 1884). Liu Bingzhang (1826–1905), the governor of Zhejiang at the time of Hu's bankruptcy, remarked that Hu had banks and pawnshops in practically 'every province and port' in the dominion.

It was his dealings on the silk market that proved to be Hu's undoing. In an audacious move, he staged an attempt to corner the world's largest export market in silk. For three years, from 1880 to 1883, he propped up the price of raw silk on the Shanghai market by continuously buying and hoarding export-grade silk, much to the ire of Western merchants, who had previously dominated the trade. In the end, a bumper Italian crop provided his rivals with an alternative source of silk and caused prices to fall precipitously. Hu was forced to dispose of his entire holding at a huge loss. A perfect storm gathered, as news of the disaster spread, and depositors flocked to his banks to withdraw their money. The effects of the collapse of his banks were so widespread and devastating that they triggered the first major financial crisis in modern Chinese history.

The authorities acted with uncommon speed, immediately stripping Hu of his official rank. An ensuing witch-hunt used trumped-up charges of embezzlement of public funds to confiscate all his remaining assets. A final blow was attempted on 18 December 1885, when the Board of Revenue petitioned the emperor to take him into custody for sentencing, but in fact the Red Hat Merchant had died twelve days earlier.

Zhiqing Hu

69. WIDOW ANWU

安吴寡婦 (1869–1908)

THE MOST SUCCESSFUL BUSINESSWOMAN IN LATE QING CHINA

A girl born in 1869 into the Zhou family of Luqiao village in Shaanxi province grew up to become one of the most successful businesswomen in Chinese history. Yet, despite her remarkable achievements, very little information about her life can be found in official written sources. We can only piece together sporadic mentions of her in local gazetteers, later personal writings and popular histories to get a fuller picture of this remarkable woman.

Although local gazetteers referred to her as Madame Wuzhou after her marriage, or Widow Anwu after her husband died, she came to be widely known in popular culture as Zhou Ying. During the Qianlong (r. 1736–1795) and Jiaqing (r. 1796–1820) periods, the Zhou family had made a fortune from porcelain production and the salt trade in Jiangxi. However, by the time of Zhou Ying's birth, they had lost much of their wealth following the Muslim wars (1862–1873) that wreaked havoc on the economy of Shaanxi and its surrounding areas. Zhou Ying's parents died when she was young. She was brought up by her elder brother and was betrothed to Wu Pin (d. c. 1885), the son of a wealthy and prominent family based in a neighbouring town. Wu Pin's father Wu Weiwen (1830–1876) was a successful salt merchant. By buying up hundreds of *yanyin* (certificates that the government sold to merchants allowing them to make and sell salt in designated areas), Wu Weiwen had ended up controlling the salt monopolies in the eastern provinces of Jiangsu, Anhui and Jiangxi. Like many of his peers, he attempted to turn his wealth into political power by gaining official posts through purchase or generous donation to local government. As his only son, Wu Pin was also granted an official post in recognition of these philanthropic activities. Zhou Ying was married to Wu Pin at the age of sixteen. He was then seriously ill, and the hope was that the wedding would dispel his illness and hasten his recovery. Unfortunately, this did not come to pass, and Wu died ten days after the marriage, leaving Zhou Ying a young widow.

As Wu Pin died childless, his widow adopted a boy from her husband's lineage as heir, which legitimized her rights to manage the household's affairs, including interests in the salt business in the east and retail shops and banks in the north-west. The Wu family had been in decline since the death of Wu Weiwen, and by the time Zhou Ying succeeded her husband as the head of household, some of their business interests were on the verge of collapse. There is no written record of how she survived the crisis and revitalized the Wu family fortunes. The epitaph on two burial tablets for Zhou Ying – written by Zhu Yifan (1867–1937), tutor to the last emperor – describe her as a wise, meticulous and diligent woman, with strong commercial acumen, who knew her employees well enough to assign jobs commensurate with their abilities. These excellent qualities won her the respect of her staff, as well as attracting capable and talented assistants. In one of the many stories about Zhou Ying told through generations, she entrusted – against the advice of others – the family tea business in Gansu to a professional tea maker called Deng Jiantang, whose improvements to the method of making brick tea made the Wu family the largest tea producer and trader in the north-west. Because in Qing China female management of business matters, and naturally of male employees, was frowned on, Zhou Ying had to sit behind a curtain when meeting her shop managers and professional staff.

Yangzhou (then a prosperous city in east China) and the Shu region (present-day Sichuan and Chongqing) were the two heartlands of Zhou Ying's commercial empire. The Wu family continued to conduct their salt business in Jiangsu, Jiangxi and Anhui, headquartering the operation at Yangzhou. In Sichuan and Chongqing, they focused on the pawnbroking business. Between 1884 and 1900, the family business, directed by Zhou Ying, reached the zenith of its fortunes. Their business concerns extended to Hubei, Jiangsu, Shanghai, Sichuan and Gansu, profiting from trade in textiles, tea, medicines, grain and salt, and the operation of banks and pawnshops.

Zhou Ying flaunted her wealth through conspicuous consumption. She built an opulent personal mansion said to be a smaller-scale replica of the Forbidden City. But she was also a generous philanthropist. According to local gazetteers and her epitaph, she was active in local charities and public services such as road construction, disaster relief, bridge maintenance, publishing and temple building. This

Twelve-panel embroidered screen, *c.* 1900–1. The screen is said to have been presented by Widow Anwu (Zhou Ying) to Empress Dowager Cixi. The upper section depicts auspicious animals and flowers; the lower section is carved with scenes from Chinese legends. On the back of the screen are hundreds of shou (longevity) characters in gold. Wood and silk. Each panel: height 350 cm, width 60 cm. Shaanxi Provincial Library, Xi'an.

philanthropy not only enhanced her reputation as a compassionate benefactor, but also won her awards from the Qing court. In 1885, she received the honoured title of Second Rank Madame (*erpin gaoming furen*) for her donation of over 40,000 silver taels (equivalent to £1.1 million today) to restore a Confucius temple destroyed in the Muslim wars of the late 19th century. In 1900, when the Eight-Nation Alliance of Western and Japanese armies invaded and occupied Beijing at the close of the Boxer siege there, Empress Dowager Cixi fled with her entourage to Xi'an in Shaanxi, remaining there until 1902. The province was under exceptional pressure at the time. In addition to incurring the huge burden of supporting the exiled court, the area was famine-stricken following a disastrous harvest. The government was therefore desperately in need of funds. Zhou Ying sent her adopted son to the exiled court in Xi'an with 100,000 silver taels and other lavish gifts. As a reward for her generosity and loyalty, an imperial edict elevated her title to First Rank Madame (*yipin gaoming furen*), an honour normally only granted to the wife of a high-ranking official. The relationship between Cixi and Zhou Ying – both widowed young, both exercising power from behind the curtain (literally) of the patriarchal order – seized the popular imagination. The much-told story that Cixi was so fond of Zhou Ying that she became her godmother, however, has never been conclusively proved.

Zhou Ying died in 1908 at the age of thirty-nine and was buried outside the Wu family cemetery. She had a son, albeit an adopted one, so she was in every sense entitled to be buried in the family cemetery, but for some reason was excluded from its precincts. Her life inspired a very popular 2017 Chinese television drama, which introduced her to a mass audience, but unfortunately focused more on a fictional love story than the details and implications of her career, which so fascinatingly challenged contemporary gender norms.

Wenyuan Xin

70. SILAS HARDOON
AND LUO JIALING

哈同 (1851–1931) 羅迦陵 (1864–1941)

SPECULATORS AND PHILANTHROPISTS

From the 1840s, foreign powers established a series of treaty ports along China's maritime coast and major waterways, zones with a separate legal system designed to protect foreigners and their businesses. These hypercolonial zones were conduits for modern ideas and technology flowing into Qing China, and quite unintentionally provided a measure of safety for Chinese revolutionaries working to reform or overthrow the imperial system.

In Shanghai, one of the first treaty ports, entrepreneurs arrived from all over the world, seeking to trade a wide variety of goods (tea, opium and many others) in the Chinese market. They took advantage of Shanghai's access to global shipping routes, and its position on the doorstep of the wealthy and culturally rich Jiangnan region of China. Many who helped build Shanghai into a prosperous city were Jews originally from Baghdad in the Ottoman Empire, who had fled an increasingly hostile political climate, migrating first to British India, and then to Hong Kong and Shanghai. They maintained close personal and professional connections with their kin across Asia, and made use of this network to set up trading and other businesses in the growing city of Shanghai. In 1874, one such Baghdadi Jew, Silas Aaron Hardoon, arrived in Shanghai, and over the next few decades he would rise to become one of the richest men in the city. Although mostly forgotten now outside China, during Shanghai's heyday in the 1920s and 1930s Hardoon was the epitome of a new class of tycoons who had risen along with Shanghai from poverty to enormous wealth.

In Shanghai Hardoon first worked for David Sassoon & Company, an enterprise set up by another Baghdadi Jewish family, and worked his way up the ranks. The company primarily dealt in importing cotton yarn and opium from British India and operated its own fleet of opium clippers; by the 1870s, it dominated the India–China opium trade. In 1886, in a ceremony which combined Jewish and Chinese elements, Hardoon married Luo Jialing (née Liza Roos), a Eurasian who had grown up on the outskirts of Shanghai. This was highly unusual among Shanghai Baghdadi Jews, who usually married within their community and religion – Luo remained a committed Buddhist her entire life. The union, however, allowed him to form connections with the Chinese merchant community of Shanghai. From 1911 onwards, Hardoon became a property trader; it is said that he helped develop Nanking (Nanjing) Road, the main commercial artery of the city, and much of his fortune was built through shrewd property trading during a period of rapid urban development in Shanghai.

Silas Hardoon and wife Luo Jialing (née Liza Roos). After Ji Fotuo, *Jianshoutang bai sa he qing shou yan* (Jianshoutang: a tale of collectively celebrating 130 years), Shanghai, 1923. SOAS Special Collections, University of London.

From 1904 to 1909, he had a 26-acre estate built on land he had purchased in the western outskirts of the international settlement. Located at the intersection of Bubbling Well Road (today's Nanjing West Road) and what became known as Hardoon Road, Aili Gardens was the site of experimental schools, academies and a Buddhist university. Luo's religious mentor, the revolutionary monk Zongyang (1861–1921), lived on the site and edited a new edition of the Chinese Buddhist canon published between 1908 and 1913, which Hardoon financed on Luo's behalf.

Hardoon and Luo both became anti-Qing activists and supported the 1911 Revolution that toppled the dynasty, giving aid to revolutionary leaders and even hosting the first president of the new republic, Sun Yat-sen (1866–1925), when he visited Shanghai in 1911. Hardoon had become a member of the Shanghai elite, sitting on the municipal councils of both the international and the French concession, but never lost his connection to the Shanghai Jewish community, building the

Beth Aaron synagogue in 1926. The pair adopted a number of children, including orphaned refugee Jews who were brought up in that faith.

Hardoon died in June 1931 at around the age of eighty, after which Luo was almost immediately embroiled in a legal battle with his extended family over control of his estate. The Hardoon Inheritance Case dragged on until it was finally decided in Luo's favour in 1937, but after her death in 1941 the estate again became the subject of an international legal dispute between Hardoon's family and their adopted children. After the Communist take-over in 1949 the estate was seized, and Aili Gardens, heavily damaged during the war, was later razed so that the Sino-Soviet Friendship Centre could be built on the grounds. Today it is the Shanghai Exhibition Centre.

Hardoon's status as the member of a minority ethnic and religious group, his role in building Shanghai into an international, multireligious and multilingual metropolis, and the rapid dissolution of his estate during the years of war and revolution, vividly illustrate the multifaceted nature of the story of modern China.

Gregory Adam Scott

71. ERNEST MAJOR

(1841–1908)

SHANGHAI PUBLISHER AND FOUNDER OF THE *SHENBAO*

Ernest Major went to China in 1861, at the age of twenty, together with his twin brother Frederick. After spending their first ten years in Ningbo, engaged in various business enterprises, he moved to Shanghai and founded the first modern Chinese-language newspaper, *Shenbao* ('Shanghai News') in 1872, followed by a major book publishing company, Shenbao Publications. These innovative and successful ventures helped establish Shanghai as China's publishing capital for decades to come.

Major was born in south London as the third of five siblings. He grew up in modest financial circumstances, but in an unusually open-minded and progressive intellectual context. His father, Ebenezer Langley Major (1802–1891), was baptized in the (dissident) Independent Church in Bull Lane in Stepney, and held minor positions in the British civil service. His mother, Emma Jones (1811–1891), was born a British subject in Calcutta (Kolkata), east India. Ernest Major was educated at the famously reform-oriented Clapham Grammar School, where he was brought up in the intellectual spirit of the Scottish Enlightenment; he also took private lessons in Chinese as a teenager, provided by a private house tutor in London. Thus, when he arrived in China, he was not only already exceptionally highly literate in Chinese, but also educated with a liberal, scientifically oriented outlook.

As publisher of the *Shenbao* and at Shenbao Publications, he is credited with the introduction of new printing technologies, but also innovative approaches that would

Dianshizhai, from Wu Youru (*c.* 1840–1894), *Scenic Views in and round Shanghai*, volume 1, part 2, 59b–60a, originally published in Shanghai by Dianshizhai, 1884. The image shows the Dianshizhai Lithographic Printing Bureau.

transform the Chinese public sphere. *Shenbao* (1872–1949) quickly established itself as a newspaper of national repute. Setting a new tone with its reform-oriented editorials and open debate (promoting the Enlightenment ideals of fair and objective discussion), it was a complete novelty on the Shanghai press market. Its overall pro-China orientation – and critical tone towards the British government – was also novel to the British community in Shanghai and beyond.

While Ernest Major was initially involved in the day-to-day editorial work, and published articles and editorials of his own, most of the paper was produced by a small Chinese editorial board of literati he brought on board from Jiangnan – a region of the south-east that had for centuries produced some of China's most brilliant writers and scholar-officials – as well as by a network of correspondents and writers of 'letters to the editor'. Under Major's editorial leadership and strict observation of fair and professional journalistic standards, this group of reform-oriented scholars produced editorials on topics relating to political reform and international law, including (among many others) anti-corruption, private and public finances in economics and trade, science and technology, women's education and anti-opium campaigns. As such, the paper not only attracted a national distribution network of subscribers among the Chinese literati and merchant community, but was also read by local officials and reached the highest imperial government ranks (China's first 'ministry of foreign affairs', the Zongli yamen in Beijing, subscribed).

Having discovered this market, Major established Shenbao Publications. The fact that many classical literary works had been lost due to large-scale destruction of books and other cultural artefacts in the Jiangnan area during the Taiping Civil War (1851–64) again inspired him to work with erudite elite Chinese scholars to find original manuscripts, which he reproduced in fine lithograph editions that were coined 'Major editions'. Shenbao Publications encompassed several companies, including the Shenchang Book and Illustration Office, the Dianshizhai Lithographic Printing Bureau and the Gujin Tushu Jicheng Publishing House. Major also published China's first literary journals, *Universal News Items* (*Yinghuan suoji*) and *Global News Items* (*Siming suoji*), catering to a cultural elite with broad interests from international political events to literary, antiquarian or entertainment pursuits. Setting a standard that would become a regular one within a few decades, the first ever translation of an English novel in China, Bulwer-Lytton's *Night and Morning* (1841), was serialized in one of Major's journals. Bringing together cutting-edge lithograph technology with international content, Major oversaw the publication of China's first illustrated journal, *Dianshizhai Pictorial* (1884–97).

The *Shenbao* was a very profitable enterprise – as were Major's other publishing ventures. However, its legal status as a Chinese paper published and owned by a British subject in the foreign concession zone of Shanghai remained uncertain. Major therefore diversified into a number of other business enterprises, which laid the foundation for Major Brothers, Ltd: these included modern manufacturing plants such as the Kiangsu Chemical Works, the Suichang Match Factory, the Major Soap Factory, the Suichang Fire Brigade and the Jiangsu Medicinal Water Plant. Again, Major was directly involved in technical and managerial innovations – aiming to provide products vital for Chinese national industrial production, which would ultimately replace costly imports from Western countries. He also engaged in investment beyond China's borders, in a tobacco plant in British Borneo and later in Sumatra. During his time in China, he was thus a businessman who travelled extensively: in China and across the borders to Japan and Southeast Asian countries, but also back to London three times in the years 1877, 1880 and 1884–85.

During his eighteen years based in Shanghai, Ernest Major built a manufacturing and publishing empire. The grand office and company buildings of his enterprises became architectural landmarks, finely reproduced in lithographs of the time. Returning to London in 1889 as a wealthy man, he moved into a spectacular villa in Waterdale, Cookham Dean. He had married Anne Margaret Nadin (1856–1937) in London in 1885. They had three children, while continuing to travel between London and China during the 1890s.

The *Shenbao* was a novelty to its Chinese readership, as it was to the Chinese and British authorities. From the outset, Major's project was subjected to attacks from not only Chinese local government but also British colonial rulers, both of whom felt their interests were misrepresented. The unruly diversity of his professional ventures is perhaps why we still lack any full historical account of Ernest Major as a person: he does not fit comfortably into either a British or a Chinese national historiography. His life and activities as described here have been reconstructed piecemeal from archival material, newspaper reports, court cases and other primary sources, as part of an (unfinished) biographical project that the late German Sinologist Rudolf G. Wagner pursued over decades.

Natascha Gentz

72. SIR ROBERT HART

(1835–1911)

INSPECTOR GENERAL OF THE IMPERIAL MARITIME CUSTOMS

Born in Portadown, County Amagh, Robert Hart arrived in China in 1854 as a student interpreter in the British consular service. He was recruited from there in 1859 to the foreign-staffed Imperial Maritime Customs Service, a Qing state agency that had been set up, initially as a temporary arrangement, to facilitate trade at Shanghai, after the city's local government collapsed in 1853 during the disorder caused by the Taiping Civil War. A gifted linguist, Hart became one of the most prominent and influential foreign servants of the Qing state. By 1861, he was acting chief of the service, and in 1863 was appointed its inspector general, a post he held until his death in 1911.

The Imperial Maritime Customs became the single most important body that mediated Qing China's relationship with foreign powers, engaging with developing currents of global trade and exchange in the latter half of the 19th century. Hart's British and American successors would administer the service until 1949, across those decades recruiting thousands of men from a cosmopolitan array of European nations, the United States and Japan, who worked under their orders as Chinese civil servants, alongside an equal number of Chinese employees.

Band practice in Beijing, c.1906. Special Collections, Queen's University Belfast.

It was always much more than a revenue assessment agency. The Customs under
Hart built a network of coastal lighthouses; mapped coasts and harbours; established
the country's Post Office; organized the representation of China at international
expositions; generated an immense body of scientific, medical and cultural data
about China, which it disseminated through a busy publication programme; and
supported the Qing's nascent overseas diplomatic presence. It was able to do this
because of its success in facilitating Sino-foreign trade, and through generating
healthy revenues that enabled the Zongli yamen, a central state body established in
1861, to deal with foreign matters, and to embark on a series of initiatives designed to
strengthen the capacity of the Qing state.

The growth of the service, and of its reach and responsibilities, also stemmed
from Hart's own wide-ranging interests and restless energy, and his very strong relations both with Zongli yamen officials – in 1861, Prince Gong described him as 'our
Hart' – and with foreign ones – in 1885, he was offered the post of British minister
(ambassador) to the Qing. He ultimately declined the position as he felt that he could
be more useful to British interests if he stayed with the Customs. Hart saw no contradiction in this, nor any conflict of interests or loyalties. He genuinely believed that
Qing and British interests were aligned, and that his work could go some way to
ensure that conflict – which he had experienced directly during the Second Opium
War (1856–60) – could be avoided.

Hart is also remembered for two other significant facets of his life. The first
stemmed from his love of music. Although there were doubtless employees with

musical talent to be found stationed at the Inspectorate General in Beijing, Hart set about forming a brass band of teenage Chinese boys trained from scratch (and led by a German postal clerk). For the following two decades, Hart's band played at private and official events, evolved to include strings, inspired the formation of similar ensembles by leading figures at court (who poached his musicians) and has a respectable place in the history of the introduction of European art music to China. More privately, in his early years in China, Hart had a long relationship with a Chinese woman, who is known to history only as Ayaou. Some details of this affair survived the destruction by his family of the relevant volumes of his voluminous diary, while descendants of two of their children live in Britain and in North America. In 1866, Hart married the daughter of a Portadown neighbour, but they lived most of the time apart. Hart was wedded to China, and to the Customs and to his control of it.

Through the Customs, Hart aimed to ensure that China was smoothly integrated into the global community. We might see this as a simple conceit, for the terms of integration were weighted mostly against the Qing, but his achievements were significant for China, nonetheless. Hart's position, and his long tenure of it – and no little amount of self-publicity – meant that he built up an international reputation. While he mostly preferred to work behind the scenes, he was ready to use his fame to appeal to an international public to understand the roots of the popular anger that fuelled the 1900 Boxer War. While under armed siege in Beijing during the conflict, Hart composed a series of essays explaining the origins of the crisis, in a bid to avert harsh retribution from the foreign powers. If he did not entirely succeed, the service he had built played a key role in securing revenues that helped the Qing quickly to recover from the destruction wrought by massive civil wars and embark on an ambitious programme of reforms thereafter. These did not save the dynasty from the Revolution of 1911, but had an impact on China's society and culture that long outlasted it.

Robert Bickers

73. THOMAS HANBURY

(1832–1907)

TRADER AND BOTANIST WHO HELPED SHAPE SHANGHAI

In September 1853, a young English Quaker businessman called Thomas Hanbury arrived at Shanghai's foreign-controlled settlement with three partners to establish a new firm, Hanbury & Co., to trade in tea and silk. 'It is but a swamp', he wrote to his brother Daniel, a naturalist and pharmacist, and he stayed first at a house called, ironically, 'Mosquito Lodge', but 'There is the finest chance here of making money with the Chinamen in various ways', and 'What capital merchants they are'. Hanbury arrived in the midst of chaotic conflict. The region had been destabilized by the then

Thomas Hanbury
in Shanghai, 1859.
Photograph taken outside
the Chartered Mercantile
Bank of India. Bath Royal
Literary and Scientific
Institution.

victorious forces of the Taiping Heavenly Kingdom, whose civil war against the Qing government would last another decade; a branch of the uprising close to home in the neighbouring Chinese walled city occasioned 'daily battles' in the vicinity.

Out of this chaos came Hanbury's substantial fortune. All foreign traders needed Chinese partners to facilitate their trade. Hanbury, unusually, pursued study of the language and of China's natural history, alongside developing his commercial interests. In addition, he worked on building very good relations with his Chinese business associates. This was shrewd, but also stemmed from a personal distaste for the mores of expatriate life in the tiny foreign settlement (which did not, however, prevent him from fathering a son with a Chinese mistress). He actively opposed the opium trade.

Hanbury was successful as a merchant, and the instability that surrounded the peace of the small British-controlled settlement created further opportunities. Initially set aside by the local Qing authorities exclusively as a site of foreign residence, it attracted wave after wave of refugees as the crisis continued. Trading associates from outside the city sought Hanbury out to protect their possessions and their capital. Many would stay, and many were rich: all needed housing. By 1864 Hanbury was the largest landowner in the foreign settlement: he served as an agent for Chinese investment, and ploughed his own profits into land purchases and property development.

Shanghai was shaped in two ways by Hanbury's efforts, one of which lasts to this day. The Shanghai row house (terraced house), set in close-packed alleyways (*lilong*), was designed to maximize the use of space on lots such as the dozens of parcels of land he owned. This amalgam of Chinese and foreign architectural forms became a distinctive feature of Shanghai's urban landscape, and while most have now been replaced by new developments, the real legacy of these row houses lies in the ways they persist in Shanghai's cultural memory.

His more obvious legacy is Shanghai's iconic riverfront Bund. Hanbury used his influence, and his capital, to lobby to protect the Bund's riverbank from commercial use, and to preserve it as an open public space. 'Public', for decades, did not extend fully to the occupants of Hanbury's own houses, for Chinese residents were excluded from using the Bund's lawns and garden until 1928. Successive developments in Shanghai have never displaced the Bund from its central position in the life and image of the city, and its essential character remains as it was, and as shaped by Hanbury.

Hanbury left Shanghai for good in 1871, and retired to La Mortola, an estate on the Italian–French border that he had purchased in 1867. There he created the striking botanical garden that bears his name, and later a botanical institute. In England, his most obvious legacy is the Wisley garden, which he bought and presented to the Royal Horticultural Society in 1903. While the degree of Hanbury's commercial success was unusual, and the resources he was able to invest in his other interests so much greater than many, he was not alone in his pursuit of knowledge about China's natural history and botany, and in contributing richly this way to cultural and scientific exchange between Europe and the Qing empire.

Robert Bickers

74. KISHIDA GINKŌ

岸田吟香 (1833–1905)

PIONEER JOURNALIST, ENTREPRENEUR AND BENEFACTOR

An important early figure in modern Sino-Japanese relations, Kishida was a cultural and commercial pioneer. Born late in the Tokugawa period (1603–1867), he was educated in the standard curriculum of Chinese learning (*Kangaku*). After working as a farmer and later a businessman, he contracted a serious eye disease in the early 1860s – probably deterioration of the ophthalmic nerve – rapidly losing his eyesight. The two traditions of medicines available in Japan at the time, Dutch and Chinese, provided no cure. In 1864, his friend Mitsukuri Rinshō (1846–1897), a well-known legal scholar, suggested he call on Dr James C. Hepburn (1815–1911), a lay missionary doctor in Yokohama, who had come to Japan in 1859, having chosen it because he was appalled by the unhealthy competition among an excess of doctors in his native United States, and because Japan was relatively untouched by Christianity. Hepburn devised a cure for Kishida's affliction, and his sight was quickly restored.

Hepburn is better known to history for his groundbreaking Japanese–English dictionary, which he was writing at that time. Greatly in the doctor's debt, Kishida was in an excellent position to help him, because, given his life experiences, he was acquainted with a broad assortment of linguistic registers of the Japanese language. Able to see again, Kishida began working with Hepburn full-time, and in late summer 1866, they completed a draft, but a serious problem remained. There was at the time no printer in Japan that used movable type; everything was still in the woodblock phase. In late October 1867, Kishida and Hepburn (along with the latter's wife) sailed to Shanghai, where the dictionary was printed at the American Presbyterian Mission Press. How is it that this missionary press had the kana syllabaries of Japanese (its hiragana and katakana phonetic alphabets, used alongside Chinese characters to produce written Japanese) – in addition, of course, to Chinese characters and the Roman alphabet? The Mission Press had in fact been able to print kana since 1861, as it was preparing to launch its work in Japan, which was only recently opened to a range of foreign activity. Were there any Japanese people in Shanghai in 1861? This remains an open question, but it seems likely.

Dr and Mrs Hepburn fell ill shortly after reaching Shanghai and returned to Japan. Kishida stayed to see the project through (though he had little good to say about the conditions he found prevailing in Shanghai at the time). In May 1867, the *Japanese–English Dictionary* (*Wa–Ei gorin shūsei*) appeared in print. The dictionary has attained a legendary reputation because the romanization system for rendering Japanese became the basis for all dictionaries thereafter. Dr Hepburn compensated Kishida for his labours by giving him the formula for his miraculous optical curative. Kishida christened it 'Essence of Water' (*Seikisui*). It was an eyewash containing zinc sulphate, which Kishida manufactured in small glass vials, revolutionizing ophthalmology in Japan. Only a few months after the dictionary rolled off the press, Kishida was producing *Seikisui* on an industrial scale. He transported immense quantities to Shanghai in 1868, and had them sold at two stores in the city, each of which bore the placard: 'On sale here the eye medicine Seikisui, expertly produced by Mr. Kishida Ginkō of Japan'. This was the first instance of direct private sales of the product to the Chinese.

Before his trip to Shanghai, Kishida met arguably the most international Japanese man of his day, Hamada Hikozō, or Joseph Heco (1837–1897). A shipwreck victim off the coast of Japan in 1850, Hamada had been saved by an American vessel and taken to California. He spent almost a decade in the United States, even meeting President Abraham Lincoln. Back in Japan in the early 1860s, Kishida briefly studied English with Hamada, who introduced Kishida to the Western concept of the newspaper. Intrigued, Kishida joined forces with Heco to start Japan's first modern newspaper, *Kaigai shinbun* ('Overseas News'), launched in the spring of 1864. A second publication followed in 1868.

Kishida founded a pharmacy in September 1875, the Rakuzendō, in Tokyo's Ginza district, branches of which soon proliferated, mainly selling *Seikisui*. In 1878 the first branch outside Japan opened in Shanghai. In 1882 he developed another

Photograph of Kishida Ginkō. Published in Sugi Kenji, ed., *Okayama-ken meikan* (Collection of biographies of famous people from Okayama Prefecture), 1911. Tsuyama Archives of Western Learning, Okayama.

pioneering commercial product: pocket-sized editions of the Chinese classics and histories, known as *xiuzhenben*, or 'sleeve volumes', because a student wearing a loose-fitting Chinese garment could slip them into the sleeves. Kishida sold these very inexpensively, meaning they were now available to virtually all students preparing for the civil service examinations. Each year he sold roughly 150,000 volumes, and soon became a wealthy man. He could have lived out his life in relative luxury, but instead he chose to funnel his profits back into ventures involving the people who had origi- nally generated his wealth: the Chinese. The most famous of his many ventures was his tireless effort to broadcast the evils of opium and establish drug rehabilitation centres in China. This idiosyncratic reinvestment business practice was subsequently dubbed 'Kishida's one-way trade'.

In the 1880s, Kishida's branch of his Rakuzendō pharmacy in Hankou (central China) became home to an operation set up by Arao Sei (1859–1896). Originally sent to China by the Japanese army as a spy, Arao soon left military intelligence and worked with other Japanese (including Kishida) and Chinese people to foster Sino- Japanese trade. In 1887 Kishida and Arao established in their Hankou pharmacy the Institute for Sino-Japanese Trade, where Chinese language, geography and other trade-related fields were taught. In 1892 the institute published *A Comprehensive Overview of China's Commerce and Trade*, a publication still used by scholars today.

Joshua A. Fogel

75. DI BAOXIAN

狄葆賢 (1873–c. 1939)

CULTURAL ENTREPRENEUR

Di Baoxian created a media ecosystem, comprised of a publishing infrastructure, newly imported print technologies and a series of influential periodicals, that helped define the look, the politics and the sensibility of the unsettled decades immediately preceding and following the fall of the last imperial dynasty in 1912.

Di was born into an elite family of poets, scholars and art collectors in Suyang, Jiangsu province, in 1873. He carried on his family lineage by passing the mid-level imperial civil service examination and becoming a *juren*, or provincial graduate, at an early age, but never took an official position in the Qing bureaucracy. He joined the reformist political fervour of the 1890s, and lived the cultural politics of the succeeding decades with an unmatched intensity. He was a man of productive contradictions: a failed revolutionary turned cultural entrepreneur, a practising Buddhist and publisher of courtesan albums, a connoisseur of fine art and promoter of new media. He sought refuge in, took inspiration from and vilified Japan. Each of his many ventures had unintended results, most of which were consequential.

The first of these ventures was his involvement in the abortive anti-Qing Independent Army Uprising in 1900. Di had financed the misadventure by selling part of his family's art collection – the casual act of a committed radical. It was when he was forced, at the turn of the 20th century, to seek refuge in Japan that he realized the value of art conservation, and the connection between an artistic and national patrimony. From this moment, privately, Di placed greater value on what was left of his family's artistic heritage, most famously Wang Meng's (*c.* 1308–1385) *Dwelling in Reclusion in the Qingbian Mountains*. He then went on to establish a publishing company in Shanghai, the Youzheng Book Company, to produce print material related to the Chinese fine arts. This included the periodical *Famous Chinese Paintings* (published 1908–30), together with exhibition catalogues, and reproductions of paintings, calligraphy, steles and rubbings.

Di's brief period of exile in Japan also set the course for his political publishing career. In Tokyo, he began to collaborate with two other famous exiles who had fled to Japan after the failed 1898 Reform Movement, Kang Youwei (1858–1927) and Liang Qichao (1873–1929). Di agreed to establish a daily newspaper to represent the views of their political faction when he returned to Shanghai. From the moment *Shibao*, or the *Eastern Times*, first went to press in 1904, it transformed the Chinese newspaper industry. The paper introduced innovations in format and layout, but more particularly in language and style. Di had an eye for talented editors, one of whom created a new short, pithy and lively essay form that revolutionized journalistic writing. Witty and sardonic political cartoons further set the tone and helped make

Photograph of Di Baoxian as a young man. After Di Baoxian, *Notes from the Pavilion of Equality*, Shanghai: Youzheng shuju, *c.* 1911–49.

Shibao the bestselling newspaper in the city, with a circulation estimated at 17,000. Di was himself a contributor. Known in literary circles as an authority on contemporary poetry, his column 'Pavilion of Equality' functioned as a focal point for the beginnings of the modern poetry movement in China. It also served as the basis of one of Di's two published works, *Comments on Poetry from the Pavilion of Equality*.

Aware that he had a winning formula in *Shibao*, Di Baoxian built on the newspaper's success by publishing a number of supplements, which eventually took on lives of their own. The first, *Eastern Times Fiction* (*Xiaoshuo Shibao*), went to press in 1909, followed in 1911 by *Eastern Times for Women* (*Funü Shibao*) – the earliest Chinese newspaper supplement dedicated to women – and in 1912 by *Buddhist Studies Magazine*, the first Chinese periodical to specialize in Buddhist content. These periodicals were integral to Di's media ecosystem. Although precise financial details are murky, it is possible that these more commercial ventures helped finance the art publications, which were significantly more costly to produce. At the same time, the Youzheng Book Company helped offset certain costs of running the periodicals: its books were awarded as prizes to winners of the women's journal's ongoing essay competitions, for example, and used to pay freelance contributors to *Shibao*.

The final critical component of Di's media conglomerate was the Minying Photography Studio. Di established the studio in 1907 or 1908 to facilitate his project of preserving China's artistic cultural traces. He equipped Minying with the most up-to-date machinery and employed Japanese experts to train their Chinese counterparts in the methods of collotype printing. Di quickly realized that the studio could serve the ends of commercial, as well as high, art. While Chinese periodicals up to that date had generally opened with copperplate illustrations of landscapes or reproductions of the calligraphy of famous artists, Di mobilized the skills of Minying's technicians to create photographs of fashionable women. These included both courtesans, whom Di's Youzheng Book Company featured in three lush volumes published between 1909 and 1914, and respectable women, who graced the opening pages of the *Eastern Times for Women*.

Di Baoxian's politics were as wide-ranging as his publications. A degree-holder who never took up an official position, he nonetheless had a deep sense of public service. While he established *Shibao* to serve a reform agenda, he ultimately took the newspaper in a more radical direction. At the same time, he had close ties with more conservative figures such as Zhang Jian (1853–1926), with whom he was involved in a number of late Qing reform organizations including the Jiangsu General Educational Association. He was also a member of the Jiangsu Provincial Assembly.

For all the traces Di Baoxian left in the worlds of politics, publishing and art, he remains an elusive character. This is particularly so in matters of personal faith, although he was known to be a devout Buddhist. He directed the *Shibao* building housing the newspaper offices (and a club where courtesans were often entertained) to be built in the form of a pagoda. He also created *Buddhist Studies Magazine*, which served as a platform for the dissemination of Buddhist scripture, and his faith apparently deepened after he lost a son early in the Republican era. By the 1930s, he was retreating from the various arenas of political and cultural life he had once been involved in, and the details surrounding his death are uncertain.

Deeply engaged in the arts, publishing and politics of this complex period, Di Baoxian's greatest asset in his business practice may, ironically, have been a religious sense of detachment from the cultural ferment that he helped to foment.

Joan Judge

7

STATESPEOPLE

CAMPAIGNERS, REFORMERS, DIPLOMATS AND PHILOSOPHERS

The institutions of the Qing state were hybrid and multi-ethnic. The basic shape of Qing government – often known as the *waijing*, the 'outer court' – was borrowed from its Ming predecessor. The highest internal executive office was the Grand Secretariat, which processed communications between the emperor and other officials, including those scattered across the provinces, dealing with day-to-day local governance. For much of the 19th century, the government was staffed by graduates of the civil service examinations, fluent in classical texts identified as upholding Confucius's core principles. These tests of Confucian orthodoxy had arbitrated the paths to wealth and social success for centuries, and had long served as the basic mechanism by which (through the promise of salary and status) scholars and writers were integrated into state machinery. Until the end of the 19th century, this culturally and politically indoctrinating system helped to hold the empire together in a community of shared educational experience and cultural aspiration.

As a Manchu conquest minority ruling an empire inhabited by a Chinese majority, the Qing also founded and relied on 'inner court' (*neiting*) institutions, which were generally not staffed by those who had come up through the civil service bureaucracy, and were dominated by Manchus. Across the 18th century, arguably the most powerful of the 'inner court' institutions was the Grand Council (*junjichu* – literally, the 'office of military planning'): an elite inner cabinet, between three and five members strong, mainly Manchu and the closest associates of the emperor. Many other choice political positions across the empire were occupied by members of the Manchu elite, including those in the 'outer court' bureaucracy, such as provincial governorships. The Manchu politician Yinghe can be seen as an archetypal representative of this official class.

The upheavals of China's 'long 19th century', however, led to two major governmental transformations: the reassertion of political power by Han Chinese statesmen, and the internationalization of the Qing state machinery. The former began in the early 1800s, when the new Jiaqing emperor limited the opaque, personal powers of members of the Manchu elite in institutions such as the Grand Council and promoted carefully educated and trained (often Han Chinese) bureaucrats with personal experience of frontier and post-conflict governance.

This increased political participation by Han elites and became one of the most significant sociopolitical developments of the 19th century, which, arguably, eventually delegitimized the Qing and culminated in the revolution of 1911–12.

Men like the trouble-shooting Lin Zexu were typical of these self-confident, highly competent Han officials. As emperors became less fertile and long-lived across the 19th century, and as the old Manchu armies began to malfunction, experienced, resourceful Chinese administrators would play key roles in maintaining a stable, functioning state. Han generals also became more prominent, and Han rank and file more numerous, in the formerly Manchu-dominated military.

Amid the generalized military crisis of the Anglo-French storming of Beijing and the Taiping conquest of south-east China in the second half of the 1850s (both of which highlighted failures by Manchu commanders), a coterie of hardworking Han Chinese officials – Zeng Guofan, Li Hongzhang, Zuo Zongtang and others – took command of anti-Taiping military campaigns and, between the 1860s and 1890s, were rapidly promoted (sometimes outside the traditional civil service hierarchy) to top government positions.

Until the 1890s, such Han reformers remained broadly loyal to the imperial system, or at least to the emperor. By the closing years of the dynasty, however, a variegated anti-imperial opposition movement had emerged, split between reformists, constitutional monarchists and revolutionaries. Some, as Zhang Zhidong, Guo Songtao and Kang Youwei did in their different ways, sought accommodations between loyalty to the old imperial and cultural system, and new forms of political organization borrowed from the modern Western nation state. Others, like Sun Yat-sen, sought to replace dynastic rule with a republic; the latter vision won the day in early 1912.

After European aggression violently cast the Qing empire into a Western-dominated international order, the empire began building up its diplomatic presence abroad. Prince Gong, brother of the Xianfeng emperor, founded the country's first de facto foreign office and training school for interpreters in the early 1860s. Although at first excoriated as 'traitors' for serving outside the empire, the Qing's earliest diplomats – trailblazers like Guo Songtao and Chen Jitong – became crucial vectors for knowledge about the outside world. In the 1900s, Qing diplomatic delegations – including the avid antiquarian Duanfang – travelled to Japan, the United States and Europe to research constitutional monarchies and other foreign political systems, as part of a radical rethink of late imperial government. By the close of the imperial period, Chinese political thought and practice had become dazzlingly hybrid, as conservatives like Duanfang and Gu Hongming negotiated between Qing China and the international world, and reformers such as Kang Youwei and Liang Qichao toggled between ancient Chinese belief systems and the institutions of Western and Japanese state-building. Elite and popular audiences even lionized the 'cross-cultural concubine' Sai Jinhua, for her (most likely fictional) mediation between China and foreign aggressors. **JL**

76. YINGHE

英和 (1771–1839)

MANCHU POLITICIAN AND MAN OF LETTERS

In 1825, Yinghe, a Manchu high official of the Socoro (Chinese: Suochuoluo) clan, devised an ingenious plan to circumvent the catastrophic blockage of grain transport at the junction of the Grand Canal and the Yellow River. In two memorials to the Daoguang emperor (r. 1821–1850), Yinghe did not hold back from pointing to the political roots of the crisis, ostensibly caused by flooding earlier that year: the extortionist practices of shippers and the cowardice of local officials fearing imperial retribution. His proposal to bring rice from Shanghai to Tianjin by sea – the first such seaborne attempt during the Qing dynasty – came to fruition the following year. Such swift and decisive action resulted from the emperor's trust in Yinghe's administrative capabilities, and particularly his position within a Manchu banner elite corps of officials who could get things done.

An 1806 portrait of Yinghe in official court dress projects his self-confidence in this milieu. Precociously, at the age of about twenty, he had already attained the top *jinshi* civil service degree. Owing in part to the skill of his father Debao in refusing to have Yinghe marry the daughter of Heshen, the Qianlong emperor's infamously corrupt minister and favourite purged by the Jiaqing emperor as soon as his father Qianlong died in 1796, Yinghe had navigated smoothly the transition to the Jiaqing era. By the time of the portrait, Yinghe had already taken up positions in the Grand Secretariat, the Board of Rites, the Board of Revenue and the Imperial Household. In March 1803, while Yinghe was serving as a private secretary to the Jiaqing emperor, the emperor had gifted to him as a token of approbation a gold-inscribed jadeite archer's thumb ring. The military resonances of this treasured object, most likely not used in actual archery training or combat, are echoed in the tiger skin draped over Yinghe's chair in the portrait. The symmetrical and front-facing composition brings to mind portraits designed for posthumous veneration by the sitter's descendants, but, in an unusual inscription to this type of painting, Yinghe indicates that he himself commissioned the work from a professional artist. Presumably he requested that the depiction include scholarly accoutrements – a brush pot and a peach-shaped water cup in carved stone, and several book volumes atop a rosewood table. Together these symbols of both Manchu martial values and Chinese cultural attainments enhance the representation of Yinghe as the archetypal cross-culturally proficient Manchu official first envisioned by the Qing founder Nurhaci in the early 17th century and further idealized by the Yongzheng and Qianlong emperors in the 18th century.

Yinghe's forthrightness, loyalty and dedication to his job would certainly have gained the emperor's trust, but also left him exposed to the emperor's ire. His career

Unidentified artist, *Portrait of Yinghe*, dated 1806. The portrait was commissioned to commemorate his thirty-sixth birthday. Hanging scroll, ink and colour on silk. Height 356 cm, width 136 cm. Arthur M. Sackler Gallery, Smithsonian Institution, Washington, DC

乾隆三十六
年辛卯四月
十四日辰時生
於粵東撫署
嘉慶丙寅年
三十有六倩
畫工寫照於
安圍

encompassed both spectacular highs and abysmal lows. His role in the decisive suppression of the sectarian Eight Trigrams rebels in 1813 led to his appointment as minister of the Board of Works. In 1826, after the implementation of the sea transport route for grain and his advice towards another successful military campaign in Xinjiang, Yinghe was concurrently president of the Board of Revenue and grand secretary, the latter a position held in previous reigns solely by imperial princes. But a seemingly minor suggestion by him to open silver mines outside the capital, Beijing, and a subsequent accusation of exorbitant rents by one of his tenants saw Yinghe stripped of his high offices, kicked out of the Imperial Study and Imperial Household, and demoted to lowlier posts in undesirable locations.

Though rehabilitated to Beijing in 1827, Yinghe got into trouble again in his assignment to build the Daoguang emperor's tomb in the Eastern Mausoleum precinct, starting in 1821. He and other officials in charge were at first praised for having completed the project in 1827 under severe budgetary constraints, but received the blame when engineering flaws caused water to seep into the underground chamber. The emperor chose to abandon that tomb and rebuild it in the Western Mausoleum precinct (both eastern and western precincts were in the remote suburbs of Beijing). Once more dismissed from his posts, Yinghe was banished to Heilongjiang (though some of his colleagues were sent out even further, to Xinjiang). After two years, he received a pardon and returned to Beijing to live in retirement until his death in 1839.

Yinghe had a prodigious literary output both in post and in exile. The Manchu literatus Shengyu (1850–1900) included many of Yinghe's works in the *Classics of Literature in the Eight Banners*, a prose anthology of writings by the banner elite. During his tenure as tomb architect, Yinghe published a biography of the philosopher, poet and calligrapher Weng Fanggang (1733–1818), also a former superintendent of the imperial tombs. While in exile in Heilongjiang, he wrote two works describing local conditions in the capital, Qiqihar. In his retirement, he produced an autobiography and a compilation of examination style essays revered by his pupils, many of whom, such as the Manchu Grand Councillor Mujangga (1782–1856), would further develop the power and perquisites of the Manchu bannermen. Before the 1806 portrait, Yinghe had already overseen two provincial examinations (in 1800 and 1801) and one metropolitan examination (1805), with another to come (1809). The commitment to higher education ran strong in, and raised the prestige of, Yinghe's Socoro clan, which produced an impressive six *jinshi* degree laureates: first his father's cousin Guanbao (1735), next Yinghe himself (1793), then, clearly under Yinghe's influence, his sons Kuiye (1811) and Kuizhao (1814), and finally his grandson Xizhi (1835).

Among Yinghe's writings we find prefaces to works by women poets, including Luo Qilan (1755–1813) and Lady Tongjia (1737–1809). The latter was related to Dorgon, regent to the Shunzhi emperor (r. 1644–1661). In his preface to her *Elegant Exercises by the Empty Window*, Yinghe highlighted the importance of women in educating children: 'Whenever she wrote a poem, she would order the Prince [her son Junying, Prince Rui] to write a matching composition, and if he showed but the slightest improvement, she would express her pleasure. Once, when the Prince followed His Imperial Majesty on a trip beyond the Wall, she still personally inscribed a white fan and sent it to him as an admonishment.' His support for banner women's artistic accomplishments extended to his wife, Jiewen of the Sakda (Chinese: Sakeda) clan, fourth daughter of Asiha, governor general of Yunnan and Guizhou in 1769. In a moving elegy he described her vivid butterflies, her practice of copying ancient landscapes, and her use of fingernails to effect exquisite detail. She especially excelled in painting birds of prey, capturing their spirit and majesty, with each of her works inscribed by Yinghe himself. Both Jiewen and Yinghe (he primarily as a calligrapher) merited entries in the *Record of Painting in the Eight Banners* (1919), a catalogue and selective history of Qing art that again extolled the idealized marrying of the martial and the cultural within the banner elite.

Nixi Cura

77. LIN ZEXU

林則徐 (1785–1850)

TROUBLESHOOTER

Lin Zexu's reputation as a determined remediator of catastrophic problems preceded his arrival in Guangzhou (Canton) on 8 January 1839. He was born into a humble but literate family in Fujian province in 1785, and achieved the highest civil service examination degree (the *jinshi*) at the relatively young age of twenty-six. His early career was varied and peripatetic. He became so noted as a crisis manager that in 1825 the imperial government called him out of his required mourning for his mother to oversee the repair of dams and dykes on the flooding Yellow River. In the following years he addressed further problems on the eastern Yellow River and the Grand Canal, as well as financial challenges in several provinces of central China and the Yangtze Delta. He earned a reputation not only for competence, but also incorruptibility and compassion.

After an exponential rise in the amount of opium imported into China in the 1830s, the court concluded that addiction had swamped the bureaucracy, the military and the aristocracy, and decided to outlaw the drug – at the time an unusual policy, but one followed by an increasing number of nations in the later 19th century. In 1838, the Daoguang emperor personally commissioned Lin Zexu to eradicate foreign opium importation through the city of Guangzhou. Lin travelled with a small entourage, giving strict instructions to his attendants to avoid accepting bribes or soliciting extravagant meals or lodging. Nevertheless, alarm spread among the Guangzhou-based Hong merchants – Chinese international trade brokers who handled Indian-grown opium among other products – who rightly feared that they would be the first target of Lin's campaign.

Lin Binri (1749–1827), Lin Zexu (1785–1850), Tang Yifen (1778–1853) and Wu Rongguang (1773–1843), *Rearing Cranes* (detail), with postscripts added over several decades, *c.* 1800–50. Lin Zexu loved this painting of his father and it travelled with him all over China. Height 29.5 cm, length 115.5 cm. Private collection.

The foreign interests with whom Lin came into conflict in Guangzhou tended to portray him as inflexible, even fanatical. Along with some subsequent journalists and historians, they cited his intransigence as a major cause of the First Opium War (1839–42). In fact Lin had proven many times to be a man of reserved and responsive judgment. He carefully researched the problems he encountered in his career, and was willing to change his mind as guided by the facts. In 1838, Lin had agreed with others that opium sale and use should not be tolerated, and that it was important to rehabilitate addicts, but his first priority was Chinese smugglers. Only late in the day, before he took up his mission to Guangzhou, did he change his mind to focus on the foreign importers.

Lin intended to use a proven method against opium smugglers and addicts: severe pressure on wrongdoers, which would be alleviated in degrees as they reformed. Because of the structure of the commercial community at Guangzhou, the most efficient path to the foreign importers was through their Chinese partners. After he had been in the city only about a week, he threatened to execute the two most influential merchants if they did not persuade the foreign importers to surrender all the opium they had on hand and sign contracts guaranteeing that no more would be imported. He and provincial officials blockaded the mouth of the Pearl River, preventing the new British trade official, Charles Elliot (1801–1875), from entering Guangzhou when he arrived only days later. Lin ordered all Chinese out of the foreign residential compounds in Guangzhou, and forbade any supply of food or medicine to the foreigners. It may have been about this time that Lin and his government colleagues wrote their famous letter to Queen Victoria, charging Britain with knowingly violating Qing law and promoting a vice that was morally condemned in Britain itself. 'Where is the conscience in this?' they concluded. Though there is no evidence that British officials, let alone Victoria, received the letter, months later a translation was printed in the British press and helped arouse public opinion supporting war with China.

Lin and Elliot sparred over legal issues and technicalities. Elliot first surrendered about a tenth of the available opium and told Lin it was the entire supply. But Lin's habit of seeking exact information allowed him to see through the ruse and demand all the contraband. For his part, Elliot now convinced the British merchants to give their opium to him before giving it to Lin, meaning that, by the time Lin received it, the opium had become British crown property, and its destruction a possible cause for war. But within weeks Lin seemed to be getting results. The British were surrendering their opium to him as it came into the city, and Lin allowed supply of food and services to be resumed. When the river was unblocked, the British fled the foreign district of Guangzhou, most going to Macao. In June 1839, Lin first prayed for protection of the fish of the Pearl River, then destroyed the thousand tons of opium he had confiscated.

Lin thought the conflict was nearly resolved. But, in July, drunken British sailors killed a Chinese fisherman in the Kowloon peninsula. Lin and the local governor demanded that the responsible sailors be surrendered for punishment, but Elliot insisted that the culprits be dealt with according to British law. Lin then forced the British in Macao to relocate to Hong Kong Island, which at the time had insufficient living quarters and food for them. The question of compensation for the opium destroyed by Lin became an issue of intense debate in the British Parliament. Elliot had implied that the British government would pay, but British officials insisted the charges be transferred to the Chinese government. In March 1840, a narrow vote in Parliament authorized war against China. When British gunboats from India reached the southern and eastern Chinese coast two months later, the war immediately went badly for the Qing. In September, the imperial court dissolved Lin's position, and before the end of the year had exiled him to a minor position in Ili, Xinjiang.

Lin's reputation as a troubleshooter was dented but not destroyed. The imperial court delayed his Xinjiang exile with an assignment to address more Yellow River problems. When he finally completed the four-month journey from Beijing to Ili in 1842, he was repeatedly drawn away again, to consult in Beijing and to act as governor in half a dozen distressed provinces. In literati circles, he became famous as a vigorous advocate for reform. While the First Opium War was raging he had defied elite opinion in Beijing by initiating the selection and translation of British works on law, geography and natural science. Lin was himself an avid writer and editor, and actively led the project. He argued that, contrary to prior assumptions, the British could defeat the Qing through naval bombardment, while rarely setting foot on land. For the empire to be secure, its coastal defences must be reinforced, and new expenditures directed towards the most urgent needs: 'ships and guns'.

Though Lin's arguments for sound knowledge of the West impressed rising reformers, including his collaborator Wei Yuan (1794–1857), it did not move the Qing court, which above all sought to avoid expense – including payment of the indemnities stipulated in the series of unequal treaties with foreign powers that followed the First Opium War. Instead of attempting to prevent problems. the court continued to deploy Lin to fix them. In 1850, he was commissioned to solve what would prove to be the greatest of all Qing crises – the Taiping uprising. But he died en route to Guangxi, before he could begin the work.

Pamela Kyle Crossley

78. BAO SHICHEN

包世臣 (1775–1855)

POLICY EXPERT

Bao Shichen was arguably the most celebrated policy consultant of the early 19th century. The offspring of a modestly prosperous Anhui family, he passed the two lower levels of the civil service examinations (the local and provincial exams) as a young man, then continued, over the rest of his life, to fail – at least a dozen times – the highest (central) level. Consequently he had virtually no official career, and instead spent his adulthood as a peripatetic policy advisor to numerous reformist officials. The reason for his repeated failure in the highest exam was hardly lack of ability or scholarly diligence, but rather that the content of his study had shifted away from the classical curriculum to less canonical, but in his view more 'useful' texts, on military strategy, social organization, agronomy, fiscal and judicial administration, and other practical subjects. In each of these policy areas, Bao combined his textual command with field observation, and with an unusual emphasis on quantitative analysis, to arrive at what was widely regarded as surpassing expertise. The 1921 *Draft History of the Qing* noted of Bao, 'All the great officials of the south, when faced with major policy decisions regarding warfare, famine, river conservancy, grain tribute, or salt administration, never failed to come humbly to him for advice, and he would expound his views with vigour.'

Bao's young adulthood coincided with the multifaceted general crisis of the early 19th century, starting during the reign of the Jiaqing emperor (1796–1820). Confronting challenges of demographic pressure, ecological decay, sectarian rebellion, official corruption, bureaucratic inertia and fiscal impoverishment – soon to be joined in the Daoguang reign (1821–1850) by an unprecedented foreign threat from

Tao Zhaosun, *Portrait of Bao Shichen*, 1775–1855. Hanging scroll, ink and colour on paper. Height 93.5 cm, width 38.4 cm, The Palace Museum, Beijing.

the maritime West – officials and private literati from the throne on down were tortured by awareness that problems that had once seemed relatively easy to solve now seemed impossibly difficult. Among these reform-minded thinkers, Bao Shichen stood out for his optimism that well-informed practical problem-solving offered a way both to save the dynasty, and to provision and enrich its people.

Among the most debated problems for which Bao offered solutions were those of grain tribute collection and the imperial salt administration. Both were areas in which a bloated bureaucracy impeded efficient management. The government monopoly on salt production and distribution was in the hands of a relatively small number of franchised official-merchants who were tasked with annual shipment of large amounts of salt along minutely prescribed routes from the production areas to specified distribution centres, where they would be sold at officially fixed prices. The unwieldiness of this system had given rise to growing smuggling rackets, which undercut the price of official salt and were clearly better meeting the needs of consumers, but cut deeply into government revenues. Bao argued that the solution was less government micro-management and an invitation to broader participation by a larger cohort of smaller-scale private merchants, shipping smaller job-lots to a wider range of distribution points, in flexible response to market demand. His proposals were adopted, with considerable success.

The issue of the grain tribute system – shipping tax-grain from the south to the court at Beijing via the Grand Canal – was more vexing. Long-term failure to conduct routine dredging of the Canal and the north China river system that fed into it had resulted in silting up of the bed of the Canal and increasingly impeded progress of government grain shipments from the south to official and military consumers in the north. By the mid-1820s, the problem had become so acute that northbound grain boats nearly all ran aground in the Canal, their cargo never reaching its intended destination. As a solution to this dilemma, Bao proposed that grain shipments from the Yangtze valley to north China be handled not by government personnel on the Canal, but instead by contracted private merchants from Yangtze delta ports such as Shanghai along the maritime coast. This sea-route policy was tried with mixed success. Tribute grain was once again successfully shipped to the north, but the problem of silting of the Canal was not effectively addressed and laid-off Canal boatmen became a persistent threat to public order.

Bao Shichen's proposed solutions to these two aspects of crisis involved both a degree of privatization of economic activity, and a reliance on merchants and the open marketplace. This has led some scholars to characterize Bao as an economic 'liberal' and an advocate of *laissez-faire* economic policy. But such a view tends to overlook that it was above all the economic interests of the state that drove Bao's concern. In both cases, he argued reliance on market forces over bureaucratic commandism would actually increase the government's fiscal revenues. Ever since his experience combatting White Lotus rebels during his early adulthood, it had been state impoverishment that, as much as anything else, worried Bao. His concern for the wealth and power of the imperial state, and his unembarrassed advocacy of policies aimed at increasing 'profit' for both public and private parties, challenged the conventional view that 'benevolent government' meant *small* government and anticipated the arguments of later 19th-century reformers such as Feng Guifen (1809–1874) and Yan Fu (1854–1921).

Bao's perceived need for a wealthy and powerful state further intensified in the face of the British threat of the 1830s. He was possibly the first Chinese observer to link British opium imports to the problems of silver outflow, destabilization of the domestic silver–copper exchange rate, and the consequent impoverishment of Qing commoners, who relied on the increasingly devalued copper coin for tax payments and purchase of daily necessities. To remedy this issue, Bao advocated a strict prohibition on opium imports and an extreme hard line on British trade, despite the real danger of war with a powerful foreign antagonist this policy presented. He counselled his friend Lin Zexu to take such a hard line in his capacity as imperial commissioner at Canton (Guangzhou), which Lin in fact did, leading to the catastrophe of the First Opium War (1839–42).

William T. Rowe

79. ZENG GUOFAN

曾國藩 (1811–1872)

VICTORIOUS GENERAL IN THE TAIPING CIVIL WAR

The most famous general of China's 19th century never intended to have a military career. Zeng Guofan was the oldest of five brothers raised on a rural farm in Hunan province. He started out in life with aspirations to become a Confucian scholar and hopefully pass the civil service examinations to become an official. However, even though the imperial Chinese examination system purported to be meritocratic, the reality was that the children of wealthy, urban scholars had enormous advantages in preparing for them. Zeng did not have such advantages and no one in his family prior to his father had ever managed to pass even the lowest level of the examinations. His father was the first in the family to study for them and would eventually pass the lowest level one after sixteen failed attempts. Fortunately for Zeng Guofan, however, he proved an exceptional student and was able to show that it was indeed possible for a young man of modest means from a rural family to succeed, if he had sufficient talent. It took him seven attempts to pass the district-level examination, but he then went on to perform brilliantly at both the provincial level and the imperial level in Beijing, where he was selected in 1838 as a Hanlin scholar. The Hanlin Academy was the government's elite academic institution, so Zeng's selection marked him as one of the top hundred or so candidates in an empire of several hundred million people.

Zeng's official career began auspiciously enough, and success in the examinations meant not just prestige but also wealth. In 1843, he was sent to supervise the imperial examinations in Sichuan province, where rich families vied for his favour by inundating him with expensive gifts. He returned to Beijing in possession of sixteen sedan chairs filled with silver, jade, furs and other treasures. But, even as he profited from the endemic corruption of the imperial bureaucracy, he grew to despise it, eventually setting a firm moral standard for himself and for the other scholars whom he counted as friends. He was fond of setting strict rules for his own conduct, governing everything from how and what he would read, to the exercise he would take after meals, to his habit of keeping a daily diary.

The turning point in his career came in 1852, when the Taiping rebels swept through his home province of Hunan on their way north out of Guangxi, shattering the imperial forces that had been sent to stop them. Usually, Zeng Guofan would not have been home in Hunan – China's imperial government traditionally feared the emergence of local bases of power, and so officials as a rule were not posted to service in their home provinces. However, his mother had died, and in that circumstance an official was expected to retire from public service and return home for an extended period of mourning. For the Xianfeng emperor (r. 1851–1861) in Beijing, this was fortuitous.

In light of the emergency posed by the Taiping, the emperor asked Zeng Guofan to begin organizing local militia forces in Hunan province, so they could provide security for the province and possibly go on campaign against the Taiping. Zeng initially did not know how to respond, because following the emperor's orders would mean abandoning his Confucian duty to continue mourning his mother. But after a period of reflection, Zeng Guofan concluded that his duty to the emperor was more urgent, so he came out of retirement and started raising an army.

What emerged over the following months and years would, by the early 1860s, become the most powerful and cohesive military force in all of China. Beginning with local militias, Zeng Guofan ultimately created an army of some 120,000 Hunanese soldiers. And he defied precedent by building it entirely along personal and local lines, so that each member of the army served under a superior with whom he had a pre-existing bond. For the generals, Zeng chose his own brothers and scholarly friends from Hunan. They in turn recruited officers from their own personal networks, and, at the lowest levels, the foot soldiers were Hunanese peasants, recruited by scholars from their own districts, and serving alongside men from their own home villages.

The Hunan Army was largely self-funded (by local gentry and transit taxes) and Zeng Guofan commanded it independently of the demands of Beijing. Because Zeng was loyal to the emperor, it fought on the imperial side. By the early 1860s, however, the Hunan Army and a smaller provincial army from Anhui, built on similar lines, were the only viable imperial forces left campaigning against the Taiping. This was a fearful prospect for the imperial government, because the Hunan Army's ultimate loyalty was to Zeng Guofan and their home province of Hunan, rather than

to the dynasty. By the time the Hunan Army extinguished the Taiping capital in Nanjing in 1864, it would have been relatively easy for Zeng to cast off the failing Qing and establish himself on the throne as China's new emperor. That he did not do so – instead serving out his years as a senior Qing official – is one of the reasons he is remembered in China as an unfailing model of Confucian loyalty.

Zeng Guofan was Qing China's great military hero of the 19th century, the general who rose up in a time of chaos to restore order to the empire. He cast a shadow over subsequent generations. As China's government changed, however, views on Zeng also changed. By the early 1900s, the Han Chinese nationalists who led the revolution against the Manchus that would bring down the Qing dynasty painted Zeng not as a hero but as a traitor: a Han Chinese general who had killed untold numbers of other Chinese (the Taiping soldiers) in order to preserve the rule of the alien Manchus. In the 1920s, Zeng was rehabilitated by 'Generalissimo' Chiang Kai-shek (founder of the Nationalist government in 1928), who saw in the Qing dynasty's war against the Taiping an analogy to his own Nationalist Party's efforts to destroy China's Communists. Chiang modelled himself after Zeng Guofan – the suppressor of internal threats – and edited Zeng's writings into a textbook for military cadets. With the victory of the Communists over the Nationalists in 1949, however, the pendulum swung again, and the Taiping were recast as the heroes – the peasant rebels who foreshadowed Mao and the 20th-century Communists – while Zeng Guofan became a villain once more. Today, in yet another reversal, Zeng has been resurrected as a model of Confucian loyalty and a restorer of order, who stood against the forces of chaos in his time.

In spite of his lasting influence over China's military culture, Zeng Guofan never wanted to be remembered as a general. To the end, it was his Confucian scholarship – his original goal in life, before the Taiping emergency – that he considered his highest calling. He wished the same for his descendants. As he wrote to his sons while he was on campaign against the Taiping: 'All you should do is pursue your studies with a single mind. You must not become soldiers. And you need not become officials either.'

Stephen Platt

80. ZUO ZONGTANG

左宗棠 (1812–1885)

MILITARY LEADER AND INDUSTRIAL INNOVATOR

Zuo Zongtang rose to become one of the most important 19th-century Qing generals and statesmen. He played a key role in carrying the state through the destructive civil war period (1850s to 1870s), and devoted his life to strengthening Qing China against enemies, both internal and external. His influence reshaped the Qing empire, and yet his career almost did not happen at all.

Zuo was born in Xiangyin county in Hunan into a moderately wealthy family of scholars. As for sons in most gentry families of the time, Zuo was educated in the Confucian classics, in the hope that he would one day pass the imperial examinations to become an official. Then, in 1830, Zuo's father died, leaving the family in difficult financial circumstances. With the patronage of the official and scholar He Changling (1785–1848), Zuo was able to enter an academy nearby. He Changling was a proponent of the 'statecraft' (*jingshi*) school, an approach that emphasized the practical application of scholarship to the work of government. He encouraged the young Zuo to read widely, in fields such as geography, agriculture and military tactics, alongside his studies in history and classics. Zuo himself developed a belief in the importance of practically orientated Confucian governance and the role that moral, self-cultivated officials should play in guiding the people towards ethical living – a form of Confucian revivalism that deeply influenced his policy-making. He passed the provincial examinations in 1832, but repeatedly failed to pass the metropolitan-level examinations that would have allowed him to become an official. Abandoning the attempt, Zuo became a local scholar and teacher, with a particular interest in the cultivation of mulberry trees. Without the crises of the 19th century, this is likely where he would have remained.

When the Taiping Civil War broke out in 1851, Zuo initially fled to the mountains. However, with Hunan falling into chaos, a friend of Zuo recommended his talents to the governor of Hunan, Zhang Liangji (1807–1871). Zuo was promptly delegated to oversee military affairs in the region, a task at which he soon distinguished himself. As the Taiping continued to ravage the area, Zuo was commanded to raise a brigade of his own in 1860, under the direction of Zeng Guofan (1811–1872). The decision to instruct local gentry to raise their own forces was a sign of how threatened the Qing were: historically, the Green Standard forces of the Qing had been structured specifically to prevent any one commander from developing a following that might be loyal to him alone. The Hunanese armies raised by Zeng and Zuo swiftly became the most effective fighting forces remaining to the Qing, with soldiers tied to their commanders through bonds of friendship, native place, religion and shared outlook. Zuo played an instrumental role in Qing victory in the Taiping Civil War, and was then transferred to Shaanxi and Gansu to defeat the Muslim rebellion there in 1866.

He was a talented administrator, with a particular gift for the logistics of war. He is often described as a member of the Self-Strengthening Movement, devoted to introducing Western science, industry and military methods into China, while

Portrait of Zuo Zongtang, from *Zuo Zongtang Recovering Hangzhou*, *c.* 1864–85. Ink and colours on silk. Height 54.7 cm, width 29.3 cm. Peking University Library.

preserving the Confucian moral core at the heart of imperial rule. While governor general of Fujian and Zhejiang in the 1860s, he founded China's first modern dockyard and naval academy at Fuzhou. Other initiatives included printing presses to distribute Confucian tracts, alongside general reconstruction work across the provinces.

Zuo's greatest impact was probably in the north-western regions of Shaanxi, Gansu and Xinjiang, where his proposals went significantly further than simply reconquest. In order not merely to bring peace but also to ensure that rebellion would never occur again, Zuo masterminded the resettlement of tens of thousands of Muslims in Shaanxi and Gansu away from their former Han neighbours. He argued forcefully for the necessity of reconquering Xinjiang and negotiated the return of occupied territory in the Ili Valley from Russia. Xinjiang was made a province in 1880 with the intention that its laws and customs be reformed to match those of the interior. In both places, a programme of education was designed to Confucianize Chinese and Turkic Muslims. These were colonial, 'civilizing' projects, designed to transform people – a programmatic intent distinct from earlier Qing approaches to the north-west, which had mostly seen maintenance of the status quo as the easiest route to stability. Although left largely unrealized, the transformative intent behind them reshaped relationships between Chinese Muslims, Turkic Muslims and the Han, hardening boundaries between groups and redefining what it meant to be Muslim in China.

Zuo's cultural programmes went hand-in-hand with a programme of development. He was clear-headed in his awareness that enduring post-war stability required an economic revival. His soldiers were directed to cultivate land when they were not at the front, an initiative that helped ease some of his supply-chain difficulties with fighting through the barren, devastated lands of the north-west. Former rebels were resettled onto empty lands, instructed to become farmers, and given seed grain and tools. Meanwhile, Zuo tried (and largely failed) to prohibit cultivation of opium. He opened wool and cotton mills in Lanzhou and encouraged cotton cultivation in Xinjiang, forging patterns of colonial development that persist into the present. He also retained his early interest in silviculture: his initiatives included an intensive tree-planting programme throughout Gansu.

Although Zuo would be made to look conservative by the generation that followed him, he was profoundly radical in both his particular Confucian zeal and his promotion of Western technologies. Without the armies he led, the Qing might never have survived the civil war period; the population transfers he engineered in the north-west can still be seen on a map today.

Hannah Theaker

81. ZHANG ZHIDONG

張之洞 (1837–1909)

ABOLISHER OF THE IMPERIAL EXAMINATIONS

In an era when many lost their titles, their reputations and even their lives on the shifting front lines between reform and revolution, Zhang Zhidong's career is a testament to the efficacy of advancing several steps behind the vanguard. After making his name as a member of the conservative 'Purification Clique' (Qingliu dang), Zhang emerged towards the end of his career as a moderate reformer arguing that China's educational advancement would salvage the fate of the dynasty, by bringing the educated men of the empire together in a community rooted in ancient traditions, while also embracing new technologies. Ironically, the educational reforms proposed by Zhang spelled the beginning of the end of the imperial civil service examination system and curriculum based on study of the Confucian canon, resulting in the alienation of a generation of young talent. After its abolition in 1905, the young and ambitious went on to advocate exactly what Zhang had spent his life trying to forestall: revolution.

Zhang, a talented student, passed the provincial – mid-level – civil service examinations at the age of fifteen, ranking first. After then being awarded third place in the metropolitan exams at age twenty-six, he accepted a position in the Hanlin Academy (the government's elite academic institution), where he served for almost a decade before being appointed governor of Shanxi in 1882. During this early phase of his career, Zhang supported the Purification Clique, which argued that the problems of the dynasty could be attributed to moral decay within, and military threats without. Early in his career, Zhang's impassioned attacks on Qing officials he deemed too weak and ineffective to stave off foreign aggression won him renown. But his support for war with France, in response to skirmishes in Annam (in modern Vietnam), would, in the mid-1880s, put Zhang and his fellow clique members out of imperial favour.

After this shift in his political fortunes, Zhang became a latter-day convert to the very Self-Strengthening Movement whose earlier proponents – such as Li Hongzhang (1823–1901) – he had previously ridiculed. In his career as governor general of Liangguang, Huguang and Liangjiang (1884–1907), he established not only several military academies but also schools for the study of torpedoes, telegraphy, mining, railroads, chemistry, agriculture, industry and commercial affairs. Like Self-Strengthening governors of earlier years, Zhang also established ironworks, mining operations and textile factories, in addition to pouring decades of effort into completing the Beijing–Hankou railway.

At the height of his Self-Strengthening phase, Zhang forged relationships with famous reformers of the time. In 1895, he formed a 'Strengthening Study Society' with Yuan Shikai (1859–1916), Xu Shichang (1855–1939), and the soon-to-be-infamous

Kang Youwei (1858–1927), who emerged at the centre of the Guangxu emperor's (r. 1875–1908) abortive Hundred Days' Reform of the summer of 1898.

By that summer, Zhang both disavowed those – like his former clique members – who only prized 'ancient learning' as well as those – like Kang – whom he dubbed too fascinated with the 'new learning' from the West to save the Chinese tradition. In his famous 1898 tract *Exhortation to Learning* (translated into English as *China's Only Hope*), Zhang argued for a middle road. On the one hand, he insisted that the foundation of all governance was education, and that the subjects of the empire must be inculcated with the ancient values that bound together the Chinese dynasties of the past, because, 'The preservation of the dynasty, the preservation of our teachings, and the preservation of our race require a sameness of heart and mind.' The centrality of ancient learning to a trans-dynastic Chinese tradition led him to dismiss those who would emulate Western institutions as 'hateful, vulgar men angry at the age' and abandon the very tradition that he saw as China's only salvation.

But changing times did warrant reform. In this, Zhang echoed earlier Self-Strengthening proponents in proposing that 'ancient learning' could remain the centre of the dynasty's educational mission, while 'new learning' from the West could be pursued in technical fields, policy and international relations. He stridently dismissed 'those literati of China who, until now, have been content with remaining unmoving and backward', refusing to learn what the West had to teach.

Zhang's recommendations – the founding of new schools throughout the empire, a renewed focus on both the classics and the technical arts, the abolition of the infamous eight-legged essay of the civil service examination, and the introduction into the examination syllabus of questions about policy matters and technical knowledge – were all well-trodden territory by the time Zhang produced the *Exhortation to Learning*. But Zhang's timely authoring of the piece won the praise and recognition of the Guangxu emperor in the summer of 1898. Guangxu, however, was not able to bring Zhang's vision to fruition. Just a few months after the throne's endorsement of his work, Zhang supported Empress Dowager Cixi's (1835–1908) coup to reclaim power. The Hundred Days' Reform ended in the flight, exile or execution of many who had advocated reform.

Zhang, spared from the purge, brought up educational reform once again in the summer of 1900, when the imperial court – in flight from Beijing after the suppression of the Boxer Rebellion – solicited advice on how to save the dynasty. Zhang proposed once more, first, the end of the eight-legged essay format and, second, the inclusion of questions about technical fields and policy issues in the exams. The Empress Dowager now belatedly endorsed the proposal and the 1902 metropolitan exam – the highest in the empire – followed this new format.

But just a year later, Zhang argued that even this measure for promoting new talent and knowledge had failed, co-authoring a joint memorial with Yuan Shikai calling the collected exams little more than 'empty words' and declaring, 'We must plan for the gradual phasing out of the civil service exams.' They proposed that

Photograph of Zhang
Zhidong, *c.* 1901–09.
Height 9.5 cm, width
6.8 cm. National Library
of Finland, Helsinki.

graduates of the new schools (with curricula featuring subjects such as science and foreign languages) cropping up throughout the empire be granted the paths to officialdom formerly monopolized by successful exam candidates.

By 1905, Zhang and Yuan finally urged the throne to immediately cease the civil service examinations, deeming further reform of the existing system impossible. Only the new schools could introduce talented young thinkers to save the age. When this memorial was approved by the Empress Dowager, the exams stopped. Two years later, Zhang retired from service in the provincial bureaucracy, taking up a post on the coveted Grand Council that advised the throne, and later serving as the head of the Qing's newly established Ministry of Education. In October of 1909, he fell ill and died, aged seventy-two.

Two years after Zhang's death, on 10 October 1911, it was in the city of Wuchang – the seat of Zhang Zhidong's governor generalship of Liangguang – that the Xinhai Revolution broke out, led by both students of the new schools, for which Zhang had so ardently advocated, and graduates of the Hubei Military Academy, where Zhang had cultivated the military talent meant to save the Qing from its enemies. When Yuan Shikai was ordered to send the Beiyang Army to recapture the city, the forces were sent into Hubei on the very railway that Zhang Zhidong had spent over a decade completing. Only two years after his death, the same achievements that Zhang had promised would secure the future of the Qing were instruments of its demise. For this dubious honour, Sun Yat-sen (1866–1925) later dubbed him 'the greatest revolutionary who never spoke of revolution'.

Maura D. Dykstra

82. PRINCE GONG

恭親王 (1833–1898)

ARCHITECT OF MODERN DIPLOMACY IN CHINA AFTER 1860

On 3 May 1898, the *Manchester Guardian* reported that 'by the death of Prince Kung (Gong)' the day before 'China loses the most powerful, if not the most prominent, of her statesmen of recent years'. Provincial officials such as Li Hongzhang (1823–1901) and Zeng Guofan (1811–1872) might be more famous in the West, but 'none of these held at any time anything like the power of the Manchu prince who has played the chief part in directing the policy of China since the day of the Treaty of Tientsin [Tianjin]' of 1858. The newspaper was not exaggerating. In 1861, the 28-year-old Prince Gong had conspired with empress dowagers Ci'an (1837–1881) and Ci'xi (1835–1908), the latter just widowed following the death of the Xianfeng emperor (r. 1851–1861), to effect the Xinyou Coup. The coup's success made the prince a powerful figure at the centre of power in Beijing until his death at the age of sixty-five.

Born in 1833, Yixin (Prince Gong) was raised in the Forbidden City together with his older half-brother, Yizhu, who would become the Xianfeng emperor. The two learned Manchu, Mongol and Chinese, and studied the Confucian Classics, history and poetry in the Imperial Library under the great statesman Jia Zhen (1798–1874), as well as archery and horsemanship. Legend has it that the less talented Yizhu was able to secure the favour of his father, the Daoguang emperor (r. 1821–1850), through clever strategies. One spring when out hunting with his father and brother, he refused to release any arrows, explaining that he did not want to kill animals in the breeding season. When it became clear that his father's days were numbered, he wailed on the ground. Having long hesitated between his two remaining senior sons, the emperor anointed Yizhu because of his humaneness and filiality. At the same time he indicated his faith in Yixin by elevating him to Prince of the First Degree.

By 1860, the survival of the dynasty was at stake. In the Yangtze river valley, the Taiping Civil War (1851–64) – whose final estimated death toll of 20 to 70 million direct and indirect lives makes it the most destructive civil war in history – had revived from internal conflict among the insurgents and now threatened Shanghai, which was rapidly growing into China's financial and commercial centre. At the end of the Second Opium War (1856–60), Britain and France marched on Beijing to avenge the Qing having taken hostage their negotiators and to enforce the ratification of the Treaty of Tianjin. This treaty required the opening of more ports to trade, the cession of Kowloon to Britain, residence of diplomats in Beijing, and the right of foreigners to be held to their own laws (extraterritoriality) rather than the Qing's. To the north, the Russian empire had massed forces along the Mongolian and Manchurian borders. The Xianfeng emperor fled Beijing for Chengde as British and French forces approached the city. He had ordered Prince Gong to stay behind to deal with the foreigners.

This Prince Gong did with audacity and intelligence. Rather than fighting the British and the French, and so run the risk that they made common cause with the Taiping, he decided to make peace with them, drawing their diplomatic representatives away from Canton (Guangzhou) and Shanghai to Beijing, and making the fight with the Taiping their war too. In Prince Gong's eyes, the Taiping were a far greater threat than foreigners who, he declared, just wanted trade opportunities. At the cost of territorial concessions in outer Manchuria, Prince Gong also made peace with Russia. Its envoy, Nikolai Ignatiev (1832–1908), helped broker the settlement that meant the British and the French stayed their hand in Beijing – that is, sacked the Summer Palace (Yuanming yuan) to the north-west of the capital rather than torch the Forbidden City at its centre – and let matters rest with the ratification of the Tianjin Treaty. Xenophobes surrounding the Xianfeng emperor were enraged at the concessions Prince Gong made. To undo these, a group of eight Manchu princes and high officials established a council of regents to take over when the hapless Xianfeng emperor died in 1861. Prince Gong conspired with Ci'an and Cixi, all three of whom had reason to fear for their lives, in arresting the council of regents. Their leader, Sushun (1816–1861), was publicly dismembered, two others were required to commit suicide, a lesser punishment, and the remainder were sent into internal exile. Prince Gong became sole prince regent.

The way now lay open for Prince Gong, together with Ci'an and Cixi (who gained consultancy rights), to push through a wide range of reform measures, which historians refer to collectively as the Self-Strengthening Movement. They included the creation of a proto-foreign office, the Zongli yamen; the training of a new Manchu force armed with Western weapons in Beijing, the Shenjiying; the hiring of foreigners to manage China's Customs Service, which helped solve a deep financial crisis; the establishment of modern arsenals; the introduction of the telegraph; and the founding of the Translator's College, which translated Western legal, scientific, philosophical and economic texts, and began the training of modern diplomats. Prince Gong also advocated for changes in the traditional examination system and sent students abroad. With the help of foreign forces, including Charles Gordon's (1833–1885) Ever Victorious Army, the Taiping were defeated by 1864. Prince Gong had sailed the Qing dynasty's ship of state through its mid-19th-century storms.

Felice Beato (1832–1909), *Prince Gong*, 1860. Albumen print. National Portrait Gallery, London.

Prince Gong's impact on the Qing's fate was as profound as (if not more profound than) that of Richard Nixon and Deng Xiaoping on the People's Republic some 110 years later. In an 1866 memorial to the Tongzhi emperor (r. 1862–1874), Prince Gong wrote that 'it is groundless to criticize [our reform policies] as "abandoning Chinese ways and following Westerners". For Western numbers actually all stem from ancient Chinese techniques of algebra, and even Western scholars view them as "techniques that came from the east". It is just that their dispositions are more meticulous.' Prince Gong became an advocate of the theory that Western science and learning had ancient Chinese sources, not as a salve to wounded pride or as emotional consolation, but, as intellectual historian Leigh Jenco has argued, to give that learning the pedigree of a prestigious intellectual lineage. It therefore demanded serious engagement and so opened up space for genuinely innovative thinking. Prince Gong, in short, not only facilitated the Qing dynasty's entry into the modern global political economy, but also helped spark its intellectual and cultural transformation.

No one is powerful without also being a threat. Prince Gong was censured by senior court enemies in 1865 and then again in 1874 on the grounds that he had not shown due respect to the emperor. On both occasions he was restored to power quickly. In 1884, he and his principal followers were ousted when Qing forces suffered defeats in the Sino-French War, and Yixuan (1840–1891), the father of the newly enthroned Guangxu emperor (r. 1875–1908), became regent. When the next crisis, war with Japan, hit in the mid-1890s, Prince Gong once more returned to power. His last major act was his refusal in 1898 to side with Kang Youwei (1858–1927) and Liang Qichao (1873–1929), when they led a campaign to turn the Qing into a constitutional monarchy. Had he done so, the Qing might well have lasted longer. Prince Gong was thus ultimately driven by maintaining his and his family's grip on power.

Chinese historians of the 20th century tended to marginalize Prince Gong as a historical figure, because anti-Manchu and anti-imperialist historiography declined to credit Manchu figures with having done anything useful. As an emblem of this disdain, in the 1950s, the bricks of his grave, which had already been robbed in the 1930s, were used to build a water reservoir. But historians began to pay attention to him once more during the relative liberalization of academic research that followed the rise of Deng Xiaoping, and Beijing's preparations for the 2008 Olympics included the restoration of the magnificent Prince Gong Mansion in Beijing. It is an appropriate monument to one of the key historical figures of the Qing dynasty in its last century.

Hans van de Ven

83. LI HONGZHANG

李鴻章 (1823–1901)

DIPLOMAT BROKERING AN INTERNATIONAL VISION OF CHINA

A diplomat, general and reformer, Li Hongzhang guided the foreign policy of the late Qing government from the late 1860s until his death in 1901. His high-profile negotiation of treaties and canny use of the media made him the best-known Chinese official outside China – as demonstrated in countless photographic portraits, where he is often posed with his diplomatic counterparts. Just as importantly, he was an early and active proponent of the Self-Strengthening Movement, a series of institutional reforms based on the pragmatic adoption of Western technology, strategy and education. Throughout his long career, Li outpaced his contemporaries in initiatives devoted to developing modern military resources, manufacturing enterprises and transportation infrastructure.

The first decades of his life were marked by a swift rise through the ranks of state officialdom, as well as the raising of the Huai Army to contain the insurgents during the Taiping Civil War (1851–64). He was buoyed by ambition, competence in military strategy, and a distinctively proactive response to Western powers. Li was a native of Hefei in Anhui province and came from a scholar-gentry family. He achieved the prestigious, top-level *jinshi* civil service degree in 1847, and was given initial postings in the elite Hanlin Academy in Beijing. He returned to his native province in 1853, where he was engaged in suppressing the Taiping, serving as an assistant to Zeng Guofan (1811–1872), founder of the Hunan Army. Distinct from the imperial armies under the direction of the Qing, the Hunan Army was a militia force based on local affiliations and loyalties, and financed by local gentry, with direct personal allegiance to Zeng. Li gained a reputation for military strategy. From 1862 to 1866, he was in Shanghai, where he served as the governor of Jiangsu, charged with founding the regional Huai Army, organized along the same localist lines as Zeng's Hunan force. The position brought Li into proximity with Western military ideas and technology. Significantly, he observed the efficacy of the Ever Victorious Army, a light infantry of European mercenaries and Chinese recruits, equipped with rifles and howitzers. Dealing with European consuls, and naval and military personnel, Li developed a new, global perspective on Chinese competitiveness in the arenas of warfare and economy. He enhanced his troops' fighting capacity through foreign-led training and the use of artillery. The Huai Army grew to 40,000 men, armed with more than 10,000 rifles and cannon. Li led it to retake Suzhou, Changzhou and other territories. As a result, he is credited in part with suppressing the Taiping army. His ability to lead and modernize the Huai Army also signified the growth of his own regional power as supported by local elites.

The mandate for the remainder of his career was set: to open up China to the world, but on Chinese terms. Amid further military campaigns quashing rebellions, Li sought to enhance China's 'wealth and strength' – or strategically adopt Western means of growing China's forces and material resources, all the while protecting against foreign encroachment. Early initiatives in Shanghai included founding two arsenals, later combined into the Jiangnan Arsenal, and securing foreign expertise in the production of munitions. In the 1870s, he was concurrently appointed viceroy of Zhili province (later Hebei province) and Beiyang trade minister, the latter a key role that gave him responsibility over commercial and state affairs in the northern ports. Despite considerable challenges to the Qing in the realm of international diplomacy, he signed treaties with Britain, Peru, Japan and France, and took the lead on Qing relations with Korea, all with varying degrees of success in negotiating for Qing China's sovereignty rights. He pursued commercial reforms that allowed for the development of modern private enterprise, such as the China Merchants' Steam Navigation Company. In the government sector, he shifted state funds to modernize the Beiyang naval fleet in north-east China, purchasing battleships from Germany and Britain; the Beiyang became the largest of the Qing regional navies. In 1875, at the death of the Tongzhi emperor (r. 1862–1874), Li led a force into the capital and effected a coup, placing the Guangxu emperor (r. 1875–1908) in power with the empress dowagers Ci'an (1837–1881) and Cixi (1835–1908) as regents. In 1885, he founded the modernized Tianjin Military Academy to train officers; also in that year, Li made an

相壽爺古

帝　天　天
君祉　子　公錫
子福為敢實方兄純
有祿尤不惟既文毆
穀不　來阿平兄有
詔崇永王衛保弍秭
孫　錫果謚　斯
子　難遠海遠祜
　老能外猾押
　既邁有辰押
　受爲載吉威
　　龍莫四儀

Unknown artist, *Portrait of Li Hongzhang in Official Robes and Fur Coat*, c. 1840–1901. Album leaf, ink and colour on paper. Height 63 cm, width 75 cm. National Museum of China, Beijing.

agreement with Japanese statesman Itō Hirobumi (1841–1909), creating a joint protectorate over Korea.

Towards the end of his career, several events resulted in mixed appraisals of Li as a mediator and emissary. The Qing empire went to war with Japan in 1894 over Korea, and he was drawn into the conflict, due to his political ties with Manchuria and his previous activities in Korea. Li's naval forces lost, and, in the resulting negotiations, the Qing ceded Taiwan and the Liaodong Peninsula to Japan, recognized Korean independence and opened new treaty ports. It also paid indemnities to Japan and accorded it the same extraterritorial privileges previously granted Western nations under the unequal treaties. In 1896, Li toured the United States and Europe, and was received by leaders such as President Grover Cleveland (1837–1908) and Queen Victoria (r. 1837–1901). While in the United States, he advocated for reform of the Chinese Exclusion Act of 1882, a xenophobic policy that restricted Chinese immigration to the United States. While in Russia, he attended the coronation of Tsar Nicolas II (r. 1894–1917), and secretly negotiated the Li–Lobanov Treaty. The treaty provided for Russian protection against future Japanese aggression, but also ceded considerable privileges to Russia in north-east China; it was met with disapproval from officials upon his return. In 1901, he signed the Boxer Protocol with the eight foreign powers who had subdued the nationalist and anti-foreign Boxer uprising. The treaty included provisions for indemnity payments that totalled almost half of the Qing annual budget. Li died two months later, purportedly of exhaustion over the negotiations.

Li was at the centre of two critical tensions in 19th-century China. The first was debate about Western ideas, technologies and their implementation; and the second was the growth of regional power among the elite classes, as demonstrated through the rise of regional armies that weakened the centralized might of the Qing imperial forces. In over five decades of service to the Qing government, Li advocated institutional innovation, in the face of the countervailing force of Confucian revivalism, which argued instead for a return to Confucian learning and classical texts as resources for confronting Western incursion. Yet his efforts were curtailed by endemic conservatism, as well as the limits of his own vision in redesigning traditional systems of government – particularly the structures that enabled his own considerable personal power. Assessments of his life and career are ongoing, but scholars concur that his personal story is uniquely entangled with China's internal and external conflicts of the period, and its contested paths to modernization.

Susan I. Eberhard

84. GUO SONGTAO

郭嵩燾 (1818 –1891)

DIPLOMAT AND FIRST CHINESE MINISTER TO BRITAIN

Guo Songtao was a scholar-official, diplomat and educator from Xiangyin county in Hunan province. Having earned his *jinshi* – top-level civil service – degree in 1847, he assisted his fellow Hunanese and close friend Zeng Guofan (1811–1872) in organizing local militia into the force that would become the Hunan Army, to defend their home province against invading Taiping forces. At Guo's suggestion, in 1853, the Hunan Army built its first naval force and expanded its revenue beyond the *lijin*, a commercial tax on local merchandise. While supporting the campaign against the Taiping, Guo read and researched widely in history and *li* 'ritual' (a core concept of Chinese statecraft, including the political and social theories of Confucius). Guo understood the latter not as rigid rules and routines, but rather as practices animated with human emotion, which underpinned proper community relationships. In the process of his research, he became deeply influenced by another, earlier Hunanese, Wang Fuzhi (1619–1692), a Ming loyalist who, after the Qing conquest of the 1640s, devoted his scholarly energies to understanding the cause of the Ming's decline. Guo came to believe that the present internal and external crisis faced by the Qing was rooted in an atrophy of ritual in local communities. He contended that ritual, as a foundation for rebuilding social order, should not remain static, but must be reformed to keep up with changing circumstances. Guo's interest in reform also extended to rebuilding local society and economy, which had been devastated by war. He believed that the court and the hardliners in foreign policy – in calling for war against the West – missed the real root of China's problems.

During the Second Opium War (1856–60), Guo was dispatched by the Xianfeng emperor to assist Mongol Prince Sengge Rinchen (1811–1865) in defending Tianjin against British and French forces. Guo was specifically tasked with increasing the army's revenue by closing tax loopholes in Shandong province and establishing more *lijin* (internal transit) tax bureaus. But he was critical of Sengge Rinchen's hawkish foreign policy and advocated a longer-term strategy focused on developing naval capability, training students in foreign languages, and treating the West with sincerity and good faith. His disagreements with prevailing views at court led to his impeachment, and he returned home in 1860.

In the aftermath of the Qing's defeat in the Second Opium War, the court was newly dominated by moderates seeking reconciliation and cooperation with Western powers. Guo's knowledge of the West and openness to Western learning attracted the attention of leaders of the Self-Strengthening Movement. Recommended by Li Hongzhang (1823–1901), another major player in the revival of Qing military forces against the Taiping, Guo served as governor of Guangdong between 1863 and 1866.

Lock & Whitfield (act. 1856–1894), *Guo Songtao*, 1880 or earlier. Woodburytype on paper mount. National Portrait Gallery, London.

Following the complete breakdown of Sino-British relations during the Second Opium War, in which tensions in the provincial capital of Guangzhou (Canton) had been the touchpaper to the conflict, Guo built good relationships with the British consuls, and mediated between the Cantonese gentry and foreigners in several local disputes. However, in 1867, Guo was removed from the position, probably due to the jealousy of his superiors and colleagues. It likely did not help that his personality had grown increasingly abrasive and that he was often openly critical of court policies.

After eight years in retirement, in 1874, Guo was recalled by the court and recruited into the Zongli yamen – the new diplomatic office established by Prince Gong (1833–1898) after 1861 – to assist with foreign affairs. The next year, the killing of British interpreter Augustus Margary (1846–1875) in Yunnan set off yet another diplomatic crisis with England, and Guo was selected to head the mission of apology to the Court of St James's and thereafter establish a permanent legation in London to represent the Qing dynasty. This was a first for the Qing, which had no prior tradition of dispatching resident diplomats to foreign countries, relying instead on imperial envoys and travelling missions when necessary. The lack of institutional precedents and clear guidelines regulating the conduct of legation staff made Guo's task difficult, confusing and vulnerable to criticism, and he resigned after less than two years of service. He was succeeded by Zeng Jize (1839–1890), the eldest son of Zeng Guofan.

Despite Guo's personal frustration while serving as the Qing's inaugural minister, the establishment of the Qing legation in London improved China's international standing and opened up an official channel of communication between Qing diplomats and the British Foreign Office, which had previously been the monopoly of British diplomats in China. With the help of his English secretary Halliday Macartney (1833–1906) and Chinese student interpreters, Guo and the legation maintained an amicable relationship with the Foreign Office, and dealt with more than a dozen major diplomatic issues, ranging from seeking redress for Qing subjects from Britons who had committed crimes in China, to offering diplomatic apologies for offences committed against Britons in China. Guo also established a Qing consulate in Singapore, and protested against a proposed poll tax on Chinese merchants and labourers in British Columbia.

The most controversial aspect of Guo's tenure came from the publication of his *A Record of a Diplomatic Mission to the West*, his personal journal recording his observations on the voyage from Shanghai to London. In this, Guo interpreted international law, British colonialism and the British parliament as moral systems, as a modern manifestation of the Confucian Way, which he believed had been in long-term decline in China since the founding of the Qin dynasty in 221 BCE; he viewed international law, for example, as a reenactment of ancient ritual, founded on 'fidelity and righteousness'. He was criticized for this view not only by his domestic opponents, but also by Dutch diplomats, who viewed his depiction of British colonialism as naively simplistic. After his resignation from London, Guo retired to Hunan and devoted his effort to educating local youth and engaging in rebuilding a moral order from the bottom up, by setting up private academies teaching new curricula. Frustrated with Qing officialdom, he shunned government service, turned his attention to local affairs and became a pioneer in the Hunan Reform Movement. His belief that 'Western learning' was not in contradiction with the Confucian Way, but rather consistent with a Chinese humanistic, moral vision, helped find Chinese accommodations for new, foreign ideas, and paved the way for the next generation of intellectuals to argue for deeper, more thoroughgoing reforms in government.

Jenny Huangfu Day

85. CHEN JITONG

陳季同 (1852–1907)

FLAMBOYANT QING EMISSARY TO FRANCE

In 1884, as the Qing empire and France became embroiled in a conflict over Vietnam, a book titled *Les Chinois peints par eux-mêmes* (The Chinese painted by themselves) by Chen Jitong, the military attaché of the Chinese legation, appeared in Paris. Covering topics such as family structure, government, education and gender relations, it presented a panoramic sweep of Chinese society and culture in a positive manner, at a moment of high political tension. Reprinted several times and translated into other European languages, it helped to transform its author from a junior diplomat into perhaps the most widely read Chinese writer in *fin-de-siècle* Europe. It also marked the beginning of a series of remarkable literary and public engagements by Chen, which shaped aspects of Qing cultural diplomacy in the late 19th century and pioneered a mode of cross-cultural mediation in modern Sino-Western exchanges.

Born to a scholar-gentry family in mid-19th-century Fuzhou, Chen Jitong belonged to a generation of writers – including the famous translators Yan Fu (1854–1921) and Lin Shu (1852–1924) – who were shaped by the twin influences of a vibrant local intellectual culture rooted in neo-Confucian academies and poetry clubs, and the new scientific and foreign language curriculum of the Fuzhou Navy Yard, a flagship institution of the late Qing Self-Strengthening Movement. Having studied naval engineering and French, Chen travelled with the first Qing government-sponsored education mission to Europe in 1877, enrolled in courses in international law at Paris's École Libre des Sciences Politiques, and was afterwards appointed attaché to the Qing legations in Berlin and Paris. Equipped with strong language skills and technical expertise, as well as with considerable personal flair, Chen Jitong used the opportunities furnished by his official duties assisting the Qing ambassador on diplomatic visits to build his own social network, while writing books for a French audience at a prolific rate.

Between 1884 and 1891, Chen published several more books in French – including a comparative study of Chinese and French theatre (*Le Théâtre Chinois*), a translation of tales from Pu Songling's (1640–1715) *Strange Tales from a Chinese Studio* (*Contes Chinois*), a novel based on a Tang-dynasty (618–907) romance (*Le Roman de l'homme jaune*), and a collection of his observations of *fin-de-siècle* Paris. By now he was a cultural celebrity: a French-speaking Chinese diplomat who frequently rubbed shoulders with the Third Republic elite. Parisian newspapers eagerly noted his appearances at social and cultural functions, and reported on his speeches at salons and congresses. As one contemporary writer noted, Chen Jitong was 'ardently attached to the pleasure of the capital'. For the French public, Chen's flamboyance as a bicultural man of letters and imperial representative added to their own perception of Paris as the cosmopolitan centre of the *fin de siècle*.

Much of Chen Jitong's literary success and fame in Paris was based on his culti-vation of an identity as a creative writer at home in both the mass press of *fin-de-siècle* Paris and in the literati values and sensibilities of late imperial China. To begin with, he constructed an authorial persona based on his official naval title – expectant colonel of brigadier-general rank (*houbu fujiang*), 'expectant' meaning that he had probably bought the rank, or been gifted it by a powerful patron – and published his books as 'General Tcheng-Ki-Tong', thereby adding a layer of transcultural-military cachet to his works. At the same time, even while purporting to challenge Western

Gaspard-Félix Tournachon (1820–1910), photograph of Chen Jitong in official robes. *c.* 1875–95. Height 14.5 cm, width 10.5 cm. Bibliothèque Nationale de France, Paris.

Charles Castellani (1838–1913), *Panorama le 'Tout-Paris'*, painted for the Universal Exhibition of 1889. In this Paris street scene Chen Jitong is depicted third from the right. Bibliothèque Nationale de France, Paris.

stereotypes and misconceptions of China, Chen borrowed from French conventions to perform his role as a cultural mediator. Notably, in titling his collection of auto-ethnographic portraits of Chinese social life after the 1841 French compilation *Les Français peints par eux-mêmes*, Chen appropriated the literary position of the French *flâneur*, or the writer of the 'literature of physiologies' who treated sociological topics. Moreover, he did not shy away from appropriating and building on the enthusiastic poetry translations and colourful portraits of China created by contemporary French poets and Sinologists such as Judith Gautier, Henri Cordier, Antoine Bazin and the Marquis d'Hervey de Saint-Denys.

Many of Chen's essays were first published in the widely circulating daily papers and magazines of *fin-de-siècle* Paris, which undoubtedly enhanced his popularity with Parisian audiences. Indeed, in *Les Parisiens peints par un Chinois* (1891), a collection of sharp vignettes drawn from the French capital, he would claim for himself the role of *boulevardier*: an elegant stroller in the streets of Paris, and a journalist who frequented cafes and restaurants, and produced a variety of pieces for the mass press. Such a persona – and the French fascination with Chen – is evidenced in *Panorama le 'Tout-Paris'*, by the painter Charles Castellani (1838–1913), which depicted groups of famous Parisians for the hundreds of thousands of visitors to the 1889 Universal Exposition in Paris. In one of the illustrations, Chen Jitong is shown in a dark robe and 'melon' hat (a kind of Chinese skullcap), his conspicuous foreignness juxtaposed with his assumed public familiarity, as he is named at the bottom of the image as a recognizable figure. Similarly, a series of studio portraits taken by the famous Nadar, or Gaspard-Félix Tournachon (1820–1910), who made a habit of photographing celebrities, shows Chen Jitong in both civilian dress and his official robes, vividly capturing his charismatic presence.

That such striking visual representations of Chen Jitong were produced demonstrates the extent to which the Chinese diplomat became a public personality beyond the page. In fact, one of the most remarkable aspects of Chen's performance as a cultural mediator was his talent for public speaking: he was an eloquent *conférencier*, who gave addresses on China at private salons, academic meetings, and as a member of several *sociétés savantes*, including the newly established French Society of Popular Traditions. By enthusiastically participating in society meetings, contributing to their official journals, and delivering speeches at international congresses organized by these groups during the Universal Exposition – an event in which the Qing state did not officially participate – Chen established a significant presence for Qing China in several transnational and non-governmental cultural organizations.

In representing China to a French audience in his writings and speeches, Chen Jitong argued against prejudiced 19th-century European accounts of despotic rule, barbaric customs, the suppression of women, and an immobile empire in poverty and decline. Instead, he portrayed China as a rational and 'harmonious' Chinese civilization, based on well-functioning Confucian values that demanded better understanding from the West. At the same time, consistent with the beliefs of a scientifically trained modern diplomat who self-identified as a *wenren* (man of letters), Chen repeatedly noted that China was capable of reconciliation with Europe, through modern scientific and technological advancements, as well as the sharing of literature.

Chen's tenure in Paris was cut short in 1891, when he was impeached for accumulating personal debts while negotiating a railway loan for the Qing government. Forced to return to China, he avoided severe punishment thanks to protection from his patron Li Hongzhang (1823–1901), but was never again able to find a secure position, spending most of the 1890s and 1900s pursuing a series of social and political projects during the crisis-laden final decades of the Qing. Following a brief stint in the short-lived Taiwan Republic of 1895, established between Qing cession and Japanese annexation of the island, Chen relocated to Shanghai, where he edited a reform-era newspaper and helped establish the first Chinese Girls' School, alongside his talented sister-in-law Xue Shaohui (1866–1911) and his French wife Maria-Adèle Lardanchet (1848–1921). After his death in 1907, Chen's adventures in Paris and transcultural romantic liaisons lived on in fascinated public memory in the writings of his student Zeng Pu (1872–1935), whose stories of 'General Chen Jitong' and fictional portrayal of Chen and his Western wives in the popular novel *Flower in the Sea of Retribution* made Chen an object of exotic interest to younger, Republican-era Chinese writers.

For the 19th century, however, Chen Jitong's story is emblematic of historically specific conditions – including the cultural confidence of Self-Strengthening elites between the 1860s and 1890s, the flexible nature of Qing diplomacy abroad in its early years, the publishing opportunities in the *fin-de-siècle* mass press, and the internationalism of learned societies and world's fairs of the 1880s and 1890s. All of these spaces provided a place for the Qing diplomat-writer to represent China on the global stage.

Ke Ren

86. SAI JINHUA

賽金花 (1864–1936)

CROSS-CULTURAL COURTESAN

The last of the old-style courtesans to make her mark on modern China, Sai Jinhua was most likely born in 1864 in or near Suzhou (though she later gave her date of birth as 1874, taking ten years off her age, and thus further sensationalizing the events surrounding her life and legend). Having begun her career as a sing-song girl on a 'flower boat' in Suzhou, she would probably have come from humble origins and her original name is disputed. A chronology compiled by her first husband Hong Jun (1840–1893) indicates her maiden name was Zhao. Depictions in poetry and fiction usually call her Fu Caiyun ('Rainbow Cloud Fu'). But Sai Jinhua ('Flower to Rival Gold') became her best-known trade name. By the early 1900s, Sai Jinhua had attained the status of living legend in Chinese popular culture, not so much for the scandal value of her alleged sexual exploits as for her unique or, perhaps more accurately, her uniquely imagined place in Sino-Western diplomacy. This was a fame that she would continue to enjoy and exploit up to her death in the 1930s.

We must rely on a combination of history, fiction, poetry and popular legend to reconstruct Sai Jinhua's remarkable career. The earliest treatment of Sai Jinhua in turn-of-the-century Chinese literature came in *The Ballad of Rainbow Cloud*, a long classical poem by the Hubei literatus Fan Zengxiang (1846–1931). The first part, written in 1899, relates early events in Caiyun's (Sai Jinhua's) life, based in part on history and in part on fictional romance. These include being unwittingly seduced into the sing-song trade from a middle-class family at the age of twelve, and the subsequent fortuitous marriage out of the profession the following year as concubine to Hong Jun, a high-ranking official thirty-five years her senior. Hong Jun was subsequently appointed in 1887 as Chinese minister to the courts of Berlin, St Petersburg, Vienna and the Hague. Because his first wife was either too old or preoccupied with running the household, and his first concubine was in ill health at the time, the first wife supposedly gave her permission for Caiyun to accompany him on his mission abroad with the same status that would have been accorded to herself. Their travels took them first to St Petersburg, then to London and Paris, and eventually to Berlin,

Sai Jinhua's wedding photograph with Wei Sijiong, her third husband, Shanghai, 1918.

where Hong Jun became permanently stationed. This much is based on and corroborated by historical fact.

The poem's next set of stories about Sai Jinhua strays into popular legend. In Berlin, she began to learn German and became much celebrated in high society for her charming deportment and appearance. While her husband devoted himself to his scholarship and attended to the affairs of state, she is said to have pursued an active social life and was even rumoured to have had a liaison with a German officer. (In fact, it was unlikely that she would have been allowed any extensive independent socializing.) At any rate, the first part of *The Ballad of Rainbow Cloud* concludes with her return to China from Europe together with her husband, a series of infidelities, the death of Hong Jun, and the decline of her fortunes. Her biographers say that she was driven out of the household by Hong Jun's sons and resumed her old trade.

The second part of the poem, written in 1904, begins with the entry into Beijing of the Eight-Nation Alliance's expeditionary forces and their suppression of the anti-foreign Boxer forces (1899–1901). Empress Dowager Cixi (1835–1908) and the Guangxu emperor (r. 1875–1908) flee west to Xi'an. The supreme commander of the allied armies, Alfred Graf von Waldersee (1832–1904), had a liaison with Caiyun some years previously in Berlin, and sends for her upon his entry into the capital. The two lived together for some months in the emperor's private quarters within the Forbidden City, playing emperor and empress.

On a number of occasions during this period, says the legend, Caiyun intercedes to dissuade Waldersee from following through with Kaiser Wilhelm's orders to cut a bloody swathe across China in revenge for the deaths of the German ambassador, Baron von Ketteler (1853–1900), as well as numerous foreign nationals and Christian converts at the hands of the Boxers. Through her intercession, lives are saved, areas of cultural importance in the capital spared, and the populace finally given grain to stave off starvation. All this earns her the appellation 'protectress of the country' (*huguo niang-niang*), as she takes up the role that the absent Cixi should have been playing. Finally, peace accords are signed, in part due to Caiyun's skilful intervention at a point of impasse. Waldersee returns to his native land, where he is disciplined by the kaiser for his scandalous conduct in China. Caiyun is left to face the wrath of her own countrymen, many of whom are quick to condemn her for consorting with the enemy commander, without pausing to examine the beneficial role she played in mitigating against violence and wholesale destruction in the capital by the occupying foreign troops.

Sai Jinhua's later life was insecure. Working as a madam, she was accused of having brought about the death of a young courtesan in her charge and imprisoned for a time in 1905, exhausting her financial resources in her legal defence. She remarried twice, in 1911 and 1918, both times to lower-level government officials; neither left her with enough money to live on. By the 1930s she was impoverished and relied on contributions from scholars such as Liu Bannong (1891–1934), who came to interview her in attempts to ascertain the real facts of her life and times. Already in the 1900s, she was the starring character in poems and fiction (most famously, Fan's epic ballad and Zeng Pu (1872–1935)'s *Flower in the Sea of Retribution*). Prior to her death in 1936, the Chinese press and academia seemed to be running a Sai Jinhua fever, which generated articles, books and plays, including one by the prominent playwright and Communist Party member Xia Yan (1900–1995), a performance of which occasioned an orchestrated riot. During the Cultural Revolution (1966–76), residual enthusiasm for her story was strong enough for political puritans to launch a movement to 'repudiate the Sai Jinhua fever'. In subsequent decades, her life has continued to inspire television series, films and spoken drama across the Sinophone world. Even though much of Sai's own testimony about the events of her life as well as different versions of the popular legend contradict each other, the power of the 'myth' – the never-fading romantic appeal of the tale of the patriotic prostitute saving an empire from destruction – as a source for storytelling inspiration has not been diminished by doubts about its authenticity.

Jon Eugene von Kowallis

87. GU HONGMING

辜鴻銘 (1857–1928)

WORLD THINKER AND ECCENTRIC LOYALIST

Noted for his ultraconservatism and eccentricity, Gu Hongming remains one of the most controversial figures in modern Chinese intellectual history. More than a century later, there is continued debate as to whether he was Confucian or Western, nationalist or cosmopolitan, anachronistic or prophetic.

Born into a wealthy Chinese family in the British colony of Penang, Gu left for Scotland, wearing a queue, at the age of fourteen. Having received a liberal arts education and a thorough classical training in Western literature and culture, he graduated from the University of Edinburgh in April 1877, and became a lifetime proponent of European Romanticism and conservatism.

After a ten-year sojourn in Europe, Gu returned to Penang in 1879. Now an adult of twenty-three who spoke fluent English, he wore a Western suit, and no longer had a queue. After a few unsatisfactory positions within British networks in Asia, Gu reached another turning point in his life in 1885, when he became a private secretary to influential Qing viceroy Zhang Zhidong (1837–1909). Gu spent the rest of his life as a Qing-dynasty loyalist and spokesman for China, who defended the Manchu monarchy, Confucian morality and Chinese traditions.

After his so-called conversion from 'an imitation Western man' to 'a Chinaman again', Gu devoted his life to translating Confucian classics into English and interpreting 'the spirit of the Chinese people' for the Western world through numerous English writings. His works were published in various languages including English, German, French and Japanese, by major publishing houses in Asia, Europe and the United States. He foresaw the disastrous long-term consequences of industrialism and imperialism, then at their peak, and called for a revival of Confucianism as the antidote to modern Western civilization.

Gu flouted the intellectual, moral and aesthetic norms of the day, and danced between critical intellectual engagements and symbolic public performance. He enjoyed a daily rickshaw ride, redisplaying his queue after the 1911 Revolution when everyone else was removing theirs and embracing Western culture as a symbol of progress. He defended concubinage with the famous analogy of one teapot (that is, a man) matching multiple teacups (women). He frequently insulted foreigners, from a random Scottish man in a cinema to faculty members of Peking University. After meeting the English writer W. Somerset Maugham, he wrote the visitor a set of love poems in calligraphy as a farewell gift. In a 1921 *New York Times* interview, he said Westerners were 'all barbarians'.

Gu's conservative ideas and eccentric, often paradoxical behaviour have posed a challenge to scholarly consensus and often provoked polarized responses. Outside

China, he emerged as the most prominent exponent of Confucianism and Chinese tradition in the first two decades of the 20th century. Hailed as a Chinese sage, he was often compared with non-Western prophets such as Tagore, Gandhi and Tolstoy. Together with the writings of other prominent advocates of 'the decline of the West', his messages about Eastern spirituality were enthusiastically welcomed and reproduced, especially in Germany. He proved to be a talented interpreter and successful popularizer of Chinese culture for a general Western audience.

In contrast, within China, Gu's ideas met with, at best, indifference, or outright hostility. Few of his writings in English were translated into Chinese or introduced to Chinese readers until the 1990s. During the May Fourth–New Culture movements (*c.* 1915–25), his works were completely discarded by modernist intellectuals, who were busy introducing Western trends and critiquing Chinese traditions. Late Qing and Republican-era Chinese intellectuals portrayed him as a reactionary, with little understanding of what China needed in modern times. In the eyes of the Chinese 'new youth' of the early 20th century, 'crazy old Gu' was nothing but an object of mockery.

Forced out of Peking University in the early 1920s, due to his outspoken opposition to the revolution, Gu taught at the Great Asiatic Culture Association in Japan between 1924 and 1927. He died in Beijing on 30 April 1928. A few months before his death, he did eventually meet the last Qing emperor, Puyi (1906–1967), in person, considering it 'the proudest day of my life'.

In mainland China, during the 1960s and 1970s, Gu was largely excluded from historical discussion, because of his political and cultural conservatism. In recent decades, however, a renewed interest in Gu has emerged among academic and popular audiences. He is today celebrated as a guru of national learning and an icon of Chinese nationalism, as China seeks to build a new 'traditional' identity in the face of continued and accelerated globalization and Sino-Western tensions. Outside China, Gu's ideas remain appealing in global intellectual discussions on civilization, religion and spirituality, reflected in new Korean, French and Turkish editions of *The Spirit of the Chinese People* being recently published.

Chunmei Du

88. KANG YOUWEI

康有為 (1858–1927)

RADICAL PHILOSOPHER AND REFORMER

Kang Youwei, a native of Guangdong born into wealth, was the pre-eminent monarchist reformer of the late Qing dynasty. Several of his forbears had passed the imperial civil service examinations to become officials, and the young Kang was quickly identified as a precocious student. However, he himself did not pass the third and final stage of the examinations – which would in theory guarantee him a high-ranking government post – until 1895.

In the 1870s and 1880s, Kang made tours of Shanghai and the new British colony of Hong Kong, which fuelled his interests in strengthening China through active Westernization. Kang founded a school in 1891 in Canton (Guangzhou) called Thatched Hall of Ten Thousand Trees with a curriculum encompassing traditional and modern, Chinese and Western subjects, such as Confucian and Buddhist studies, geography, mathematics, calligraphy and public speaking. Among his students was Liang Qichao (1873–1929), a reformist thinker in his own right. Also in 1891, Kang published *An Examination of the Forged Classics of the Xin Dynasty*, which won him fame (and notoriety) by claiming that the versions of classic Confucian texts that literati had studied as their canon for 2,000 years had been forged in the early years of the first millennium CE. From here, Kang argued, the Sinophone literary and philosophical heritage needed to be completely reinterpreted – an argument that fitted neatly with his own vision for reforming late Qing politics and culture.

Xu Beihong (1895–1953), *Pleasures of Mr Nanhai* [Kang Youwei] *at Sixty*, c. 1916. Watercolour on paper. Height 81.5 cm, width 117.5 cm. Private collection.

China's humiliating defeat in the First Sino-Japanese War (1894–95) convinced Kang Youwei that superficial imports of Western skills could not protect China from foreign imperialism. In the second half of the 1890s, Kang at last attained a position of political importance when his reformist proposals won the ear of the Guangxu emperor (r. 1875–1908), under whose aegis Kang engineered the Hundred Days' Reform (June to September 1898). He sought sweeping transformation in education, infrastructure, transportation, commerce and industry.

After an unsuccessful coup to remove Empress Dowager Cixi (1835–1908) from power, Kang's brother Kang Guangren (1867–1898), Tan Sitong (1865–1898) and four other allies in the cause of reform were executed. Kang Youwei fled the country and became one of China's first world travellers. While in exile, he continued to champion constitutional monarchy and completed the manuscript of his famously utopian *Book of Great Harmony* (published posthumously), which studied foreign histories to find useful models for China. At the same time, he rallied international support for the Guangxu emperor and an enlightened constitutional monarchy after the model of the Meiji Restoration in Japan. Towards this goal, Kang founded in 1899 the Society for the Protection of the Emperor in Victoria, British Columbia, which eventually expanded into at least 200 chapters with a membership of possibly 100,000 worldwide. This was the largest Chinese transcultural organization at the time. Kang's celebrity in overseas Chinese communities soared. One of his unrealized plans was to establish a 'New China' in industrialized Mexico, a country which – unlike the United States and other European societies – welcomed Chinese immigrants. Besides continuing to make his mark as a political writer, Kang devoted much energy towards fundraising and business investments. A self-defined 'sage' (*shengren*), he was both admired and ridiculed for his faith in improving the imperial system from within. Due to his reluctance to join Sun Yat-sen's (1866–1925) campaign to overthrow the Qing government, he was largely treated as an anachronism after the Republican Revolution of 1911. Nonetheless, Kang returned to China in 1913, channelling his political energies into the cultural arena.

In addition to being a political activist and revisionist philosopher, Kang was a gender activist (founder of two Anti-Foot Binding Societies in 1887 and 1895), a distinguished calligrapher, a leading theorist of the Stele school (which looked to ancient inscriptions for calligraphic inspiration), a champion of pictorial realism through East–West synthesis, and mentor to young artists such as Xu Beihong (1895–1953), Liu Haisu (1896–1994) and the female calligrapher Xiao Xian (1902–1997). In the same year as the Hundred Days' Reform, Kang published *Investigation of Confucius as a Reformer*, a book that was soon banned, due to its depiction of Confucius as an opponent of authoritarian government.

During his foreign exile, Kang discovered 'form-likeness' in the Italian Renaissance, especially Raphael, viewing it as the ideal in techniques of representation in Western art. He was impressed by the period's depictions of three-dimensional form on a two-dimensional surface, and prescribed greater incorporation of a similar principle in modern Chinese painting, without advocating the overthrow of artistic tradition. Whether discussing politics, education, religion, mass communication or art, Kang always returned to his core priority of engineering change. His direct contributions to art history included an 1891 calligraphy treatise titled *Extended Paired Oars for the Boat of Art* and his 1917 *Catalogue of Collected Paintings from the Thatched Hall of Ten Thousand Trees*, a record of his personal art collection with a preface that lamented what he perceived as the downward trajectory of Chinese art after the Song dynasty (960–1126). This latter work was completed while in temporary asylum at the American embassy in Shanghai, to escape the fallout from his backing of Zhang Xun's (1854–1923) abortive attempt to restore the last emperor, Puyi (r. 1909–1912) to the throne in 1917. Kang's preface deplored painting in China as having become utterly degenerate by the Qing dynasty, as flavourless as 'chewed wax'. His proposed solution was to revive the marvellous beauty of certain Chinese painting styles, while harmonizing with Western methods, emphasizing greater representationalism over formulaic brushwork. Kang's characterization reflected a biased and incomplete view of art history, which was nevertheless consistent with his reformist ideology (that resonated with many of his contemporaries).

Kang exerted a profound influence on the early Republican discourse of *gailiang* (correcting and bettering) articulated by art writers. His calligraphy treatise has been criticized for empirical inaccuracies, but it was a bestseller that gave concrete advice on how to practise, collect and improve calligraphy. (It was also a disguised piece of political propaganda against conservatism and national weakness.) Kang's own calligraphy passed through several phases – his dynamic running script is particularly admired – progressively absorbing the aesthetics of antique stone inscriptions to create a distinct personal style. He spent the last decade and a half of his life in comfort surrounded by his large family, while continuing to court controversies.

Aida Yuen Wong

89. LIANG QICHAO

梁啟超 (1873–1929)

CHINA'S FIRST PUBLIC INTELLECTUAL

An academic prodigy, Liang Qichao passed the first level of the Qing's imperial civil service examinations at the age of eleven. Born into an educated farming family near Guangzhou, he no doubt thought he was headed for a distinguished official career. Instead, he became a leader of China's modern intellectual revolution. Liang became an indefatigable writer who might be considered modern China's first public intellectual. From the 1890s to the 1910s, no one did more to introduce and popularize Western political concepts such as nationalism, constitutionalism, liberty and democracy to the Chinese reading public.

Liang passed the higher provincial level examinations at the age of sixteen, the youngest successful candidate of that year, but he failed to go on to pass the highest, metropolitan examinations. Meanwhile, he began studying with the excitingly radical Confucian scholar-activist Kang Youwei (1858–1927) in 1890. Liang helped Kang rewrite the history of Confucianism in ways that legitimated radical reform; he read Western history and political theory; and he began editing and writing for new journals. Qing China's military loss to Japan in 1895 provoked a protest movement among the elite men gathered in Beijing at the time to take the civil service examinations, which Liang helped to mobilize and lead. After the crises of the Second Opium War (1856–60) and the Taiping Civil War (1851–64), the Qing had undertaken a series of limited reforms, which were now deemed to have been inadequate. Powerful reformist statesmen noticed Liang; perhaps not entirely aware of just how radical his views were becoming, they were willing to sponsor his journalism and give him a position at the new School of Current Affairs (Shiwu xuetang) in Changsha, Hunan province. Liang spoke to his students about democracy and parliaments and even suggested that the Qing, as a Manchu foreign conquest dynasty, was illegitimate (at twenty-four, Liang was not much older than his pupils).

At this time, Liang published a series of essays *On Reform*, which spoke of the need to industrialize and encourage commerce, to establish newspapers and other voluntary associations, and to modernize China's educational institutions, including introducing formal education for women. Following his teacher Kang, Liang advocated reform in the name of Confucianism, positing that Confucius himself had envisioned a future marked by progress. He also developed an innovative and lively writing style that used classical grammar flavoured with colloquial phrases.

Events moved quickly. In June 1898, the young Guangxu emperor (r. 1875–1908), inspired by Kang Youwei, started issuing a series of reform edicts to reshape the bureaucracy, and Liang was brought back to the capital to join the endeavour. Feeling threatened, conservative officials and Manchu grandees convinced the old Empress Dowager to stage a coup against the emperor, her nephew, in September. Kang and Liang escaped China with a price on their heads. Relocating to Japan, then some thirty years into its own modernization programme, Liang began the most spectacular phase of his journalistic career. He read voraciously, particularly in Japanese, and transmitted much of his new learning in articles that circulated clandestinely but widely in China. One of his first self-appointed tasks was to explain and justify the aborted 'reform movement of 1898', further amplifying his fame. In Japan, Liang came into his own as an intellectual. Although he marked a break from Kang by declaring, 'I love Confucius, but I love the truth more', he retained a strong commitment to Confucian and Buddhist morality and character discipline. Over the next few years, Liang visited Australia, Hawaii and North America.

An anti-Qing republican revolutionary movement was growing, but Liang supported reform instead, hoping that China could become a constitutional monarchy. Over the next few years, he attacked China's autocratic imperial traditions on the one hand, and the revolutionaries' attempts to overthrow it root and branch on the other. Yet both Qing officials and the revolutionaries – many of whom were

Photo of Liang Qichao taken in Boston, 1903. SOAS, University of London.

Cover for Liang Qichao's paper *New Citizen Journal* (*Xinmin congbao*), Yokohama, 1903.

China's brightest students – largely acquired their ideas about race and nationalism, democracy and equality, and liberty and individualism from Liang. A very youthful Mao Zedong (1893–1976) for example, growing up in Hunan, deep in the Chinese interior, encountered Liang's writings, later admitting that, as a sixteen-year-old, he 'worshipped' the older man. Liang called on the Chinese people to become 'new citizens' able to strengthen and stabilize their rapidly declining country. He declared that the Chinese had never developed national consciousness as politics was monopolized by the imperial clan and a few officials. Democracy, rights, popular sovereignty and constitutionalism thus formed the basis of Liang's teaching on how to create national unity and strength.

Liang believed the world followed the laws of social Darwinism – the stronger races and nations took what they wanted while the weak perished – as shaped by the new 'national imperialism'. No longer were strong, resilient empires created by charismatic military conquerors; only when the entire strength of the nation (through the forging and bettering of citizens) was mobilized could such empires be formed – or resisted. 'The state is an aggregation of the people as a whole,' Liang wrote. 'If the people of a state govern, legislate and plan for the interests of the whole state and stave off disturbances that might threaten the state, then the people cannot be bullied and the state cannot be overthrown.' It was partly based on this vision of the whole people that Liang opposed a revolution driven by ethnic resentment that would divide Han Chinese from Manchus. His 'new citizen' was defined more by civic responsibilities than ethnicity. But Liang remains the father of Chinese popular sovereignty, and what might be called his anti-anti-Manchuism foreshadowed later attempts to remake the empire into a multi-ethnic nation state.

In the wake of the 1911 Revolution, Liang Qichao returned to China, founded a political party, and supported the new strongman president Yuan Shikai (1859–1916). But Liang's hopes for a political career soon went sour. He turned against Yuan when the president tried to make himself a new emperor. During the years of the warlords, who carved up between themselves political control of China through the 1910s and 1920s, Liang remained a significant public intellectual. But now his voice was merely one among many. On a trip to Europe in the wake of World War I, in 1918–19, Liang wrote more critically of the West's material accomplishments and more explicitly on the need to integrate the accomplishments of East and West. As his attention returned to China, in effect Liang began a second major career as a scholar of ancient Chinese philosophy and Buddhism, writing important works on cultural history and historiography. Liang died in 1929 at the age of fifty-six; his life both influenced and reflected the tumultuous changes China underwent in the late 1800s and early 1900s.

Peter Zarrow

90. DUANFANG

端方 (1861–1911)

MANCHU STATESMAN, REFORMER AND ART CONNOISSEUR

John C. Ferguson (1866–1945), old China hand, former foreign advisor to the late Qing government, and collector and procurer for major American art museums in the early 20th century, vividly recalled evenings in the Nanjing office mansion of Duanfang, then the viceroy of Jiangsu and Jiangxi (1906–9), during which the latter would show off the latest antiquities he had acquired. Duanfang impressed the missionary-turned-foreign-advisor with his knowledge of, and passion for *jinshi*, (literally 'metal and stone'), or the study of ancient vessels and stone steles. Although, after his untimely death in 1911, Duanfang left behind a full catalogue of his exceptional collection for Ferguson to refer to, in his reminiscences the American still missed 'the flashing eyes and nervous movements of the great connoisseur as I can remember him when handling his wonderful bronze'.

China's 19th-century antiquarianism sprang from the rise of 'evidential learning' in the previous century, which sought empirical foundations for knowledge through undertaking meticulous analysis of ancient texts. Evidentialists used inscribed ancient bronzes and steles as the basis for their philological studies. By the last decade of the Qing, this scholarship incorporated study of a wider range of artefacts, especially following the discovery by European explorers of Buddhist manuscripts, paintings and sculptures in the caves at Dunhuang, and the identification of oracle bones from Anyang (north China) as bearing inscriptions of the oldest Chinese characters. A highly sociable practice, *jinshi* involved gatherings at which rubbings and antiquities were viewed by like-minded friends. Among such antiquarians, Duanfang was exceptional for the range of his collecting interests (which he combined with a successful political career), in pursuit of which he crossed ethnic and national boundaries.

Duanfang was born to a prominent Manchu family of the Tohoro clan in the White Banner. But he also had Han Chinese ancestors, who had joined Manchu armies during their 17th-century conquest of China and served as government officials for several generations. He inherited a mid-level civil service degree and went on to take up posts in multiple government departments.

Duanfang was a nifty political operator. During the Guangxu emperor's (r. 1875–1908) short-lived 1898 Hundred Days' Reforms aiming to modernize government, Duanfang was appointed superintendent in the new Bureau of Agriculture,

Photograph of Duanfang and colleagues with bronze altar set now in the Metropolitan Museum of Art in New York, c. 1907. Freer Gallery of Art and Arthur M. Sackler Gallery Archives, Smithsonian Institution, Washington, DC.

Rubbing of an ancient Egyptian stone carving with Duanfang's inscription. Egypt, 1906. Handscroll, ink on paper. Maidstone Museum.

Industry and Commerce. When court conservatives and Empress Dowager Cixi (1835–1908) quashed the reforms, placed Guangxu under house arrest and executed or exiled his radical advisors, Duanfang used his connections in the antiques trade to bribe Cixi's favourite eunuch Li Lianying (1848–1911) with antiquities and wrote the Empress Dowager a flattering poem. Far from being punished, Duanfang was promoted to a senior provincial posting. The antiques trade saved Duanfang's career, and possibly his life.

When in 1900 Cixi and Guangxu fled Beijing for Xi'an during the foreign invasion that ended the Boxer War, Duanfang, then acting governor of Shanxi, both ensured the safety and comfort of the imperial family and their entourage, and protected foreigners in his jurisdiction. His career (and international reputation) flourished. While governor of several regions from 1901 to 1904, he supported Zhang Zhidong's (1837–1909) moderate reform policies: modernizing education and military systems, building modern libraries and industries, and trying to open a trading port. He dispatched more than two hundred Hubei students to study in Japan, Europe and the United States. He even sent women to Japan to train as primary school instructors.

In 1905, Duanfang was chosen by the court as one of five special commissioners to travel to Western countries to observe their political and cultural institutions, in preparation for constitutional government in China. Over the course of an eight-month tour of the United States and Europe, Duanfang visited – in addition to government buildings, schools and libraries – many museums, such as the Metropolitan Museum of Art in New York and the Field Museum in Chicago. Again, his collection of antiquities helped him connect with the world. He proposed to the newly established Field Museum that he would donate a rare ancient Chinese inscribed stone tablet in his collection. He also arranged a trip to Egypt, where he purchased some ancient inscribed and carved stones. He later gifted rubbings of the stones, some containing hieroglyphs, to diplomatic friends such as the Japanese

Ma Shaoxuan (1894–1932), inside-painted rock-crystal snuff bottle with a portrait of Duanfang wearing a fur hat and fur-trimmed jacket, c. 1900–10. Height 6.2 cm. Water, Pine and Stone Retreat Collection. Photograph by Nick Moss.

statesman Inukai Tsuyoshi (1855–1932), who visited Duanfang in 1907. Like contemporary Western collectors, Duanfang embraced the global circulation of antiquities.

Soon after his return to China, Duanfang was promoted again, and, at the end of the 1900s, helped organize the Nanyang Industrial Exposition in Nanjing, the first international exposition held in China – an important moment in Qing China's self-presentation to the world. He became an increasingly innovative cataloguer of his extraordinary collection of antiques. The book of his bronze collection, *Catalogue of the Auspicious Metals of Tao Studio*, published in 1908, was the first catalogue to use photolithography to reproduce line-drawn images of the bronzes and their rubbings. Highly conscious of the power of photography, Duanfang was one of the most photographed officials of the Qing, probably second only to Li Hongzhang (1823–1901). He also avidly used photography to promote and advertise his collection. A photograph of Duanfang with other senior officials standing in front of the Confucius Temple in Beijing with his most prized items, a group of Western Zhou altar bronzes excavated in Baoji in 1901, became arguably as iconic as the antiques themselves.

The modern technology of photography not only made Duanfang an international celebrity; it also caused his downfall. Duanfang was dismissed from office soon after the death of Empress Dowager Cixi, apparently for showing disrespect to the deceased empress by taking photographs of her funeral procession. In 1911, the court reinstated Duanfang to suppress anti-Qing dissent not long before the revolution that would bring the dynasty down. In late autumn, amid nationwide revolutionary army mutinies against the Qing, Duanfang's own men assassinated their commander. His murderers were officers in the New Armies: the modernized, educated force that Duanfang himself had promoted through his work in office, but which became the chief recruiting ground for anti-Qing revolutionaries in the final years of the dynasty.

As one of the most significant late Qing collectors of bronzes, jades, stone steles, rubbings, painting and calligraphy, Duanfang – with the help of his entourage – systematically catalogued his collection and navigated global art networks. After his death, his collections made their way to major museums in the West, notably the Metropolitan Museum of Art in New York, the Freer Gallery in Washington, DC, and the Nelson-Atkins Museum of Art in Kansas City, laying the foundation for Chinese art history as a modern discipline in the United States and later in China.

Yu-chih Lai

91. SUN YAT-SEN

孫逸仙 (1866–1925)

CHINA'S FIRST PRESIDENT

On 1 January 1912, Sun Yat-sen was inaugurated as the first president of the provisional government of the Republic of China. But politics in the new republic moved fast. On 12 February, Yuan Shikai (1859–1916), prime minister and Qing strongman, persuaded the last emperor of China to abdicate. The following day, acknowledging Yuan's stronger power base (over the previous twenty years, Yuan had built up the New Armies, whose mutinies had driven the previous year's Republican Revolution), Sun resigned the presidency to Yuan. For years Sun Yat-sen had dreamed of China becoming a republic, a sovereign nation free from Manchu rule and Western imperialism. He may have been president of a provisional government for only forty-five days, but his vision for a modern republic changed China forever. Today, in global Chinese communities (and on both sides of the Taiwan Strait), he is known as the 'Father of the Nation' (*Guofu*).

Sun was born on 12 November 1866 in Cuiheng, a village in Xiangshan county, Guangdong province, where it was not uncommon for family members to work overseas and send money home. At the age of thirteen, Sun was sent to live with his brother in Hawaii. Sun enjoyed his new Western education but showed too much interest in Christianity for his brother's liking. When Sun Yat-sen wanted to be baptized, his brother sent him back home. Frustrated by returning to the restrictions of rural life, Sun and a friend smashed a temple statue and fled to Hong Kong. Sun stayed on the island from 1883 to 1894, where he attended school and medical college, was baptized, and met radical critics of the Manchu dynasty. It was there that he took the name Sun Yat-sen (the Cantonese pronunciation of Sun Yishan). In 1894 he took a petition to the leading Qing statesman Li Hongzhang (1823–1901), hoping to present and gain support for his ideas for modernizing China, but was not granted an audience. Thereafter, he seems to have leaned increasingly towards revolution. Sun went back to Hawaii and, on 24 November 1894, founded China's first revolutionary organization, the Revive China Society in Honolulu.

Elliott & Fry (act. 1863– 1962), *Sun Yat-sen*, 1911. Bromide print. Photographs Collection, National Portrait Gallery, London.

Sun returned to Hong Kong in early 1895 to launch an uprising out of Guangzhou. The insurrection failed, and Sun escaped from Qing China with a price on his head. He was also barred from Hong Kong for five years. He spent time in Europe, the United States, Canada and Japan, networking, rallying support and raising funds. Japan, as an East Asian neighbour that had engaged in a highly successful, wide-ranging modernization programme since the 1870s, was of particular interest to modernizing Chinese rebels. It was in Japan that he acquired the name Sun Zhongshan (based on the Chinese pronunciation of his Japanese pseudonym, Kikori Nakayama), by which he is best known in China today.

In 1896, Sun made a trip to Britain that almost cost him his life. Tipped off about Sun's arrival, the Qing Chinese legation in London hired a detective to follow his movements. The legation was housed in an unmarked building on Portland Place, a few minutes' walk from the home of Dr Cantlie, an old friend of Sun's from Hong Kong. On 11 October, Sun – under circumstances that remain unclear – was apparently kidnapped by Qing officials and locked in an upstairs room, prior to planned extradition to China, where he would likely be executed. A few days later, he managed to get a note to Dr Cantlie, who alerted the British authorities and the press. The incident gained notoriety (and much sympathetic and helpful publicity for Sun as an opponent of the Qing) in British and international newspapers. Sun was eventually freed on 23 October, and, thanks to Dr Cantlie, remained in the spotlight for a while. He spent the next eight months in London, reading in the British Museum, witnessing spectacular displays of imperial power at Queen Victoria's jubilee celebrations, and shaping in his mind the modern Chinese republic he dreamed of.

In 1905, Sun tried to unify China's fragmented revolutionary movement by founding in Japan, where student revolutionaries were concentrated, the Revolutionary Alliance (Tongmenghui) against the Qing. After 1911, the Revolutionary Alliance would become the Guomindang, or Nationalist Party – one of the two major mass political parties of 20th-century China, and long-time rivals of the Chinese Communist Party. Between 1900 and 1911, numerous revolutionary upris-ings were attempted in China by Sun's and other secret organizations, with varying success. Sun was known best for his international fundraising ability, and for keeping the spirit of revolution alive through public speaking and networking, in multiple continents. He was not, however, a superlative organizer of military operations and his attempts at revolutionary insurrection suffered badly from problems of communication and supply. When the revolution finally succeeded, it took everyone – including Sun – by surprise. On 9 October 1911, a group of revolutionaries in the Qing army making bombs in Hankou, a city in central China, accidentally detonated one of their explosives. As the Qing government began hunting down the conspira-tors, revolutionaries in the neighbouring city of Wuchang decided to mutiny before they were arrested. Forces loyal to the Qing were quickly defeated, and the revolt spread through army headquarters up and down the country. On 1 November, the Qing court appointed Yuan Shikai, founder of the dynasty's most effective military force, the Beiyang Army, as prime minister, and authorized him to negotiate with the revolutionaries. Sun Yat-sen was thousands of miles away, fundraising in the United States, where he first read about the uprising in a newspaper. He returned to China in time to become the first president of the Republic on 1 January 1912, in recognition of his status as the longest-standing proponent of and agitator for the revolution.

Sun's political career in the Republic remained tumultuous. After ceding the presidency to Yuan Shikai, Sun spent several further years in exile, following the assassination of China's first democratically elected prime minister Song Jiaoren (1882–1913) and Yuan's suppression of the Revolutionary Alliance's successor organization, the Nationalist Party (Guomindang), in 1913. After Yuan's death, regional militarists (sometimes referred to as warlords) fragmented central political control and Sun struggled to gain support for his vision of a unified, modern Chinese republic. Although he had limited success in building the state he dreamed of, he was a tireless public speaker and political activist, able to inspire individuals and groups from a wide range of backgrounds and classes to support and donate to revolutionary activity. He also had ambitious plans for modernizing China's government, industry and infrastructure. At the heart of that vision were his 'Three Principles of the People' (*San min zhuyi*): the people's nationalism/self-determination (*minzu zhuyi*), democracy/power of the people (*minquan*), and the people's economic livelihood (*minsheng*). While Sun was willing to borrow political and technical innovations from the West, he also passionately attacked Western imperialism, and the financial and political damage it had wrought on China.

Sun Yat-sen died of cancer in Beijing in 1925, aged fifty-nine. Chiang Kai-shek (1887–1975), his brother-in-law and self-appointed political heir, reinvented Sun as a saintly political sage, a symbolic national figurehead around which the country and Nationalist Party should unify. Following a new revolutionary war to unify the country, Chiang in 1928 founded a Nationalist government headquartered in Nanjing. In spring 1929, Chiang reinterred Sun, with enormous ceremony, at a magnificent mausoleum in the suburbs of the new capital, not far from the tomb of the Hongwu emperor (r. 1328–1398), the first emperor of the Ming dynasty. The choice of burial site was perhaps designed to invite associations between the two: Hongwu had begun life as a peasant and wandering beggar, before ousting foreign (Mongol) rulers to found the Ming, often considered one of the most powerful of Han Chinese dynasties.

Helen Wang

8

MAKERS

CRAFTSPEOPLE, FOLKLORISTS AND SCIENTISTS

Histories of 19th-century China used to dismiss the period as one of stagnation, reiteration and decline, including in craft and science, until the arrival of modern methods and ideas from the West and Japan after the First Opium War (1839–42) transformed theory and practice. The lives presented here tell a different story: of Confucian scholars from the start of the century, men like Wu Qijun, turning their highly disciplined minds to empirical investigation of the natural world; of exceptional artisans transforming their crafts with fusions of traditional and new, foreign-learned skills; of scholars turning classical antiquarianism into a scientific, artefact-focused archaeology. This widespread revival and repurposing of ancient traditions in craft and scholarship can arguably be seen as a renaissance of Chinese cultural heritage in parallel with broader, coterminous currents of cultural nationalism.

Through much of imperial history, potters had very low status; most ceramicists are lost from the historical record. By the late Qing, Jingdezhen had been China's porcelain capital for nearly a thousand years, mass-producing tableware and figures for domestic and foreign markets. But in the mid-19th century, it was devastated by natural disasters and the violence of the Taiping Civil War (1851–64). The ceramics industry recovered from these disasters, however, to innovate and assert a new professional self-confidence. Artists at Jingdezhen collaborated with potters to produce landscape paintings in overglaze enamels on white tiles and vessels. Teapot makers at Yixing in Jiangsu, working with natural-coloured clays, sculptors of glossy white porcelain at Dehua in Fujian, and modellers of heavy stonewares at Shiwan in Guangzhou all signed their work and were celebrated as creative artists during their lifetimes. For the first time, individual potters such as Su Xuejin were recognized internationally, for example receiving awards from craft exhibitions. Although some Peking Opera celebrities left their mark on written histories, far more musicians – singers and players of classical Chinese instruments such as the *erhu* or *pipa* – have sadly been effaced from the record. But the traces of this lost world of music can be detected in the canonized repertoire of Abing, one of the few performers of the late imperial period whose work was preserved in the modern era.

Textile production changed dramatically in the 19th century. Embroidery, which until 1800 had largely been a small-scale domestic craft for women, over the ensuing hundred years developed into a large-scale industry employing men, women and children. It innovated as an art form, using new technologies, dyes and materials. The celebrated embroiderer Shen Shou worked with a potential palette of 745 colours. Some of her compositions were based on Western oil paintings, Christian imagery or portraits of foreigners. Women wrote new embroidery manuals, and the expansion of a modern publishing industry meant that designs could circulate rapidly in response to images in illustrated books and magazines, and in stage performances. As production methods modernized after the 1860s, textile industries such as cotton were industrialized. Imported machine-made cottons from India and Japan stimulated Chinese entrepreneurs such as Zhang Jian to set up cotton factories. Reflecting new trends in philanthropy and public service, such individuals often took over responsibility for building community infrastructure and providing welfare that had previously been the preserve of the state.

After China's defeat in the Sino-Japanese War of 1894–95, educated Chinese people sought to modernize the Qing state. But 19th-century intellectual life was also characterized by a fervent antiquarianism; by the turn of the century, this was starting to morph into a scientific archaeology, a discipline that during the 20th and 21st centuries would play a central role in governments' and individuals' quests to define a Chinese cultural identity. In the late 19th century, texts on ancient animal bones discovered in north-central China were identified as the earliest form of Chinese writing; epigraphists like Luo Zhenyu and Liu E prolifically collected, studied and deciphered their inscriptions, an endeavour that established – for the first time, using empirically researched material evidence – the earliest Chinese historical records and underpinned subsequent archaeological excavation and research.

The import of European and American ideas about medicine – especially surgery and public health – drove innovations in clinical practice within the Qing empire. The late 19th century witnessed major public health projects, and the earliest modern medical associations. But traditional Chinese medicine was practised in this period alongside Western and Japanese medicine; a situation that persists today in China, and many other countries. Patent medicine adverts in the new Shanghai press combined older Chinese and newer Western ideas about the body and disease. Male and female Chinese students began studying medicine abroad. Individuals like Ida Kahn, the adopted daughter of an American missionary who studied in the United States and Britain, returned to China where she led the fields of clinical practice and administration, founding new hospitals specifically for women and children, and campaigned for female education. Such individuals mediated, with great energy and skill, between diverse communities and identities: China and the West; missionary Christianity and local community; revolutionary politics and civil society. JHH

92. SU XUEJIN

蘇學金 (1869–1919)

PRIZE-WINNING POTTER FROM DEHUA

Su Xuejin was a sculptor-potter active in the late 19th and early 20th centuries. Born in Dehua, Fujian province, Su was an important maker in the lineage of the *blanc de chine* ceramic tradition, famous for not only his artistic creations but also his contribution to the development of the ceramics industry in Dehua.

Blanc de chine, literally 'white from China', is the name given by European connoisseurs to white porcelain objects made in Dehua, a centre of ceramics that has flourished since the 11th century, making figures and vessels from local *kaolin* clay. Rich in potassium oxide, this special clay gives objects dense, pure and lustrous qualities distinct from products of any other kiln site. Dehua craftsmanship reached its zenith in the 17th century. Famous potters such as He Chaozong (act. *c.* 1580–1620) created elegant religious effigies, such as figures of Guanyin and her attendants, and began to stamp their individual marks on their work, suggesting that their craft was now perceived as a fully fledged art. The style and techniques of He Chaozong and his contemporaries profoundly influenced the subsequent three centuries of Dehua potters.

By the 19th century, blue-and-white wares had taken over as Dehua's dominant ceramic product, and the *blanc de chine* sculptural tradition had gone into decline. It was the emergence of Su Xuejin that reversed this process. Su's father, Su Deming (n.d.), had been a wood and stone carver who worked mainly for temples and private households, and occasionally at ceramic workshops. Accompanying his father on his many commissions, Su Xuejin gradually perfected his own carving skills and turned his hand to making porcelain religious figurines. Like most other Dehua potters, Su Xuejin imitated the stylistic signatures of the late Ming master sculptors, for example in his figurines' serene expressions and graceful postures. Indeed, his imitation was so perfect that his works were sometimes mistaken for authentic 17th-century pieces. Interestingly, the earlier master He Chaozong had also initially worked as a carver for temples. Working almost three centuries apart, both makers were able to transfer their sculptural skills from wood and stone to clay (a very different medium). Su Xuejin was apparently very proud of being seen as inheriting the great Ming tradition, to the extent that he used the mark *boji yuren* ('the vastly accomplished fisherman'), which – it is thought – was originally the mark of a Ming sculptor of uncertain identity.

While continuing the Ming stylistic tradition, Su Xuejin also developed and promoted a new category of product, the porcelain plum-blossom tree. Plum blossom is one of the most common motifs used on Dehua porcelains, mainly as an ornament in the form of relief applied to vessels such as cups and teapots. Sometime in the 18th

Figure of a *luohan* (disciple of Buddha), made by Su Xuejin, Dehua, *c.* 1890–1919. Porcelain with white glaze. Height 16.5 cm. Victoria and Albert Museum, London.

century, Dehua potters began to transform this motif from an essentially two-dimensional, secondary decoration into a three-dimensional format. Each porcelain plum-blossom tree sits on a porcelain pot or a base, and is to be displayed and appreciated more or less as one would a bonsai (Chinese: *penjing*). Su Xuejin further refined this new form, making it a piece of sculptural art in its own right. He made porcelain flowers with techniques such as pinching, that recreated the delicacy of prunus blossom in glassy white porcelain. A *blanc de chine* plum-blossom tree earned Su Xuejin a gold medal in the Panama–Pacific International Exposition in 1915; he was the first Dehua potter to receive this honour. Local history tells that the Dehua magistrate presented Su with a plaque to celebrate his achievement.

In addition to his artistic accomplishment, Su Xuejin was also an entrepreneur. Possibly around the beginning of the 20th century, he founded his own commercial studio, naming it the Yunyu studio, after his courtesy name Su Yunyu. A little earlier, in the late 19th century, Western collectors had developed a revived interest in Chinese porcelains. Somewhat jaded by the modest quality of export *blanc de chine* wares, which had begun to be traded to Europe a couple of centuries earlier, collectors now newly discovered and were astounded by the refined figurines made by Ming master sculptors. Su Xuejin clearly benefited from this wave of enthusiasm. His commercial studio took on commissions from a variety of clientele, and many of his works entered public and private collections outside China. Su Xuejin's studio was significant not only for the products it generated, but also for continuing the long lineage of *blanc de chine* manufacture. After his first two apprentices sadly died young, Su Xuejin apprenticed another young craftsman Xu Youyi (1887–1940), who became a close friend. After Su died of illness in 1919, Xu Youyi effectively fostered and raised Su's young son Qinming (1910–1969). Su Qinming learned the craft of porcelain from Xu and ended up marrying Xu's adopted daughter, before returning to his own home and restarting his father's old business. The friendship and collaboration between the Su and the Xu clans played an important role in the revival of the Yunyu studio, which is now a landmark in the ceramics industry at Dehua.

Xiaoxin Li

93. CHEN WEIYAN

陳謂岩 (1868–1926)

SHIWAN POTTER WHO EXPERIMENTED WITH PORCELAIN

Chen Weiyan was one of the most experimental ceramic sculptors working in China at the turn of the 20th century. His early career in the 1880s and 1890s proved his talent working with clay and grounded him in the Shiwan stoneware sculpting tradition, named after the town Shiwan, near Foshan, Guangdong province, where the kilns were located. However, it was his opportunities later in life that allowed him to experiment with different materials and develop the skills that made him a remarkable ceramic sculptor.

Chen grew up in Kuilongli, near Shiwan. He came from a humble family but received a good education, attending private school when he was young. He later worked as a teacher, excelled in calligraphy and was known for his seal carving. He was, however, more drawn to working with clay and was one of the very few Shiwan sculptors with a formal education. Chen's repertoire included artistic utilitarian wares, such as bonsai and brush pots, but it was his sculptural works that made him famous. By the 18th and 19th centuries, the kilns in Shiwan were already renowned for their sculptures. However, Chen's works captured a realism and sensitivity that took the tradition to a new level of artistry, and clearly distinguished his sculptures from those of his contemporaries. Throughout his lifetime, Chen sought inspiration from others but depended on his own skills in executing works that reflected his own style. It is said that he would often call on the famous Shiwan sculptor Huang Bing (1815–1894), famous for his depictions of animals. During these visits, Chen surreptitiously noted technical secrets and studied unfinished works. He then quickly recreated these works himself and put them on sale before the originals by Huang were even finished.

Chen's artistic talent further developed between 1900 and 1910, when he studied at the celebrated porcelain-making centre of Jingdezhen, along with his student Pan Yushu (1889–1936), attempting to infuse porcelain work with the sculptural qualities of Shiwan wares. While there, Chen learned porcelain techniques from various masters. Although detailed and sensitively executed, the experimental results of this fusion could not capture the more expressive *gongzai* (which, translating from the Cantonese understanding of the term, can be roughly rendered as 'doll-like') quality for which Shiwan sculptures of humans and deities were celebrated. However, Chen was able to capture a sensitive and interior depiction of emotion in his sculptures, for which Jingdezhen porcelain was a better medium than Shiwan stoneware clay

Chen Weiyan (1868–1926), *Self-Portrait*, c. 1888–1926. Glazed porcelain. Height 37.5 cm. Macao Museum of Art.

(the latter excelled more at capturing the dynamic immediacy of movement). Chen also mastered the use of enamels, which allowed him a wider and brighter colour palette than typical Shiwan glazes. In some of these experimental works, Jingdezhen enamels were also applied to wares fired from Shiwan clays.

In 1915, Chen Weiyan and a few associates founded the Yuhua Ceramic Industrial Company. That same year, a pair of sculptures of the sun and moon deities made by Chen was exhibited at the Panama–Pacific International Exposition in San Francisco. Chen then worked at the Guangdong Ceramics Industry Company as an engineer from 1920 until its closure in 1922. By now, Chen was also receiving private commissions. In 1920, he collaborated with Pan Yushu to create seven or eight larger-scale figures measuring between forty-eight and ninety-one centimetres in height for the Portuguese barrister, professor and Sinologist, Manuel da Silva Mendes (1867–1931). Da Silva Mendes is the earliest-known Westerner to have studied and collected Shiwan wares, and invited Chen and Pan to discuss the commission in Macao, where he lived. Six of these works are currently held by the Macao Museum of Art.

Chen suffered from a serious illness in the early 1920s. His mother vowed at the Buddhist Guangxiao Temple in the city of Guangzhou that Chen would produce one hundred sculptures of Huineng, the Sixth Patriarch of Chan Buddhism, if he were to recover. After recuperating in 1923, Chen duly honoured the promise with statues copied from the mummified body of Huineng at Nanhua Temple in northern Guangdong province.

Towards the end of his life and career, Chen Weiyan, along with Pan Yushu, sculpted figures for the Lee Gardens, an important commercial development in Hong Kong. The largest figures were nine feet tall, too large to be easily fired from stoneware. Therefore, the figures of Lee Gardens were instead made from painted plaster sculpted over an armature. The sculptures represented well-known religious and mythological figures, including Guanyin, Bodhidharma and various Daoist immortals. Unfortunately, these works survive only in photographs, as the Lee Gardens fell into disrepair in the 1940s and were levelled after World War II for redevelopment.

Chen Weiyan passed away in Macao in 1926 at the age of fifty-eight. His thirst for learning and for experimentation, as well as his mastery of various media, enabled him to stand out from his predecessors and contemporaries. A self-portrait sculpture in the Macao Museum of Art illustrates his skills. Coated in a dark glaze meant to imitate patinated bronze, the figure's precise but fluid lines exemplify his realistic style. His best-known works are held by museums in Guangdong, Hong Kong and Macao, as well as in various private collections.

Michel Lee

94. WU QIJUN

吴其濬 (1789–1847)

BOTANIST, GOVERNOR AND TECHNOCRAT

In the autumn of 1843, Wu Qijun departed Beijing for Yunnan, where he had been appointed provincial governor. Yunnan, on the south-western frontier of the Qing empire, was known for its ethnic diversity, biodiversity and rich mineral resources. Wu Qijun was most interested in the latter two. As a lifelong botanical researcher, he had examined a large variety of highland and tropical plants, which he had never seen in China proper. Meanwhile, as a governor, he had taught himself the technical knowledge to administer the mining industry – an important source of the Qing empire's wealth.

Two years later, Wu left Yunnan with a long list of achievements. In addition to career success, in 1844, he had published a mining treatise, *An Illustrated Account of Mines and Smelters of Yunnan*, which documented details of the province's mining technology. He had also collected information about the flora and fauna in south-west China, which was eventually to appear in his 1848 *Illustrated Investigation of the Names and Facts of Plants*. Both treatises were beautifully illustrated, well-organized, and grounded in empirical evidence. In addition, they were written without contact with Western science and technology. His books on mining and botany, published by the Qing government, were to receive international attention. Western scientists and Sinologists in China sent them to major libraries in Europe and America, and translated them into several languages.

Although Wu Qijun is now celebrated as a pioneer in the history of science, he was originally trained as a scholar specializing in Confucian classics. What motivated him to write about scientific and technical matters? How can we explain his transition from traditional Confucian scholar to technocrat and botanist?

Wu was born to a prominent gentry family from rural Gushi county, in Henan province. Members of the Wu family had been extremely successful in the civil service examinations. Both his father and elder brother climbed the ladder to become compilers at the elite Hanlin Academy in Beijing – a fast-track position for new scholar-officials – to rise to important positions. In 1817, Wu Qijun was the highest-scoring candidate in the top-level, metropolitan examinations, and was appointed to a prestigious position in the Hanlin Academy, like his father and elder brother.

However, Wu Qijun's promising career stalled in the early 1820s due to the death of his parents. From 1821 to 1828, he took leave and returned to his hometown in Henan to complete the standard period of filial mourning. Wu used this period to manage his family's affairs and to indulge his personal interest in botany. In 1822, he purchased a farm and named it 'Eastern Villa'. While at the villa, he probably spent much time studying plants with local farmers. In his botanical treatise, Wu Qijun constantly refers to himself as 'the farmer of Yulou' – Yulou is an archaic name for his hometown. His description of plants is notable for its considerable empirical observation and first-hand experience, indicating his deep personal engagement in agriculture.

Wu was summoned back to work in 1829. He spent around ten years supervising the empire's provincial examinations and was promoted to important positions in the Grand Secretariat, the Board of Revenue and the Board of War. After 1841, Wu Qijun became even busier: he was dispatched to several provinces across the Qing empire to suppress rebellions, investigate corrupt officials, establish new garrisons, and reform mining and salt administration.

Wu Qijun wrote his mining treatise because of the urgent need to generate more revenue for the empire. Since the early 19th century, the Qing empire had been plagued by fiscal disorder caused by natural disasters, rebellions and a corrupt bureaucracy. When Wu was in Yunnan, he was expected to increase tax revenue by intensifying the exploitation of the province's mineral resources. Previous copper administration manuals had tended to focus on tax regulations, but Wu's mining treatise covered the day-to-day operation of mines, including the equipment used,

Wu Qijun (1789–1847), illustration of a cactus plant and its blossoms, from *An Illustrated Investigation of the Names and Facts of Plants, juan 15,* 1848. Leiden University Libraries.

Wu Qijun (1789–1847), illustration of underground mining, from *An Illustrated Account of Mines and Smelters of Yunnan*, 1844. Miners and the structure of the mining tunnel are depicted. Harvard Yenching Library, Cambridge, MA.

labour organizations, and the cost of shipping from Yunnan to Beijing. The technical details were intended to educate scholar-officials who had little knowledge of mining, so that corrupt government clerks could no longer meddle in the administration.

As in his botanical research, Wu emphasized empirical knowledge in his book on mining. He included illustrations of tools and maps created by a local magistrate. One section of the book was based on a survey, in which county magistrates described the shape and colours of ores, tools and the smelting process. Making use of this technical data, Wu increased the number of mining sites and reduced administrative costs. His work became a guidebook for future administrators and researchers. Wu Qijun was an exemplarily successful 19th-century official – a Confucian scholar who was capable of absorbing technical knowledge quickly.

While the mining treatise reflects Wu's administrative skills, the botanic treatise shows his scholarly side. *An Illustrated Investigation of the Names and Facts of Plants* was the product of a lifetime's research. Wu conducted research whenever he had leisure time. His appointments across the empire provided him the opportunity to examine plants that were unknown in traditional pharmaceutical scholarship. For instance, he was the first to describe and illustrate cactus blossoms – cacti were not native to China, having originated from the Americas. The content of the book was also different from traditional pharmaceutical natural history. Traditional *materia medica* cover all types of materials, including not only plants, but also animals and insects. In contrast, Wu's book was limited to plants, making him a true pioneer of botanical science in China. Moreover, Wu's methodology diverged from 18th-century trends in scholarship, which focused on the study of ancient texts. As a scientific investigator, Wu instead prioritized above all empirical, in-the-field observation and first-hand information from farmers, vendors and cooks. Wu's approach to plants made him closer to a modern botanist.

Wu Qijun passed away from illness in 1847, while holding the office of the governor of Shanxi province. The emperor bestowed prestigious posthumous honours on Wu and conferred official positions on his sons. Born at the end of the most prosperous era of the Qing dynasty, he died after the First Opium War (1839–42), which had ushered in a new, even more turbulent period in Chinese history.

Wu's life and work demonstrate the transitions that Chinese scholar-officials underwent in an age of crisis and change. Wu Qijun trained himself to become a technocrat adept at administering the empire, and his scholarly interests expanded from classical learning to first-hand, evidence-based knowledge. He was not alone in this. At this phase in late imperial history, many of his peers – men like He Changling (1785–1848), Bao Shichen (1775–1855) and Lin Zexu (1785–1850) – also began to value practical knowledge over abstract scholarship, in their efforts to improve the governance of the country. Wu and his peers laid the foundation for post-1860 reforms that brought industrialization and modernization to China. Thanks to trailblazers like Wu, when exposure to Western science and technology (through the arrival in greater numbers of Protestant missionaries and foreign engineers) intensified in the late 19th century, many scholar-officials were ready to embrace these new ideas and practices.

Yijun Wang

95. ZHANG JIAN

張謇 (1853–1926)

MODERNIZING INDUSTRIALIST, EDUCATOR
AND PHILANTHROPIST

Best-known as an industrialist, Zhang Jian was also an educator, conservationist and philanthropist. One of the last generation of classically educated Chinese men, he was a transitional figure, who straddled the Qing empire (1644–1912) and Republican China (1912–49). Moving between official and business circles, he made important contributions to modernizing China through a tumultuous period.

Born into a well-off farming family in Haimen, a district of Nantong, Jiangsu province, he demonstrated early academic promise and was selected from several brothers to begin the lengthy education required to become a scholar-official. This culminated in him securing at the age of forty-one the *jinshi* – highest civil service

– qualification in the 1894 palace examinations. His academic training and achievement as the top-scoring candidate provided him with a reputation and a network of high-level connections, both of which would underpin his later business success. Exposed, like other moderate reformers, to Western and Japanese models of industrial and technological development, he grew convinced of the urgent need for Qing China to modernize. The 1895 Treaty of Shimonoseki, following China's defeat in the First Sino-Japanese War (1894–95), which gave foreigners the right to establish factories in China, spurred Zhang to abandon his fledgling official career to return to Nantong, and focus on local modernization projects as a means of helping his country.

His entrepreneurship began with the Dasheng (Dah Sun) Cotton Mill, established in 1895 in Tongzhou district, Nantong – the first cotton-spinning mill to be established in a rural setting. Lying north-west of Shanghai and less rich in natural resources than areas south of the Yangtze River, Nantong was underdeveloped, but nonetheless a well-chosen location. Both nationally and locally, the Qing government was encouraging the gentry to establish textile factories to compete with the foreign enterprises enabled by the treaty. The huge increase in Indian and Japanese cotton-yarn imports had demonstrated the demand for machine-spun yarn, and, by the end of the 19th century, China was consuming large quantities of foreign cotton goods. Since cotton was a staple crop in Nantong, Dasheng was assured of a steady supply of high-quality raw material, as well as benefiting from cheaper wages than in Shanghai (where many cotton mills had been established), good logistics and a ready local market. Despite all these advantages, the cotton sector was still seen as a risky endeavour, and Zhang faced an arduous process of securing capitalization. Like many industrial ventures of this period, the mill was initially established as a 'government-supervised, merchant-operated' (*guandu shangban*) enterprise, but several early backers pulled out, and Zhang had to be tenacious in obtaining funds from local investors.

Zhang Jian introduced modern technology and management to the cotton mill, assisted by Zhang Cha (1851–1939), his brother and close associate, and initially Dasheng was successful, providing employment to thousands of workers (mostly women) in the region, and profits to its investors. They expanded to create a large-scale regional enterprise spanning four cotton-spinning mills, and several subsidiary companies, including an oil mill, flour mill, publishing house, steamship line, silk filature and iron works, which became a single corporate entity, the Nantong Industrial Company, in 1907. Once Dasheng was stable, Zhang Jian used its profits and reputation to branch out into his many other areas of interest.

He began, in 1902, by establishing the first normal school in China, Tongzhou Normal College, to train teachers, but his vision was a comprehensive schooling system in Nantong. Under his plan, what became the Nantong County Educational Association developed hundreds of primary schools across the district, funded through private donations and public tax levies, and administered by local self-government associations. He also established professional schools, including a

medical school, an agricultural school and a textile school – at the latter, the famed embroiderer Shen Shou (1874–1921) ran embroidery classes.

Zhang's other primary areas of interest were coastal land reclamation and water conservancy. He sought to transform the saline coastal land of northern Jiangsu, long used for salt production, into agricultural land for growing cotton to better supply his mills. This would have relieved population pressures and increased agricultural production. However, the land reclamation companies he established encountered a complex set of challenges: existing land ownership; opposition from vested interests, in the form of the salt merchants and salt commissioner, who obstructed his plans; and serious natural disasters common to the area. He was also interested in water management and in preventing natural disasters by controlling the Huai River, whose flooding had long plagued parts of Jiangsu province, including Nantong. He established surveying and hydraulic engineering classes to train a new generation of home-grown experts, so that the country would no longer depend on foreign expertise. However, he ultimately struggled to secure funding in the face of political instability. Though often close to political events, he always skirted the arena of political activity and held appointments only briefly: president of the Jiangsu Provisional Assembly in 1909, and minister of agriculture and commerce from 1913 to 1915.

All his areas of interest connected with Nantong in some way, and, in 1915, he resigned all official positions to focus his attention on civic and philanthropic projects there, including homes for the destitute, aged and disabled (funded partly by sales of his calligraphy); medical clinics; modern theatre (a keen opera buff, Zhang was a key patron of the Beijing opera star, Mei Lanfang); a library; and the first museum in mainland China, Nantong Museum, established in 1905. He also built roads and parks, planted trees, and introduced gas illumination. Nantong, once backward, became a leader in education and culture, known as a 'model county'. However, despite his aims of local self-government and self-strengthening through education and industry, these efforts were mostly funded by Zhang and his brother, and without official support – the 'Nantong Model' was short-lived.

Later, Dasheng also failed, partly due to the poor business climate facing the Chinese textile industry in the 1920s, but also because of Zhang's various forms of financial mismanagement. Especially problematic was his habit of using capital from the Dasheng mills to finance other ventures, often without permission from share-holders or transparent accounting. Overextended bank loans took Dasheng close to bankruptcy, and it was taken over by a Shanghai bank. Dasheng's path mirrored the times: in 1904, it had been one of the first limited liability companies to be formed in China; in the 1950s, the socialist government turned it into a state-owned enterprise.

Zhang's reputation has gone through similar ups and downs. Vilified as an exploitative capitalist during the Cultural Revolution (1966–76), he was celebrated as a dynamic entrepreneur during the 1990s. Ultimately, his legacy is mixed. He was undoubtedly a man of enormous vision, energy and determination, yet many of his ventures failed to achieve long-term success, partly because he took on so many tasks in so many disparate areas, and partly because of the political instability of the late Qing and early Republic. His career reflects both the possibilities and difficulties of this period. Like other elite figures who attempted local models of experimental modernization, he strove to fill a vacuum created by the absence of strong central government, but his efforts were ultimately undone by that absence.

Rachel Silberstein

96. SHEN SHOU

沈壽 (1874–1921)

INNOVATIVE EMBROIDERER

Daughter of an antiques dealer in Suzhou, Shen Shou was born one decade after the Taiping Civil War (1851–64) decimated the fabled gardens and workshops of her hometown. By 1881, when the seven-year-old came of age, the clattering of silk looms again filled its alleyways and barges loaded with rice and cotton clogged its canals. Like other ordinary Suzhou girls, Shen's homeschooling began with embroi-dery, as soon as her mind grew steady and her eyes discerning. The mother of all feminine arts, embroidery was a profitable skill. Confucian thinkers considered the legendary 'tilling farmer and weaving maid' co-contributors to the economic and moral foundations of civilization. In Suzhou and its environs, women's textile work brought in as much as one third of the cash needed by an average household. Girls were valued at home; the handful of formal schools ran by missionaries attracted mostly orphans or indigents.

The Suzhou-style embroidery Shen Shou learned from her mother and elder sister was of the highest calibre in artistic and technical demands. Instead of utilitarian garments or purses, the embroiderer produced pictorial works intended to be mounted or framed, effectively treating the needle as a painting brush and the extra-fine silk floss as ink or colour pigments. Identified as 'boudoir embroidery' in the market, such works fetched the highest prices as objects of art. Seven years into her tutelage, the teenage daughter accrued fame, attracting not only buyers but also a suitor, an irrepressible painter by the name of Yu Jue (1868–1951). In 1894, when Shen turned twenty, her father finally agreed to the marriage.

A consummate operator, Yu applied himself to fostering his wife's career. Their big break came ten years later, when Yu worked his connections to convey twelve embroidered gifts, probably including an eight-panelled human-sized standing screen, to Empress Dowager Cixi, on the occasion of her seventieth birthday in 1904. The collection took Shen and a team of eight women one year to produce (a record speed considering the magnitude). The august patroness of the arts was so pleased that she bestowed upon the couple two calligraphic scrolls by her own hand. The outside world opened for Shen when railway tracks were laid linking Suzhou to the metropolis of Shanghai. An invitation arrived from the Empress Dowager in 1904: Yu and Shen were to pack immediately for a two-month trip to Japan. Their mission was to survey the new art schools, textile workshops and retailers, to help modernize the embroidery trade in China.

Shen Shou was not impressed by Japanese embroidery, nor the woven pictorial hangings featuring hounds and horses then popular at the world expos. She was struck, however, by close viewings of watercolours and oil paintings – the latter represented an art form new to her. She also perceived the creative synergy between fine-art painters and embroiderers, who collaborated in the art schools and workshops. Later, in designing the curricula of embroidery schools in China, she would engage painters to train students in art appreciation and brush painting. Her husband, in turn, was awed by the business acumen of kimono manufacturers in Kyoto. Both realized that Japan was a formidable competitor to latecomer China in the global textiles market.

Subsequently, in 1907, the Empress Dowager summoned Shen to the capital to open China's first state-sponsored embroidery school. Appointed chief instructor, Shen drew a hefty monthly salary of 50 taels of silver, a large sum for a semi-literate woman. Her new position reflected shifting priorities among Qing's ruling elites. As China strove to modernize its economy, female livelihoods became an urgent concern; reformers harboured hopes that if all 200 million pairs of female hands were put to work for the country, instead of for family patriarchs, national wealth and power would ensue.

Photograph of Shen Shou, c. 1912. From *Embroidered Portrait of Jesus: Exhibited by Mrs. Yu Shen-sheo, China*, Shanghai, Chung Hwa Book Co., c. 1914.

One of these reformers was Zhang Jian (1853–1926), an industrialist who later invited Shen to run a girls' handicrafts school in his hometown Nantong (105 kilometres from Shanghai), taking over from Yu Jue the role of Shen's promoter in the last seven years of her life. Zhang also urged Shen to dictate lessons from her sick bed and published them as *Manual of Embroidery* by Xueyi (a name he conferred on Shen). When they met, Zhang was an official in charge of selecting products from the various provinces to represent China at world expos. He recognized in Shen's recent works a winning product, one that showcased the refinement of traditional Chinese craft, while appealing to collectors of European art.

After her return from Japan, Shen experimented with naturalistic portraits based on oil paintings or photographs, but executed with Suzhou-boudoir stitching techniques. ('Boudoir embroidery' was an artistically prestigious style associated with the work of skilled, educated women working at home.) She described her approach as follows: 'Shadows are born of light, and light has a *yin* aspect and a *yang* aspect.

I concentrate my mind on discerning the *yin* from the *yang*, using this new awareness to execute the old familiar way of embroidery. I began to produce something new.... As time went on, I came to realize that although there are myriad forms and gestures under heaven, whatever enters my eyes…can be entered into my embroidery.' Shen branded this new genre 'Embroidery that imitates life.' An early exercise, a portrait of Italian Queen Elena of Montenegro, made a stir at the International Expo in Turin in 1909, and was subsequently presented to the queen herself as a diplomatic gift by the newly minted Republic of China.

Shen's masterpiece, however, is *Jesus*, which won First Honors at the Panama–Pacific International Expo in San Francisco in 1915. In this portrait, to emulate the veristic shading effects of an oil painting, Shen Shou used ultra-fine split floss of 111 colours, the majority of which she dyed herself. For the concave or shady areas on Jesus's face and neck, she invented the 'swirling stitch', whereby one short satin stitch radiates from the previous one, thus diffusing light. For the convex or bright areas, she applied the 'mixed straight stitch', the mainstay of boudoir embroidery. Despite a period of illness caused by the intensity of the work involved, she completed the embroidery in thirteen months.

Shen Shou (1874–1921), *Jesus*, 1913–14. Embroidery exhibited at the Panama–Pacific International Exposition. Height 54.8 cm, width 32.7 cm. The seal reads 'Yu Shen Shou'. Nanjing Museum.

Shen Shou's serene and magnanimous bearing, as shown in a photograph, of about 1912, belies the relentless pressure of deadlines and competition which attended her journey from an ordinary daughter to career woman, national celebrity and 'world artist' (an accolade etched on her tombstone). Posing behind a European-style chair and a standing embroidery frame, she is decked out in modern fashionable silk jacket, ankle-length skirt, Japanese-style coiffure and leather shoes. The two awards on her chest are the Decoration of the Fourth Order medal bestowed by the Guangxu emperor (viewer's left) and a gold watch bearing the emblem of the House of Savoy gifted by Italian Queen Elena of Montenegro (viewer's right). (The original English caption reads, 'Photograph of Mrs. Yu Shen-sheo, completing her work on the Portrait of Jesus after her recovery from weakness of brains during the last month of her work.')

By the time of her later death, aged forty-seven, Shen had embroidered over a hundred signed or unsigned works, taking Suzhou-style embroidery from the boudoir to the global market and helping engineer its transition from traditional craft to modern art. Although the dream of enriching the national coffers by exporting embroidery did not materialize, students from the four schools she founded continued to teach and stitch, nurturing embroidery artists who are still flourishing today.

Dorothy Ko

97. ABING

阿炳 (c. 1893–1950)

CHINA'S GREATEST FOLK MUSICIAN

Only one, albeit iconic, photograph of the folk musician Abing (below) survives today. In the image, a pair of round, blackened, lopsided glasses both conceals, and alerts the viewer to, the musician's blindness. He is best known for six pieces of music, three each for the two-stringed fiddle *erhu* and the four-stringed lute *pipa*. He lived and worked in Wuxi, a city in the Jiangnan region (the Yangtze delta region), famous for its rich cultural life and traditions of string music. He led an impoverished existence at the margins of Chinese society – yet he was celebrated, after 1950, as China's greatest folk musician. The music associated with him has become part of the standard concert repertoire in China for traditional Chinese music.

This transformation from impoverished street musician to canonical figure – the making of a musical giant – has as much to do with the 19th-century musical culture from which Abing sprang, as it does with the changes that Chinese society experienced on its path to political, social, intellectual, artistic and musical modernization in the 20th century. Although his music helped define and create what is perceived today as traditional Chinese music, it was the canon-forming processes of the 20th

Abing's identity card, used during the Japanese occupation of Wuxi after 1937. It is now the only surviving image of the musician.

century (and their transformation of oral musical traditions into a modernized concert repertoire) that made Abing such a key figure.

As one might expect for such a socially marginal individual, little historical evidence about Abing's life survives. Over the course of the 20th century, his life was recounted and thus reinterpreted various times, each retelling revealing as much about the evolution of history and historiography in China, as it did about Abing's actual life. The earliest biography of Abing – written by Yang Yinliu (1899–1984) in 1952 – emphasizes the importance of class conflict to his life experiences. Much later, during the Cultural Revolution years of the 1960s, discussion of him was discouraged by the Communist establishment. After all, Abing's biography defied the simple binary categories dominant during Mao's last revolution, and his music was 'out of tune' with the harmonic language of the era. This changed in the late 1970s when Abing's life was re-excavated in academic texts, a biography, a movie and at least two comic books.

Abing was born Hua Yanjun, most likely in 1893. After his mother died when he was still an infant, he grew up with his father (who might have been his stepfather), in whose footsteps he followed as a musician in a Daoist temple. In his thirties, Abing went blind, possibly after contracting venereal disease, and left (or was forced to leave) the Daoist community. Sources vary as to the reasons for his leaving the temple:

his blindness, his acquaintance with street musicians, or – as the later texts reveal – his frequenting brothels and opium dens.

Shortly before his death in December 1950, the two musicologists Cao Anhe (1905–2004) and Yang Yinliu (1899–1984) travelled to Jiangnan, as part of a larger campaign launched by the government to record the folk music(s) of China. These coordinated efforts were in tune both with attempts begun in the early 20th century to standardize and modernize Chinese music, and with an interest on the part of intellectuals in China's folk traditions. These efforts also harmonized with Mao Zedong's famous injunctions (in his 1942 lectures on literature and art) that culture should serve politics. Folk songs could be used with new texts to propagate Communist ideology and instrumental music was important to the creation of a new national music. As Yang had known Abing during his youth in Wuxi, he and Cao recorded six pieces by the blind musician. The conditions of the recording session were anything but ideal; Abing's health was deteriorating, and he had been unable to practise for two to three years on account of turmoil resulting from the civil war between Communists and Nationalists. Cao and Yang transcribed and published these pieces in 1952. Of the *erhu* pieces, *The Moon Reflected on the Second Springs* is the most famous and most widely performed; of the *pipa* pieces, it is *Great Waves Washing the Sand*.

While these are considered formalized compositions today, they originated from a context of musical improvisation. Jonathan Stock has shown that the *erhu* pieces are in fact three improvisations on similar musical material. They are not the performance of three distinct, memorized, fixed creations. These pieces, together with the compositions for *erhu* by the music reformer, teacher and composer Liu Tianhua (1895–1932) and a few others, form the core repertoire of *erhu* practice in conservatoires and concert halls in China today. Abing's *pipa* performances are similarly core to that instrument's concert repertoire.

The publication of the music scores in 1952 marked the beginning of Abing's posthumous fame and the inclusion of his music in the new musical canon of the People's Republic of China (founded 1949). With this, Cao and Yang also set off a process by which Abing's improvised music slowly acquired the status of an *opus* by Western standards: now written down, his works were included in standard collections and authoritative syllabi of *erhu* and *pipa* music. The works were furthermore adapted for other solo instruments and different accompaniments, ranging from traditional Chinese ensembles, to piano and fully fledged Western symphony orchestras. These different arrangements were recorded by countless musicians, in different interpretations, and are based on Cao and Yang's notated music, not on Abing's performance. In many performances by later artists, the listener can hear an intensification of the music through changes in tempo and instrumentation, and through omissions and additions to the musical script. Interestingly, these performance adaptations have manifested a certain degree of standardization, as several of these later performances feature the same divergences from the original text – as if these differences are functioning as favourite, canonical cadenzas. But these adaptations also point to the remnants of oral musical traditions which allow performers a certain leeway with a particular musical text. Lastly, they point to the continued, creative fascination that Abing's music holds for performers and listeners in China alike. They suggest, arguably, that China's 'greatest folk musician' was created not only by the histories and hagiographies written about him, but also by the power of his melodies and the amplifying effect of musical recordings. China's 'greatest folk musician' was thus created by the vigour and appeal of traditional 19th-century musical practices, in concert with the political, canonizing culture of the 20th century.

Lena Henningsen

98. LUO ZHENYU

羅振玉 (1866–1940)

ANTIQUARIAN AND ARCHAEOLOGICAL PIONEER

Agronomist, educationalist, reformer, antiquarian, epigrapher, entrepreneur, art dealer, Qing loyalist, Japanese collaborator, Luo Zhenyu embodies the transformations and contradictions of intellectual and political life at the end of the Qing and in the early decades of the Republic. He was recognized during and after his lifetime as one of the great collectors and interpreters of the earliest verified Chinese-language texts, using archaeological evidence for the first time to confirm the antiquity of the Chinese state. This verification of an ancient 'Chinese nation' made possible a modern archaeology that the Nationalist government after 1928 hoped would promote national morale in the face of Japanese invasion. But Luo had to finance his scholarship by selling artistic masterpieces to wealthy Japanese customers and ended his life in the service of the Japanese army's puppet Manchurian state in the north-west.

Luo was born into a literary family of very modest means in south-east China. Demonstrating early academic talent, by the age of three he could recognize some thousand Chinese characters; as a teenager, he sought out celebrated antiquarians, such as the novelist Liu E (1857–1909). At the age of eighteen, he published his first scholarly book on ancient inscriptions, and would complete dozens more before his death. After failing the second rung of the civil service examinations, however, Luo abandoned hope of progressing further, and tried to make a living from tutoring.

Shocked (like many of his contemporaries) by Japan's defeat of the Qing empire in the 1894–95 Sino-Japanese War, Luo threw himself into reform activities. He moved to Shanghai – centre of a booming press – and founded publishing houses specializing in agricultural science and modern education (while still finding time to research 2,000-year-old calligraphy). In 1900, Zhang Zhidong (1837–1909) – governor of Hubei province, and one of the most powerful officials in the empire – invited Luo into government service, to modernize agriculture and education, a role that took Luo to

Photograph of Luo Zhenyu
published in *Jiaoyu shijie*
(Educational World), no. 69,
1904.

Japan for a nine-week study mission. This elevation into official circles brought Luo into contact with some of the wealthiest and most successful art collectors of the era.

Luo's antiquarian connections drew him into an extraordinary archaeological and epigraphic discovery. The story goes that, in the summer of 1899, an antiquarian collector called Wang Yirong (1845–1900) suffering from malaria bought a remedy from a Beijing pharmacy called 'dragon bones'. When he looked more closely at the ancient bones to be ground into medicine, he discovered some inscriptions that resembled Chinese characters. Further research revealed that they came from the village of Xiaotun, in Anyang county, Hebei, where farmers dug up ancient bones, called them dragon bones or dragon teeth, and sold them on to urban pharmacies for use in traditional medicines. A cluster of passionate antiquarians, among whom Luo Zhenyu was one of the most dedicated, embarked on collecting and deciphering the inscribed fragments. In the first two decades of the 20th century, Luo published multiple catalogues and studies of the bones (in addition to books about documents, paintings, murals, coins and other artefacts). He proved that the bones were authentic objects from the Shang dynasty (the second oldest royal house recorded in ancient Chinese historiography), written as divination tools during the second millennium BCE; verified the historical existence of the dynasty; and elucidated some of the bones' insights about royal chronology, ritual, geography and etymology. In 1928, trained Chinese archaeologists undertook the first large-scale systematic archaeological dig in Anyang, to unearth the ancient capital of the Shang. The light that antiquarians had already cast on the 'oracle bone' inscriptions provided a crucial database of knowledge for this first major Chinese excavation.

Luo's contribution to the evolution of China's millennia-old tradition of anti-quarianism into archaeology went beyond deciphering oracle bones. Before Luo, most educated Chinese collectors were uninterested in ancient objects without text. But Luo was adamant that any artefact – mirrors, statues, bricks, tools – could be a repository of history, culture and religion, and, like every archaeologist, he wanted to know exactly where an item that caught his attention had been dug from. He collected so many tomb figurines – models buried with the deceased to stand in for the servants and animals whose company they would need in the afterlife – that friends nicknamed his home 'the studio of the dead'.

Although Luo was a passionate (and sometimes wily) private collector, he was also an early campaigner for public preservation of antiquities in museums and libraries. In 1907, he urged officials to found institutes of national learning in every province (to encompass libraries, museums and research institutes), but the project was side-lined and delayed by the other crises pressing in on the Qing. A similar attempt by Luo failed in the 1920s.

After the fall of the dynasty in 1911, Luo remained a loyalist (he never cut off his queue); he seems to have concluded that the imperial state could best preserve the ancient Sinophone culture that he cherished. Feeling alienated from the new Republican state, Luo left for eight intensely productive years in Japan, working on his vast collection of antiquities and documents. In one year alone, he published fourteen books, on topics varying from Shang inscriptions to Qing coins. But with no family money or official salary, he had to support himself and his large family through dealing in arts and antiques, mainly to well-heeled Japanese clientele. This conflict of interest – between Luo the scholar and Luo the dealer – clouded his reputation, both during and after his lifetime, for some suspected that his academic authentications of objects were designed to inflate their market value.

In 1919, he returned to China and joined the 'little court' of the last, abdicated Qing emperor, Puyi. In the late 1920s, Luo was persuaded by Japanese colonial officers resident in north-east China that they would restore Puyi to the emperorship in the old Qing homeland of Manchuria. Convinced in turn by Luo, Puyi arrived in late 1931, not long after the 'Mukden Incident' made clear the Japanese empire's ruthlessly expansionist aims; he remained trapped as puppet ruler of Japan's colony in north-east China until Japanese surrender in 1945. Five years after Luo died of heart failure in 1940, at the chaotic close of World War II his remarkable collections were scattered between Japanese collectors, Russian armies, Chinese Communist functionaries and the streets of Port Arthur.

Julia Lovell

99. LIU E

劉鶚 (1857–1909)

HYDROLOGIST, ANTIQUARIAN, NOVELIST

Liu E was a hydrologist, industrialist, epigraphist and *littérateur* of the late Qing period. During his life, he used several pseudonyms including 'Scholar of a Hundred Temperings from Hongdu' (Hongdu bailian sheng), under which his celebrated novel *The Travels of Laocan* was serialized, and 'Owner of the Studio for Hugging Remnants and Preserving Fragments' (Baocan shouque zhaizhu).

Liu E was born in Liuhe county, Jiangsu province, on 18 October 1857, and died in Ili, Xinjiang, on 23 August 1909. The Liu family was originally from Yan'an in Shaanxi, and claimed as an ancestor Liu Yanqing (*c.* 1068–1127), a commander of the Northern Song dynasty. Several descendants of the Liu clan had distinguished military careers. Liu E's father, Liu Chengzhong (1818–1884), gained his *jinshi* – top-level degree – in the imperial civil service examinations of 1852, and for years served as a government official in Henan, where he specialized in management of the Yellow River and was well-known for his probity, at a time when government corruption was an acknowledged problem. Liu senior was also entrusted, in 1868, with the task of dredging the Huiji River at Chuitai, Kaifeng, and the following year was appointed supervisor for a project building European-style waterwheels.

Liu E was a precocious child. He started to learn characters and poems at the age of three under the guidance of his second-eldest sister. In 1865, when he was eight, he began to accompany his father on official postings around Henan province. By the time of Liu E's marriage to a woman surnamed Wang in 1873, he had built himself a broad social network. In summer 1876, Liu E failed the provincial – second-level – examination in Nanjing, after which he gave up practising for the complex, highly conventionalized 'eight-legged essay' necessary to pass the civil service examinations, and instead immersed himself in the family library, which contained books on a wide range of subjects, including hydrology, astrology, astronomy, musicology, medicine and military science as well as Chinese translations of Western and Japanese books collected by his father and his elder brother. This reading programme prepared him well for his future hydrological work. After his father died in 1884, Liu E explored a few business ventures in Jiangsu, including a tobacco shop in Huai'an, a bookshop in Shanghai and a medicine practice in Yangzhou, all of which, however, proved short-lived.

In September 1887, the Yellow River overran its dykes near Zhengzhou in Henan province, causing a levee breach over 1,000 metres wide and huge damage across north China. In 1888, Liu E was offered a position in Henan by Wu Dacheng (1835–1902), the director general of the Grand Canal and also a renowned antiquarian, to combat the Yellow River flood. His dyke-building programme proved effective. As he discarded his official robes and set to work as industriously as any of the labourers, Liu E became famous for his diligence and practical acumen. That winter, the repair work was completed, and over the next six years Liu published two important river management manuals.

In 1895, following the Qing's catastrophic defeat by Japan, Liu began work in the Zongli yamen, the government's equivalent of a foreign office. An admirer of Western technical knowhow and a follower of Taigu philosophy (which believed in progress through modern commerce and industry), Liu E advocated opening mines and building railways, and volunteered to help build a railway line between north and central China. However, conservative opposition blocked the project.

In 1897, Liu E explained in a report the benefits of using foreign loans for mining projects, and became the Shanxi manager of the London-based Peking Syndicate, a firm that bought mining rights in China. But in 1898 the entrepreneurial Liu E was impeached for granting privileges to foreigners and returned to Beijing. One of his detractors even demanded the death penalty, on the charge of colluding with foreigners, but Liu was exempted as he was living in extraterritorial Shanghai at the time. When foreign armies invaded and occupied Beijing in 1900, at the close of the Boxer siege of the capital, Liu E raised money for and personally delivered famine relief to Beijing, whose grain supplies had been cut off. His final years remained turbulent. In 1908 Yuan Shikai (1859–1916) accused him of embezzling mining profits, illegally selling imperial grain and running a private salt transportation company. Liu was arrested then banished to Xinjiang, where he began to write a medical handbook, *Collected Diagnoses and Treatments for Longevity and Wellbeing*, and compiled his earlier antiquarian writings into *Records of the Study of Bronze and Stone*. There, Liu E died of a stroke in 1909.

Although Liu E spent so much time and energy on government work, he is probably best remembered as a scholar and writer. Alongside other passionate antiquarian contemporaries, including Wu Dacheng, Luo Zhenyu (1866–1940) and others, he carried out pioneering research on Chinese antiquities: bronzes, ceramics, lutes, seals, currency, coin moulds, eaves tiles, diquan (land contracts) and rubbings. He was a path-breaking epigrapher, decoding bronze inscriptions from the early first millennium BCE. He was also one of the earliest collectors and scholars of oracle bones, the fragments of ox and turtle bones from Henan (north central China) – first discovered by Wang Yirong (1845–1900) around 1899 – on which the earliest versions of Chinese characters were identified. After Wang committed suicide during the foreign occupation of Beijing in 1900–1, his collection of around a thousand oracle-bone fragments came into Liu E's possession. With the help of Luo Zhenyu, Liu E compiled and published the first monograph on the oracle bones, including rubbings of 1,058 pieces from his collection. Although the book has many errors, it was the first to declare that oracle bones showed the script used by the inhabitants of Yin (the capital of one of China's earliest dynasties, the Shang, of the late second millennium BCE).

Between 1903 and 1907, Liu E also wrote *The Travels of Laocan*, one of the best-known satirical novels of the late Qing. Set in Shandong province, in north-east China, the novel stars an itinerant doctor called Laocan. On his journeys around China, Laocan repeatedly witnesses the cruelty and incompetence of local officials, and the injustices and suffering they inflict on ordinary people. Since it was published, the novel has been celebrated by critics and historians as a reflection of the political and social malaise of the final years of imperial China.

Guo Yongbing

100. IDA KAHN

康愛德 (1873–1931)

MEDICAL LEADER AND MISSIONARY

Ida Kahn was a missionary and doctor who seemed to embody the ideals of modern Chinese womanhood. During her lifetime, she actively participated in an international movement of Christian women, advocated for women's education, founded a women's hospital and gained the support of not only missionaries but also local gentry to fund her work in China. She accomplished all this while acknowledging the effects of class and gender, and questioning the racial hierarchies around her.

Many accounts emphasize just one aspect of Kahn's life. In 1897, the reformer Liang Qichao (1873–1929) acclaimed her, due to her studies in Western medicine, as an exemplar of the 'new Chinese woman' (which he contrasted rhetorically with his perception of a bound-foot 'traditional' woman, emblematizing the backwardness of imperial China). He paid no attention to her missionary connections. Meanwhile, the missionary community portrayed her not as a convert from a poor family who had become a missionary, but as a Chinese woman from a 'good family', who descended from the line of Confucius. In contrast to such one-dimensional representations, Kahn was a mediator and cultural translator. She did not simply exist in separate Chinese or American spheres, nor can she be confined to either missionary or revolutionary contexts. Her complex identity is reflected in the names by which she has been known. Having first been called Kang Aide, she later took the English name of Ida Kahn and used the literary name of Kang Cheng for her Chinese writings.

Kang Aide was born in Jiujiang, Jiangxi province (south-east China), in 1873. She was the sixth daughter to parents of modest means and came close to being betrothed when she was just two months old. Gertrude Howe (1847–1928), an American Methodist Missionary in Jiujiang, heard about the baby's predicament and adopted her. Howe was one of the first missionaries of the Woman's Foreign Missionary Society of the Methodist Episcopal Church, which was formed in 1869. She was not conventional by any means: Howe was an abolitionist who adopted a Chinese baby, and raised her bilingually and biculturally, at a time when this was hardly accepted within the missionary community. As she transgressed the boundaries of segregation by adopting Ida and other Chinese children, Howe was marginalized within missionary circles. These difficulties were not limited to their life in China. During the time of the Chinese Exclusion Act (instituted in 1882), Howe took Ida Kahn and Mary Stone (Shi Meiyu), the daughter of a local convert and pastor, to the United States to study medicine. In 1896, when Ida Kahn and Mary Stone received their medical degrees with distinction from the University of Michigan and returned to China, they were warmly welcomed and celebrated.

In 1903, Kahn went to practise medicine in Nanchang, the Jiangxi provincial capital, having been invited by a member of the Chinese gentry, and, soon after, Howe joined her daughter there. Kahn worked as a 'self-supporting' missionary there, which meant that missionary funds were limited to her own salary. Her refusal to cut ties with the Methodist Episcopal mission board meant that the local gentry provided less funding for her medical work than she had expected. The financial situation improved by 1907, as she gained more support from the local gentry as well as the missionary community, and she was approved for furlough in 1907, which she spent in the United States and England. In 1909, Howe oversaw the building of her daughter's hospital, which was ready by 1911, when Kahn returned to China.

Between 1908 and 1911, while on furlough from missionary work, Kahn studied literature at Northwestern University in Chicago. She also took a course at the School of Tropical Diseases in London. Around this time, Kahn prepared *An Amazon in Cathay* (1912), a pamphlet issued by the Woman's Foreign Missionary Society in

Medicine chest packed with ointments, powdered plants, dried insects, lizards, seahorses and written charms to speed recovery, 1890–1910. Height 8 cm, width 62 cm, depth 45.5 cm. Great North Museum, Newcastle.

Boston. In this publication, Kahn explored class dynamics, and promoted a hospital for women and children as being the ideal way to serve the Chinese state. Ida Kahn believed in the importance of women's education. Soon after writing *An Amazon in Cathay*, when the Rockefeller Foundation urged her to integrate her hospital with that of a male medical missionary in Nanchang, she reaffirmed the importance of the education and medical treatment of women. Following on from this, she spent two years in Tianjin running a government hospital for women, and returned to Nanchang in 1918.

At one level, Kahn's activities seemed to resonate with the ideas of Chinese revolutionaries. After all, she worked to create a new China – which, to her, involved the promotion of Western medicine. In Kahn's view, the medical work of women in women-led institutions could strengthen the Chinese nation. Following the 1911 Revolution, she hosted a banquet for Sun Yat-sen (1866–1925), the figurehead of the revolution and the Republic's first president, during his visit to Nanchang (1912). Yet, contrary to dominant revolutionary ideas in this era, she believed that women's activities should remain distant from the battlefield.

Through her work, Kahn managed to assume administrative positions in hospitals at a time when notions of racial superiority allowed for the conversion of Chinese women and their acceptance into missionary circles, but not their representation as heads of institutions. Kahn's ability to appeal to American missionaries as well as Chinese revolutionaries and local gentry provided her with unique opportunities. Yet this multiplicity of ties also created obstacles for her.

In Kahn's article 'The Place of Chinese Christian Women in the Development of China' (1919), we can see that she believed that the Anglo-Saxon world had achieved its relatively favourable condition through Christianity. She perceived conversion as a way to equalize the hierarchies between races and pave the way for the Chinese state to progress, and for the people to advance in their work. Although she believed in the transnational movement of women missionaries, Kahn did not shy away from critiquing the racial hierarchies and managerial practices that structured the lives of those in the missionary communities.

Kahn lived at a time when frameworks of Chinese and Western medicine were reshaping one another, and in a context where patients often explored options for a range of medical therapies. She participated in early associational ventures by Chinese practitioners of Western medicine. For example, in 1915 she spoke on 'Hygiene in the Home' at the first conference of the National Medical Association of China. Her presentation preceded a paper on the 'Foundations of Modern Hygiene in China' by the eminent doctor of public health, Wu Lien-teh (1879–1960). However, Ida Kahn was not inclined to broker knowledge exchange between Chinese and Western medicine. Following her medical education at the University of Michigan – at a time before American medical institutions included learning on alternative or holistic medicines – she continued to hold the view that Western medicine alone could carry the nation to the modern world.

It is a challenge to neatly put Ida Kahn in a single category. Doing so would be a disservice to the range of causes and groups she was involved in. She was a missionary, a doctor, and a visionary who embraced revolutionary ideals. Ida Kahn's voice shines through at the junctures that forced her to mediate between the different worlds she inhabited. She believed that a stronger nation would be born through women's education, and thought that conversion to Christianity would render racial hierarchies obsolete. To Kahn, medicine was both a vehicle for conversion and a means for educating women. Understanding Ida Kahn helps to make sense of the long 19th century in all its complexity, by considering its multifaceted nature and its global connections.

Sare Aricanli

Above. Xu Beihong, *Portrait of He Zhanli (1891–1915)*, 1915. This portrait depicts Lily Haw (He Zhanli), a Chinese-American woman who became the third wife of intellectual reformer Kang Youwei (see pages 286–89). The daughter of Hakka immigrants, Lily spoke Chinese, English and Spanish. Married aged 15 to Kang who was in his late 40s, together they travelled the world. Xu was commissioned to represent Lily as she had appeared to Kang in a dream, 10 days after her death from scarlet fever, aged only 24. Watercolour and gouache on paper. Height 127.1 cm, width 65 cm. Shanghai Museum.

Opposite. Ren Xiong, *Autumn Shadow in Liangxi (Wuxi)*, 1840–57. In 1855, at the peak of his creativity, Ren Xiong (see pages 140–44) painted this portrait for the poet and painter Yao Xie (1805–1864), representing one of Yao's wives. Hanging scroll; ink and colours on silk. Height 126 cm, width 60 cm. Michael Yun-Wen Shih Collection.

331

FURTHER READING

1. Jiaqing

Fung Ming-chu 馮明珠 and Chen Lung-kuei 陳龍貴. *Jiaqing jun you Taiwan* 嘉慶君遊台灣 (Lord Jiaqing and the journey to Taiwan: A special exhibition on cultural artifacts of the Qing Emperor Renzong), bilingual edition. Taipei: National Palace Museum, 2016.

Guan Wenfa 關文發. *Jiaqing huangdi* 嘉慶皇帝 (The Jiaqing emperor). Changchun: Jilin wenshi chubanshe, 1993.

McMahon, Daniel. *Rethinking the Decline of China's Qing Dynasty: Imperial Activism and Borderland Management at the Turn of the Nineteenth Century.* London and New York: Routledge, 2015.

Mosca, Matthew W. 'The Literati Rewriting of China in the Qianlong–Jiaqing Transition'. *Late Imperial China* 32.2 (2011): 89–132.

Rowe, William T. *Speaking of Profit: Bao Shichen and Reform in Nineteenth-Century China.* Cambridge, Mass.: Harvard University Press, 2018.

Wang, Wensheng. *White Lotus Rebels and South China Pirates: Crisis and Reform in the Qing Empire.* Cambridge, Mass.: Harvard University Press, 2014.

2. Daoguang

Mao Haijian 茅海建. *Tianchao de bengkui: Yapian zhanzheng zai yanjiu* 天朝的崩潰：鴉片戰爭再研究 (The collapse of the celestial dynasty: A re-examination of the Opium War). Beijing: Zhongguo qingnian chubanshe, 2014.

Ni Yuping 倪玉平. *Daoguang wangchao* 道光王朝 (The Daoguang court). Beijing: Xinlian shudian, 2008.

Qing shilu: Xuanzong cheng huangdi shilu 清實錄·宣宗成皇帝實錄 (Veritable records of the Qing during the Daoguang reign). Beijing: Zhonghua shuju, 1986–7.

3. Xianfeng

Meyer-Fong, Tobie. *What Remains: Coming to Terms with Civil War in 19th Century China.* Stanford: Stanford University Press, 2013.

Rawski, Evelyn S. *The Last Emperors: A Social History of Qing Imperial Institutions.* Berkeley: University of California, 1998.

Spence, Jonathan D. *The Search for Modern China.* New York: Norton, 1990.

Xu Liting 徐立亭. *Xianfeng Tongzhi di* 咸丰同治帝 (The Xianfeng and Tongzhi emperors). Changchun Shi: Jilin wenshi chubanshe, 1993.

Ye Xiaoqing. 'Imperial Institutions and Drama in the Qing', *European Journal of East Asian Studies* 2.2 (2003): 329–64.

4. Tongzhi

Li Li 立禮. *Tongzhi: Muhou yuyi xia de zhongxing zhi zhu* 同治：母后羽翼下的中興之主 (Tongzhi: The ruler of the restoration under the protection of the Empress Dowager). Nanchang: Jiangxi meishu chubanshe, 2020.

Ma Dongyu 馬東玉. *Qingchao tongshi: Xianfeng Tongzhi chao* 清朝通史·咸豐同治朝 (Comprehensive history of the Qing dynasty: The reigns of Xianfeng and Tongzhi). Beijing: Zijincheng chubanshe, 2008.

Wright, Mary Clabaugh. *The Last Stand of Chinese Conservatism: The Tung-Chih Restoration, 1862–1874.* Stanford: Stanford University Press, 1957.

Xu Liting 徐立亭. *Qingdi liezhuan: Xianfeng Tongzhi di* 清帝列傳·咸豐同治帝 (Biographies of the Qing emperors: Xianfeng and Tongzhi). Jilin: Jilin wenshi chubanshe, 1993.

Zhu Saihong 朱賽虹, *Qingshi tudian: Xianfeng Tongzhi chao* 清史圖典·咸豐同治朝 (Illustrated compendium of Qing history: The reigns of Xianfeng and Tongzhi). Beijing: Zijincheng chubanshe, 2002.

5. Guangxu

Feng Yuankui 馮元魁. *Qingdi liezhuan: Guangxu di* 清帝列傳·光緒帝 (Biographies of the Qing emperors: The Guangxu emperor). Jilin: Jilin wenshi chubanshe, 1993.

Karl, Rebecca E. and Peter Zarrow (eds). *Rethinking the 1898 Reform Period: Political and Cultural Change in Late Qing China.* Cambridge, Mass.: Harvard University Asia Center, 2002.

Qing shilu: Dezong jing huangdi shilu 清實錄·德宗景皇帝實錄 (Veritable records of the Qing during the Guangxu reign). Beijing: Zhonghua shuju, 1986–7.

Sui Lijuan 隋麗娟. *Mingjia shuo qingshi: Guangxu huangdi* 名家說清史·光緒皇帝 (Famous scholars' lectures on Qing history: The Guangxu emperor). Beijing: Gugong chubanshe, 2016.

Sun Xiao'en 孫孝恩 and Ding Qi 丁琪. *Guangxu Zhuan* 光緒傳 (Biography of the Guangxu emperor). Bejing: Renmin chubanshe, 1997.

Xu Che 徐徹. *Guanxu di benchuan* 光緒帝本傳 (Draft biography of the Guangxu emperor). Shenyang: Liaoning guji chubanshe, 1996.

6. Keshun

Chen Yishun 陳煒舜. *Bei wuren de lao zhaopian* 被誤認的老照片 (Misidentified old photographs). Hong Kong: Zhonghe chuban youxian gongsi, 2021.

Hu Sijing 胡思敬. *Guowen beicheng* 國聞備乘 (Stories of the state). N.p., *c.* 1911

Ju Xuanya 橘玄雅. 'Fenghuang yu fei: Qingdai wuci huangdi dahun yu qi beihou de gushi' 鳳凰于飛: 清代五次皇帝大婚與其背後的故事 (Male and female phoenixes flying together: Five weddings of Qing dynasty emperors and the stories behind them). *Zijincheng* 4 (2019): 15–25.

Qingshigao jiaozhu 清史稿校注 (Draft history of the Qing, collated and annotated). Taipei: Guoshiguan, 1986.

Shang Yanying 商衍瀛. 'Zhen Fei qiren' 珍妃其人 (Consort Zhen the person). In *Wenshi ziliao xuanji* 文史資料選輯 (Selections of literature and history) 92: 195–200. Beijing: Zhongguo wenshi chubanshe, 1999.

7. Empress Dowager Cixi

Chang, Jung. *Empress Dowager Cixi: The Concubine Who Launched Modern China*. New York: Alfred A. Knopf, 2013.

Huters, Theodore. *Bringing the World Home: Appropriating the West in Late Qing and Early Republican China*. Honolulu: University of Hawai'i Press, 2005.

Judge, Joan. *The Precious Raft of History: The Past, the West, and the Woman Question in China*. Stanford: Stanford University Press, 2008.

Peng, Ying-chen. *Artful Subversion: Empress Dowager Cixi's Image Making*. New Haven: Yale University Press, 2023.

Wang, Daisy Yiyou and Jan Stuart (eds). *Empresses of China's Forbidden City: 1644–1912*. Salem, Mass., and Washington, DC: Peabody Essex Museum and Freer Gallery of Art and Arthur M. Sackler Gallery, Smithsonian Institution, 2018.

8. Puyi and Wanrong

Aisin Gioro Puyi. *From Emperor to Citizen: The Autobiography of Aisin-Gioro Pu Yi*. W. J. F. Jenner tr. Beijing: Foreign Languages Press, 1989.

Liu, Beisi 劉北汜 and Xu Qixian 徐啟憲. *Gugong zhencang renwu xiezhen huicui* 故宮珍藏人物寫真薈萃 (A compilation of the photographic portraits in the Palace Museum collection). Beijing: Zijincheng chubanshe, 1994.

McMahon, Keith. *Celestial Women: Imperial Wives and Concubines in China from Song to Qing*. Lanham: Rowman & Littlefield, 2016.

Rawski, Evelyn. *The Last Emperors: A Social History of Qing Imperial Institutions*. Berkeley: University of California Press, 2009.

Wang, Daisy Yiyou and Jan Stuart. *Empresses of China's Forbidden City, 1644–1912*. Salem, Mass., and Washington DC: Peabody Essex Museum and Freer Gallery of Art and Arthur M. Sackler Gallery, Smithsonian Institution, 2018.

9. Li Lianying

Anderson, Mary. *Hidden Power: The Palace Eunuchs of Imperial China*. Buffalo: Prometheus Books, 1990.

Cai Shiying 蔡世英. *Da taijian Li Lianying* 大太監李連英 (Grand Eunuch Li Lianying). Beijing: Zijincheng chubanshe, 2011.

Dale, Melissa S. *Inside the World of the Eunuch: A Social History of the Emperor's Servants in Qing China*. Baltimore: Project Muse, 2019.

Li, Yuhang. 'Oneself as a Female Deity: Representations of Cixi Posing as Guanyin'. *Nan Nü: Men, Women, and Gender in China* 14.1 (2012): 75–118.

Rawski, Evelyn S. *The Last Emperors: A Social History of Qing Imperial Institutions*. Berkeley: University of California Press, 1998.

10. Yu Rongling

Hayter-Menzies, Grant. *Imperial Masquerade: The Legend of Princess Der Ling*. Hong Kong: Hong Kong University Press, 2008.

Ma, Nan. 'Dancing into Modernity: Kinesthesia, Narrative, and Revolutions in Modern China, 1900–1978'. PhD thesis, University of Wisconsin–Madison, 2015.

Wilcox, Emily. 'Beyond Internal Orientalism: Dance and Nationality Discourse in the Early People's Republic of China, 1949–1954'. *The Journal of Asian Studies* 75.2 (May 2016): 363–86.

Yu, Derling (Princess Der Ling). *Two Years in the Forbidden City*. London: Unwin, 1924.

———. *Lotos Petals*. New York: Dodd, Mead, 1930.

Yu Rongling 裕容齡. 'Qingmo wudaojia Yu Rongling huiyilu' 清末舞蹈家裕容齡回憶錄 (Memoir of Yu Rongling, a dancer of the late Qing), *Wudao* 2 (March 1958): 44–5.

11. Tan Xinpei

Byrne, Emily Curtis. *Reflected Glory in a Snuff Bottle: Chinese Snuff Bottle Portraits*. New York: Soho Bodhi, 1980.

Chen, Liana. *Staging for the Emperors: A History of Qing Court Theatre, 1683–1923*. Amherst, NY: Cambria Press, 2021.

Goldstein, Joshua. *Drama Kings: Players and Publics in the Re-Creation of Peking Opera 1870–1937*. Berkeley and Los Angeles: University of California Press, 2007.

Huang Dequan 黃德泉. 'Xiqu dianying *Dingjun shan* zhi youlai yu yanbian' 戲曲電影《定軍山》之由來與演變 (The origins and evolution of the Chinese opera film *Dingjun Mountain*). In Robert C. Allen and Douglas Gomery, *Dianyingshi: Lilun yu shijian (zuixin xiudingban)*《電影史：理論與實踐》（最新修訂版）(Film History: Theory and Practice, revised ed.), Li Xun 李迅 tr.: 381–98. Beijing: Beijing lianhe chubanshe, 2016.

Rolston, David L. *Inscribing Jingju / Peking Opera: Textualization and Performance, Authorship and Censorship of the 'National Drama' of China from the Late Qing to the Present*. Leiden and Boston: Brill, 2021.

12. Wang Yaoqing

Goldman, Andrea S. *Opera and the City: The Politics of Culture in Beijing, 1770–1900*. Stanford: Stanford University Press, 2012.

Goldstein, Joshua L. *Drama Kings: Players and Publics in the Re-Creation of Peking Opera, 1870–1937*. Berkeley: University of California Press, 2007.

Li, Hsiao-t'i. *Opera, Society, and Politics in Modern China*. Cambridge, Mass.: Harvard University Asia Center, 2019.

Sun Hongxia 孫紅俠. *Wang Yaoqing pingzhuan* 王瑤卿評傳 (A critical biography of Wang Yaoqing). Shanghai: Shanghai guji chubanshe, 2013.

Wu Xinmiao 吳新苗. *Liyuan siyu kaolun: Qingdai lingren shenghuo, yanju ji yishu chuancheng* 梨園私寓考論:清代伶人生活、演劇及藝術傳承 (Research on the brothels of the Pear Garden: The livelihood, performance and artistic transmission of actors in the Qing dynasty). Beijing: Xueyuan chubanshe, 2017.

13. Min Yide

Esposito, Monica. *Creative Daoism*. Wil and Paris: UniversityMedia, 2013.

Goossaert, Vincent. 'The Jin'gaishan network'. In *Daoism in Modern China: Clerics and Temples in Urban Transformations, 1860–Present*, Vincent Goossaert and Liu Xun (eds): 83–119. London: Routledge, 2021.

———. *Making the Gods Speak: The Ritual Production of Revelation in Chinese History*. Cambridge, Mass.: Harvard University Asia Center, 2022.

Liu Xun. 'An Intoning Immortal at the West Lake: Chen Wenshu and his Daoist Pursuits in Late Qing Jiangnan'. *Cahiers d'Extrême-Asie* 25 (2016): 77–111.

Min Yide 閔一得 (ed.). *Gushu yinlou cangshu* 古書隱樓藏書 (Books from the pavilion storing old works). Beijing: Zongjiao wenhua chubanshe, 2010.

14. Wanyan Linqing

Arlington, Lewis Charles and William Lewisohn. *In Search of Old Peking*. Peking: Henri Vetch, 1935. Hong Kong: Oxford University Press, 1987 (reprint).

Dodgen, Randall A. *Controlling the Dragon: Confucian Engineers and the Yellow River in Late Imperial China*. Honolulu: University of Hawaii Press, 2001.

Fang, Chao-ying. 'Lin-ch'ing'. In *Eminent Chinese of the Ch'ing Period (1644–1912)*, Arthur Hummel Sr (ed.): 506–7. Washington, DC: United States Government Printing Office, 1943.

Hecken, J. L. van and W. A. Grootaers. 'The Half-Acre Garden, Pan-Mou Yuan'. *Monumenta Serica* 18 (1959): 360–87.

Leys, Simon. *Other People's Thoughts: Idiosyncratically Compiled by Simon Leys for the Amusement of Idle Readers*: 54. Melbourne: Black Inc., 2007

Liu Xun. 'Immortals and Patriarchs: The Daoist World of a Manchu Official and his Family in Nineteenth-Century China'. *Asia Major* 17.2 (2004): 161–218.

Wanyan Linqing. 'Tracks in the Snow: Episodes from an Autobiographical Memoir by the Manchu Bannerman Lin-ch'ing (1791–1846), with Illustrations by Leading Contemporary Artists', Yang Tsung-han tr., John Minford (ed.), foreword by Liu Ts'un-yan. *East Asian History* 6 (1993): 105–42.

Yang, Tsung-han and Christina Sanderson tr., Wanyan Linqing. *Wild Goose Tracks in the Snow: An Illustrated Record of my Preordained Life*, John Minford (ed.). Forthcoming.

15. Yang Wenhui

Chan, Sin-wai. *Buddhism in Late Ch'ing Political Thought*. London: Routledge, 2019.

Scott, Gregory Adam. *Building the Buddhist Revival: Reconstructing Monasteries in Modern China*. Oxford: Oxford University Press, 2020.

Tarocco, Francesa. *The Cultural Practices of Modern Chinese Buddhism: Attuning the Dharma*. London: Routledge, 2007.

Welch, Holmes. *The Buddhist Revival in China*. Cambridge, Mass.: Harvard University Press, 1968.

Wu, Yankan. 'Yang Renshan and the Jinling Buddhist Press'. *The East Asian Library Journal* 12.2 (2006): 49–98.

16. Yusuf Ma Dexin

Atwill, David G. *The Chinese Sultanate: Islam, Ethnicity and the Panthay Rebellion in Southwest China, 1856–1873*. Stanford: Stanford University Press, 2006.

Gelvin, James and Nile Green (eds). *Global Muslims in the Age of Steam and Print*. California: University of California Press, 2013.

Lipman, Jonathan N. *Familiar Strangers: A History of Muslims in Northwest China*. Seattle: University of Washington Press, 1997.

Ma Dexin 馬德新. *Chaojin tuji* 朝覲途記 (Record of the pilgrimage journey). Ma Anli tr. Ningxia: Ningxia renmin chubanshe, 1988.

Petersen, Kristian. *Interpreting Islam in China: Pilgrimage, Scripture and Language in the Han Kitab*. Oxford: Oxford University Press, 2017.

17. Hong Xiuquan

Meyer-Fong, Tobie. *What Remains: Coming to Terms with Civil War in 19th Century China*. Stanford: Stanford University Press, 2013.

Platt, Stephen R. *Autumn in the Heavenly Kingdom: China, the West and the Epic Story of the Taiping Civil War*. London: Atlantic Books, 2013.

Spence, Jonathan D. *God's Chinese Son: The Taiping Heavenly Kingdom of Hong Xiuquan*. New York: Norton, 1996.

ter Haar, Barend. *Religious Culture and Violence in Traditional China*. Cambridge: University Press, 2019.

Zhang, Daye. *The World of a Tiny Insect: A Memoir of the Taiping Rebellion and its Aftermath*. Xiaofei Tan tr. Seattle: University of Washington Press, 2014.

18. Liang Fa

Bohr, P. Richard. 'Liang Fa's Quest for Moral Power'. In *Christianity in China: Early Protestant Missionary Writings*, Suzanne Wilson Barnett and John King Fairbank (eds): 35–46. Cambridge, Mass.: Committee on American–East Asian Relations of the Department of History and Council of East Asian Studies/Harvard University, 1985.

Kim, Sukjoo. 'Liang Fa's *Quanshi liangyan* and its Impact on the Taiping Movement'. PhD thesis, Baylor University, 2011.

Liang Fa 梁發. *Quanshi liangyan* 勸世良言 (Good Words to Admonish the Age: Being Nine Miscellaneous Christian Tracts, by Leangafa, of the London Missionary Society). Taipei: Taiwan xuesheng shuju, 1965. [Original: Guangzhou: LMS/Harvard University Blockprint Collection for Guangzhou, 1832.]

Liang Fa suiyue: Zhonghua Jidu jiaohui Liang Fa jinian Libai tang 50 zhounian jinian 梁發歲月: 中華基督教會梁發 紀念禮拜堂50週年紀念 (The Life of Liang Fa: The 50th anniversary of the Liang Fa Memorial Chapel of the Christian Church in China). Hong Kong: Zhonghua Jidu jiaohui Liang Fa jinian Libai tang, 2013.

McNeur, George Hunter. *China's First Preacher: Liang A-Fa 1789–1855*. Shanghai: Kwang Hsueh Publishing House & Oxford University Press (China Agency), 1934.

Seitz, Jonathan A. *Builders of the Chinese Church: Pioneer Protestant Missionaries and Chinese Church Leaders*. Cambridge: Lutterworth Press, 2015.

19. Nergingge

Cosmo, Nicola Di. 'Did Guns Matter? Firearms and the Qing Formation'. In *The Qing Formation in World-Historical Time*, Lynn A. Struve (ed.). Leiden: Harvard University Asia Center, 2004.

Heath, Ian. *Armies of the Nineteenth Century: Asia, China*. St Peter Port: Foundry, 1998.

Lovell, Julia. *The Opium War: Drugs, Dreams and the Making of China*. London: Picador, 2011.

Xue Fucheng 薛福成. *Yongan biji* 庸庵筆記 (Notes from a commonplace hut). Chongqing: Chongqing chubanshe, 1999.

Zhang Jixin 張集馨. *Dao Xian huanhai jianwenlu* 道咸宦 海見聞録 (Records from official circles during the Daoguang and Xianfeng reigns). Beijing: Zhonghuashuju, 1981.

20. Shi Yang

Antony, Robert. *Like Froth Floating on the Sea: The World of Pirates and Seafarers in Late Imperial South China*. Berkeley: University of California Press, 2003.

_____. *Unruly People: Crime, Community, and State in Late Imperial South China*. Hong Kong: University of Hong Kong Press, 2016.

Dalrymple, Sir John C. *The Suppression of Piracy in the China Sea, 1849*. London: Edward Stanford, 1889.

MacKay, Joseph. 'Pirate Nations: Maritime Pirates as Escape Societies in Late Imperial China', *Social Science History* 37.4 (Winter 2013): 551–73.

Murray, Dian. 'Sea Bandits: A Study of Piracy in Early Nineteenth Century China'. PhD thesis, Cornell University, 1979.

_____. 'One Woman's Rise to Power: Cheng I's Wife and the Pirates'. *Historical Reflections/Réflexions Historiques* 8.3 (Fall 1981): 147–61.

21. Wei Yuan

Leonard, Jane Kate. *Wei Yuan and China's Rediscovery of the Maritime World*. Cambridge, Mass.: Council on East Asian Studies, Harvard University Press, 1984.

Li Hu 李瑚. *Wei Yuan yanjiu* 魏源研究 (Research on Wei Yuan). Beijing: Zhaohua chubanshe, 2002.

Mosca, Matthew W. *From Frontier Policy to Foreign Policy: the Question of India and the Transformation of Geopolitics in Qing China*. Stanford: Stanford University Press, 2013.

Polachek, James. *The Inner Opium War*. Cambridge, Mass.: Harvard University Press, 1992.

Wang Jiajian 王家儉. *Wei Yuan nianpu* 魏源年譜 (Chronology of Wei Yuan). Taipei: Zhongyang yanjiuyuan jindaishi yanjiusuo, 1981.

Wei Yuan 魏源. *Haiguo tuzhi* 海國圖志 (Illustrated treatise on the maritime kingdoms), 2nd edn. Taipei: Chengwen chubanshe, 1967.

22. Sengge Rinchen

Bagen 巴根. *Senggelinqin Qinwang* 僧格林沁親王 (Prince Sengge Rinchen). Beijing: Wenhua meishu chubanshe, 1993.

Lovell, Julia. *The Opium War: Drugs, Dreams and the Making of China*. London: Picador, 2011.

Teng, Ssu-yü. *The Nien Army and their Guerrilla Warfare 1851–1868*. Westport, Connecticut: Greenwood Press, 1961.

———. *The Taiping Rebellion and the Western Powers: A Comprehensive Survey*. Oxford: Clarendon Press, 1971.

Williams, Samuel Wells and Frederick Wells Williams. *The Life and Letters of Samuel Wells Williams, LL.D., Missionary, Diplomatist, Sinologue*. New York: Putnam, 1889.

23. MG Charles Gordon

Chappell, Jonathan. 'Some Corner of a Chinese Field: The Politics of Remembering the Foreign Veterans of the Taiping Civil War'. *Modern Asian Studies* 52.4 (2018): 1134–71.

Faught, C. Brad. *Gordon: Victorian Hero*. Dulles: Potomac, 2008.

Platt, Steven R. *Autumn in the Heavenly Kingdom: China, the West and the Epic Story of the Taiping Civil War*. New York: Knopf, 2018.

Smith, Richard J. *Mercenaries and Mandarins: The Ever Victorious Army in Nineteenth Century China*. New York: KTO Press, 1978.

Wilson, Andrew. *'Ever Victorious Army': A History of the Chinese Campaign under Lt. Col. C.G. Gordon C.B. R.E. and the Suppression of the Tai-Ping Rebellion*. London: Blackwood, 1868.

24. Huang Shuhua

Fong, Grace. 'Signifying Bodies: The Cultural Significance of Suicide Writings by Women in Ming–Qing China'. *Nan Nü* 3.1 (2001): 105–42.

Huntington, Rania. 'The Captive's Revenge: The Taiping Civil War as Drama'. *Late Imperial China* 35.2 (December 2014): 1–26.

Mann, Susan. 'The Lady and the State: Women's Writing in Times of Trouble During the Nineteenth Century'. In *The Inner Quarters and Beyond: Women Writers from Ming through Qing*, Grace S. Fong and Ellen Widmer (eds). Leiden: Brill, 2010. 281–313

Meyer-Fong, Tobie. *What Remains: Coming to Terms with Civil War in 19th Century China*. Stanford: Stanford University Press, 2013.

Wang, Guojun. *Staging Personhood: Costuming in Early Qing Drama*. New York: Columbia University Press, 2020.

Xu E 徐鄂. 'Lihua xue' 梨花雪 (Snow on the pear blossom/The pear blossom rights wrongs). In *Songdi zhai qu* 誦荻齋曲 (Plays from the studio of chanting on reeds). Shanghai: Datong shuju, 1887.

25. Yuan Shikai

Chen, Jerome. *Yuan Shih-kai*. Stanford: Stanford University Press, 1972.

MacKinnon, Stephen R. *Power and Politics in Late Imperial China: Yuan Shikai in Beijing and Tianjin, 1901–1908*. Berkeley: University of California Press, 1980.

Shan, Patrick Fuliang. *Yuan Shikai: A Reappraisal*. Vancouver: The UBC Press, 2018.

Spence, Jonathan. *The Search for Modern China*. New York: W. W. Norton, 1990.

Young, Ernest P. *The Presidency of Yuan Shikai: Liberalism and Dictatorship in Early Republican China*. Ann Arbor: University of Michigan Press, 1977.

26. Qiu Jin

Dooling, Amy D. and Kristina M. Torgeson. *Writing Women in Modern China: An Anthology of Women's Literature from the Early Twentieth Century*. New York: Columbia University Press, 1998.

Hu, Ying. *Burying Autumn: Poetry, Friendship and Loss*. Cambridge, Mass.: Harvard University Asia Center, 2016.

Judge, Joan. *The Precious Raft of History: The Past, the West, and the Woman Question in China*. Stanford: Stanford University Press, 2008.

Lu Xun. 'Medicine'. In *The True Story of Ah Q and Other Tales of China: The Complete Fiction of Lu Xun*, Julia Lovell tr.: 37–45. London: Penguin Classics, 2009.

Rankin, Mary Backus. 'The Emergence of Women at the End of Ch'ing: The Case of Ch'iu Chin [Qiu Jin]'. In *Women in Chinese Society*, Margery Wolf and Roxane Witke (eds): 39–66. Stanford: Stanford University Press, 1975.

27. Deng Shiru

Chen Shuo 陳碩. 'Zhizao Deng Shiru: Cong Deng Shiru yu Cao Wenzhi de jiaoyou kan *Wanbai shanren zhuan* zhong de xiangguan wenti' 製造鄧石如：從鄧石如與曹文埴的交遊看《完白山人傳》中的相關問題 (The fabrication of Deng Shiru: From the friendship between Deng Shiru and Cao Wenzhi to the *Biography of the Mountain Man of Wanbai*). *Taiwan daxue meishushi yanjiu jikan* 48 (2020): 241–96, 300.

_____. 'Chongsu chuantong: Deng Shiru yu qing zhongqi shufashi de biange' 重塑傳統：鄧石如與清中期書法史的變革 (Reshaping tradition: Deng Shiru and the transformation of mid-Qing dynasty calligraphy). PhD thesis, Zhejiang University, 2020.

Masahiro Endoh 遠藤昌弘. 'Tō Sekijo nenpu shōkō' 鄧石如年譜詳考 (A thorough study of the biographical chronology of Deng Shiru). *Daidō s hodō kenkyū* 15 (2007): 64–116.

Meng Ying 孟瀅 and Xu Zhenxuan 許振軒 (eds). *Deng Shiru shufa zhuanke quanji* 鄧石如書法篆刻全集 (Complete works of calligraphy and seal engraving by Deng Shiru). Hefei: Anhui meishu chubanshe, 1993.

Mu Xiaotian 穆孝天 and Xu Jiaqiong 許佳瓊 (eds). *Deng Shiru yanjiu ziliao* 鄧石如研究資料 (Research materials on Deng Shiru). Beijing: Renmin meishu chubanshe, 1988.

28. Yi Bingshou

Fu, Shen. *Traces of the Brush: Studies in Chinese Calligraphy*. New Haven: Yale University Art Gallery, 1977.

Ho Pik Ki 何碧琪. 'Qingdai lishu yu Yi Bingshou' 清代隸書與伊秉綬 (Qing-dynasty clerical script and Yi Bingshou). MA thesis, Chinese University of Hong Kong, 2001.

McNair, Amy. 'Engraved Calligraphy in China: Recension and Reception'. *The Art Bulletin* 77.1 (1995): 106–14.

Tan Pingguo 譚平國. *Yi Bingshou nianpu* 伊秉綬年譜 (Chronology of Yi Bingshou). Shanghai: Dongfang chubanshe, 2017.

Zhou Hanyun 周寒筠. 'Yi Bingshou shufa yanjiu' 伊秉綬書法研究 (Research on Yi Bingshou's calligraphy). PhD thesis, China Academy of Art, 2014.

29. Ruan Yuan

Lefebvre, Eric. '"L'image des antiquités accumulées" de Ruan Yuan, la représentation d'une collection privée en Chine à l'époque pré-moderne'. *Arts Asiatiques* 63 (2008): 61–71.

Miles, Stephen. B. *The Sea of Learning: Mobility and Identity in Nineteenth Century Guangzhou*. Cambridge, Mass.: Harvard University Asia Center, 2006.

Ruan Yuan 阮元. *Ruan Yuan ji* 阮元集 (Collected works of Ruan Yuan). Yangzhou: Guangling shushe, 2021.

Wei, Betty Peh-t'i. *Ruan Yuan, 1764–1849: The Life and Work of a Major Scholar-official in Nineteenth-Century China Before the Opium War*. Hong Kong: Hong Kong University Press, 2006.

Yangzhou Museum 揚州博物館. *Ruan Yuan yanjiu guoji xueshu yantaohui lunwenji* 阮元研究國際學術研討會論文集 (Proceedings of the International Symposium on Ruan Yuan Research). Beijing: Wenwu chubanshe, 2016.

30. Liuzhou

Brown, Shana J. *Pastimes: From Art and Antiquarianism to Modern Chinese Historiography*. Honolulu: University of Hawai'i Press, 2011.

Hatch, Michael J. 'Outline, Brushwork, and the Epigraphic Aesthetic in Huang Yi's Engraved Texts of the Lesser Penglai Pavilion (1800)'. *Archives of Asian Art* 70:1 (April 2020): 23–49.

Lawton, Thomas. 'Rubbings of Chinese Bronzes'. *Bulletin of the Museum of Far Eastern Antiquities* 67 (1995): 5–48.

Wang Yifeng 王屹峰. *Gu zhuan hua gong: Liuzhou yu 19 shiji de xueshu he yishu* 古磚花供：六舟與 19 世紀的學術與藝術 (Ancient bricks and flower offering: Liuzhou and 19th-century scholarship and art). Hangzhou: Zhejiang renmin meishu chubanshe, 2017.

Yang, Chia-ling. 'Power, Identity, and Antiquarian Approaches in Modern Chinese Art'. *Journal of Art Historiography* 10 (2014): 1–33.

31. Sun Mingqiu

Berliner, Nancy. *The 8 Brokens: Chinese Bapo Painting*. Boston: MFA Publications, Museum of Fine Arts, 2018.

_____. 'The "Eight Brokens", Chinese Trompe-l'oeil Painting'. *Orientations* 23.2 (February 1992): 61–6.

_____. 'From Bits and Pieces: Constructing a Biography for a Lost Talent'. *Orientations* 49.4 (July/August 2018).

_____. 'Questions of Authorship in "Bapo": Trompe l'oeil in Twentieth-century Shanghai'. *Apollo* (March 1998): 17–22.

Wang Yifeng 王屹峰. *Gu zhuan hua gong, Liuzhou yu shijiu shiji de xueshu he yishu* 古磚花供：六舟與 19 世紀的學術與藝術 (Ancient tiles and flower offerings: Monk Liuzhou and the learning and art of the 19th century). Hangzhou: Zhejiang renmin meishu chubanshe, 2017.

32. Zhang Yin

Lu Jiugao 陸九臯. 'Zhang Xi'an de shengping he yishu' 張夕庵的生平和藝術 (Zhang Yin's life and art), *Art Research (Meishu yanjiu)* 1 (1984): 70–5.

Wan Qingli 萬青力. *Bingfei shuailuo de bainian*) 並非衰落的百年 (A century in which art did not decline). Guilin: Guangxi shifan daxue chubanshe, 2008.

Zhao Li 趙力. *Jingjiang huapai yanjiu* 京江畫派研究 (Research on the Jingjiang school). Changsha: Hunan meishu chubanshe, 1994.

_____. 'Jiangnan fengxiang – cong Zhang Xi'an de *Jingkou sanshan tujuan* tan wanqing huatan de yidong' 江南風象 – 從張夕庵的《京口三山圖卷》談晚清畫壇的異動 (The trend in Jiangnan – changes in late Qing painting as seen in Zhang Yin's *Three Mountains in Jingkou*). *Meishu yanjiu* 1 (2000): 69–73.

Zhao Qibin 趙啟斌. 'Jingjiang huapai de huihua tezheng jiqi lishi diwei – xia' 京江畫派"的繪畫特徵及其歷史地位（下）(The characteristics of Jingjiang school paintings and their role in history – part two). *Rongbaozhai* 2007 (1): 64–77.

33. Qian Du

Chou, Ju-hsi. 'Qian Du to Zhang Jing'. *Phoebus* 8 (1998): 38–66.

Hatch, Michael J. (as He Yanhui 何彥暉). 'Qian Du, Zhang Yin yu shijiu shiji chuqi dui wupai huajia de xingqu' 錢杜，張崟與十九世紀初期對吳派畫家的興趣 (Qian Du, Zhang Yin and the early 19th-century interest in Wu school painters). In *Gudian de fuxing: xike jiulu cang Ming Qing huihua yanjiu* 古典的復興：溪客舊廬藏明清文人繪畫研究, Zhang Hui 章暉 and Fan Jingzhong 范景中 (eds): 22–6. Shanghai: Shanghai shuhua chubanshe, 2018.

Hatch, Michael J. 'Lineages and the Posthumous Lives of Chinese Paintings'. In *Posthumous Art, Law and the Art Market*, Sharon Hecker and Peter J. Karol (eds): 189–99. New York: Routledge, 2022.

Qian Du 錢杜. *Songhu hua zhui* 松壺畫贅 (Songhu's superfluous words on painting) and *Songhu hua yi* 松壺畫意 (Songhu's reflections on painting). In *Hushu Qian shi jia ji* 湖墅錢氏家集 (Collected writings of the Qian clan of Hushu), Qian Xibin 錢錫賓 (ed.), vol. 11. 1896.

34. Cao Zhenxiu

Cao Zhenxiu 曹貞秀. *Xieyun xuan xiaogao* 寫韻軒小稿 (Drafts from the Pavilion for Writing Rhymes). 1815 revised edition. In *Ming–Qing Women's Writings Digitization Project* (McGill-Harvard website) https://digital.library.mcgill.ca/mingqing/ (accessed on 30 January 2022).

Chang Chun 長春. 'Qingdai nüxing shufa jiaoliu lüekao' 清代女性書法交流略考 (Summary of exchanges between female calligraphers of the Qing dynasty). *Zhongguo shufa* 302 (March 2017): 174–6.

Lee, Lily Xiao Hong, A. D. Stefanowska, Sue Wiles and Clara W. Ho. *Biographical Dictionary of Chinese Women*, vol. 1, *The Qing Period, 1644–1911*. London: Routledge, 2015.

Ruitenbeek, Klaas (ed.) *Faces of China: Portrait Painting of the Ming and Qing Dynasties (1368–1912)*. Museum für Asiatische Kunst, Staatliche Museen zu Berlin. Michael Imhof Verlag, 2017.

Yan Cheng 嚴程. 'Qingdai guixiu shufa fengshang' 清代閨秀書法風尚 (Calligraphy practices among gentlewomen of the Qing dynasty). *Zhongguo shufa* 290 (September 2016): 172–4.

Yang Binbin. *Heroines of the Qing: Exemplary Women Tell Their Stories*. Seattle: University of Washington Press, 2019.

35. Fei Danxu

Brown, Claudia. *Great Qing: Painting in China 1644–1911*. Seattle: University of Washington Press, 2014.

Fei Danxu 費丹旭. *Fei Danxu ji* 費丹旭集 (Anthology of Fei Danxu). Hangzhou: Zhejiang renmin meishu chubanshe, 2016.

Huang, Yongquan 黃湧泉. *Fei Danxu* 費丹旭 (Fei Danxu). *Zhongguo huajia congshu* 中國畫家叢書 (Series on Chinese painters). Shanghai: Renmin meishu chubanshe, 1962.

_____ and Sun Yuanchao 孫元超. *Fei Xiaolou chuanshen jiapin* 費曉樓傳神佳品 (Excellent portraits by Fei Danxu). Beijing: Renmin meishu chunbanshe, 1959.

Koon, Yeewan. *A Defiant Brush: Su Renshan and the Politics of Painting in Early Nineteenth-Century Guangdong*. Honolulu: University of Hawai'i Press, 2014.

Meyer-Fong, Tobie. 'Packaging the Men of Our Times: Literary Anthologies,

Friendship Networks, and Political Accommodations in Early Qing'. *Harvard Journal of Asiatic Studies* 64.1 (2004): 5–56.

36. Tang Yifen

Bao Zhihong 鮑志宏. 'Tang Yifen yanjiu' 湯貽汾研究 (A study of Tang Yifen). MA thesis, Zhejiang University, 2011.

Sun Chao 孫超. 'Tang Yifen shoubei Yangzhou qijian de wenxue chuangzuo' 湯貽汾守備揚州期間的文學創作 (The literary creations of Tang Yifen during his service as military commander in Yangzhou). MA thesis, Heilongjiang University, 2014.

_____. 'Cong Da Chongguang *Huaquan* dao Tang *Yifen Huaquan xilan*' 從笪重光《畫筌》到湯貽汾

《畫筌析覽》 (From Da Chongguang's *Painting Methods* to Tang Yifen's *Analytical Examination on Painting Methods*). *Xueshu jiaoliu* 7 (2018): 143–9.

_____. 'Tang Yifen guitian yinqing kao' 湯貽汾歸田隱情考 (The hidden story of Tang Yifen's retirement to his homeland). *Jianghai xuekan* 6 (2019): 203.

Wang Limeng 王黎夢. 'Tang Yifen *Huangquan xilan kaoshu*' 湯貽汾《畫筌析覽》考述 (The examination and interpretation of Tang Yifen's *Analytical Examination of Painting Methods*). *Meishu daguan* 8 (2017): 76–7.

Yang Yuan 羊原. 'Jiandan pingshi jian youxian – Tang Yifen de *Qiuping xianhua tu*' 簡淡平實見悠閒 – 湯貽汾的《秋坪閒話圖》 (Leisure from simplicity and plainness – Tang Yifen's *Chit-Chat on an Autumn Plain*). *Zhongguo shuhua* 11 (2005): 178.

37. Dai Xi

Brown, Claudia and Ju-hsi Chou (eds). *Transcending Turmoil: Painting at the Close of China's Empire, 1796–1911*. Phoenix: Phoenix Art Museum, 1992.

Jian Songcun 簡松村. 'Qing zhongye huihua sixiangjia: Dai Xi' 清中葉繪畫思想家 – 戴熙 (The mid-Qing painting theorist Dai Xi). *Gugong wenwu yuekan* 51 (1987): 108–17.

Mei Yutian 梅雨恬. '"Qiwei" de ronghe: lun Dai Xi dui Yun Shouping de shifa' '氣味'的融合 – 論戴熙對惲壽平的師法 (A fusion of 'tastes': On Dai Xi's study of Yun Shouping). *Wenhua yishu yanjiu* 8.3 (July 2015): 132–8.

Tu, Lien-che. 'Dai Xi'. In *Eminent Chinese of the Ch'ing Period (1644–1912)*, Arthur W. Hummel (ed.), vol. 2: 700–1. Taipei: Ch'eng Wen Publishing, 1970.

Zhou Yongliang 周永良. 'Qian xi Dai Xi huihua yishu de shanbian: Jianji *Xiku zhai huaxu* jinian ben de faxian' 淺析戴熙繪畫藝術的嬗變 – 兼及《習苦齋畫絮》紀年抄本的發現 (A preliminary analysis of Dai Xi's evolution as a painter, with recourse to the newly discovered chronologically arranged edition of his *Idle Thoughts on Painting from the Studio for Being Accustomed to Hardship*). *Gugong bowuyuan yuankan* 4.96 (2001): 51–9.

38. Su Renshan

Faure, David and Helen Siu (eds). *Down to Earth: The Territorial Bond in South China*. California: Stanford University Press, 1995.

Kao, Mayching (ed.). *The Art of Su Liupeng and Su Renshan*. Hong Kong: Chinese University of Hong Kong and Guangzhou Art Gallery, 1990.

Koon, Yeewan. *A Defiant Brush: Su Renshan and the Politics of Painting in Early 19th Century Guangdong*. Hong Kong: University of Hong Kong Press, 2014.

Ryckmans, Pierre. *The Life and Work of Su Renshan: Rebel, Painter and Madman 1814–1849*, Angharad Pimpaneau tr. Paris and Hong Kong: University of Paris, 1970.

Wakeman, Frederick Jr. *Strangers at the Gate: Social Disorder in South China, 1839–1861*. Berkeley and Los Angeles: University of California Press, 1966.

39. Ju Chao

Chuang Shen 莊申 (ed.). *Cong baizhi dao baiyin: Qingmo Guangdong shuhua chuangzuo yu shoucang shi* 從白紙到白銀：清末廣東書畫創作與收藏史 (From paper to silver: A history of creating and collecting painting and calligraphy in late Qing Guangdong). Taipei: Dongda tushu gongsi, 1997.

Croizier, Ralph. *Art and Revolution in Modern China: The Lingnan (Cantonese) School of Painting, 1906–1951*. Berkeley: University of California Press, 1988.

Guangzhou Museum of Art and Hong Kong Museum of Art 廣州藝術博物院、香港藝術館. *Gu yuan shi xiang – Ju Chao, Ju Lian huihua* 故園拾香 – 居巢、居廉繪畫 (Strolling in the fragrant garden: Paintings of Ju Chao and Ju Lian). Guangzhou: Lingnan meishu chubanshe, 2008.

Ju Chao 居巢. *Jinxi'an shichao* 今夕盦詩鈔 (Poem collection from the Hut of Tonight), Qiu Weixuan 邱煒萲 (ed.). 1900.

Zhu Wanzhang 朱萬章. *Duihua xiezhao: Ju Chao Ju Lian huayi* 對花寫照：居巢居廉畫藝 (Taking likenesses of flowers: The painting of Ju Chao and Ju Lian). Guangzhou: Guangdong renmin chubanshe, 2016.

40. Yao Xie

Erickson, Britta. 'Uncommon Themes and Uncommon Subject Matters in Ren Xiong's Album after Poems by Yao Xie'. In *Visual Culture in Shanghai 1850s–1930s*, Jason Kuo (ed.): 29–54. Washington, DC: New Academia Publishing, 2007.

Hong Keyi 洪克夷. *Yao Xie pingzhuan* 姚燮评传 (Critical Biography of Yao Xie). Hangzhou: Zhejiang guji chubanshe, 1987.

Wue, Roberta. *Art Worlds: Artists, Images, and Audiences in Late Nineteenth-Century Shanghai*. Hong Kong: Hong Kong University Press, 2014.

Yao Xie 姚燮. *Yao Xie ji* 姚燮集 (Collected Works of Yao Xie), Lu Wei 路偉 and Xin Cao 曹鑫 (eds). Zhejiang wencong, vols. 257–63. Hangzhou: Zhejiang guji chubanshe, 2014.

41. Ren Xiong

Cahill, James. 'Ren Xiong and His Self-Portrait'. *Ars Orientalis* 25 (1995): 119–32.

Cai Zhaochu 蔡照初 and Ren Xiong 任熊. *Ren Weichang mu ke hua si zhong* 任渭長木刻畫四種

(Four types of woodcut pictures by Ren Weichang).
Beijing: Xueyuan chubanshe, 2000.

Erickson, Britta. 'Zhou Xian's Fabulous Construct:
The Thatched Cottage of Fan Lake'. *Phoebus 8:
Art at the Close of China's Empire* (1998): 67–93.

Nie Chongzheng 聶崇正. 'Ren Xiong ji qi *Shiwan tu
ce* 任熊及其《十萬圖》冊 (Ren Xiong and his
Ten Myriads album). *Gugong bowuyuan yuankan* 1 (1983):
61–4, and pls. 1–3.

Pang Zhiying 龐志英 and Wu Changshuo 吳昌碩.
Yao Damei shi yi tu ge 姚大梅詩意圖冊 (Ren Xiong's
album after the poems of Yao Xie). Shanghai:
Shanghai renmin meishu chubanshe, 2010.

42. Ren Yi or Ren Bonian

Lai, Yu-chih. 'Remapping Borders: Ren Bonian's
Frontier Paintings and Urban Life in 1880s
Shanghai'. *The Art Bulletin* 86.3 (September 2004):
550–72.

Vinograd, Richard. *Boundaries of the Self: Chinese Portraits:
1600–1900*. Cambridge: Cambridge University Press,
1992.

———. 'Satire and Situation: Images of the Artist in
Late Nineteenth-Century China'. *Phoebus* 8 (1998):
110–33.

Wue, Roberta. *Art Worlds: Artists, Images, and Audiences
in Late Nineteenth-Century Shanghai*. Hong Kong and
Honolulu: University of Hawai'i Press, 2014.

Yang Chia-ling 楊佳玲 (Translator Yang En-hao 楊恩
豪). *Hua meng Shanghai: Ren Bonian de bimo shijie* 畫夢上
海：任伯年的筆墨世界 (New wine in old bottles:
The art of Ren Bonian in 19th-century Shanghai).
Taipei: Diancang shuhua jiating, 2011.

43. Zhao Zhiqian

Wang Jiacheng 王家誠. *Zhao Zhiqian zhuan* 趙之謙傳
(Biography of Zhao Zhiqian). Taipei: National
History Museum, 2002.

Wu, Chao-jen. 'Between Tradition and Modernity:
Strange Fish of Different Species, Products
of Wenzhou by Zhao Zhiqian (1829–1884)
and their Relationship to the Epigraphic Studies
of Late Qing'. PhD thesis, University of Kansas,
2002.

Zhang Xiaozhuang 張小莊. *Zhao Zhiqian yanjiu* 趙之謙
研究 (Study of Zhao Zhiqian). Beijing: Rongbaozhai
chubanshe, 2008.

Zhao Erchang 趙爾昌. *Zhao Zhiqian zhuzuo yu yanjiu* 趙
之謙著作與研究 (Life and writing of Zhao Zhiqian).
Hangzhou: Xiling yinshe, 2008.

Zhao Zhiqian 趙之謙, *Zhang'an zashuo* 章安雜說
(Miscellanea from Zhang'an). Shanghai: Shanghai
renmin meishu chubanshe, 1989.

Zou Tao 鄒濤. *Zhao Zhiqian nianpu* 趙之謙年譜
(Chronology of Zhao Zhiqian). Beijing:
Rongbaozhai chubanshe, 2003.

44. Wu Changshi

Chen Zhenlian 陳振濂. *Xiandai Zhongguo shufa shi* 現代中
國書法史 (A history of modern Chinese calligraphy).
Zhengzhou: Henan meishu chubanshe, 1993.

Erickson, Britta and Craig L. Yee. *Modern Ink: The Art
of Wu Changshi*. Honolulu: University of Hawai'i
Press, 2018.

Fong, Wen C. *Between Two Cultures: Late-Nineteenth- and
Early-Twentieth-Century Chinese Paintings from the Robert
H. Ellsworth Collection in The Metropolitan Museum of Art*.
New York: The Metropolitan Museum of Art, 2001.

Kuo, Jason C. (ed.). *Visual Culture in Shanghai 1850s–1930s*.
Washington, DC: New Academia Publishing, 2007.

Shen Kuiyi. 'Wu Changshi and the Shanghai Art World
in the Late Nineteenth and Early Twentieth
Centuries'. PhD thesis, Ohio State University, 2000.

45. Qingkuan

Li Junwen 李駿雯. *Suojian Qingkuan shiliao zhi chubu shuli*
所見慶寬史料之初步梳理 (A preliminary survey
of the historical documents I have seen about
Qingkuan). N.p., manuscript, 2014.

Lin Chi-hung 林志宏. *Minguo nai diguo ye: Zhengzhi
wenhua zhuanxing xia de Qing yimin* 民國乃敵國也：政
治文化轉型下的清遺民 (The Republic is an enemy:
Qing loyalists during a transitional period of political
culture). Taipei: Lianjing chuban shiye gufen youxian
gongsi, 2009.

Liu Xiaomeng 劉小萌. *Qingdai Beijing qiren shehui* 清代北
京旗人社會 (The Bannermen society in Qing
Beijing). Beijing: Zhongguo shehui kexue chuban
she, 2008.

Qi Meiqin 祁美琴. *Qingdai neiwufu* 清代內務府 (The
Qing Imperial Household Department). Liaoning:
Liaoning minzu chubanshe, 2009.

Zhang, Hongxing. 'Studies in Late Qing Dynasty Battle
Paintings'. *Artibus Asiae* 60.2 (2000): 265–96.

46. Wu Youru

Hay, Jonathan. 'Painters and Publishing in Late
Nineteenth-Century Shanghai'. In *Art at the Close
of China's Empire*, Ju-hsi Chou (ed.): 134–88. Arizona:
Arizona State University Press, 1998.

Reed, Christopher A. *Gutenberg in Shanghai: Chinese Print
Capitalism, 1876–1937*. Vancouver, Toronto: University
of British Columbia Press, 2004.

Wagner, Rudolf G. (ed.). *Joining the Global Public: Word,
Image, and City in Early Chinese Newspapers, 1870–1910*.
Albany: State University of New York Press, 2008.

Ye Xiaoqing. *The Dianshizhai Pictorial: Shanghai Urban Life 1884–1898*. Ann Arbor: University of Michigan Center for Chinese Studies, 2003.

Zhang, Hongxing. 'Studies in Late Qing Dynasty Battle Paintings'. *Artibus Asiae* 60.2 (2000): 265–96.

47. Li Shutong

Kao, Mayching. 'Reforms in Education and the Beginning of the Western-Style Painting Movement in China'. In *A Century in Crisis: Modernity and Tradition in the Art of Twentieth-Century China*, Julia F. Andrews and Kuiyi Shen (eds): 146–61. New York: Solomon R. Guggenheim Foundation, 1998.

'Li Shutong youhua *Banluo nüxiang* de faxian yu chukao' 李叔同油畫《半裸女像》的發現與初考 (The discovery and early examination of Li Shutong's oil-painting *Semi-Nude Woman*). https://www.cafamuseum.org/exhibit/newsdetail/2404

Ōno Kimika 大野公賀. 'Kōitsu hōshi (Ri Shukudō) to Nihon' 弘一法師（李叔同）と日本 (Master Hongyi [Li Shutong] and Japan)'. *Tōyō bunka kenkyūjo kiyō* 160 (2011): 39–78.

Yoshida Chizuko 吉田千鶴子. *Kindai higashi ajia bijutsu ryūgakusei no kenkyū* 近代東アジア美術留学生の研究 (Modern East Asian art students in Japan). Tokyo: Yumani Shobō, 2009.

Zhen Xing 陳星, Cao Bula 曹布拉 et al. (eds) *Hongyi dashi yishu lun* 弘一大師藝術論 (On great master Hongyi's art). Hangzhou: Xiling yinshe, 2001.

48. Lai Fong

Bennett, Terry. *History of Photography in China: Chinese Photographers, 1844–1879*. London: Bernard Quaritch, 2013.

Cody, Jeffrey W. and Frances Terpak (eds). *Brush and Shutter: Early Photography in China*. Los Angeles: Getty Research Institute, 2011.

Hu Zhichuan 胡志川 and Ma Yunzeng 馬運增 (eds). *Zhongguo sheying shi, 1840–1937* 中國攝影史 1840–1937 (A history of Chinese photography, 1840–1937). Beijing: Zhongguo sheying chubanshe, 1987.

'Lai Fong (Afong Studio)'. *Historical Photographs of China*. At https://www.hpcbristol.net/photographer/lai-fong-afong-studio (accessed on 26 January 2022).

Wue, Roberta. 'Picturing Hong Kong: Photography through Practice and Function'. In *Picturing Hong Kong: Photography, 1855–1910*, 27–47. New York: Asia Society Galleries, 1997.

49. Yun Zhu

Epstein, Maram. 'The Argument for a Woman's Authorship of the *Hou honglou meng*'. *Nan Nü: Men, Women and Gender in China* 22 (2020): 223–64.

Mann, Susan. *Precious Records: Women in China's Long Eighteenth Century*. Berkeley: University of California Press, 1997.

'Ming Qing Women's Writings'. McGill University Digital Collections. https://digital.library.mcgill.ca/mingqing/.

Shen Shanbao 沈善寶. *Mingyuan shihua* 名媛詩話 (Remarks on poetry by notable women). Beijing: Hongxuelou, 1879.

50. Gu Taiqing

Grant, Beata. 'The Poetess and the Precept Master: A Selection of Daoist Poems by Gu Taiqing'. In *Text, Performance, and Gender in Chinese Literature and Music: Essays in Honor of Wilt Idema*, Maghiel van Crevel et al. (eds): 325–40. Leiden: Brill, 2009.

Idema, Wilt L. and Beata Grant. *The Red Brush: Writing Women of Imperial China*. Cambridge, Mass.: Harvard University Press, 2004.

Jin Qicong 金啟孮. *Gu Taiqing yu Haidian* 顧太清與海淀 (Gu Taiqing and Haidian). Beijing: Beijing chubanshe, 2001.

_____ and Jin Shi 金適 (eds). *Gu Taiqing ji jiaojian* 顧太清集校箋 (Edited and annotated collected writings of Gu Taiqing). Beijing: Zhonghua shuju, 2012.

Widmer, Ellen. *The Beauty and the Book: Women and Fiction in Nineteenth-Century China*. Cambridge, Mass.: Harvard University Press, 2006.

51. Wu Songliang

Qin Fang 秦芳 and Chen Yiyuan 陳飴媛. 'Wu Songliang zhushu kaolüe' 吳嵩梁著述考略 (Investigation of Wu Songliang's writing). *Zaozhuang xueyuan xuebao* 34 (2017): 20–4.

Waley, Arthur. *Yuan Mei: Eighteenth-Century Chinese Poet*. London: Allen and Unwin, 1956.

Wu Songliang 吳嵩梁. *Xiangsu shanguan quanji* 香蘇山館全集 (Complete works of the Xiangsu mountain lodge), 57 *juan*. Baixi fang cang ban, 1843.

Xu Guohua 徐國華. 'Qingdai "Shi Fo" Wu Songliang pingshu' 清代"詩佛"吳嵩梁評述 (Evaluation of the 'lyrical Buddha' Wu Songliang). *Zhongwen zixue zhidao* 1 (2005): 58–61.

Ye Yanlan 葉衍蘭 and Ye Gongchuo 葉恭綽. *Qingdai xuezhe xiangzhuan heji* 清代學者像傳合集. (Collected illustrated biographies of Qing scholars). Shanghai: Shanghai guji chubanshe, 1989.

52. Wu Jianren

Huters, Theodore. *Bringing the World Home: Appropriating the West in Late Qing and Early Republican China*. Honolulu: University of Hawai'i Press, 2005.

_____. 'Wu Jianren'. In *Dictionary of Literary Biography, 328: Chinese Fiction Writers, 1900–1949*, Thomas Moran (ed.): 212–19. Detroit: Thomson, Gale, 2007.

Jones, Andrew F. *Developmental Fairy Tales: Evolutionary Thinking and Modern Chinese Culture*. Cambridge, Mass.: Harvard University Press, 2011.

Wu Jianren. *The Sea of Regret: Two Turn-of-the-Century Chinese Romantic Novels*, Patrick Hanan tr. Honolulu: University of Hawai'i Press, 1995.

53. Jakdan

Bosson, James and Hoong Teik Toh. 'Jakdan and his Manchu Poetry'. In *Proceedings of the First North American Conference on Manchu Studies* vol. 1, Stephen Wadley and Carsten Naeher (eds): 13–25. Wiesbaden: Otto Harrassowitz, 2006.

Chiu, Elena Suet-Ying. *Bannermen Tales (zidishu): Manchu Storytelling and Cultural Hybridity in the Qing Dynasty*. Cambridge, Mass.: Harvard University Asia Center, 2018.

Nappi, Carla. *Translating Early Modern China: Illegible Cities*. Oxford: Oxford University Press, 2021.

Porter, David. 'Bannermen as Translators: Manchu Language Education in the Hanjun Banners'. *Late Imperial China* 40.2 (2019): 1–43.

Söderblom Saarela, Mårten. *The Early Modern Travels of Manchu: A Script and its Study in East Asia and Europe*. Philadelphia: University of Pennsylvania Press, 2020.

54. Manchu Teacher of the 'One Hundred Lessons'

Crossley, Pamela Kyle. *Orphan Warriors: Three Manchu Generations and the End of the Qing World*. Princeton: Princeton University Press, 1990.

Elliott, Mark C. *The Manchu Way: The Eight Banners and Ethnic Identity in Late Imperial China*. Stanford: Stanford University Press, 2001.

Fraser, Michi Forbes Anderson. *Tanggu Meyen and Other Manchu Reading Lessons*. London: Luzac & Co., 1924.

Stary, Giovanni et al. *On the Tracks of Manchu Culture, 1644–1994: 350 Years after the Conquest of Peking*. Wiesbaden: Harrassowitz, 1995.

Takekoshi Takashi 竹越孝. *Ichi yaku jyō, Seibun yubiyō taishōhon* 一百條, 清文指要 対照本 (Comparison of the *Tanggū Meyen* and *Qingwen zhiyao*). Kobe: Kobe Foreign Languages University Editions, 2018.

Zarrow, Peter. 'The New Schools and National Identity: Chinese History Textbooks in the Late Qing'. In *The Politics of Historical Production in Late Qing and Republican China*, Tze-ki Hon and Robert Culp (eds): 21–53. Leiden: Brill, 2007.

55. Injannasi

Bawden, Charles. 'The First Systematic Translation of Hung Lou Meng: Qasbuu's Commented Mongolian Version'. *Zentralasiatische Studien* 15 (1981): 241–306.

Clunas, Craig. 'The Prefaces to Nigen Dabqur Asar and their Chinese Antecedents'. *Zentralasiatische Studien* 14.1 (1980): 139–94.

_____. 'The Tümed and the Physical World of Injanasi (1837–1892)'. *Journal of the Anglo-Mongolian Society* 7.1 (1981): 73–84.

Elverskog, Johan. *Our Great Qing: The Mongols, Buddhism, and the State in Late Imperial China*. Honolulu: University of Hawai'i Press, 2008.

Hangin, John Gombojab. *Köke Sudur (The Blue Chronicle): A Study of the First Mongolian Historical Novel by Injannasi*. Asiatische Forschungen, Band 38. Wiesbaden: Otto Harrassowitz, 1973.

56. Lu Xinyuan

Brown, Shana J. *Pastimes: From Art and Antiquarianism to Modern Chinese Historiography*. Honolulu: University of Hawaii Press, 2011.

Shan, Fred Yi. 'Making Rare Books Public: the Jiangsu Provincial Guoxue Library in the Nanjing Decade (1927–1937)'. *East Asian Publishing and Society* 10.2 (2020): 125–58.

Xu Zhenji, *Cangshu jia Lu Xinyuan* 藏書家陸心源 (Lu Xinyuan: Book collector). Xi'an: Shaanxi renmin chubanshe, 2007.

57. Mūsā Sayrāmī

Baytur, Änwär. 'Mulla Musa Sayrami sheirliridin tallanma'. *Bulaq* 15 (1985): 194–227.

Hamada Masami. 'Jihâd, hijra et "devoir du sel" dans l'histoire du Turkestan oriental'. *Turcica* 33 (2001): 35–61.

Kim, Hodong. *Holy War in China: The Muslim Rebellion and State in Chinese Central Asia, 1864–1877*. Stanford: Stanford University Press, 2004.

Schluessel, Eric. *Land of Strangers: The Civilizing Project in Qing Central Asia*. New York: Columbia University Press, 2020.

_____. *The World as Seen from Yarkand: Ghulām Muhammad Khan's 1920s Chronicle, Mā Tītayni wāqi'asi*. Tokyo: NIHU Program Islamic Area Studies, 2014.

58. Wang Tao

Cohen, Paul A. *Between Tradition and Modernity: Wang T'ao and Reform in Late Ch'ing China*. Cambridge, Mass.: Harvard University Press, 1987.

Lai Moushen 賴某深. 'Wang Tao: zaoqi Zhongying wenhua jiaoliu de youhao shizhe' 王韜：早期中英

文化交流的友好使者 (Wang Tao: A friendly messenger of early Sino-British cultural exchange). *Shiie wenhua* 2 (2021): 39–42.

Li Dong 李棟 and Yang Ying 楊瑩. 'Yangwu yundong shiqi Wang Tao duidai xifang fazheng zhishi de renzhi yu luoji' 洋務運動時期王韜對待西方法政知識的認知與邏輯 (The logic and understanding in Wang Tao's knowledge of Western laws and politics during the Westernization movement). *Guangdong shehui kexue* 2 (2019): 220–7.

Qu Wensheng 屈文生 and Wan Li 萬立. 'Wang Tao de xixue yu zhongxue fanyi shenfen, renzhi yu shijian' 王韜的西學與中學翻譯身份、認知與實踐 (Identity, cognition and practice in Wang Tao's translation of Western learning and Chinese learning). *Beijing xingzheng xueyuan xuebao* 3 (2021): 114–121.

Sun Qiaoyun 孫巧雲. 'Cong "xixue jicun liuzhong" kan Wang Tao xixue bishuzhe shenfen de zhuanbian' 從《西學輯存六種》看王韜西學"筆述者"身份的轉變 (The changing identity of Wang Tao as a writer as seen in *Six Volumes of Western Studies*). *Zhejiang shehui kexue* 11 (2018): 129–134.

59. Shan Shili

Hu, Ying. 'Re-configuring Nei/Wai: Writing the Woman Traveler in the Late Qing'. *Late Imperial China* 18.1 (1997): 72–99.

———. 'Would that I were Marco Polo: The Travel Writings of Shan Shili (1856–1943)'. In *International Journal of Travel and Travel Writing*, Traditions of East Asian Travel, Special Issue, Joshua Fogel (ed.) (2004): 119–41.

Qian Shan Shili 錢單士厘. *Guimao lüixing ji* 癸卯旅行記 (Record of a journey in the year 1903) and *Guiqian ji* 歸潛記 (Writings in retirement). In *Zouxiang shijie congshu* 走向世界叢書 (Marching towards the world series), Yang Jian (ed.). Changsha: Hunan renmin chubanshe, 1981.

Shan Shili (Sen Tanshiri) 單士厘. *Kibō ryokōki yakuchū: Sen Tōson no haha no mita sekai* (Record of a journey in the year 1903: The world as seen by the mother of Qian Daosun), Suzuki Tomō 鈴木智夫 tr. Tokyo: Kyūko shoin, 2010.

Widmer, Ellen. 'Foreign Travel through a Woman's Eyes: Shan Shili's *Guimao lüixing ji* in Local and Global Perspective'. *The Journal of Asian Studies* 65.4 (November 2006): 763–91.

60. Li Gui

Chaplin, Joyce E. *Round About the Earth: Circumnavigation from Magellan to Orbit*. New York: Simon & Schuster, 2012.

Desnoyers, Charles A. tr. *A Journey to the East: Li Gui's A New Account of a Trip Around the Globe*. Ann Arbor: University of Michigan Press, 2004.

Goodman, Matthew. *Eighty Days: Nellie Bly and Elizabeth Bisland's History-Making Race Around the World*. New York: Ballantine Books, 2014.

Li Gui 李圭. 'Huanyou diqiu xinlu' 環游地球新錄 (The new record of a trip around the world). In *Zou xiang shijie congshu* 走向世界叢書 (Walking toward the world collectanea), Zhong Shuhe 鍾叔河 (ed.): 169–362. Changsha: Yuelu shushe, 1985.

———. 'Sitong Ji' 思痛記 (A Record of Pondering Pain). In *Taiping Tianguo* 太平天國 (Taiping Heavenly Kingdom), Zhongguo shixue hui 中國史學會 4 (ed.): 463–98. Shanghai: Shanghai renmin chubanshe, 1957.

Meyer-Fong, Tobie. *What Remains: Coming to Terms with Civil War in 19th Century China*. Stanford: Stanford University Press, 2013.

van de Ven, Hans J. *Breaking with the Past: The Maritime Customs Service and the Global Origins of Modernity in China*. New York: Columbia University Press, 2014.

61. Huang Zunxian

Arkush, R. David and Leo O. Lee (eds). *Land Without Ghosts: Chinese Impressions of America from the Mid-Nineteenth Century to the Present*. Oakland, CA: University of California Press, 1993.

Huang Zunxian 黃遵憲 and Qian Zhonglian 錢仲聯 (eds). *Renjinglu shicao jianzhu* 人境廬詩草箋注 (Notes and commentary on poems written in the hut within the human realm). Shanghai: Guji chubanshe, 1981.

Kamachi, Noriko. *Reform in China: Huang Tsun hsien and the Japanese Model*. Cambridge, Mass.: Harvard University Press, 1981.

Martin, Helmut. 'A Transitional Concept of Chinese Literature 1897–1917: Liang Ch'i-chao on Poetry Reform, Historical Drama and the Political Novel'. *Oriens Extremus* 20 (1973): 196–7.

Schmidt, Jerry Dean. *Within the Human Realm: The Poetry of Huang Zunxian, 1848–1905*. Cambridge: Cambridge University Press, 2007.

62. Yan Fu

Fröhlich, Thomas and Axel Schneider (eds). *Chinese Visions of Progress, 1895 to 1949*. Leiden and Boston: Brill, 2020.

Huang, Max K. W. *The Meaning of Freedom: Yan Fu and the Origins of Chinese Liberalism*. Hong Kong: The Chinese University Press, 2008.

Huang Kewu 黃克武 (Huang, Max K. W.). *Bixing shanhe: Zhongguo jindai qimengren Yan Fu* 筆醒山河：中國近代啟蒙人嚴復 (Yan Fu: the man who

enlightened China with his pen). Guilin: Guangxi
shifan daxue chubanshe, 2022.

Pusey, James Reeve. *China and Charles Darwin.*
Cambridge, Mass.: Harvard University Asia Center,
1983.

Schwartz, Benjamin I. *In Search of Wealth and Power:
Yen Fu and the West.* Cambridge, Mass.: Belknap Press
of Harvard University Press, 1964.

63. Sarah Pike Conger

Conger, Sarah Pike. *Letters from China: With Particular
Attention to the Empress Dowager and the Women of China.*
London: Hodder and Stoughton, 1909.

_____. *Old China and Young America.* Chicago: F. G.
Browne and Co., 1913.

Hayter-Menzies, Grant. *The Empress and Mrs. Conger:
The Uncommon Friendship of Two Women and Two Worlds.*
Hong Kong: Hong Kong University Press, 2011.

Hoe, Susanna. *Women at the Siege, Peking 1900.* London:
Holo Books, 2000.

Hunter, Jane. *The Gospel of Gentility: American Women
Missionaries in Turn-of-the-Century China.* New Haven:
Yale University Press, 1984.

64. Zhang Taiyan

Laitinen, Kauko. *Chinese Nationalism in the Late Qing
Dynasty: Zhang Binglin as an Anti-Manchu Propagandist.*
London: Curzon, 1990.

Murthy, Viren. *The Political Philosophy of Zhang Taiyan:
The Resistance of Consciousness.* Leiden: Brill, 2011.

Shimada, Kenji. *Pioneers of the Chinese Revolution*, Joshua
Fogel tr. Stanford: Stanford University Press, 1990.

Wang, Hui. *Becoming Chinese: Passages to Modernity and
Beyond.* Berkeley: University of California Press, 2000.

Wong, Young-Tsu. *Search for Modern Nationalism: Zhang
Binglin and Revolutionary China, 1869–1936.* Oxford:
Oxford University Press, 1989.

65. Naitō Konan

Fogel, Joshua A. *Politics and Sinology: The Case of Naitō
Konan (1866–1934).* Cambridge, Mass.: Council
on East Asian Studies, 1984.

Mitamura Taisuke 三田村泰助. *Naitō Konan* 内藤湖南.
Tokyo: Chūō kōronsha, 1972.

*Naitō Konan and the Development of the Conception of
Modernity in China History*, Joshua A. Fogel tr.
Special issue of *Chinese Studies in History* (Fall 1983).

Zhou Yiliang 周一良. 'Riben Neiteng Hunan
xiansheng zai Zhongguo shixueshang zhi gongxian'
日本內藤湖南先生在中國史學上之貢獻 (The
contributions to Chinese historical studies of
Professor Naitō Konan of Japan). *Shixue nianbao*
2.1 (September 1934): 155–72.

66. Wu Bingjian

He Chi 賀痴 and Lü Jingxia 呂靜霞. *Qingdai shijie shoufu
Wu Bingjian de caifu rensheng* 清代世界首富伍秉鑑的
財富人生 (The richest man in the world during the
Qing dynasty: Wu Bingjian and his wealthy life).
Beijing: Zhongguo zhigong chubanshe, 2010.

Richard, Josepha. 'Uncovering the Garden of the
Richest Man on Earth in Nineteenth-Century
Canton: Howqua's Garden in Honam, China'.
Garden History 43.2 (2015): 168–81.

Wang, Shuo. *Negotiating Friendships: A Canton Merchant
Between East and West in the Early 19th Century.* Munich:
De Gruyter Oldenbourg, 2020.

Wong, John D. *Global Trade in the Nineteenth Century:
The House of Houqua and the Canton System.* Cambridge:
Cambridge University Press, 2016.

Zhang Xiaoli 張曉立. *Wanqing shoufu Wu Bingjian* 晚清
首富伍秉鑑 (Wu Bingjian: The richest man in the
late Qing dynasty). Wuhan: Huazhong Kejidaxue
chubanshe, 2014.

67. Sir Jamsetjee Jejeebhoy

Palsetia, Jesse S. 'The Parsis of India and the Opium
Trade in China'. *Contemporary Drug Problems* 35.4
(2008): 647–78.

Siddiqi, Asiya. 'The Business World of Jamsetjee
Jejeebhoy'. *The Indian Economic & Social History
Review* 19.3–4 (1982): 301–24.

Thampi, Madhavi. *Indians in China, 1800–1949.*
New Delhi: Manohar Publishers, 2005.

_____. *China and the Making of Bombay.* Mumbai:
KR Cama Oriental Institute, 2009.

68. Hu Xueyan

Cheng, Linsun. *Banking in Modern China: Entrepreneurs,
Professional Managers, and the Development of Chinese
Banks, 1897–1937.* Cambridge: Cambridge University
Press, 2003.

Goetzmann, William N. *Money Changes Everything: How
Finance Made Civilization Possible.* Princeton: Princeton
University Press, 2016.

Hao, Yen-p'ing. *The Commercial Revolution in Nineteenth-Century
China: The Rise of Sino-Western Mercantile Capitalism.*
Berkeley: University of California Press, 1986.

69. Widow Anwu

Li Gang 李鋼. *Shaanxi shangbang shi* 陝西商幫史
(The history of the Shaanxi merchants' group).
Xi'an: Shaanxi remin jiaoyu chubanshe, 1997.

Liu Maoguan 劉懋官 and Song Bolu 宋伯魯 (eds).
Chongxiu jingyang xianzhi 重修涇陽縣志 (Revised
gazetteer of Jingyang county), *juan* 15. Tianjin:
Huaxin yinshuaju, 1911.

Song Bolu 宋伯魯 (ed.). *Xuxiu shaanxi tongzhigao* 續修陝西通誌稿 (The sequel to the draft of the Shaanxi provincial gazetteer), *juan* 124. Xi'an: Shaanxi sheng zhengfu qianyin, 1934.

Wu Mi 吳宓. *Wumi riji xubian* 吳宓日記續編 (Sequel to the diary of Wu Mi), vol. 5. Beijing: Sanlian shudian, 2006.

Yang Jurang 楊居讓. *Bude bushuo de Anwu guafu Zhou Ying* 不得不說的安吳寡婦周瑩 (The story of Widow Anwu (Zhou Ying) that must be told). *Tangu xuekan* 26.5 (2010): 108–10.

70. Silas Hardoon and Luo Jialing

Betta, Chiara. 'Silas Aaron Hardoon and Cross-Cultural Adaptation in Shanghai'. In *The Jews of China, Volume One: Historical and Comparative Perspectives*, Jonathan Goldstein (ed.): 216–29. Armonk, NY: M. E. Sharpe, 1999.

Bickers, Robert and Isabella Jackson (eds). *Treaty Ports in Modern China: Law, Land and Power*. London: Routledge, 2016.

Carter, Jay. *Champions Day: The End of Old Shanghai*. W. W. Norton & Company, 2020.

Scott, Gregory Adam. 'The 1913 *Pinjia Canon* and the Changing Role of the Buddhist Canon in Modern China'. In *Reinventing the Tripitaka: Transformation of the Buddhist Canon in Modern East Asia*, Jiang Wu and Greg Wilkinson (eds): 95–125. Lanham: Lexington Books, 2017.

Shen Ji 沈寂. *Shanghai daban: Hatong waizhuan* 上海大班哈同外傳 (The Shanghai chairman: An anecdotal biography of Hardoon). Shanghai: Xuelin chubanshe, 2002.

71. Ernest Major

Vittinghoff [Gentz], Natascha. *Die Anfänge des Journalismus in China, 1860–1911*. Wiesbaden: Harrassowitz, 2002.

Wagner, Rudolf G. (ed.). *Joining the Global Public: Word, Image and City in the Early Chinese Newspapers 1870–1910*. New York: SUNY, 2007.

———. *The Life and Times of a Cultural Broker: Ernest Major and his Shenbao Publishing House in Shanghai (1872–1889)*, Natascha Gentz and Cathy V. Yeh (eds). New York: Columbia University Press, forthcoming.

Xu Zaiping 徐載平 and Xu Duanfang 徐端芳. *Qingmo sishinian Shenbao shiliao* 清末四十年申報史料 (Forty years of historical material on the *Shenbao* in the Late Qing). Beijing: Xinhua Press, 1988.

Ye, Xiaoqing. *The Dianshizhai Pictorial: Shanghai Urban Life 1884–1898*. Ann Arbor: University of Michigan Center for Chinese Studies, 2003.

72. Sir Robert Hart

Bickers, Robert. *The Scramble for China: Foreign Devils in the Qing Empire, 1832–1914*. London: Penguin, 2011.

Fairbank, John King and Katherine F. Bruner (eds). *The I. G. in Peking: Letters of Robert Hart, Chinese Maritime Customs, 1868–1907*, 2 vols. Cambridge, Mass.: The Belknap Press of Harvard University Press, 1975.

Hart, Robert. *These from the Land of Sinim: Essays on the China Question*. London: Chapman and Hall, 1901.

van de Ven, Hans. *Breaking with the Past: The Maritime Customs Service and the Global Origins of Modernity in China*. New York: Columbia University Press, 2014.

73. Thomas Hanbury

Bickers, Robert. *The Scramble for China: Foreign Devils in the Qing Empire, 1832–1914*. London: Penguin, 2011.

Hanbury, Thomas. *Letters of Sir Thomas Hanbury*. London: West, Newman & Co., 1913.

Hibbard, Peter. *The Bund Shanghai: China Faces West*. London: Hong Kong, 2007.

Moore, Alasdair. *La Mortola: In the Footsteps of Thomas Hanbury*. London: Cadogan Guides, 2004.

74. Kishida Ginkō

Amano Hiroshi 天野宏, Saitō Akemi 斎藤明美 and Sugihara Masayasu 杉原正康. 'Meiji shoki no yakugyōkai ni kōken shita Kishida Ginkō' 明治初期の薬業界に貢献した岸田吟香 (Kishida Ginkō's contributions to the medical world in the early Meiji period). *Yakushigaku zasshi* 24.1 (1989): 47–54.

Etō Shinkichi 衛藤瀋吉. 'Chūgoku kakumei to Nihonjin: Kishida Ginkō no baai' 中国革命と日本人：岸田吟香の場合 (The Chinese revolution and the Japanese: The case of Kishida Ginkō). In *Nihon no shakai bunka shi* 日本の社会文化史 (Social and cultural history of Japan), vol. 7: *Sekai no naka no Nihon* 世界の中の日本 (Japan in the world), Miwa Kimitada 三輪公忠 (ed.). Tokyo: Kōdansha, 1974.

Fogel, Joshua A. *Articulating the Sinosphere: Sino-Japanese Relations in Space and Time*. Cambridge, Mass.: Harvard University Press, 2009.

Jansen, Marius. *The Japanese and Sun Yat-sen*. Cambridge, Mass.: Harvard University Press, 1954.

Sugiura Tadashi 杉浦正. *Kishida Ginkō, shiryō kara mita sono isshō* 岸田吟香：資料から見たその一生 (Kishida Ginkō: A life seen through documents). Tokyo: Kyūko shoin, 1996.

75. Di Baoxian

Judge, Joan. *Print and Politics: Shibao and the Culture of Reform in Late Qing China*. Stanford: Stanford University Press, 1996.

_____. *Republican Lens: Gender, Visuality, and Experience in the Early Chinese Periodical Press*. Berkeley: University of California Press, 2015.

Scott, Gregory Adam. 'Conversion by the Book: Buddhist Print Culture in Early Republican China'. PhD thesis, Columbia University, 2013.

Vinograd, Richard. 'Patrimonies in Press: Art Publishing, Cultural Politics, and Canon Construction in the Career of Di Baoxian (1873–1941)'. In *The Role of Japan in Modern Chinese Art*, Joshua A. Fogel (ed.): 244–72. Berkeley: University of California Press, 2012.

Wang Cheng-hua. 'New Printing Technology and Heritage Preservation: Collotype Reproduction of Antiquities in Modern China, Circa 1908–1917'. In *The Role of Japan in Modern Chinese Art*, Joshua A. Fogel (ed.): 273–308. Berkeley: University of California Press, 2012.

76. Yinghe

Idema, Wilt L. *Two Centuries of Manchu Women Poets: An Anthology*. Seattle: University of Washington Press, 2017.

Leonard, Jane Kate. *Stretching the Qing Bureaucracy in the 1826 Sea-Transport Experiment*. Boston: Brill, 2018.

Stuart, Jan and Evelyn Sakakida Rawski. *Worshiping the Ancestors: Chinese Commemorative Portraits*. Washington, DC: Freer Gallery of Art and Arthur M. Sackler Gallery, Smithsonian Institution; Stanford: Stanford University Press, 2001.

77. Lin Zexu

Chang, Hsin-pao. *Commissioner Lin and the Opium War*. Cambridge Mass.: Harvard University Press, 1964.

Chen, Shunyi. 'Translation and Ideology: A Study of Lin Zexu's Translation Activities'. *Meta* 62.2 (2017): 313–32.

Madancy, Joyce. *The Troublesome Legacy of Commissioner Lin: The Opium Trade and Opium Suppression in Fujian Province, 1820s to 1920s*. Cambridge Mass.: Harvard University Press, 2004.

Polacheck, James. *The Inner Opium War*. Cambridge Mass.: Harvard University Press, 1991.

Shao Xueping 邵雪萍 and Lin Benchun 林本椿. 'Lin Zexu he ta de fanyi banzi' 林则徐和他的翻譯班子 (Lin Zexu and his translation team). *Shanghai keji fanyi* 4 (2002): 47–9.

78. Bao Shichen

Han, Seunghyun. *After the Prosperous Age: State and Elites in Early Nineteenth-Century Suzhou*. Cambridge, Mass.: Harvard University Asia Center, 2016.

Jones, Susan Mann and Philip A. Kuhn. 'Dynastic Decline and the Roots of Rebellion'. In *Cambridge History of China*, vol. 10, *Late Ch'ing, 1800–1911*, part 1, John King Fairbank (ed.): 107–62. Cambridge: Cambridge University Press, 1978.

Leonard, Jane Kate. *Controlling from Afar: The Daoguang Emperor's Management of the Grand Canal Crisis, 1824–1826*. Ann Arbor: University of Michigan Center for Chinese Studies, 1996.

Lin Man-houng. *China Upside Down: Currency, Society, and Ideologies, 1808–1856*. Cambridge, Mass.: Harvard University Asia Center, 2006.

Rowe, William T. *Speaking of Profit: Bao Shichen and Reform in Nineteenth-Century China*. Cambridge, Mass.: Harvard University Asia Center, 2018.

79. Zeng Guofan

Guo, Yingjie and Baogang He. 'Reimagining the Chinese Nation: The "Zeng Guofan Phenomenon"'. *Modern China* 25.2 (April 1999): 142–70.

Hail, William James. *Tseng Kuo-fan and the Taiping Rebellion: With a Short Sketch of his Later Career*. New Haven: Yale University Press, 1927.

Platt, Stephen. *Provincial Patriots: The Hunanese and Modern China*. Cambridge, Mass.: Harvard University Press, 2007.

_____. *Autumn in the Heavenly Kingdom: China, the West, and the Epic Story of the Taiping Civil War*. New York: Knopf, 2012.

Zeng Guofan 曾國藩. *Zeng Guofan quanji* 曾國藩全集 (The complete works of Zeng Guofan), 16 vols. Beijing: Zhongguo zhigong chubanshe, 2001.

80. Zuo Zongtang

Kuhn, Philip. *Rebellion and its Enemies in Late Imperial China: Militarization and Social Structure, 1796–1864*. Cambridge, Mass.: Harvard University Press, 1970.

Lavelle, Peter B. *The Profits of Nature: Colonial Development and the Quest for Resources in Nineteenth-Century China*. New York: Columbia University Press, 2020.

Piassetsky, Pavel. *Russian Travellers in Mongolia and China*, J. Gordon-Cummings tr. London: Chapman & Hall, 1884.

Platt, Stephen R. *Provincial Patriots: the Hunanese and Modern China*. Cambridge, Mass.: Harvard University Press, 2007.

Schluessel, Eric T. *Land of Strangers: The Civilizing Project in Qing Central Asia*. New York: Columbia University Press, 2020.

Zuo Zongtang 左宗棠. *Zuo Zongtang quan ji* 左宗棠全集 (Complete Works of Zuo Zongtang), Liu Yangyang 劉泱泱 (ed.), 15 vols. Changsha: Yuelu shu she, 2009.

81. Zhang Zhidong

Ayers, William. *Chang Chih-tung and Educational Reform in China.* Cambridge, Mass.: Harvard University Press, 1971.

Bays, Daniel H. *China Enters the Twentieth Century: Chang Chih-tung and the Issues of a New Age, 1895–1909.* Ann Arbor: University of Michigan Press, 1978.

Chang, Chih-tung. *China's Only Hope: An Appeal by her Greatest Viceroy, Chang Chih-tung, with the Sanction of the Present Emperor, Kwang Sü,* Samuel I. Woodbridge tr. New York: F. H. Revell Co., 1900.

Fan Shuyi 苑書義 et al. (eds). *Zhang Zhidong quanji* 張之洞全集 (Complete collected writings of Zhang Zhidong). Shijiazhuang shi: Hebei renmin chubanshe, 1998.

Zhang Zhidong 張之洞. *Quan xue pian* 勸學篇 (An exhortation to learning), Feng Tianyu 馮天瑜 and Jiang Hailong 姜海龍 (eds). Beijing: Zhonghua shuju, 2016.

82. Prince Gong

Fan Baichuan 樊百川. *Qingji de yangwu xinzheng* 清際的洋務新政 (The new policy towards foreign affairs in the Qing dynasty). Shanghai: Shanghai shudian, 2009.

Hao, Yen-P'ing and Erh-Min Wang. 'Changing Chinese views of Western relations, 1840–95'. In *The Cambridge History of China* vol. 11, John K. Fairbank and Kwang-Ching Liu (eds): 142–201. Cambridge: Cambridge University Press, 1980.

Jenco, Leigh. *Changing Referents: Learning Across Space and Time in China and the West.* New York: Oxford University Press, 2015.

Li Wenjie 李文傑. 'Chuilian tingzheng, xunzheng, guizheng yu wan Qing de zouzhe chuli' 垂簾聽政，訓政，歸正與晚清的奏摺處理 (Ruling from behind the curtain, instructions in governance, resumptions of regular procedure and the management of memorials to the emperor). *Jindaishi yanjiu* 2 (2018): 45–67.

van de Ven, Hans. *Breaking with the Past: The Maritime Customs Service and the Global Origins of Modern China.* New York: Columbia University Press, 2014.

83. Li Hongzhang

Bland, J. O. P. *Li Hung-chang.* New York: Henry Holt and Company, 1917.

Chu, Samuel C. and Liu, Kwang-Ching (eds). *Li Hung-Chang and China's Early Modernization.* London and New York: Routledge, 1994.

Gu Tinglong 顧廷龍 and Dai Yi 戴逸 (eds). *Li Hongzhang quanji* 李鴻章全集 (Collected papers of Li Hongzhang), 39 vols. Hefei: Anhui jiaoyu chubanshe, 2008.

Spector, Stanley. *Li Hung-Chang and the Huai Army: A Study in Nineteenth-Century Chinese Regionalism.* Seattle: University of Washington Press, 1964.

Wue, Roberta. 'The Mandarin at Home and Abroad: Picturing Li Hongzhang'. *Ars Orientalis* 43 (2013): 140–56.

84. Guo Songtao

Day, Jenny Huangfu. *Qing Travelers to the Far West: Diplomacy and the Information Order in Late Imperial China.* Cambridge: Cambridge University Press, 2018.

_____. 'Searching for the Roots of Western Wealth and Power: Guo Songtao and Education in Victorian England'. *Late Imperial China* 35.1 (2014): 1–37.

Frodsham, J. D. *The First Chinese Embassy to the West: The Journals of Kuo Sung-T'ao, Liu Hsi-Hung and Chang Te-yi.* Oxford: Clarendon Press, 1974.

Wagner, Rudolf. 'The Shenbao in Crisis: The International Environment and the Conflict between Guo Songtao and the Shenbao'. *Late Imperial China* 20.1 (1999): 107–43.

Wang Rongzu 王榮祖. *Zouxiang shijie de cuozhe: Guo Songtao yu Dao Xian Tong Guang shidai* 走向世界的挫折:郭嵩燾與道咸同光時代 (Frustrations in encountering the world: Guo Songtao and the era of the Daoguang, Xianfeng, Tongzhi and Guangxu emperors). Changsha: Yuelu shushe, 2000.

85. Chen Jitong

Qian, Nanxiu. *Politics, Poetics, and Gender in Late Qing China: Xue Shaohui and the Era of Reform.* Stanford: Stanford University Press, 2015.

Ren, Ke. 'Fin-de-Siècle Diplomat: Chen Jitong (1852–1907) and Cosmopolitan Possibilities in the Late Qing World'. PhD thesis, Johns Hopkins University, 2014.

_____. 'Chen Jitong, *Les Parisiens peints par un Chinois,* and the Literary Self-Fashioning of a Chinese Boulevardier in Fin-de-siècle Paris'. *L'Esprit Créateur* 56.3 (Fall 2016): 90–103.

_____. 'The Conférencier in the Purple Robe: Chen Jitong and Qing Cultural Diplomacy in Late Nineteenth-Century Paris'. *Journal of Modern Chinese History* 12.1 (2018): 1–21.

Yeh, Catherine Vance. 'The Life-style of Four Wenren in Late Qing Shanghai'. *Harvard Journal of Asiatic Studies* 57.2 (December 1997): 419–70.

86. Sai Jinhua

McAleavy, Henry. *That Chinese Woman: The Life of Sai-chin-hua.* London: George Allen and Unwin, 1959.

von Kowallis, Jon Eugene. *The Subtle Revolution: Poets of the 'Old Schools' during late Qing and early Republican China.* Berkeley: California University Press, 2006.

von Minden, Stephan. *Die Merkwürdige Geschichte der Sai Jinhua: Historisch-Philologische Untersuchung zur Entstehung und Verbreitung einer Legende aus der Zeit des Boxeraufstands.* Stuttgart: Franz Steiner Verlag, 1994.

Wei Shaochang 魏紹昌. 'Guanyu Sai–Wa gongan de zhenxiang' 關於賽瓦公案的真相 (Concerning the true facts of the Sai–Waldersee controversy). *Shinmatsu shōsetsu kenkyū* 4 (1980): 73–84.

Wu Deduo 吳德鐸 (ed.). *Sai Jinhua benshi* 賽金花本事 (Source material on Sai Jinhua). Changsha: Yue Lu shushe, 1985.

87. Gu Hongming

Du, Chunmei. *Gu Hongming's Eccentric Chinese Odyssey.* Philadelphia: University of Pennsylvania Press, 2019.

Furth, Charlotte (ed.). *The Limits of Change: Essays on Conservative Alternatives in Republican China.* Cambridge, Mass.: Harvard University Press, 1976.

Ku Hung-Ming [Gu, Hongming]. *The Conduct of Life or the Universal Order of Confucius.* London: John Murray, 1912.

———. *The Spirit of the Chinese People: With an Essay on 'The War and the Way Out'.* Taipei: Committee for the Publication of Dr. Ku Hung-ming's Works, 1956.

Liu, Lydia. *The Clash of Empires: The Invention of China in Modern World Making.* Cambridge, Mass.: Harvard University Press, 2004.

88. Kang Youwei

Baohuanghui Scholarship. At https://baohuanghui.blogspot.com/ (accessed 5 January 2022).

Brusadelli, Federico. *Confucian Concord: Reform, Utopia and Global Teleology in Kang Youwei's Datong Shu.* Leiden: Brill, 2020.

Kang Youwei 康有為. *Guang yizhou shuangji* 廣藝舟雙楫 (Extended Paired Oars for the Boat of Art], with reading guide by Gong Pengcheng 龔鵬程. Taipei: Jinfeng chubanshe, 1999.

Wan, Zhaoyuan. *Science and the Confucian Religion of Kang Youwei (1858–1927): China Before the Conflict Thesis.* Leiden: Brill, 2021.

Wong, Aida Yuen. *The Other Kang Youwei: Calligrapher, Art Activist, and Aesthetic Reformer in Modern China.* Leiden: Brill, 2016.

Zarrow, Peter. *Abolishing Boundaries: Global Utopias in the Formation of Modern Chinese Political Thought, 1880–1940.* Albany: SUNY Press, 2021.

89. Liang Qichao

Chang, Hao. *Liang Ch'i-ch'ao and Intellectual Transition in China, 1890–1907.* Cambridge, Mass.: Harvard University Press, 1971.

Hazami Naoki 狹間直樹 (ed.). *Kyōdō kenkyū Ryō Keichō: Seiyō kindai shisō juyō to Meiji Nihon* 共同研究 梁啓超: 西洋近代思想受容と明治日本 (Collaborative research on Liang Qichao: The reception of modern Western thought and Meiji Japan). Tokyo: Misuzu shobō, 1999.

Levenson, Joseph R. *Liang Ch'i-ch'ao and the Mind of Modern China.* Berkeley: University of California Press, 1970.

Tang, Xiaobing. *Global Space and the Nationalist Discourse of Modernity: The Historical Thinking of Liang Qichao.* Stanford: Stanford University Press, 1996.

Zhang Pengyuan 張朋園. *Liang Qichao yu Qingji geming* 梁啟超與清際革命 (Liang Qichao and the late Qing revolution). Taipei: Zhongyang yanjiu yuan jindaishi yanjiu suo, 1982 [1964].

90. Duanfang

Hummel, Arthur W. Sr (ed.). 'Tuan-fang'. *Eminent Chinese of the Ch'ing Period,* vol. 2, 780–2. United States Government Printing Office, 1943.

Lawton, Thomas. *A Time of Transition: Two Collectors of Chinese Art.* Kansas: The University of Kansas, 1991.

Netting, Lara Jaishree. *A Perpetual Fire: John C. Ferguson and his Quest for Chinese Art and Culture.* Hong Kong: Hong Kong University Press, 2013.

Pearlstein, Elinor. 'Early Chicago Chronicles of Early Chinese Art'. In *Collectors, Collections and Collecting the Arts of China: Histories and Challenges,* Jason Steuber and Guolong Lai (eds): 7–42. Florida: University Press of Florida, 2014.

Rhoads, Edward J. M. *Manchus and Han: Ethnic Relations and Political Power in Late Qing and Early Republican China, 1861–1928.* Seattle: University of Washington Press, 2000.

Zhang, Jun. 'Spider Manchu: Duanfang as Networker and Spindoctor of the Late Qing New Policies, 1901–1911'. PhD thesis, University of California at San Diego, 2008.

91. Sun Yat-sen

Bergère, Marie-Claire. *Sun Yat-sen,* Janet Lloyd tr. Stanford: Stanford University Press, 1998.

Harrison, Henrietta. *China.* London: Arnold, 2001.

Sun Yat-sen. *San Min Chu I: The Three Principles of the People,* Frank W. Price tr. Shanghai: Commercial Press, 1928.

Wells, Audrey. *The Political Thought of Sun Yat-sen: Development and Impact.* New York: Springer Link, 2001.

Wong, J. Y. *The Origins of an Heroic Image: Sun Yatsen in London, 1896–1897.* Oxford: Oxford University Press, 1986.

Wongsurawat, Wasana. 'Sun Yat-sen'. In *Demystifying China: New Understandings of Chinese History*, Naomi Standen (ed.): 163–70. Lanham: Rowman and Littlefield, 2012.

92. Su Xuejin

Ayers, J. et al. *Blanc de Chine: Divine Images in Porcelain*. New York: China Institute Gallery, 2002.

Donnelly, P. J. *Blanc de Chine: The Porcelain of Têhua in Fukien*. London: Faber and Faber, 1969.

Kerr, Rose and John Ayers. *Blanc de Chine: Porcelain from Dehua*. Singapore: Asian Civilisations Museum, 2002.

Liu Youzheng 劉幼錚. *Zhongguo Dehua baici yanjiu* 中國德化白瓷研究 (Research into Chinese porcelain from Dehua). Beijing: Kexue chubanshe, 2007.

Sun Bin 孫斌. *Yunyu ci zhuang: Su Qinming zhuan* 蘊玉瓷莊:蘇勤明傳 (Yunyu ceramics workshop: A biography of Su Qinming). Ha'erbin: Heilongjiang meishu chubanshe, 2014.

93. Chen Weiyan

Chan, Hou Seng, Staci Ieong Choi and Isabel Carvalho (eds). *Shiwan Ceramics: Collection of the Macao Museum of Art*. Macao: Macao Museum of Art, 2009.

Chan, Kuen On. 'Painted Plaster Figures of Lee Garden, Hong Kong'. In *Rustic Images: Shiwan Ware from the Eryi Caotang Collection*, Kuen On Chan (ed.): 268–71. Hong Kong: Art Museum, The Chinese University of Hong Kong, 2003.

Fung Ping Shan Museum. *Exhibition of Shiwan Wares*. Hong Kong: Fung Ping Shan Museum, University of Hong Kong, 1979.

Wong, Anita ed. *Gathering of Earthly Gods: Shiwan Wares from the Collections of the International Shiwan Ceramics Association*. Hong Kong: University Museum and Art Gallery, The University of Hong Kong. 2004.

Zou Hua 鄒華. 'Shiwan taosu san da mingren zhiyi de Chen Weiyan' 石灣陶塑三大名家之一的陳渭岩 (Chen Weiyan, one of the three famous masters of Shiwan pottery sculpture), in *Guangzhou wenshi ziliao* 廣州文史資料 (Guangzhou Literature and History), vol. 38. Guangzhou: Guangdong renmin chubanshe, 1988.

94. Wu Qijun

Bian, He. *Know Your Remedies: Pharmacy and Culture in Early Modern China*. Princeton: Princeton University Press, 2022.

Elman, Benjamin A. *On Their Own Terms: Science in China, 1550–1900*. Cambridge, Mass.: Harvard University Press, 2005.

Rowe, William. *Speaking of Profit: Bao Shichen and Reform in Nineteenth-Century China*. Cambridge, Mass.: Harvard University Asia Center, 2018.

Sun, E-tu Zen. 'Wu Ch'i-Chün: Profile of a Chinese Scholar-Technologist'. *Technology and Culture* 6.3 (1965): 394–406.

Wang, Yijun. 'From Tin to Pewter: Craft and Statecraft in China, 1700–1844'. PhD thesis, Columbia University, 2019.

95. Zhang Jian

Bastid, Marianne. *Educational Reform in Early Twentieth-Century China*. Michigan: University of Michigan, 1987.

Chu, Samuel C. *Reformer in Modern China: Chang Chien, 1853–1926*. New York: Columbia University Press, 1965.

Claypool, Lisa. 'Zhang Jian and China's First Museum'. *Journal of Asian Studies* 64.3 (2005): 567–604.

Köll, Elizabeth. *From Cotton Mill to Business Empire: The Emergence of Regional Enterprises in Modern China*. Cambridge, Mass.: Harvard University Press, 2003.

Qin Shao. *Culturing Modernity: The Nantong Model, 1890–1930*. Stanford: Stanford University Press, 2004.

96. Shen Shou

Fong, Grace S. 'Female Hands: Embroidery as a Knowledge Field in Women's Everyday Life in Late Imperial and Early Republican China'. *Late Imperial China* 25.1 (June 2004): 1–58.

Ko, Dorothy. *Every Step a Lotus: Shoes for Bound Feet*. Berkeley: University of California Press, 2001.

Li, Yuhang. *Becoming Guanyin: Artistic Devotion of Buddhist Women in Late Imperial China*. New York: Columbia University Press, 2020.

Mann, Susan S. *The Talented Women of the Zhang Family*. Berkeley: University of California Press, 2007.

Silberstein, Rachel. *A Fashionable Century: Textile Artistry and Commerce in the Late Qing*. Seattle: University of Washington Press, 2020.

97. Abing

Ah Bing, *Minzu yinyuejia Hua Yanjun (Abing) jinian zhuanji* 民族音樂家華彥鈞（阿炳）紀念專輯 (Commemoration of the renowned folk musician Hua Yanjun (Ah Bing)). CD audio. Hongkong, ROI Productions Ltd., RC-961002-2C, 1996.

Cheung, Joys Hoi Yan. 'Chinese Music and Translated Modernity in Shanghai, 1918–1937'. PhD thesis, University of Michigan, 2008.

Jones, Andrew F. *Yellow Music, Media Culture and Colonial Modernity in the Chinese Jazz Age*. Durham: Duke University Press, 2001.

Jones, Stephen. *Folk Music of China, Living Instrumental Traditions*. Oxford: Clarendon Press, 1995.

Liu, Terence M. 'The Development of the Chinese Two-Stringed Lute *Erhu* Following the New Culture Movement (*c.* 1915–1985)'. PhD thesis, Kent State University, 1988.

Stock, Jonathan. *Musical Creativity in Twentieth-Century China: Abing, his Music, and its Changing Meanings*. Rochester: University of Rochester Press, 1996.

Yang Yinliu 楊陰瀏 and Cao Anhe 曹安和 (eds). *Xiazi Abing qu ju* 瞎子阿炳曲集 (Works by the blind Abing). Shanghai: Wanye shudian, 1952.

98. Luo Zhenyu

Brown, Shana. *Pastimes: From Art and Antiquarianism to Modern Chinese Historiography*. Hawai'i: University of Hawai'i Press, 2011.

Fiskesjo, Magnus and Chen Xingcan. *China Before China: Johan Gunnar Andersson, Ding Wenjiang and the Discovery of China's Prehistory*. Stockholm: Museum of Far Eastern Antiquities, 2004.

Jacobs, Justin. *The Compensations of Plunder: How China Lost its Treasures*. Chicago: University of Chicago Press, 2020.

Mitter, Rana. *A Bitter Revolution: China's Struggle with the Modern World*. Oxford: Oxford University Press, 2004.

Yang, Chia-Ling and Roderick Whitfield (eds). *Lost Generation: Luo Zhenyu, Qing Loyalists and the Formation of Modern Chinese Culture*. London: Saffron Books, 2012.

99. Liu E

Kwong, Luke S. K. 'Self and Society in Modern China: Liu E (1857–1909) and Laocan youji'. *T'oung Pao* LXXXVII.4-5 (2001): 360–92.

Liu Delong 劉德隆, Zhu Xi 朱禧 and Liu Deping 劉德平. *Liu E xiaozhuan* 劉鶚小傳 (Biography of Liu E). Tianjin: Tianjin renmin chubanshe, 1987.

Liu Delong 劉德隆 and Liu Yu 劉瑀 (eds). *Liu E nianpu changbian* 劉鶚年譜長編 (Chronology of Liu E). Shanghai: Shanghai jiaotong daxue chubanshe, 2019.

Liu E 劉鶚. *Liu E ji* 劉鶚集 (The collected works of Liu E). Changchun: Jilin wenshi chubanshe, 2007.

Wang, David Der-Wei. *Fin-de-siecle Splendor: Repressed Modernities of Late Qing Fiction, 1849–1911*. Stanford: Stanford University Press, 1997.

Yuan Tingdong 袁庭棟. *Liu E ji Laocan youji ziliao* 劉鶚 及《老殘遊記》資料 (Research materials relating to Liu E and his novel *The Travels of Laocan*). Chengdu: Sichuan renmin chubanshe, 1985.

100. Ida Kahn

Burton, Margaret E. *Notable Women of Modern China*. Charleston: BiblioLife, 2007.

Hu, Ying. 'Naming the First "New Woman"'. In *Rethinking the 1898 Reform Period: Political and Cultural Change in Late Qing China*, Rebecca Karl and Peter Zarrow (eds) Cambridge, Mass.: Harvard University Press, 2002.

Shemo, Connie A. *The Chinese Medical Ministries of Kang Cheng and Shi Meiyu, 1872–1937: On a Cross-Cultural Frontier of Gender, Race, and Nation*. Bethlehem: Lehigh University Press, 2011.

_____. '"So Thoroughly American": Gertrude Howe, Kang Cheng, and Cultural Imperialism in the Woman's Foreign Missionary Society, 1872–1931'. In *Competing Kingdoms: Women, Mission, Nation, and the American Protestant Empire, 1812–1960*, Barbara Reeves-Ellington, Kathryn Kish Sklar and Connie A. Shemo (eds) London: Duke University Press, 2010.

Ward, David and Eugune Chen. *The University of Michigan in China*. Ann Arbor: Michigan Publishing, 2017.

CONTRIBUTORS

1. Ricarda Brosch 瑞琦 Assistant Curator, East Asia, Victoria and Albert Museum, London, United Kingdom

2. Zhao Chengling 趙晨嶺 Associate Researcher, Qing History Compilation and Research Centre, Ministry of Culture and Tourism, China

3. Jan Stuart 司美茵 Melvin R. Seiden Curator of Chinese Art, National Museum of Asian Art (Freer Gallery of Art and Arthur M. Sackler Gallery), Smithsonian Institution, Washington, DC, United States

4. Zhu Saihong 朱賽虹 Research Fellow, Palace Museum, Beijing, China

5. Ren Wanping 任萬平 Deputy Director and Research Fellow, Palace Museum, Beijing, China

6. Yingbai Fu 傅盈白 PhD candidate, History of Art and Archaeology, SOAS University of London, London, United Kingdom

7. Ying-chen Peng 彭盈真 Assistant Professor of Art History, American University, Washington DC, United States

8. Daisy Yiyou Wang 王伊悠 Deputy Director, Hong Kong Palace Museum, Hong Kong, China

9. Yuhang Li 李雨航 Associate Professor, Department of Art History, University of Wisconsin–Madison, Madison, United States

10. Anne Witchard 安妮·韋查德 Reader in English Studies, School of Humanities, University of Westminster, London, United Kingdom

11. Judith T. Zeitlin 蔡九迪 William R. Kenan, Jr. Professor in East Asian Languages and Civilizations and Theater and Performance Studies, University of Chicago, Chicago, United States

12. Andrea S. Goldman 郭安瑞 Associate Professor, Department of History, University of California, Los Angeles, United States

13. Vincent Goossaert 高萬桑 École Pratique des Hautes Études (EPHE, PSL), Paris, France

14. Christina Sanderson 盛佳靈 PhD candidate, Australian National University, Canberra, Australia

15. James Robson 羅柏松 James C. Kralik and Yunli Lou Professor of East Asian Languages and Civilizations, Harvard University, Boston, United States.

16. Hannah Theaker 何娜 Lecturer in History and Politics, University of Plymouth; Visiting Fellow to the KB Chen China Centre, University of Oxford, Oxford, United Kingdom

17. Barend ter Haar 田海 Professor of Chinese Studies, University of Hamburg, Hamburg, Germany

18. Lars Laamann 勞曼 Senior Lecturer in the History of China, SOAS, University of London, London, United Kingdom

19. Fresco Sam-Sin 京以成 Research Associate at Leiden University and Research Fellow at Research Centre for Material Culture RCMC, Leiden, Netherlands

20. Jessica Harrison-Hall 霍吉淑 Head of the China Section, Curator of Chinese Ceramics, Decorative Arts and the Sir Percival David Collection at the British Museum, London, United Kingdom

21. Zou Zhenhuan 鄒振環 Professor of History, Department of History, Fudan University, Shanghai, China

22. Juul Eijk 韋書 PhD candidate, Leiden University, Leiden, Netherlands

23. Jon Chappell 金山森 Independent Scholar, London, United Kingdom

24. Rania Huntington 韓瑞亞 Professor of Chinese Literature, University of Wisconsin–Madison, Madison, United States

25. Patrick Fuliang Shan 單富良 Professor of History, Grand Valley State University, Allendale, United States

26. Hu Ying 胡纓 Professor of Chinese Literature, University of California, Irvine, United States

27. Chen Shuo 陳碩 Assistant Researcher, Research Centre for Literary Theory and Aesthetics, Shandong University, Jinan, China

28. Yan Weitian 閆緯天 Assistant Professor, Department of Art History, Indiana University, Bloomington, United States

29. Eric Lefebvre 易凱 Director, Musée Cernuschi, Paris, France

30. Michele Matteini 米凱 Professor of Art History, New York University, New York City, United States

31. Nancy Berliner 白鈴安 Wu Tung Senior Curator of Chinese Art, Boston Museum of Fine Arts, Boston, United States

32. Li Lan 李蘭 Deputy Head of the Paintings Department, Shanghai Museum, Shanghai, China

33. Michael J. Hatch 何彥暉 Assistant Professor of Art and Architecture History, Department of Art, Miami University, Ohio, United States

34. Luk Yu-ping 陸於平 Basil Gray Curator: Chinese Paintings, Prints and Central Asian Collections, British Museum, London, United Kingdom

35. Marion S. Lee 李松華 Associate Professor, School of Art and Design, Ohio University, Athens, United States

36. Pan Qing 潘晴 Deputy Head of International Department and Chief Curator for International Exhibitions, National Museum of China, Beijing, China

37. Joseph Scheier-Dolberg 史耀華 Oscar Tang and Agnes Hsu-Tang Associate Curator of Chinese Paintings, The Metropolitan Museum of Art, New York City, United States

38. Yeewan Koon 官綺雲 Associate Professor of Art History, University of Hong Kong, Hong Kong, China

39. Xiong Xin 熊歆 PhD candidate, Chinese University of Hong Kong, Hong Kong, China

40. Michael J. Hatch 何彥暉

41. Richard Vinograd 文以誠 Christensen Fund Professor in Asian Art, Department of Art and Art History, Stanford University, Stanford, United States

42. Richard Vinograd 文以誠

43. Chia-ling Yang 楊佳玲 Professor of Chinese Art, University of Edinburgh, Edinburgh, United Kingdom

44. Shane McCausland 馬嘯鴻 Percival David Professor of the History of Art and Head of the School of Arts, SOAS, University of London, London, United Kingdom

45. Hongxing Zhang 張弘星 Senior Curator of East Asia, Victoria and Albert Museum, London, United Kingdom

46. Hongxing Zhang 張弘星

47. Akiko Yano 矢野明子 Mitsubishi Corporation Curator of Japanese Collections, British Museum, London, United Kingdom

48. Stephen McDowall 馬蒂文 Senior Lecturer in Cultural & Social History, University of Edinburgh, Edinburgh, United Kingdom

49. Grace S. Fong 方秀潔 Professor, R. C. & E. Y. Lee Chair in Chinese Cultural Studies, Department of East Asian Studies, McGill University, Montreal, Canada

50. Annie Luman Ren 任路漫 Postdoctoral Fellow, Australian National University, Canberra, Australia

51. Charles Aylmer 艾超世 Former Head of the Chinese Department, Cambridge University Library, University of Cambridge, Cambridge, United Kingdom

52. Theodore Huters 胡志德 Professor Emeritus of Chinese, University of California, Los Angeles, United States and Chief Editor, *Renditions*

53. Sarah Jessi Bramao-Ramos 潘心結 PhD candidate, Harvard University, Cambridge, United States

54. Lars Laamann 勞曼

55. Craig Clunas 柯律格 Professor Emeritus of the History of Art, University of Oxford, Oxford, United Kingdom

56. Devin Fitzgerald 馮坦風 Curator of Rare Books and the History of Printing, UCLA Library Special Collections, University of California, Los Angeles, United States

57. Eric Schluessel 許臨君 Assistant Professor, History and International Affairs, George Washington University, Washington, DC, United States

58. Pan Qing 潘晴

59. Ellen B. Widmer 魏愛蓮 Mayling Soong Professor of Chinese Studies and Professor of East Asian Studies, Wellesley College, Wellesley, MA, United States

60. Tobie Meyer Fong 梅爾清 Professor of History, Johns Hopkins University, Baltimore, United States

61. Gregory B. Lee 利大英 Founding Professor of Chinese Studies, University of St Andrews, Scotland, United Kingdom

62. Max K. W. Huang 黃克武 Institute of Modern History, Academia Sinica, Taipei

63. Jeffrey Wasserstrom 華志堅 Chancellor's Professor of History, University of California Irvine, Irvine, United States

64. Viren Murthy 慕唯仁 Professor of History, University of Wisconsin–Madison, Madison, United States

65. Joshua A. Fogel 傅佛果 Professor, Department of History, York University, Toronto, Canada

66. Tang Hui 唐慧 Independent Scholar

67. Madhavi Thampi 瑪妲玉 Honorary Fellow, Institute of Chinese Studies, New Delhi, India

68. Zhiqing Hu 胡之青 PhD candidate, Birkbeck, University of London, London, United Kingdom

69. Wenyuan Xin 辛文元 Project Curator, British Museum, London, United Kingdom

70. Gregory Adam Scott 史瑞戈 Senior Lecturer in Chinese Culture and History, University of Manchester, Manchester, United Kingdom

71. Natascha Gentz 費南山 Chair of Chinese Studies, The University of Edinburgh, Edinburgh, United Kingdom

72. Robert Bickers 畢可思 Professor of History, University of Bristol, Bristol, United Kingdom

73. Robert Bickers 畢可思

74. Joshua A. Fogel 傅佛果

75. Joan Judge 季家珍 Professor in the Department of History, York University, Toronto, Canada

76. Nixi Cura 黃巧巧 Honorary Research Fellow, University of Glasgow, Glasgow, United Kingdom

77. Pamela Kyle Crossley, Charles and Elfriede Collis Professor of History, Dartmouth College, Hanover, United States

78. William T. Rowe 羅威廉 John and Diane Cooke Professor of Chinese History, Johns Hopkins University, Baltimore, United States

79. Stephen Platt 裴士鋒 Professor of History, University of Massachusetts, Amherst, United States

80. Hannah Theaker 何娜

81. Maura D. Dykstra 戴史翠 Assistant Professor of History, California Institute of Technology, Pasadena, United States

82. Hans van de Ven 方德萬 Vice President and Professor of Modern Chinese History, University of Cambridge, Cambridge, United Kingdom and Chair Professor, Department of History, Peking University, Beijing, China

83. Susan I. Eberhard 爾蘇珊 PhD candidate, University of California, Berkeley, United States

84. Jenny Huangfu Day 皇甫崢崢 Associate Professor of History, Skidmore College, Saratoga Springs, United States

85. Ke Ren 任可 Assistant Professor of History, College of the Holy Cross, Worcester, United States

86. Jon Eugene von Kowallis 寇志明 Professor of Chinese Studies, The University of New South Wales, Sydney, Australia

87. Chunmei Du 杜春媚 Associate Professor of History, Lingnan University, Hong Kong, China

88. Aida Yuen Wong 阮圓 Nathan Cummings and Robert B. and Beatrice C. Mayer Chair in Fine Arts and Professor of Fine Arts, Brandeis University, Waltham, United States

89. Peter Zarrow 沙培德 Professor of History, University of Connecticut, Storrs, United States

90. Yu-chih Lai 賴毓芝 Associate Research Fellow, Institute of Modern History, Academia Sinica, Taipei

91. Helen Wang 汪海嵐 Curator of East Asian Money, British Museum, London, United Kingdom

92. Xiaoxin Li 李曉欣 Curator, East Asia, Victoria and Albert Museum, London, United Kingdom

93. Michel Lee 李東 Curator, National Museums of World Culture, Sweden

94. Yijun Wang 王懿君 Assistant Professor of History, New York University, New York City, United States

95. Rachel Silberstein 蘇瑞麗 Independent Scholar

96. Dorothy Ko 高彥頤 Professor of History, Barnard College, Columbia University, New York City, United States

97. Lena Henningsen 韓儼娜 Professor at the Institute for Chinese Studies, University of Freiburg, Germany

98. Julia Lovell 藍詩玲 Professor of Modern China, Birkbeck, University of London, London, United Kingdom

99. Guo Yongbing 郭永秉 Unearthed Document Centre, Fudan University复旦大学出土文献中心, Shanghai, China

100. Sare Aricanli 李瑞 Assistant Professor of Early Modern and Modern Chinese History, Durham University, Durham, United Kingdom

CREDITS

The publisher would like to thank the copyright holders for granting permission to reproduce the images illustrated. Every attempt has been made to trace accurate ownership of copyrighted images in this book. Any errors or omissions will be corrected in subsequent editions provided notification is sent to the publisher.

Unless otherwise stated, copyright in photographs belongs to the institution mentioned in the caption. All images of British Museum objects are © 2023 The Trustees of the British Museum, courtesy the Department of Photography and Imaging.

IMAGES

Frontispiece British Museum, 1982,1217,0.296 **Page 4** *Battle Scene from the Muslim Rebellions in Shanxi, Gansu and Xinjiang Provinces,* ink and colour on silk, Mactaggart Art Collection (2004.19.92), University of Alberta Museums, Gift of Sandy and Cécile Mactaggart **Page 15** Provided by the Palace Museum **Page 18** Provided by the Palace Museum **Page 21** Provided by the Palace Museum **Page 25** Provided by the Palace Museum **Page 28** Provided by the Palace Museum **Page 31** Provided by the Palace Museum **Page 34** Provided by the Palace Museum **Page 36** Provided by the Palace Museum **Page 40** Cixi, Empress Dowager of China, 1835–1908, Photographs, FSA.A.13, Freer Gallery of Art and Arthur M. Sackler Gallery Archives , Purchase, 1966, Photographer: Xunling, FSA A.13 SC-GR-246 **Page 42** SOAS Library C Per /82379, University of London P**age 46** The Water Pine and Stone Retreat Collection of Snuff Bottles **Page 50** The Water Pine and Stone Retreat Collection of Snuff Bottles **Page 55** Courtesy of the Chinese University of Hong Kong Library **Page 58** Copyright of The University of Manchester **Page 59** Copyright of The University of Manchester **Page 62** Jinling Buddhist Press (Jinling kejingchu) **Page 64** Reproduced by kind permission of the Syndics of Cambridge University Library **Page 65** British Library, London, UK © British Library Board. All Rights Reserved/Bridgeman Images **Page 67** Courtesy of Nanjing Museum Administration **Page 68** The Bodleian Libraries, University of Oxford, (OC) 246 c.83, frontispiece **Page 70** History and Art Collection / Alamy Stock Photo **Page 74** Courtesy of the Chinese University of Hong Kong Library **Page 78** Copyrights by Hong Kong Maritime Museum **Page 80** National Museum of China **Page 83** The Picture Art Collection / Alamy Stock Photo **Page 87** Royal Engineers Headquarters Mess, Kent **Page 89** Harvard-Yenching Library of Harvard College Library, Harvard University **Page 93** Image courtesy of Donald and David Grant, and Special Collections, University of Bristol Library (www.hpcbristol.net) **Page 95** National Museum of China **Page 96** Wisconsin Historical Society, WHI-111120 **Page 97** Zhejiang Provincial Museum **Page 101** Anhui Provincial Museum **Page 103** National Museum of China **Page 104** © 2023 Princeton University Art Museum / Photo Scala, Florence **Page 105** The Metropolitan Museum of Art, New York, Purchase, Friends of Asian Art Gifts, 2015 **Page 106** The Metropolitan Museum of Art, New York, Gift of Julia and John Curtis, 2015 **Page 107** National Library of China **Page 108** Zhejiang Provincial Museum **Page 112** British Museum, 1973,0917,0.59.44 **Page 114** Provided by the Palace Museum **Page 116** Provided by the Palace Museum **Page 117** Tianjin Museum **Page 119** Provided by the Palace Museum **Page 120** The Metropolitan Museum of Art, New York, Purchase, Bequests of Edna H. Sachs and Flora E. Whiting, by exchange; Fletcher Fund, by exchange; Gifts of Mrs. Harry Payne Bingham and Mrs. Henry J. Bernheim, by exchange; and funds from various donors, by exchange, 2016 **Page 123** Zhejiang Provincial Museum **Page 125** National Museum of China **Page 127** Provided by the Palace Museum **Page 128** Courtesy of The Cleveland Museum of Art **Page 130** National Museum of China **Page 132** left Guangzhou Museum of Art **Page 132** right Guangzhou Museum of Art **Page 135** Photo supplied by the Hong Kong Museum of Art **Page 138** Provided by the Palace Museum **Page 139** Provided by the Palace Museum **Page 142** Provided by the Palace Museum **Page 143** Provided by the Palace Museum **Page 145** left Provided by the Palace Museum **Page 145** right Courtesy of The National Art Museum

ACKNOWLEDGMENTS

This book has been a delight to bring together. Through it, we have aimed to 'humanize' China's 19th century for a broad audience who would like to understand better Chinese history through its very diverse people, and to create an international network of late Qing scholars. The book was begun at the time of the Covid pandemic when we were unable to travel and have in-person dialogues with scholars of China, so as editors we especially appreciated the vibrant way in which our many contributors brought the characters of China's 19th century to life.

We would like to thank all the contributors who have written the 100 chapters for this book. They are listed separately (*see* pp.351–53) but represent a wonderfully varied team from fourteen different countries and many different institutions. For our UKRI Arts and Humanities Research Council project (*Cultural Creativity in Qing China 1796-1912*, grant reference AH/T001895/1, 2020–24) we set out to create this kind of international and interdisciplinary network of many ages and backgrounds, that could help future students and members of the public better understand late Qing China. We warmly thank the UKRI Arts and Humanities Research Council for making possible our work on China's 19th century, and our institutions – Birkbeck College, University of London and the British Museum – for their support.

We are also extremely grateful to those who did not write but who either steered us in the direction of other authors or characters to include or offered support in other ways. These scholars are too many to note but warm thanks go especially to Jonathan Hay, John Minford and J. D. Hill. For close peer review of the manuscript we thank Klaas Ruitenbeek and Henrietta Harrison. They provided a masterclass in how to re-examine a text.

The volume would not have been possible without Wenyuan Xin's many contributions: not only her careful translations from Chinese into English of eight essays in the book but also her diligence and creativity in sourcing so many images that felt at times almost impossible to track down. We would also like to thank Claudia Bloch and Laura Meachem for their support throughout the publishing process, especially the picture research, and colleagues in the British Museum for conservation and photography.

From Thames & Hudson there are many people who have transformed this project into a reality. Julian Honer believed in the merit of the book from the very beginning and offered his tireless support to shepherd it through to completion. Melissa Mellor and Rosalind Horne have kept the project on track, accommodating endless changes based on picture availability or new discoveries. Peter Dawson has, as usual, created the most beautiful, appealing design for the book. Sarah Waldram, an outstanding copy-editor, was a pleasure to work with; we thank her for her attention to detail and thoughtful additions. Howard Watson has taken on a complex proofread, and Avni Patel and Susanna Ingram have attended to the final stages of the design and production of the book with great care and precision.

We could have added hundreds of further essays to this volume as the 19th century teems with so many other interesting, significant characters. Given the current dynamism of late Qing scholarship inside and outside China, we are confident that this book will be succeeded by many more biographies of the remarkable individuals that inhabited the late Qing empire.

Below. Xugu (1823–1896), *Bronze Gui with Three Friends of Winter*, c. 1850–96. This image of pine, prunus and bamboo within an ancient bronze ritual food vessel represents the steadfast qualities admired by the well-educated. A red seal impression inside belonged to Ruan Yuan (1764–1849), a celebrated antiquarian and official (see pages 105–7). Hanging scroll, ink and colours on paper, 94.7 x 54.6 cm. Nanshun Shanfang, Singapore.

CHRONOLOGY

Rulers

The Jiaqing Emperor
(*r.* 1796–1820)

The Daoguang Emperor
(*r.* 1821–1850)

The Xianfeng Emperor
(*r.* 1851–1861)

The Tongzhi Emperor
(*r.* 1862–1874)

The Guangxu Emperor
(*r.* 1875–1908)

Empress Dowager Cixi
(1835–1908)

Aisin Gioro Puyi
(*r.* 1909–1912)

Conflicts

White Lotus Insurrection
(1794–*c.* 1806)

First Opium War
(1839–42)

Taiping Civil War
(1851–64)

Second Opium War
(1856–60)

Nian Rebellion
(1851–68)

First Sino-Japanese War
(1894–95)

Hundred Days' Reform
(11 June–21 September 1898)

Boxer War
(1899–1901)

Xinhai Revolution
(1911)

INDEX

First published in the United Kingdom in 2023 by
Thames & Hudson Ltd, 181A High Holborn, London WC1V 7QX,
in collaboration with the British Museum

First published in the United States of America in 2023 by
Thames & Hudson Inc., 500 Fifth Avenue, New York, New York 10110

Creators of Modern China: 100 Lives from Empire to Republic 1796–1912
© 2023 The Trustees of the British Museum/Thames & Hudson Ltd, London

Text © 2023 The Trustees of the British Museum

Design by Peter Dawson, gradedesign.com

British Library Cataloguing-in-Publication Data
A catalogue record for this book is available from the British Library

Library of Congress Control Number 2022945756

ISBN 978-0-500-48080-9

Printed and bound in Slovenia by DZS Grafik, d.o.o.

MIX
Paper from
responsible sources
FSC® C106600

Research and publication supported by the Arts and Humanities Research Council

Arts and
Humanities
Research Council